THE FREEMASON AT WORK

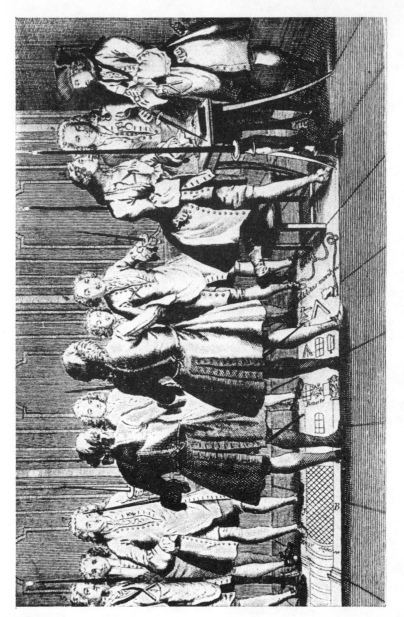

Detail from a French engraving, 1745.

HARRY CARR

With All Good Wishes

THE FREEMASON AT WORK

BY

HARRY CARR

Past Junior Grand Deacon

*P.M., (Secretary and Editor 1961–1973) of the
Quatuor Coronati Lodge, No. 2076, London*

P.M., 2265, 2429, 6226, 7464

Honorary Member of 236, 2429, 2911, 3931, 7998, 8227

*Fellow of the American Lodge of Research, N.Y., Honorary Member of
Ohio Lodge of Research, Masonic Research Lodge of Connecticut,
Loge Villard d'Honnecourt, No. 81 Paris (France),
Mizpah Lodge, Cambridge, Mass., Arts and Crafts Lodge, No. 1017, Illinois,
Walter F. Meier Lodge of Research, No. 281, Seattle, Washington,
Research Lodge of Oregon, No. 198, Portland,
Victoria Lodge of Education and Research, Victoria, B.C.*

Honorary P.A.G.D.C. Grand Lodge of Iran

Ian Allan Group

LONDON

LEWIS MASONIC

© Harry Carr 1976
First Published in Great Britain in 1976
Sixth and revised edition 1981
Reprinted 1983

Published by
A Lewis (Masonic Publishers) Ltd
Terminal House, Shepperton, Surrey
who are members of the *Ian Allan Group*, and printed
by *Ian Allan Printing Ltd* at their works at
Coomblelands in Runnymede, England

ISBN 0 85318 126 8
Carr, Harry
The Freemason at Work — 6th revised edition
1. Freemasons
1. Title
366'.1   HS395

FOREWORD

By R.W.Bro. Sir Lionel Brett, P.Dist.G.M., Nigeria

THOSE who hold that good wine needs no bush may feel that a Foreword to this book is superfluous. There is some force in this view for the generation of readers who have known Bro. Harry Carr in person or by reputation, and grown accustomed to a regular flow of articles under his name, but Masonic books have a way of surviving in lodge bookshelves long after they have gone out of print, and it seems certain that this one will be read, quoted and discussed by generations who have not had those advantages. A Foreword will justify itself if it helps future generations to put Bro. Carr in his proper class as a trustworthy guide, and this Foreword may be regarded as addressed to them.

The United Grand Lodge of England makes little provision for organized Masonic instruction. Every member receives a copy of the *Book of Constitutions*, but apart from the annual Prestonian Lectures the rest is left to the efforts of lodges or individuals. The novice with an inquiring mind will not be content for long with a printed ritual and will demand further information, whether on the practice in lodge, or on the form of the after-proceedings, or on some aspect of the history of operative or speculative Freemasonry. If he consults an individual, he will be fortunate to find a Preceptor or other informant as well equipped all round as Bro. Carr. If he turns to a book, there are a number in print which he can profitably study, but he may not always know where to look for an answer to his particular question. The distinguishing feature of this book is that it deals with questions that were actually exercising brethren over a period of twelve years.

Bro. Carr describes the genesis of the book in his Introduction. It was largely thanks to him that the material it contains came to be included in the Summonses and *Transactions* of a lodge formed by and for erudite scholars, and the variety of his Masonic experience made him exceptionally well qualified to provide the material. As Deputy Preceptor and later Preceptor of a Lodge of Instruction for many years he was in close touch with the needs of brethren at the start of their Masonic careers. As a member of the Board of General Purposes of

Grand Lodge he had direct experience of the administration of the affairs of the governing body of English Freemasonry. He first showed his interest in Masonic research in 1936, and his election to full membership of the Quatuor Coronati Lodge in 1953 is proof of the standing he already enjoyed as a Masonic scholar.

Over the years Bro. Carr has made many contributions to Masonic literature, both as author and editor. During the period when he was Secretary of the Quatuor Coronati Lodge and Editor of its *Transactions* his publications in *AQC* included full-scale papers presented to the Lodge and articles of varying length in *Miscellanea Latomorum* and 'Papers and Essays' as well as answers to Queries. They all display the same pattern: facts first; conclusions, if any, later; and no concessions to those who prefer myth to history.

The queries Bro. Carr was asked to deal with vary greatly in complexity as well as in subject-matter. Where a pure issue of fact is concerned the answer may be accepted as authoritative. Where someone has put the insoluble question, why a particular expression is used in the ceremonies, Bro. Carr's historical exposition provides as satisfactory an answer as the case admits; he might have cited what Justice Holmes said in an analogous case—'The life of the law has not been logic; it has been experience.' Where the question involves expressing a preference between two or more possible solutions, Bro. Carr has not been afraid to follow a statement of the relevant facts with an expression of his own opinion, but he has not done so dogmatically, or claimed to have said the last word. Bro. Carr's opinion on any Masonic question must carry weight, but he would certainly not wish anyone to adopt it merely on the authority of his name, and the most important thing is that he provides material for informed discussion.

The reader a hundred years hence may confidently take it that on the matters it deals with this book accurately shows the state of Masonic knowledge, and the opinions that an unusually well informed Freemason could reasonably hold, at the time of its publication, and it is a great privilege to be associated with the book, if only in the ancillary capacity of writer of the Foreword.

LIONEL BRETT

CONTENTS

For particular subjects please use the Index

ix

For particular subjects please use the Index

For particular subjects please use the Index

For particular subjects please use the Index

For particular subjects please use the Index

List of Illustrations and Diagrams

For particular subjects please use the Index

LIST OF ABBREVIATIONS

A.: Answer

A. & A.S.R.: Ancient and Accepted Scottish Rite

Antients: The Grand Lodge of England according to the Old Institutions, 1751–1813

AQC: *Ars Quatuor Coronatorum.* (Transactions of the Quatuor Coronati Lodge)

Asst.: Assistant

Bd.: Board

B.G.P.: Board of General Purposes

B. of C.: *Book of Constitutions*

B. of I.M.: Board of Installed Masters

Brn.: Brethren

Cand.: Candidate

Catéchisme: *Le Catéchisme des Francs-Maçons, 1744*

C.C.: Correspondence Circle (of the Q.C. Lodge)

Claret: *The Ceremonies of Initiation, Passing and Raising* . . . 1838, etc.

D.C.: Director of Ceremonies

Deg.: Degree

Démasqué: *Le Maçon Démasqué,* 1751

Dep.G.: Deputy Grand

Dist.G.: District Grand

E.C.: English Constitution

E.F.E.: *The Early French Exposures,* 1971

E.M.C.: *The Early Masonic Catechisms,* by Knoop, Jones and Hamer, 2nd edn., 1963

E.R.H.MS.: *The Edinburgh Register House MS.,* 1696

F.C.: Fellowcraft

F.P.O.F.: Five Points of Fellowship

G.: Grand

G.L.: Grand Lodge

G.M.: Grand Master

H.A.: Hiram Abif

I.G.: Inner Guard

J. & B.: *Jachin and Boaz* . . . 1762

K.S.T.: King Solomon's Temple

L.G.R.: London Grand Rank

Leics.: The Leicester Lodge of Research, No. 2429

L. of I.: Lodge of Instruction

L. of R.: Lodge of Research

Miller, A.L.: *Notes on Hist.* . . . *of the Lodge of Aberdeen.* . . (1919)

Misc. Lat.: *Miscellanea Latomorum*

M.M.: Master Mason

Moderns: The premier Grand Lodge, 1717–1813

M.W.: Most Worshipful

Ob.: Obligation

O.E.D.: *The Oxford English Dictionary*

O.T.: The Old Testament

P.: Past

Pen. Sn.: Penal Sign

p.g.: pass grip

P.M.: Past Master

Pres.: President

Prov.: Provincial

p.w.: password

Q.: Question

Q. and A.: Question and Answer

Q.C.: Quatuor Coronati (Lodge)

Q.C.A.: *Quatuor Coronatorum Antigrapha* (Masonic Reprints)

R.A.: Royal Arch

R.W.: Right Worshipful

S.C.: Scottish Constitution

Sec.: Secretary

Secret: *Le Secret des Francs-Maçons, 1742*

Sn.: Sign

T.D.K.: *Three Distinct Knocks,* 1760

Tn.: Token

Trahi: *L'Ordre des Francs-Maçons Trahi, 1745*

U.G.L.: United Grand Lodge of England

Vernon, W.F.: *Hist. of Free-masonry in the Province of Roxburgh* . . . (1893)

V.S.L.: Volume of the Sacred Law

INTRODUCTION

THE origins of this book are, in fact, a part of the history of the Quatuor Coronati Lodge and it is fitting that I begin by paying a richly deserved tribute to my predecessor in office, the late Bro. John Dashwood. He had been appointed Secretary of the Lodge and Editor of its *Transactions* in 1952, at a time when the membership of the Correspondence Circle had reached its supposed peak, around 3,000, and the production of the annual volumes had fallen several years in arrears.

By slimming the volumes severely during the next few years, he managed to catch up on arrears of publication. In 1960, the Lodge Standing Committee was compelled to deal with its most urgent problem, i.e., a substantial increase in income, necessitating a rapid expansion in the membership of the Correspondence Circle, which was practically its only source of revenue.

As a very junior Past Master of the Lodge, I had been arguing for some time that we were concentrating on scholarly material in the *Transactions* which could only be appreciated by the select few, and I urged that we should bring into our publications a few simple Lectures, Questions and Answers, etc., that would be suitable for 'the boys at Lodge of Instruction'. This suggestion caused some dismay at first, and there were murmurings about 'the lowering of standards'. I protested that *the new material would be in addition to our main work*, so that it would not in any way affect the quality of the *Transactions*, but would simply make them attractive to a completely new field of readers.

John Dashwood sympathized with my views and eventually the opposition was won over. For the proposed addition to the volumes, it was resolved to revive *Miscellanea Latomorum*, a Masonic magazine which had ceased publication in 1950. The copyright belonged to the Quatuor Coronati Lodge. In its new form, as an eight-page pamphlet, it would be sent annually to all members without extra charge. The first issue contained a short paper by Bro. John Rylands on 'The Ancient Landmarks', followed by fifteen questions, including some that were very abstruse. Only eight of them were answered, leaving seven that necessarily remained in limbo until the next year's volume! As to 'lowered standards', it is amusing to note that the first issue was loosely inserted in the *Transactions* as a separate pamphlet, to ensure that its contents would not contaminate the main volume with which it was posted!

The results were far better than we dared to hope, and the end of that year showed a satisfying increase in membership and funds. Unfortunately Bro. Dashwood did not live to enjoy the fruits of his labours. He went into hospital in May 1961, and died after a very brief illness. There was no successor ready to replace him, and after a few months' trial period (doing the editorial work at home, at night and week-ends) I retired from business in September 1961, to become Secretary and Editor, and to start on the happiest and most productive twelve years in a long and busy lifetime.

Uneasy and diffident, because I had had no preliminary training for the work, it was an incident in the first week of that trial period that determined me to accept the office and to make a success of it. In one day's post there were two letters, one from Alaska asking for guidance on the correct procedure for balloting in lodge and the other was from Australia requesting a ruling on a piece of 'floor-work'. I knew, of course, that there were members of the Correspondence Circle in many parts of the world; but two questions in one day from places almost as far apart as it was possible to be, made me realize suddenly how important our educational programme could become if it was handled properly. From that day onwards the Questions and Answers for the new venture became a major concern. But, in future, the items selected for publication were to be of the highest popular appeal, on subjects that would stimulate discussion and prove both instructive and entertaining, especially to those Brethren who know little or nothing of the background of Freemasonry beyond what they have seen or heard in lodge.

As part of the same programme, the Lodge Summonses were enlarged from two pages to four, the additional space being used for shorter Questions and Answers. As the Summonses were posted six times a year, it was hoped that they would help to maintain a closer contact with the Brethren for whom they were designed.

The first version of *Misc. Lat.*, produced under my supervision, was bound in with *AQC*, Vol. 74, and contained four short Lectures designed for use in lodge, with a block of Questions, Answers and Notes, twenty-eight pages in all, under a new heading 'THE SUPPLEMENT'. It created something of a sensation; clearly we had opened up a Masonic gold-mine! Soon, we were averaging more than 1,000 new members each year. In 1973 the membership of the Correspondence Circle was 12,440.

Eventually letters began to come in, urging us to publish the whole collection of Questions and Answers in book form. As author of nearly all the answers, I was eager to fulfil these requests, but that could not be done at once. Because of our rapid expansion and limited staff, much of the material had been written under pressure, with the printers waiting for every page. The Answers, especially in the Lodge Summonses, had often been skimped because of limited space and, after publication, many of the items had brought comments from readers, raising points of high interest that deserved to be included in a 'collected edition'.

Although the original material was already in print, it was clear that a great deal of editorial work would need to be done to prepare it for the new publication; but that had to wait until my retirement from office. Here are the results, the fruits of twelve years work.

THE QUESTIONS AND THEIR TREATMENT

The questions that come to us at Q.C. deal, almost invariably, with matters on which there is no Grand Lodge ruling, or on which the printed rituals and their rubrics afford little or no explanation. They fall mainly into two classes:

> Those which ask for the meaning and purpose of a specific item of ritual or procedure, or how and why it arose.
>
> Those which describe two different versions of ritual or procedure and ask 'Which is correct?'

Generally I believe the historical approach is the most rewarding, i.e., tracing the item in question from its earliest appearance, and following its development and changes up to the time when our ritual and procedures were more-or-less standardized in the early 1800s. When, as often happens, no definite conclusion is possible, this method sets out the information that may lead to a probable answer and, at the very least, it gives the enquirer a wider knowledge and a better understanding of the problems that are involved.

Because the printed pieces were intended for a world-wide circulation, my answers always tried to give a little more than the questioner had asked. I make no apology for that, since we had strong encouragement from our readers, and the regular yearly figures of increasing membership were ample proof of a steadily growing demand for our work.

Among the questions that are not easily answered, are those that ask for explanations of incidents and details in the Craft legends and allegories, in which the enquirers treat each item as though it is proven fact, supported by Holy Writ! I remember the day, more than forty years ago, when a Grand Officer—looking me straight in the eye— assured me that Moses was a Grand Master! My grounding in Old Testament refuted this utterly, but I was a young Master Mason and one does not shatter a man's illusions lightly. In dealing with questions of this kind, it is imperative to separate legend from fact; the difficulty lies only in framing the answers so that they do no hurt or damage.

Inevitably, there are questions on esoteric matters of ritual and procedure that cannot be discussed in print and those are often of the highest interest. In such cases, the only practicable course is to go back to the earliest version of the item in question, tracing its development throughout the centuries, but stopping short at the final standardization and changes that were made in the 19th century, when most of the forms in use today were established. This does not answer the question, it only points the way so that the enquirer may be enabled to find the answer for himself. I must, therefore, repeat a warning which has been given on many similar occasions:

> In dealing with certain ritual and procedural matters, the reader's attention is particularly directed to the fact that the articles in this volume quote from documents of the 14th–18th centuries, and that *the details that are described belong only to the dates that are assigned to them.* They take no account of the changes and standardization that took place in the 19th century, and it is emphasized that, except in a few innocuous cases, they do not describe— or attempt to describe—present-day practices.

Finally, the articles in this book were never intended to be the last word on those subjects. They are simply a collection of careful answers, at an elementary level (often only my own opinion) on the queries and problems that arise in the lodge room, from Brethren who are eager for a better understanding of the things that they say and do in the course of their Masonic duties. That explains the title, 'The Freemason at Work'. It is hoped that the whole collection will furnish an ample choice of subjects for discussion in lodges and Study Groups, and bring new pleasures to Brethren who enjoy their Masonry.

THE INDEX

In every work of this kind, the Index is as important as the book itself. For every reader in pursuit of a particular theme, it will be invaluable. All the Questions are numbered for easy reference, but for the reader in search of a particular theme or subject, the Index will be the most speedy guide.

COPYRIGHT

For copyright reasons, the present volume contains only my own work, supplemented in many instances by quotations from other writers with their permission, and with due acknowledgment.

Recognized lodges, Study Groups and individual Brethren have full permission to make use of the contents, but none of the articles may be reproduced or published without written permission from the author.

ACKNOWLEDGMENTS

I take this opportunity to express my indebtedness to the Librarians of Grand Lodge and their Assistants during the past twenty years, for their generous and unstinted help at all times and, especially, to the present Librarian, Bro. T. O. Haunch. My thanks also to Bro. Roy A. Wells, my successor in office and to Bro. Colin F. W. Dyer who furnished valuable additions to several of the answers, which are gratefully acknowledged here and in the text. I am particularly indebted to Bro. Frederick Smyth for the very comprehensive Index and to R.W.Bro. Sir Lionel Brett for his kindness in writing the Foreword to the book and for his ready help in Latin and other editorial problems during the years. Lastly, my thanks to the Board of General Purposes of the United Grand Lodge of England for their kind permission to quote from the *Constitutions* and other official documents and from rare manuscripts in the Grand Lodge Library.

LONDON   H.C.
December 1975

THE FREEMASON AT WORK

1. THE QUATUOR CORONATI

Q. What does the name 'Quatuor Coronati' mean?

A. The Latin words mean 'the four crowned ones' and allude to the Christian Church's Festival of the Four Crowned Martyrs, which is celebrated on 8 November annually.

The Quatuor Coronati
From the Isabella Missal, *c.* 1500. Brit. Mus. Add. Mss. 18,851.

There are numerous versions of the legend of the *Sancti Quatuor Coronati,* all very much alike, though they differ considerably in important details such as their nationality, their number, and even their names.

The story, in brief outline, is that in A.D. 302 four stone-carvers and their apprentice were ordered by the Emperor Diocletian to carve a statue of Aesculapius, which, since they were secretly Christians, they evaded doing. For disobedience to the Emperor's commands they were put to death on 8 November. During the year 304 Diocletian ordered that all Roman soldiers should burn incense before a statue of the same god, when four who were Christians refused to do so, for which they were beaten to death. This was also said to have been on 8 November, though two years later than the stone-carvers.

Melchiades, who was Pope from A.D. 310 to 314, ordained that these two sets of four and five martyrs were to be commemorated on

1

November 8, under the single name of *Quatuor Coronati*. The Sacramentary of Pope Gregory, two hundred years later, confirmed that date and Pope Honorius built a church in their honour in the seventh century. They are to be found to this day, depicted in sculpture and painting, in many mediaeval and later churches in Europe.

The Saints are referred to in the earliest known version of the *Old Charges*, the *Regius MS.*, which is dated *c*. 1390 and there is good evidence that they were venerated by English masons, notably in an ordinance of the London masons, dated 1481 and still preserved in the Guildhall archives, which prescribed that

> ... every freeman of the Craft shall attend at Christ-Church [Aldgate] on the Feast of the *Quatuor Coronati*, to hear Mass, under a penalty of 12 pence.

The founders of our Lodge, nine in number, of whom four were soldiers, chose *Quatuor Coronati* as the name of the Lodge and November 8 has been the date of the annual Festival and Installation meeting since its foundation.

---

2.   THE BRIGHT MORNING STAR

Q. When we are exhorted, in the Third Degree, to 'lift our eyes to that bright morning star, whose rising brings peace and salvation . . .' are we referring to a particular star, or is this pure symbolism?

A. The various aspects of this problem may be best envisaged, perhaps, from the following quotations, beginning with some extracts from *Miscellanea Latomorum*, (Series ii) Vol. 31, pp. 1–4:

> It is argued that this reference to 'that bright Morning Star' is an allusion to the Founder of Christianity, and as such should never have been included in, or retained in, the ritual of an Association professing entire freedom from denominational creed or dogma, outside of the simple basic belief in the existence of a Supreme Being. This attitude has unfortunately been bolstered up by a frequent misquotation of the wording, the phrase 'whose rising brings peace and tranquillity' being often rendered as 'peace and salvation', which is erroneous and decidedly mischievous. [N.B. *Emulation, Stability* and *Logic* use the word 'salvation'; *Exeter* says 'tranquillity'.]
>
> As a symbol, the Morning Star is indeed most appropriate to the ceremonial incident just previously enacted; so apt, in fact, that it may be confidently asserted that no other symbol could be found which would so perfectly fit the circumstances of the case. Astronomically the Morning Star is the herald of the dawning of a new day, just as its opposite, the Evening Star, presages the coming of night. The latter foretells the dying of another day; the approach of the time when man can no longer work; when darkness covers the face of the earth. Darkness has ever been associated with

evil, and in its sombre, unknown possibilities is a fitting emblem of death. On the other hand, the rising Morning Star brings joy and gladness with its promise of yet another day, of light once more, in which man may work and renew his association with his fellow-man in business or in pleasure. In short, with the new-born day, man rises to a new life. What more fitting symbol, then, than this of the promise of new life after death—of the immortality of the soul.

The late Dr. E. H. Cartwright, in his *Commentary on the Freemasonic Ritual*, (2nd edn., 1973, p. 186), wrote, with customary forthrightness:

'That bright morning star'. It should, of course be 'that bright and morning star', the phrase being a quotation from The Revelation, xxii, 16. The reference is definitely to Christ and is a relic of the time when the Craft was purely Christian. The allusion apparently escaped the notice of the revisers at the Union, when Christian references generally were excised. Some hold that, as we are not now exclusively Christian, but admit Jews, Moslems and others who, though monotheists, are not Christians, this reference should be deleted, as others of a like nature have been. If the phrase be objected to, the *Revised Ritual* provides an appropriate alternative rendering, namely, 'and lift our eyes to Him in whose hands are the issues of life and death, and to whose mercy we trust for the fulfilment of His gracious promises of Peace and Salvation to the faithful etc.'

My own view is that the reference to the 'Bright Morning Star' would be quite inexplicable if we read it in an astronomical sense, to imply that a particular star can bring peace, or tranquillity, or salvation, to mankind. As a Christian reference, moreover, this passage must cause embarrassment to Brethren who are not of that Faith and in two of my Lodges (of mainly Jewish Brethren) where this point arose, we now use the following:

. . . and lift our eyes to Him whose Divine Word brings Peace and Salvation to the faithful, etc.

This form of wording has two great advantages:

1. It provides a definite meaning to the passage instead of an ambiguous one.

2. It is in full accord with Masonic teaching and respects the religious beliefs of all the participants.

---

3. THE COMPASSES AND THE GRAND MASTER

Q. Why are the Compasses said to belong to the Grand Master?

A. Early official documents, i.e., the *Books of Constitutions* and the Grand Lodge Minutes, afford no information on this point. Jewels are mentioned in the *Constitutions* from 1738 onwards and frequently in the Grand Lodge Minutes from 1727 onwards, but the Grand Master's Jewel was not described in detail until the 1815 *B. of C.* It was to be of 'gold or gilt' and made up as follows:

> The compasses extended to 45°, with the segment of a circle at the points and a gold plate included, on which is to be engraven an irradiated eye within a triangle.

The Grand Master's Jewel
By courtesy of the Board of General Purposes

Nowadays, the triangle is also irradiated. It should be noted, however, that from 1815 onwards the Jewel contains several items in addition to the compasses.

The only hint, in a more-or-less official publication, suggesting that the compasses belong to the Grand Master, appears in the frontispiece to the first *Book of Constitutions*, 1723, which shows the Duke of Montagu handing a pair of compasses and a scroll to his successor, the Duke of Wharton, and there are no other tools in the picture. It would be unsafe to draw any firm conclusions from this item, because there are several documents from this period which show that the compasses belonged to the Master, not to the Grand Master. The earliest of these is the *Dumfries No.* 4 *MS., c.* 1710[1] (i.e. seven years before the election of the first Grand Master):

---

[1] See p. 5, footnote 1.

Q. would you know your master if you saw him?
A. yes
Q. what way would ye know him?
A. by his habit
Q. what couller is his habit?
A. yellow & blew meaning the compass w^c is bras & Iron

Very crude, but twenty years later the same theme appeared in better detail in a newspaper exposure, now generally known as *The Mystery of Free-Masonry*, 1730[1]:

Q. How was the Master cloathed?
A. In a Yellow Jacket and Blue Pair of Breeches.*

* N.B. The Master is not otherwise cloathed than common; the *Question* and *Answer* are only emblematical, the Yellow Jacket, the Compasses, and the Blue Breeches, the Steel Points.

Two months later, in October 1730, Prichard, in his *Masonry Dissected*, repeated this Q. and A., almost word for word, omitting only the first half of the N.B., i.e., he discarded the emblematical suggestion, thereby implying that the compasses were indeed part of the Master's regalia. Elsewhere, however, he had a note that the Master, at the opening of a Lodge, had 'the Square about his neck'. The *Wilkinson MS.*, c. 1727, agreed with Prichard on the compasses but omitted the reference to the Square.

In 1745, a popular French exposure, *L'Ordre des Francs-Maçons Trahi*, in which the catechism was substantially based on Prichard, dealt more fully with the same question:

Q. Have you seen the Grand Master? [= the W.M.]
A. Yes.
Q. How is he clothed?
A. In gold & blue. Or rather; In a yellow jacket, with blue stockings.

This does not mean that the Grand Master is dressed like that: but the yellow jacket signifies the head and the upper-part of the Compasses, which the Grand Master wears at the bottom of his Cordon, & which are made of gold, or at least gilt; & the blue stockings, the two points of the Compasses, which are of iron or steel. That is what they mean also, when they refer to the gold & blue.

The title 'Grand Master' was used quite loosely, in this text and in French practice at that period, to mean the Worshipful Master and the context of this quotation proves this beyond doubt.

It was not until the last quarter of the 18th century that the earliest English texts began to say that the compasses belonged to the Grand Master. The first of these was probably William Preston's version, in

[1] Reproduced in *The Early Masonic Catechisms*, 2nd edn. (1963) publ. by the Quatuor Coronati Lodge, London.

his 'First Lecture of Free Masonry' (which was reproduced by Bro. P. R. James, in *AQC* 82, pp. 104–149):

> Why are the compasses restricted to the Grand Master? The compasses are appropriated to Master Masons [*sic*] because it is the chief instrument used in the delineation of their plans and from this class all genuine designs originate. . . . As an emblem of dignity and excellence the compasses are pendent to the breast of the Grand Master to mark the superiority of character he bears amongst Masons. (See *AQC* 82, p. 138)

Preston wrote with his customary verbosity and his reference to Master Masons is rather confusing. The date of this version is uncertain, probably around 1790–1800. Later writers were more specific. Browne's *Master Key* (2nd ed.) appeared, mainly in cipher, in 1802:

> Why the Compasses to the Grand Master in particular? The Compasses being the chief instrument made use of in all plans and designs in Geometry, they are appropriated to the Grand Master as a mark of his distinction. . . .

Richard Carlile, in the *Republican*, 15 July 1825, wrote:

> The compasses belong to the Grand Master in particular, and the square to the whole craft.

Claret, 1838, also dealt with this question, and his answer has become standard in most modern versions of the Craft Lectures:

> That being the chief instrument made use of in the formation of all Architectural plans and designs, is peculiarly appropriated to the Grand Master, as an emblem of his dignity, he being the chief head and ruler of the craft.

Nowadays, a reference to the Jewels illustrated in the *Book of Constitutions* will show that the Compasses form a part of the Jewel of all the following:

1. The Grand Master
3. Pro Grand Master
5. Deputy Grand Master
7. Prov. or Dist. Grand Master
9. Grand Inspector

2. Past Grand Master
4. Past Pro Grand Master
6. Assistant Grand Master
8. Past Prov. or Dist. Grand Master
10. Past Grand Inspector

---

4. IT PROVES A SLIP

Q. 'It proves a slip'. How did those words arise?

A. Those words are the last relic of something that was a distinct feature of all early versions of the third degree. If one were challenged today to describe the lessons of the third degree in three words, most Brethren would say 'Death and Resurrection', and they would be right;

but originally there were three themes, not two, and all our early versions of the third degree confirm three themes, 'Death, *Decay* and Resurrection'. Any Brother who has a compost heap in his garden will see the significance of this 'life-cycle'.

Eventually, the decay theme was polished out of our English ritual, but 'the slip' which is directly related to that theme remains as a reminder of the degree in its early days.

The first appearance of 'the slip' in a Masonic context was in Samuel Prichard's *Masonry Dissected*, of 1730. That was the first exposure claiming to describe a system of three degrees and it contained the earliest known version of a Hiramic legend. Prichard's exposure was framed entirely in the form of Question and Answer and the main body of his legend appears in the replies to only two questions.

Many other and better versions have appeared since 1730, but *Masonry Dissected* (though it gives no hint of a long time-lag which might have caused decay) was the first to mention 'the slip' and to indicate that the cause was decay. The words occur in a footnote to the so-called 'Five Points of Fellowship'.

> N.B. When Hiram *was taken up, they took him by the Fore-fingers, and the Skin came off, which is called the Slip;* . . .

The next oldest version of the third degree was published in *Le Catéchisme des Francs-Maçons*, in 1744, by a celebrated French journalist, Louis Travenol. It was much more detailed than Prichard's piece, and full of interesting items that had never appeared before. In the course of the story we learn that nine days had passed when Solomon ordered a search, which also occupied a 'considerable time'. Then, following the discovery of the corpse,

> . . . One of them took hold of it by one finger, & the finger came away in his hand: he took him at once by another [finger], with the same result, & when, taking him by the wrist it came away from his arm . . . he called out *Macbenac*, which signifies among the Free-Masons, *the flesh falls from the bones. . . .*[1]

In 1745, Travenol's version was pirated in *L'Ordre des Francs-Maçons Trahi*, but there were a few improvements:

> . . . *the flesh falls from the bones or the corpse is rotten* [or decayed][2]

The English exposure *Three Distinct Knocks*, of 1760, used the words 'almost rotten to the bone', but before the end of the 18th century the

---

[1] *Early French Exposures*, pp. 97–8.
[2] *E.F.E.*, p. 258.

decay theme seems to have gone out of use in England, so that 'the slip', in word and action, remains as the last hint of the story as it ran in its original form. But the decay theme is not completely lost; several ritual workings, in French, German, and other jurisdictions, still retain it as part of their legend.

One more document must be quoted here, because it has particularly important implications. The *Graham MS.*, of 1726, is a unique version of catechism plus religious interpretation, followed by a collection of legends relating to various biblical characters, in which each story has a kind of Masonic twist. One of the legends tells how three sons went to their father's grave

> for to try if they could find anything about him ffor to Lead them to the vertuable secret which this famieous preacher had. . . . Now these 3 men had allready agreed that if that if they did not ffind the very thing it self that the first thing that they found was to be to them as a secret . . . so came to the Grave finding nothing save the dead body all most consumed away takeing a greip at a ffinger it came away so from Joynt to Joynt so to the wrest so to the Elbow so they R Reared up the dead body and suported it setting ffoot to ffoot knee to knee Breast to breast Cheeck to cheeck and hand to back and cryed out help o ffather . . . so one said here is yet marow in this bone and the second said but a dry bone and the third said it stinketh so they agreed for to give it a name as is known to free masonry to this day. . . . (*E.M.C.*, pp. 92–3).

The decay theme again, but the important point about this version is that the 'famieous preacher' in the grave was not H.A., but Noah, and the three sons were Shem, Ham, and Japheth. The appearance of this legend in 1726, *full four years before the earliest H.A. version by Prichard*, implies, beyond doubt, that the Hiramic legend did not come down from Heaven all ready-made as we know it today; *it was one of at least two (and possibly three) streams of legend* which were adapted and tailored to form the main theme of the third degree of those days.

---

5.   WHY TWO WORDS FOR THE M.M.?

Q. At a certain stage in the M.M. degree two words are uttered by the W.M. Why two?

A. There is ample evidence, from *c.* 1700 onwards, that *only one word was conferred originally*, though it appears in vastly different spellings and pronunciations. The earliest known version, in the *Sloane MS.*, of *c.* 1700, certainly belongs to the period when only two degrees were practised and, in the study of the evolution of the ritual, it is extremely interesting to find a feature of the original second degree making its appearance, ultimately, in the third.

At the end of 1725 there were already four different versions of the word in existence (two in manuscript and two in print) and before 1763 no fewer than eight versions had appeared in England alone. Whatever they were originally, by the time we find them in our early documents it would be fair to describe them as non-words, because they do not belong to any known language. As examples of debasement, *Sloane* gives the word(s) as Maha–Byn, half in one ear and half in the other; it was apparently used in those days as a test word, the first half requiring the answer 'Byn'. Other early versions were 'Matchpin', 1711, and 'Magbo and Boe', 1725.

It is generally agreed that the words were probably of Hebrew origin (in which case each of them would be a combination of two words, i.e., verb and noun); but from the time of their first appearance, either in MS. or print, they were already so debased, through ignorance or carelessness, that it is impossible to say how they were written or pronounced in their original form.

There are various printed exposures of 1760, 1762 and later, which suggest that the word was pronounced differently by adherents of the rival Grand Lodges, i.e., that the 'Moderns' used a form ending in a CH, CK, or K sound, while the 'Antients' used a form which finished with an N sound. This would seem to be a generalization that must be discounted, because there were three N versions in *c.* 1700, 1711 and 1723 respectively, decades before the Antients' Grand Lodge was founded.

Whether or not the rival Grand Lodges kept strictly to those forms (and we have to take note of the MS. catechisms and the printed exposures simply because there were no official pronouncements), the available evidence suggests that those were the two main forms in use in the English lodges throughout the 18th century.

Soon after the Lodge of Promulgation was erected (in 1809) to prepare the way for the union of the two Grand Lodges, this point came into question while dealing with the form of 'Closing the Lodge in the Third Degree', when the word is to be spoken aloud; but which word? It must have been a difficult problem, even for the distinguished members of that 'Moderns' body, partly because none of them could be certain that the form to which they were accustomed was correct, but also because it was necessary to make allowance for the form in use by the 'Antients'. This predicament gave rise to a Resolution that they made on 16 February 1810, which is a model of wisdom and tolerance:

> ... but that Masters of Lodges shall be informed that such of them as may be inclined to prefer another known method of communicating the s [*sic.*? secrets] in the closing ceremony will be at liberty to direct it so if they should think proper to do so. (*AQC* 23, p. 42.)

The special Lodge of Promulgation was a Moderns' body, but one of its members, Bro. Bonnor, was acknowledged to have an accurate knowledge of the Antients' ritual, and it is possible that this resolution was framed out of respect for the rival body, or because no compromise was possible.

Many of us must have heard some of the extraordinary pronunciations given to those 'Words' in our present-day Lodges, and I am inclined to believe that the alternate forms were approved simply because nobody could be sure which of them, if any, was correct.

---

6. APPRENTICE AND ENTERED APPRENTICE

Q. As used in Freemasonry today, are the terms Apprentice and Entered Apprentice interchangeable?

A. Under Art. ii of the Articles of Union, it was '. . . declared and pronounced that pure Ancient Masonry consists of three degrees, and no more; *Vizt.* those of the Entered Apprentice, the Fellow Craft . . .', etc. Strictly speaking, therefore, the only title for the first grade in the Craft nowadays is *Entered Apprentice*, and the title Apprentice could only stand as an abbreviation.

It is necessary to go back to early operative practice to explain the real difference between the two terms. Apprentices were usually indentured to their Masters for seven years, and in Scotland there is evidence that the Masters undertook to 'enter their apprentices' in the Lodge *during that period.*[1] In Edinburgh, it was the rule that all apprentices had to be 'booked' in the town's *Register of Apprentices*, at the beginning of their indentures. The *Register* survives from 1583 and shows that the 'bookings' recorded the names of the apprentice and his father, the father's trade and place of residence, the name, trade and residence of the master, the date of the 'booking' and (rarely) the actual date of the indentures—if there had been any delay in the 'booking'.

---

[1] See 'Apprenticeship in England and Scotland up to 1700', by H. Carr, *AQC* 69, pp. 57/8, 67/8); also 'The Mason and the Burgh', *AQC* 67.

These carefully detailed municipal records become valuable indeed when, from 1599 onwards, there are minutes for the Lodge of Edinburgh (Mary's Chapel), *in which it is possible to identify more than a hundred apprentices and to check the dates when they were admitted into the Lodge as 'entered apprentice'.* This usually happened some two to three years after the beginning of their indentures, and that marked the beginning of their career *within the Lodge.*

They would normally pass F.C. about seven years after they were made E.A., or roughly ten years from the commencement of their training. If for any reason they failed to pass F.C., they retained their Lodge status as E.A., even after their term of service had finished and they were already working as journeymen.

The Edinburgh system of introducing the apprentice into the Lodge *during* his apprenticeship did not exist in 1475, when the Masons and Wrights Incorporation [= Gild] was founded, but it was already fully established in 1598 when the earliest surviving Lodge minutes begin. The two to three-year time lag between 'booking' and E.A. may have been longer in other places. Unfortunately, it is only Edinburgh that still possesses the dual town-and-Lodge records, that enable us to verify their practice.

It is curious that the term 'entered apprentice' does not appear in English documents until the 1720s.

---

7.   THE TITLES OF THE UNITED GRAND LODGE OF ENGLAND

Q. What is the official title of the Grand Lodge of England? Here in the U.S.A. our Grand Lodges are F. & A.M., or A.F. & A.M., and this carries on down to the local Lodges. My own Lodge is commonly known as St. John's Lodge, No. 17, A.F. & A.M., yet I can find no reference to the full titles of Lodges operating under English jurisdiction. I find many references to the United Grand Lodge, but the United Grand Lodge of what?

A. The United Grand Lodge was erected in 1813 by a union of the so-called Antients' and Moderns' Grand Lodges under the Articles of Union, a lengthy document which outlined the conditions agreed for the government of the new body. The Articles were signed on 25 November 1813, and ratified by both Grand Lodges meeting independently six days later. Article vi declared that:

> ... the Grand Incorporated Lodge shall ... be opened ... under the stile and title of the United Grand Lodge of Ancient Freemasons of England.

On 27 December 1813, a Grand Assembly of Freemasons was held to give effect to the union, and the new organization was duly proclaimed under that title.

The first *Book of Constitutions* to be published after the union appeared in 1815, and the General Regulations were headed by a brief statement which gave a new title to the Grand Lodge:

> THE public interests of the fraternity are managed by a general representation of all private lodges on record, together with the present and past grand officers, and the grand master at their head. This collective body is stiled the UNITED GRAND LODGE OF ANTIENT FREE AND ACCEPTED MASONS OF ENGLAND ...

The earlier title, incorporating the expression 'Antient Freemasons of England' (but with the word 'Antient' spelt with a 't' instead of a 'c'), appeared in the printed record of Grand Lodge proceedings of March, May, June and September 1814, the word Free-Mason having a hyphen in May, June and September. It reappeared with a hyphen in the record of an Especial Grand Lodge in February 1815.

In May 1814, the Duke of Sussex was proclaimed as Grand Master of the United Grand Lodge of 'Antient Free-Masons of England', and in December 1814, he was proclaimed as G.M. of the United Grand Lodge of Ancient Free and Accepted Masons of England.

The reasons for the changes in nomenclature at this period are not apparent, but it must be inferred that the change from the expression 'Ancient Freemasons' of 1813 to the 'Antient Free and Accepted Masons' of 1815 was deliberate—a change which has been preserved in all subsequent editions of the *Book of Constitutions* to the present day. (Extracts from Notes compiled by Bro. W. Ivor Grantham.)

Strictly speaking, all English Lodges should add the A.F. & A.M. to their titles, but the practice is extremely rare.

---

8.   EVERY BROTHER HAS HAD HIS DUE

Q. What is the real meaning of the Senior Warden's words in closing the lodge, '. . . to see that every Brother had had his due.'?

A. This is an archaic survival, almost meaningless today. Yet the principle upon which it is based is one of the oldest in the English Craft, and its origins are to be found in our earliest operative documents, the *Old Charges*, or *MS. Constitutions*, which afford useful information on the management of large-scale building works in the 14th and 15th centuries.

To appreciate the full significance of these words, we may forget the lodge for the present, and go to the site where the works were in progress. In those days, the Warden (and there was only one Warden) was a kind of senior charge-hand, or overseer. Nowadays, we might call him a 'progress-chaser' and it was a part of his duties to ensure that nothing disturbed the smooth progress of the work.

If a dispute arose between any of the masons in his charge, he had to mediate and try to settle it on the spot and with absolute fairness, so that 'every Brother had his due'. If the trouble was too difficult to be settled at once, he had to fix what was called a 'loveday', which was a day appointed for the amicable settlement of disputes; but meanwhile, everyone had to get on with his work. The regulations specified that *the 'loveday' was to be held on a 'holy day', not a working day, so that the works would not suffer to the employer's detriment.* (*Cooke MS.*, c. 1400, Point vi.) The same text, at Point viii continues:

> . . . if it befall him for to be warden under his master that he be true mene [= mediator] between his master and his fellows and that he be busy in the absence of his master to the honour of his master and profit of the lord [= employer] that he serves.[1]

The *Regius MS.*, c. 1390, does not mention the warden in this context, but speaks of one who has taken a position of responsibility under his master:

> A true mediator thou must need be,
> To thy master and thy fellows free,
> Do truly all [good?] that thou might,
> To both parties, and that is good right.[1]

The same theme runs regularly through many of the old *Constitutions*, requiring the wardens to preserve harmony amongst the men under their care, by mediating fairly in any dispute that might arise, and thereby ensuring 'that every Brother had his due'.

Finally, there are many versions of these words in our modern rituals, including one which runs '. . . to pay the men their wages and see that every Brother has had . . .'. A careful examination of the texts

---

[1] From *The Two Earliest Masonic MSS.*, pp. 122–5. By Knoop, Jones and Hamer. Quotations word for word, but in modern spelling.

that deal with the Warden's duties show that wages have nothing to do with this particular question.

----

9.   ARMS OF THE GRAND LODGE

Q. What is the origin of the Arms of the United Grand Lodge of England?

A. The modern Arms are directly descended from three separate bodies, and their story begins in the 14th century, more than 300 years before the first Grand Lodge was founded.

THE LONDON MASONS' COMPANY

There are records at Guildhall in London which show that the Masons' Company was in existence in 1375. It was the first English Gild of the Mason trade and, in 1376, it elected representatives of the trade to serve on the Common Council, which was the organ of city government, proof of its status as one of the important city Companies.

The exact date of its foundation is unknown, but the roots of the Fellowship of Masons in England go back much further than that, to the year 1356, when twelve skilled master masons came before the Mayor and Aldermen at Guildhall, in London, to settle a demarcation dispute, and to draw up a code of trade regulations, because their trade had not, until then, 'been regulated in due manner, by the government of folks of their trade, in such form as other trades' were.

This was the true beginning of mason trade organization in England, which gave rise to the 'Hole Crafte & Felawship of Masons', later the London Masons' Company.

In 1472 it was given a Grant of Arms, which marked the highest form of official recognition of the Craft as one of the City Companies. The text of the Grant (with a few Anglo-Norman words rendered in modern English) runs as follows:

> To all Noblemen and gentlemen these present Letters hearing or seeing, William Hawkeslove, otherwise called Clarenceux King of Arms of the South Marches of England, sends humble and due Recommendation as appertaineth.
>
> For so much as the 'Hole Crafte and Felawship of Masons' heartily moved to exercise and use gentle and commendable guidance in such laudable manner and form as may best appear unto the gentry, by the Which they shall move with God's grace to attain unto honour and worship, have desired and prayed me, the said King of Arms, that I, by the power and

Arms of the Masons Company as stamped on the covers of the
MS. Account and Court Books.

authority and by the King's good grace to me in that behalf committed should devise A Cognisance of Arms for the said Craft and fellowship which they and their successors might boldly and dutifully occupy, challenge and enjoy for ever more, without any prejudice or rebuke of any estate or gentlemen of this Realm. At the instance and request of whom, I, the said King of Arms, taking respect and consideration unto the goodly intent and disposition of the said Craft and fellowship, have devised for them and their successors the Arms following, that is to say,

A field of Sable, a Chevron of Silver,[1] grailed,
three Castles of the same, garnished with doors and windows of the field,
In the Chevron, a Compass of Black,

which Arms, I of my said power and authority, have appointed, given and granted to, and for, the said Craft and fellowship and their successors. And by these my present Letters, appoint, give and grant unto them the same, To have, challenge, occupy and enjoy, without any prejudice, or impeachment, for evermore.

In witness whereof, I, the said King of Arms, to these presents have set my seal of Arms, with my sign Manual.

Given at London, the year of the Reign of King Edward the fourth, after the Conquest the xijth.

Clarenceux Kings of Arms
W.H.

---

[1] Note: it is a chevron, not a square.

This document gives us the earliest description of the design in black and silver, and, since 1472, the Arms reappear regularly—with occasional minor modification—in all sorts of Masonic documents. Many of the earliest versions of the *MS. Constitutions*, or *Old Charges*, from the 16th century onwards have the Arms emblazoned at their head. They are depicted in Stow's *Survey of London*, 1633, and we find them on tombstones, stained glass windows, and in architectural decoration, all over England. They are also depicted in the frieze of Arms of the City Companies which decorate the walls of Guildhall in London.

The original Grant contained no motto, and the earliest record of a motto attached to the Arms appears on the tomb of William Kerwin, dated 1594, in St. Helen's Church, Bishopsgate. It reads:

'God Is Our Guide'

The Company, indeed, has no authorized motto, but since the early 17th century, it appears to have used the words:

'In The Lord Is All Our Trust'

Arms Of The First Grand Lodge 1717–1813

There is evidence that the premier Grand Lodge, founded in 1717, began to use the Masons' Company's Arms soon after its foundation, though the early minute books are silent on this subject. In 1729–30, Thomas, 8th Duke of Norfolk, became Grand Master and, during his term of office, he presented to the Grand Lodge the Sword of State which is now borne in procession in Grand Lodge. Its silver-gilt hilt and mountings and the scabbard were made in 1730 by George Moody, the Royal Armourer, who was the first Sword-bearer of Grand Lodge, and the scabbard bears, *inter alia*, a reproduction of the Arms of the Masons' Company.

Despite the absence of any official record of the Arms being adopted by the Moderns' Grand Lodge, it was certainly using the 'Three Castles, Chevron and Compass' as the central theme of its Seal before 1813, and a less ornate version as its 'Office Seal'. Both are illustrated in Gould's *History*, 1951 edn., vol. II, fac. p. 275.

Arms Of The 'Antients' Grand Lodge 1751–1813

The Most Ancient and Honourable Society of Free and Accepted Masons according to the Old Institutions was founded in London in July 1751. At that time it consisted of only six Lodges with a total membership of some eighty Brethren. They were mainly artisans, tailors, shoemakers and painters 'of an honest Character but in low Circumstances'; many of them were immigrants from Ireland or of Irish extraction.

In 1752, Laurence Dermott became their Grand Secretary and he held that office until 1771 when he became Deputy Grand Master. He was already Past Master of a Dublin Lodge and a recent immigrant from Ireland, originally a journeyman painter, but later a successful wine merchant. A man of some education and a born leader, he compiled *Ahiman Rezon*, the first Book of Constitutions of the new Grand Lodge and published it in 1756. Boasting always of their adherence to the 'old System free from innovation' they soon became known as the 'Antients' and they thrived.

Arms of the Antients' Grand Lodge, 1751–1813.

The Arms of the Antients made their first appearance as the frontispiece to the 1764 edition of *Ahiman Rezon*, in which Dermott explained their origin at length:

N.B. The free masons arms in the upper part of the frontis piece of this book, was found in the collection of the famous and learned hebrewist, architect and brother, Rabi Jacob Jehudah Leon. This gentleman . . . built a model of Solomon's temple . . . This model was exhibited to public view . . . at Paris and Vienna, and afterwards in London, . . . At the same time . . . (he) . . . published a description of the tabernacle and the temple, . . . I had the pleasure of perusing and examining both these curiosities. The arms are emblazoned thus, quarterly per squares, counterchanged Vert. In the first quarter Azure a lyon rampant Or, in the second quarter Or, an ox passant sable; in the third quarter Or, a man with hands erect, proper robed, crimson and ermin; in the fourth quarter Azure, an eagle displayed Or. Crest, the holy ark of the covenant, proper, supported by Cherubims. Motto, Kodes la Adonai, i.e., Holiness to the Lord.

. . . Spencer says, the Cherubims had the face of a man, the wings of an eagle, the back and mane of a lion, and the feet of a calf.

. . . Ezekiel says, . . . a man, a lion, an ox, and an eagle.

. . . Bochart says, that they represented the nature and ministry of angels, by the lion's form is signified their strength, generosity and majesty; by that of the ox, their constancy and assiduity in executing the commands of God; by their human shape their humanity and kindness; and by that of the eagle, their agility and speed.

It seems probable that Rabbi Leon had indeed sketched designs more or less related to this one which Dermott had adapted, but Leon cannot have designed the Motto, which was printed in faulty Hebrew.

The Masonic significance of the design (apart from the working-tools at its foot) is closely related to the Royal Arch, and this was emphasized by Dermott's closing words on the subject:

As these were the arms of the masons that built the tabernacle and the temple, there is not the least doubt of their being the proper arms of the . . . fraternity of free and accepted masons, and the continual practice, formalities and tradition, in all regular lodges, from the lowest degree to the most high, i.e., The Holy Royal Arch, confirms the truth hereof.

ARMS OF THE UNITED GRAND LODGE

After 1751, the Antients' and Moderns' Grand Lodges existed side by side, not always without display of intense rivalry. In the late 1700s, however, there were many prominent Masons who held high rank in both bodies and in the early 1800s efforts were being made, behind the scenes, to effect a union. Eventually, and with the help of three Royal Brothers, all sons of George III, the negotiations proved successful and the Union took place in December 1813.

The Arms of the United Grand Lodge of England were a combination of the Arms of the Antients and Moderns, preserving the best features

Arms of the United Grand Lodge of England.
By courtesy of the Board of General Purposes.

of each, and the Hebrew inscription was corrected. In 1919, the shield was enhanced by a wide border bearing eight lions, suggesting the Arms of England and marking the long association of King Edward VII and many other members of the Royal Family with the Craft.

---

10.   L.F. ACROSS THE LODGE

Q. Why do we tell the Candidate in the First Deg. to 'Place your left foot across the Lodge and your r... f..., etc., heel to heel,' with similar but reverse procedure in the second? They seem to be awkward postures for the Cand. while he listens to the W.M.'s exhortation.

A. This is a survival from the time (probably before 1813) when it was customary to have the rough and smooth ashlars on the floor of the

Lodge, in the N.E. and S.E. corners, and not on the Wardens' pedestals, where they usually lie nowadays.

At the proper moment the Cand. was required to place his feet so that they formed a square on two sides of the ashlar, thus:

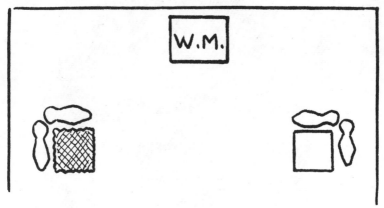

The N.E. corner   The S.E. corner

The ashlars in the N.E. and S.E. corners, as shown in our sketch, are still to be seen there in many of our old English lodges, but rather rarely in London, where we have succumbed to modern customs. The postures, however, are still in use in most English lodges (*not in all of them*) even when the ashlars rest on the Wardens' pedestals.

The reason for the postures is, undoubtedly, purely symbolical and it can best be explained in the words of a writer (Fort Newton, I believe) who said that we enter the Craft in order 'to build spiritual Temples within ourselves'. *When we stand at the N.E. or S.E. corners to hear the exhortation from the W.M., we are participating in the dedication of our own spiritual Foundation-stone.*

There appears to be no satisfactory explanation for the awkward posture. It could be avoided, of course, if the Cand. stands facing E., or if the W.M. comes on to the floor for the exhortation.

It has been suggested that in earlier times, the N.E. and S.E. positions were at the immediate right and left of the W.M., so that the Candidates standing at those positions would have been more comfortably placed than they are today. The fact is that most of these procedures are inherited practices and we tend to preserve them, even when the reasons that gave rise to them are lost in the mists of time.

11.   RAISING AND LOWERING THE
                         WARDENS' COLUMNS

Q. Why do the Wardens in a Craft Lodge raise and lower their
Columns? The usual explanations in the Lectures, etc., seem trivial, in
view of the importance many Brethren seem to place on the Columns
being moved at the right time and placed in the right position.

A. To find an acceptable answer to this question, we have to go back
to early ritual. There was a time in 18th century English practice when
both Wardens stood (or sat) in the West; this is confirmed by a passage
in *Masonry Dissected*, 1730:

> Q. Where stands your Wardens?
> A. In the West.

Incidentally there are several Masonic jurisdictions in Europe which
retain this ancient practice; but some time between 1730 and 1760 there
is evidence that the J.W. had moved to the South, as shown in *Three
Distinct Knocks*, 1760, and *J. & B.*, 1762, both using identical words:

> Mas. Who doth the Pillar of Beauty represent?
> Ans. The Junior Warden in the South.

The business of raising and lowering the Wardens' Columns made its
first appearance in England in *Three Distinct Knocks*, in which we have
the earliest description of the procedure for 'Calling Off' from labour
to refreshment and 'Calling On'. The 'Call-Off' procedure was as
follows:

> The Master whispers to the senior Deacon at his Right-hand, and says,
> 'tis my Will and Pleasure that this Lodge is called off from Work to
> Refreshment during Pleasure; then the senior Deacon carries it to the
> senior Warden, and whispers the same Words in his Ear, and he whispers
> it in the Ear of the junior Deacon at his Right-hand, and he carries it to the
> junior Warden and whispers the same to him, who declares it with a loud
> Voice, and says it is our Master's Will and Pleasure, that this Lodge is
> called from Work to Refreshment, during Pleasure;

At this point we find the earliest description of the raising and lowering of the columns and the reason for this procedure.

> then he sets up his Column, and the senior lays his down; for the Care
> of the Lodge is in the Hands of the junior Warden while they are at
> Refreshment.

> N.B. The senior and junior Warden have each of them a Column in their Hand,
> about Twenty Inches long, which represents the Two Columns of the Porch at
> *Solomon's* Temple, BOAZ and JACHIN.

J. & B. gives almost identical details throughout.

Unfortunately, apart from the exposures, there are very few Masonic writings that deal with the subject of the Wardens' Columns during the 18th and early 19th centuries. Preston, in several editions of his *Illustrations*, 1792–1804, in the section dealing with Installation, allocates the Columns to the Deacons [*sic*]. It is not until the 1804 edition that he speaks of the *raising* of the Columns, and then only in a footnote, as follows:

> When the work of Masonry in the lodge is carrying on, the Column of the Senior Deacon is raised; when the lodge is at refreshment the Column of the Junior Deacon is raised. [There is no mention of 'lowering'.]

Earlier, in the Investiture *of the Deacons*, Preston had said:

> Those columns, the badges of your office, I entrust to your care . . .

Knowing, as we do, that the Columns had belonged to the Wardens since 1760, at least, and that many of the Craft lodges did not appoint Deacons at all, Preston's remarks in the extracts above, seem to suggest that he was attempting an innovation (in which he was certainly unsuccessful).

The next evidence on the subject comes from the Minutes of the Lodge of Promulgation, which show that in their work on the Craft ritual in readiness for the union of the two rival Grand Lodges, they considered 'the arrangements of the Wardens' Columns' on 26 January 1810, but they did not record their decision. We know, however, that most of our present-day practices date back to the procedures which that Lodge recommended and which were subsequently adopted—with occasional amendments—and prescribed by its successor, the Lodge of Reconciliation. It is thus virtually certain that our modern working in relation to the raising and lowering of the Columns was then adopted, following the 1760 pattern, not only for 'Calling Off and On' but also for Opening and Closing generally.

Up to this point we have been dealing with facts; but on the specific questions as to why the Columns are raised and lowered, or why the care of the Lodge is the responsibility of the J.W. while the Brethren refresh themselves, we must resort to speculation.

In the operative system, *c.* 1400, when the Lodge was a workshop and before Lodge furniture was standardized, there was only one Warden. His duty was to keep the work going smoothly, to serve as a mediator in disputes and to see that 'every brother had his due'. We have documentary evidence of this in the *Regius* and *Cooke MSS* of *c.* 1390 and *c.* 1410, and this idea apparently persisted into the Speculative system where the S.W.'s duty in 1730 now included closing the Lodge and 'paying the men their wages'.

But in the Speculative system there were two Wardens, with the Senior, by ancient tradition, in charge of the Lodge (or the Brn.) while at work. It seems likely that in order to find a corresponding job for the J.W., he was put in charge of the Lodge (or the Brn.) while at refreshment.

There was no mention of *Wardens'* Columns, or procedures relating to them, in the exposures of 1730 or earlier. We may assume therefore that they were a more or less recent introduction in the period between 1730 and 1760, that the 'raising and lowering' procedures came into practice at about the same time and were subsequently authorized at the Union in 1813.

The 1760 explanation is still in use today. It may seem inadequate, but that is invariably the case with such problems as 'one up and one down', 'left-foot, right-foot', 'left-knee, right-knee', etc., because each interpretation has to give a satisfactory explanation for a particular procedure and for the reverse of that procedure, which is virtually impossible. The only satisfying explanation in this case is the simplest of all, i.e., the procedure was laid down to mark a distinction between the Lodge when open, and when it is closed or 'Called Off'.

During the 18th century, there is ample evidence that much of the Lodge work *was conducted at table*, punctuated by 'Toasts' and drinking, *while the Lodge was still Open*. If the Lodge was 'Called Off', while a meal (as distinct from liquid refreshment) was to be taken, and the Brethren remained in their seats at table, then some signal—recognizable at a glance—would have to be shown, to indicate whether the Lodge was at work, or at refreshment. (I am indebted to Bro. Colin Dyer for this final paragraph, which emphasizes the practical reasons for Columns up, and down.)

---

12. ORIENTATION OF THE BIBLE AND OF THE SQUARE AND COMPASSES

Q. Should the Bible be placed so that it can be read by the W.M., or the Candidate?

A. This question would not arise in Ireland, Scotland, U.S.A., or in the many jurisdictions which have their Altars at a distance from the W.M., usually in the middle of the lodge. In such cases the V.S.L. is always arranged to face the Candidate, i.e., so that it can be read from the West.

In English Masonic practice, however, the Master's pedestal is, in most cases, the Altar, so that when a Candidate is taking his Obligation, both are near enough to the Holy Book to be able to read it; hence the question.

In all regular Masonic jurisdictions the V.S.L. is an essential part of the lodge while it is in session; but in English practice there is no official rule as to which way it should be turned. My own view is that it does not matter at all which way the Bible is facing on a night when the Brethren are listening to a lecture, or when the lodge is conducting business *without a Candidate*. But on a night when a Candidate is to be obligated, the question becomes vastly more important.

Under English Masonic law, our lodges are required to provide for each Candidate that particular version of Holy Writ which belongs to his faith. The precise words are extremely interesting and will bear repetition:

> 4. The Bible, referred to by Freemasons as the Volume of the Sacred Law, is always open in the Lodges. *Every Candidate is required to take his Obligation on that book or on the Volume which is held by his particular creed to impart sanctity to an oath* or promise taken upon it.[1]
>
> (*Aims and Relationships of the Craft*, 1949)

A similar regulation, adopted in 1929, is still in force, although it omits the alternative:

> 3. That all Initiates shall take their Obligation on or in full view of the open Volume of the Sacred Law, by which is meant *the revelation from above which is binding on the conscience of the particular individual who is being initiated.*[1]
>
> (Basic Principles For Grand Lodge Recognition, 1929.)

This means that for a Jew we must provide an *Old Testament*; for a Mohammedan, a *Koran*; for a Hindu, a *Bhagvada Gita*, etc., etc. It might well happen that a Mohammedan or a Hindu, to avoid embarrassment, would say 'Don't worry; a *New Testament* will do just as well'. If we allowed that, we would be compounding a Masonic felony! We are bound to obligate him on the Holy Book which is sacred to his faith. In the best sense of the words it will be his Book and there can be no doubt that, for the Obligations, at least, the Book should be so arranged that he can easily recognize and read it.

---

[1] Author's italics.

For those who would like to have an official example as a check on their own practice, in our own Grand Lodge of England the V.S.L. is always opened facing westwards, with the points of the Compasses towards the foot of the page.

It may be interesting at this point to observe the procedure in two other jurisdictions:

Bro. G. L. Austin, Local Secretary for Q.C. in New Zealand, writes: In the New Zealand Ritual there is a rubric instructing that the Volume shall be placed '. . . so as to be read from the E., . . .', i.e., it faces the W.M. It is the custom of the Lodges in this Constitution to present to each newly raised Candidate a copy of the V.S.L. This copy measures about 6 in. × 4 in. It is placed between the large Volume and the Candidate in all three Degrees, and most Masters place it so that it may be read from the W., i.e., by the Candidate. He uses the same Volume for each Degree and seals his Ob. on the small Book, which is presented to him after Raising.

Bro. R. E. Parkinson writes: In Ireland the V.S.L. rests on the Altar in the middle of the Lodge Room, and it is placed so as to be read by the Candidate. In the Grand Lodge Room in Dublin, and in some old Lodges (including my own, No. 367, in Downpatrick), each of the principal officers also has a copy on his pedestal, and one of these should always be open, i.e., as the J.W. declares the Lodge open he closes his copy: the S.W. and W.M. in turn open theirs. Similarly, at closing, the J.W. opens his copy, and the S.W. and W.M. close theirs in turn.

There is another aspect of the use of the V.S.L. which may have a bearing on our problem. A number of our old documents contain details of the manner in which the Obligation was administered. In many of the *Old Charges*, we find an instruction, often in Latin, which runs:

Then one of the Seniors holds the book and he or they [that are to be admitted] put their hands upon the book while the Charges ought to be read.

(Translated from the *Thorp MS.*, c. 1629, *AQC*, Vol. 11, p. 210.)

The *Beaumont MS.*, c. 1690, precedes this instruction with a heading:

The Manno^r of taking an Oath att the Making free Masons.

But the *Old Charges* do not say which way the 'book' was facing.

The *Edinburgh Register House MS.*, 1696, and its two sister texts, furnish different details:

Imprimis you are to take the person to take the word [i.e., the Mason Word] upon his knees and after a great many ceremonies to frighten him you make him take up the bible and laying his right hand on it you are to conjure him to sec[r]ecie . . . [followed by the form of the oath].

It is clear that the Candidate lifted the Bible, holding it in or on his left hand, with his right hand upon it and it would seem safe to assume that he held the Book so that he could read it, not upside-down.

Yet another method is described in Prichard's *Masonry Dissected*, 1730. The catechism indicates that the Candidate was shewn 'how to walk up (by three steps) to the Master' and the Candidate's posture for the Obligation is described as follows:

> With my bare-bended Knee and Body within the Square, the Compass extended to my naked Left Breast, my naked Right Hand on the Holy Bible; there I took the Obligation . . .

The *Mason's Confession* (published in 1755–6, but claiming to describe the ceremony of *c.* 1727) gives an unusual posture:

> . . . the open compasses pointed to his breast, and his bare elbow on the Bible with his hand lifted up; and he swears . . .

Later, in the same text, we find:

> After the oath, a word in the scriptures was shewed me, which, said one, is the mason-word. The word is in I Kings vii. 21 . . .

Since the Candidate was invited to read the passage, we may fairly conclude that the V.S.L. was placed facing him.

It has been suggested that in the earlier years of Speculative Masonry under the premier Grand Lodge, the Bible on the Master's pedestal would be arranged to face him, as 'the source of light and instruction', and that the Antients generally administered the Obligation in the West, with the Bible resting between the Candidate's hands. Both practices were certainly in use, but there are two important and influential exposures which show that there was no such clear-cut distinction.

Three Distinct Knocks, 1760, which claimed to describe the practice of the Antients, contained a diagram showing that the Candidate took his Obligation facing the Master, but standing just one pace in front of the S.W. in the West, and the posture is described in excellent detail, as follows:

> . . . my left Knee bare bent, my Body upright, my right Foot forming a Square, my naked right Hand upon the Holy Bible, with the Square and Compass thereon, my Left-Hand supporting the same; . . .

It is virtually certain that in this posture, in the West and away from the Master's pedestal, the V.S.L. was held by the Candidate so that he could read it.

J. & B. was first published in 1762, claiming to represent Moderns' practice, but on this point the rival procedures are word-for-word identical.

These two documents were exposures, not official publications, and despite their apparent uniformity there can be no doubt that other forms were in use. The best evidence for this is in Wm. Preston's *First Lecture of Free Masonry*, which describes the body and knee positions as in *Three Distinct Knocks*, but then continues:

right hand voluntarily laid on the Holy Law, left hand either supporting the Law [i.e., the V.S.L.] or holding the compasses in the form of a square and one point extended at the n . . . . l . . . b . . . . .

(*AQC*, Vol. 82, p. 125.)

Preston's *First Lecture* is the only version I have been able to trace which gives full sanction to both forms and shows that both were in general use.

Browne's *Master Key*, 1802, had the left hand supporting the Compasses, and that posture seems to have been adopted at the union of the Grand Lodges; but no regulation was made as to the orientation of the V.S.L., and there is not a single document that affords instruction on that point.

These notes are not intended to conflict with established practice, or with any particular working that contains a ruling on the subject. Unfortunately, most of our modern workings fail to provide any such directions.

One final note; whichever way the Bible faces, the *Compass-points must always be towards the foot of the page*. Otherwise, something is noticeably upside-down.

---

13. THE POINTS OF FELLOWSHIP

Q. Are the Points of Fellowship of operative or speculative origin? Did they have any kind of symbolic explanation when they first appeared?

A. The Points of Fellowship make their first appearance in Masonic documents in 1696, some twenty years before the creation of the first Grand Lodge and long before there is any real evidence of Speculative Freemasonry. They appear during the next thirty-five years in a number of documents from different parts of Britain, suggesting that they were widely known among masons long before the date of the first version, 1696.

There is a particular attraction in trying to trace the old practices of the Craft, not merely for their antiquity, but because it is so interesting to see how far they differed from modern procedures and to notice, occasionally, their close resemblance.

The 'Points' are described for the first time in the *Edinburgh Register House MS.*, in a section which relates to the ceremony for the 'master mason or fellow craft', which was the second degree in the two-degree system, at a time when only two degrees were known to the Craft. The text at one stage speaks of '. . . the posture [in which] he is to receive the word . . .' Elsewhere, there are two questions:

Q. 1. Are you a fellow craft?
A.   yes
Q. 2. How many points of the fellowship are ther?
A.   fyve *viz*. foot to foot Knee to Kn[ee] Heart to Heart, Hand to Hand and ear to ear . . .

There are six texts in all, from 1696 to *c*. 1727, which have the five Points in exactly the same detail as those described above, but the last of them, 'A Mason's Confession', which claims to record the practice in a Scottish operative lodge in 1727, begins 'Hand to Hand . . .' and two of them speak of 'proper Points' without any mention of Points of Fellowship.

There are, moreover, two texts in which the procedure consists of *six* Points, instead of five, i.e.,

The 'Mason's Examination', which was the first printed exposure, published in a London newspaper in 1723:

Q. How many Points be there in Fellowship?
A. Six; Foot to Foot, Knee to Knee, Hand to Hand, Ear to Ear, Tongue to Tongue, Heart to Heart.

The Grand Mystery Laid Open, a folio broadsheet, printed in 1726, speaks of six 'Spiritual Signs':

What are these Signs, The first is Foot to Foot, the second is Knee to Knee, the third is Breast to Breast, the fourth is Hand to Back, the fifth is Cheek to Cheek, the sixth is Face to Face.

The Graham MS., 1726, does not mention Points of Fellowship, but in its description of the raising of Noah (the earliest raising in a Masonic context) it lists five items, including the 'hand to back' theme:

. . . and suported it [the corpse] setting ffoot to ffoot knee to knee Breast to breast Cheeck to cheeck and hand to back . . .

In addition to all these versions, there are three early descriptions of *postures* which seem to be related to the Points of Fellowship, though it is obvious that the writers were ignorant of precise details:

Standing close With their Breasts to each oth^{er} the inside of each oth^{ers} right Ancle Joynts the mast^{ers} grip by their right hands and the top of their Left hand fingers thurst [thrust?] close on ye small of each oth^{ers} Backbone ... till they whisp^{er} ...

(*Sloane MS*. 3329, *c*. 1700.)

The Trinity College, Dublin, MS. dated 1711, contains the shortest and most amusing version, described as 'The Masters sign':

Squeese the Master by ye back bone, put your knee between his, & say ...

The third of these postures is a much more complex affair. It appears in the 'Mason's Examination', of 1723, which, as noted above, also contains a 'six Points' version:

To know a Mason privately, you place your Right Heel to his Right Instep, put your Right Arm over his Left, and your Left under his Right, and then make a Square with your middle Finger, from his Left Shoulder to the middle of his Back, and so down to his Breeches.

One further version of the Points must be included here, from Samuel Prichard's *Masonry Dissected*, 1730, because it was then, for the first time, embodied in the third degree and directly linked with a Hiramic legend:

Hand to Hand, Foot to Foot, Cheek to Cheek, Knee to Knee, and Hand in Back.

As to the question of explanation of the Points, the late Bro. Douglas Knoop, in his Prestonian Lecture on 'The Mason Word', discussed possible sources and cited three Biblical examples 'of miraculous restoration to life ... by ... complete coincidence between the living and dead'; [Elijah, in 1 Kings, xvii, 17–23; Elisha, in 2 Kings, iv, 34–35; St. Paul, Acts, xx, 9–12]. He concluded:

It is thus not impossible that the original stories of Noah and Hiram may have been those of attempts to restore these men to life, because their secrets had died with them. (See *Collected Prestonian Lectures*, pp. 255/6. Publ. by the Q.C. Lodge, 1965.)

It is strange that none of the early texts up to 1730 contains a single word of *explanation* of the Points and this applies equally to the *Graham MS.*, 1726, and *Masonry Dissected*, 1730, in both of which the Points were linked to legends. It was not until the 1760s, when a whole new stream of English exposures began to appear, that we find explanations attached to each of the Points. They are reproduced here as the earliest known version, from *Three Distinct Knocks*, which appeared in 1760:

Mas[ter] ... Pray will you explain them.

Ans. 1st. Hand in Hand is, that I always will put forth my Hand to serve a Brother as far as lies in my power.

2d. Foot to Foot is, that I will never be afraid to go a Foot out of my way to serve a Brother.

3d. Knee to Knee is, that when I kneel down to Prayers, I ought never to forget to pray for my Brother as well as myself.

4th. Breast to Breast, is to show I will keep my Brother's secrets as my own.

5th. The Left-hand supporting the Back, is that I will always be willing to support a Brother as far as lies in my power.

We are fortunate in being able to compare these ancient practices of nearly 300 years ago with our modern procedures. They were certainly of operative origin, but their speculative symbolism arose in the 18th century.

---

14.   THE SECOND PART OF THE THREEFOLD SIGN

Q. Is it the Sn. of Prayer or Perseverance? I believe that the vast majority of modern rituals use the term 'perseverance', though it is difficult to see why that word was adopted.

A. In Exodus xvii, v. 8–13, we have the source to which the sign is most frequently attributed. The story tells of the Israelites in battle with the Amalekites, on the road to the Promised Land. Moses climbed to the top of the hill looking down on the battle, and 'when Moses held up his hand . . . Israel prevailed; and when he let down his hand, Amalek prevailed'. Later, both his hands were supported until victory was won and, although the word 'prayer' is not mentioned during this incident, there is little doubt that the posture, one hand or two, was a posture of prayer.

In the description of the origins of this particular sign, there are several English rituals which refer to the sun standing still and continuing the 'light of day' etc. The rubrics in these rituals usually refer this incident, correctly, to Joshua, x, v. 6–14; but it is difficult to see in what way it is related to the sign. A careful reading of the text shows that Joshua spoke, or prayed, to God, and he [Joshua] commanded the sun 'to stand still', i.e., to continue the light of day etc. There is positively no mention of a sign, and no hint that he made any kind of sign.

A third famous case of hands lifted in prayer is in I Kings viii, v. 22, when Solomon 'spread forth his hands toward heaven' at the dedication of his Temple, and again in v. 54, when he arose 'from kneeling on his knees with his hands spread up to heaven'. There is no clue to the idea of 'perseverance' in any of these cases.

Many of the Provincial workings do not use the word 'perseverance' as the distinctive name of the sign in question, but call it the Sn. of Prayer, and the emergence of the sign is a problem in itself. There is an unusual note in 'A Mason's Confession' (published in 1755–6, but claiming to describe the practices of *c.* 1727) which describes the Candidate's posture for the E.A. Obligation thus:

> . . . the open compasses pointed to his breast, and his bare elbow on the Bible with his hand lifted up;

This seems to be a confusion of two separate procedures, and it must be emphasized that a rather curious sign which appears at a later stage in the text is not the sign in question, nor is it named. (See *E.M.C.*, pp. 100, 102.)

The second part of the Threefold Sign seems to have been quite late in coming into general practice, and the earliest details I can find in our ritual documents are in *Three Distinct Knocks*, 1760, and *J. & B.*, 1762. Both texts indicate that it formed part of the F.C. Candidate's posture while taking his Obligation, and later in the ceremony he was entrusted with that part of the sign, though *it did not yet have its distinctive name.*

Preston, in his *Second Lecture of Free Masonry*, was almost certainly describing pre-union practice when he used that sign as part of the Candidate's posture, and in the subsequent catechism, he used the word 'perseverance', a title which probably came into use in the last two decades of the 18th century. The *Shadbolt MS.* has 'perseverance' as the name of the sign. That text is now accepted as an early record of post-union practice, representing the ritual and procedures after the Lodge of Reconciliation had made its final revisions.

Cartwright dealt with the title 'Perseverance' at length (in his *Commentary on the Freemasonic Ritual*, pp. 170–1); he believed that the Emulation school introduced it in order to distinguish that sign from what they call the Sn. of Prayer (i.e. the S. of F. with the thumb closed). We know now that this was incorrect, because that name was already in use long before the Emulation Lodge of Improvement came into existence, in 1823.

The customary definitions of 'perseverance', i.e. 'steadfast pursuit of an aim' and 'tenacious assiduity or endeavour' are very appropriate, and they are supported by extracts from Preston's *Second Lecture*, First Section, Clauses I and III. In the preliminaries to the Candidate's admission for the F.C. Degree, (Cl. I) he is announced in a very long speech, as:

A Bro. Mason who has been initiated into the First Degree of the Order, *has behaved well, served faithfully* and is *desirous of becoming more expert* ...; that he, being regularly proposed and approved by the Master ... as a candidate for preferment, honoured by them with the Test of Merit, properly prepared by Craftsmen and comes of his own free will humbly to solicit, not to demand. the secrets and privileges of the Second Degree *as a reward for his past industry.*

(Several phrases have been shown here in italics, only to draw attention to Preston's emphasis on assiduity).

Later, in Cl. III, relating to the entrusting, the text runs:

> What is the first secret?
> It is the three-fold sign.
> Give the first part. Gives it [i.e. the Pen. Sn.]
> To what does it allude?
> To the penalty of the Obligation.
> Give the second part. Gives it [i.e. the S. of F.]
> To what does it refer?
> To the fidelity of a Craftsman.
> Give me the third part. Gives it.
> To what does it refer?
> To the perseverance of a Craftsman.

(See *AQC*, Vol. 83, pp. 202, 205.)

These two passages from Preston's Lecture, when taken together, show that the word 'perseverance', which later became one of the names of that sign, was directly related to the Candidate's behaviour, service, zeal and industry, so that the conferment of the F.C. Degree was in fact a reward for 'Perseverance'.

It seems a pity that these passages have disappeared from our modern versions of the Lecture, and nowadays we describe the supposed Biblical source of the sign, without adequate explanation of its name and meaning.

Finally, the $64,000 question, which was not posed in this instance. Should the hand, when seen from the front, be seen flat, or edgewise? This question arises constantly, especially from Brethren who have witnessed both forms. Once again, there is no official ruling, and the innumerable printed versions of the ritual afford no information on this point. It is not possible, therefore, to determine that either version is correct, or incorrect.

Dr. Cartwright held that 'without doubt' the flat position was the original, and he supported it with a quotation from the *Bristol* working, in which the Master directs that the hand should be held p . . m to the f . . . t. The *Bristol* working has never been published by any authorizing body, and the instruction is an oral one; but the *Bristol* ritual is certainly one of the oldest versions in continuous use in England, and on that ground alone it must command attention. Many, if not most of the Provincial lodges follow Bristol fashion; the London lodges generally show the hand edgewise, which Dr. Cartwright described as an innovation.

As a Preceptor, I have taught the 'edgewise' position for many years, because my Mother Lodge inherited that practice, but I firmly believe that the Bristol usage is much older, and probably more 'correct'.

---

15.   DIVIDED LOYALTIES?
THE SOVEREIGN—PLACE OF RESIDENCE—NATIVE LAND

Q. The Charge in the First Degree under New South Wales Constitution has two (possibly conflicting) principles expressed in one sentence:

> . . . You are to pay obedience to the laws of any country or state which may, even for a time, become your place of residence, or afford you its protection; and, above all, let me especially charge you never to forget the allegiance due to the ruler of your native land, remembering that nature has implanted in your breast a sacred and indissoluble attachment to the country whence you derived your birth and infant nurture.

Thus, on the one hand the Candidate is required to be a lawful citizen of his place of residence and on the other to remember the allegiance due to his native land and its ruler. Could you give me some guidance on the emergence of the 'lawful citizen' principle and the 'infant nurture—native land' idea?

A. The Mason's duty to be a law-abiding citizen is drawn directly from Anderson's Charge II of the 'Charges of a Free-Mason' under the heading *Of the* CIVIL MAGISTRATE *supreme* and *subordinate*, and with only minor modifications it appears under the same headings in the English *Book of Constitutions* to this day:

> A *Mason* is a peaceable Subject to the Civil Powers, wherever he resides or works, and is never to be concern'd in Plots and Conspiracies against the Peace and Welfare of the Nation nor behave himself undutifully to inferior Magistrates . . .
> (Anderson's *B. of C.*, 1723.

> In the State, a Mason is to behave as a peaceable and dutiful Subject, conforming cheerfully to the Government under which he lives . . .
> (Smith's *Pocket Companion*, 1735 'Charge to . . . new Brethren'.)

... He is cheerfully to conform to every lawful authority . . .
(*B. of C.*, U.G.L. of England, p. 4, 1970.)

As to the question on loyalty and duty to your native land, loyalty to the King is one of the oldest injunctions in the Craft. The earliest surviving version of the *Old Charges*, the *Regius MS.* of *c.* 1390, prescribed (word for word in modern spelling):

And to his liege lord the King
To be true to him over all thing

The *Cooke MS.* of *c.* 1410:

... and they shall be true to the King of England and the realm . . .

and loyalty to the King, without treason or treachery, is prescribed in every version of the *Old Charges*—often as part of the candidate's composite obligation of loyalty to the King, his Masters and Fellows.

I suggest it was the *Cooke MS.*, *c.* 1410, which first drew attention to the mason's duty to his native land with its reference to the 'King of England *and the realm* . . .' and Anderson implied much the same in his reference to the 'Welfare of the Nation . . .' quoted above.

It was Preston in his 1796 *Illustrations* who added to the 'loyalty to sovereign and country' the new idea:

... yielding obedience to the laws which afford you protection, and never forgetting *the attachment you owe to the spot where you first drew breath* . . .

In his 1801 edition, Preston rearranged his words without improving them:

... never forgetting the attachment you owe to the place of your nativity, or the allegiance due to the sovereign and protectors of that spot.

The 1804 English edition and the 1st American edition published in that year had the same wording as in 1801. Likewise the 1821 edition, which was published three years after Preston's death, and Dr. Oliver's editions of 1829 and 1840 retained those words unchanged.

The change to our present wording seems to have made its first appearance in print in Richard Carlile's exposure, *The Republican*, dated Friday, 8 July 1825:

... and, above all, by never losing sight of the allegiance due to the Sovereign of your native land: ever remembering that nature has implanted in your breast a sacred and indissoluble attachment to that country, from which you derived your infant birth and nurture . . .

When this question was first posed to me in 1962, it dealt specifically with possible conflict of loyalties and the examples then quoted included Englishmen resident in America during the War of Independence, or

Masons residing in any country that might be at war with their native land. I found that difficult to answer, since the early versions of our Charges and later Masonic Regulations etc., apparently did not envisage emigration.

If I dare to answer now with a little more confidence than before, it is only because I am quite sure that in such a conflict of loyalties the Mason's duty must be first of all to the land in which he resides and which 'affords him protection'.

---

16.   SQUARING THE LODGE

Q. In our working, we square the lodge; but I have visited lodges in which that is not done. Why do we square the lodge?

A. It is almost certain that the practice arose unintentionally. In the early 1730s, the 'lodge', i.e. the Tracing Board, was drawn on the floor, usually within a border, or else the 'floor-cloth' (then just coming into use) was rolled out in the middle of the floor. In the small tavern rooms which were the principal places of meeting there cannot have been much space left for traversing the lodge and, if the 'drawing' or 'floor-cloth' was to be protected, a certain amount of squaring was inevitable. Of course, it was not the 'heel-clicking' type of precise squaring, but simply a natural caution to avoid disturbing or spoiling the design.

There is a minute, dated 1734, of the Old King's Arms Lodge, now No. 28, which mentions 'the Foot Cloth made use of at the Initiation of new members', but the earliest pictures of 'floor-cloths' in use, are dated 1744, and they show fairly large designs laid out to cover most of the floor of a small lodge room, with all the Brethren grouped around. Looking at those engravings, one can see that squaring was almost obligatory. (See illustration on p. ii.)

The earliest record I can find describing perambulations round the 'floor-cloth' is in *Réception d'un Frey-Maçon*, 1737, which says that the Candidate was

> . . . made to take three tours in the Chamber, around a space marked on the Floor, where . . . at the two sides of this space they have also drawn in crayon a great J. & a great B. . . .

(*E.F.E.*, p. 6.)

Most workings nowadays square the Lodge, clockwise, during the ceremonies, but the exaggerated squaring, which requires all movements to be made clockwise round the floor of the Lodge and forbids crossing diagonally even during ordinary business, probably arose in the mid-1800s. The word exaggerated is used deliberately here, because the practice is often carried to extremes, which are a waste of valuable time. I cite only one example; there are many more:

> In English Lodges the Secretary sits on the N. side of the Lodge, facing the J.W. in the S. The S.D. sits in the N.E. corner and, after the minutes have been read and confirmed, it is his duty to collect the Minute-book from the Secretary's desk, some ten feet away (anti-clockwise), and take it to the W.M. for signature. Then, to take the book back to the Secretary and return to his own place. All perfectly neat and simple; but in lodges that worship the clockwise procedure, this would not be permitted. The S.D. must cross the lodge from N.E. to S.E., then down to the J.W. in the South, then cross again, South to North, to take the book from the Secretary's table and lastly, with the book, to the W.M. After the W.M. has signed the Minutes, the S.D. is still only ten or twelve feet away from the Secretary's table, but he is not allowed to walk there anti-clockwise; he must do the whole tour again! The S.D. may look like a demi-god and march like a guardsman, but the whole business is still tedious and a waste of time.

The practice of squaring is wholly admirable, because it adds much to the dignity of the ceremonies, so long as it is not carried to extremes.

---

17.   THE WINDING STAIRS

Q. In Craft Masonry all movements are made clockwise, 'with the sun', but in the Second Degree, the five steps up the Winding Stairs are made anti-clockwise. Why?

A. There is an exaggeration in this question, which demands comment. The clockwise procedure is custom, not law, even in those Lodges where clockwise movements have become a fetish.

In English Lodges, the Altar is in the East, forming a pedestal in front of the W.M. When the Candidate in the Second Degree is led up to it to take his Obligation, he is supposedly copying our ancient Brethren who went into the Temple by an entrance on the south side and made their way, by a Winding Stair, to the 'middle chamber', whose precise location is not specified. But the majority of English workings relating to those steps start the Candidate at the N.E., and lead him to the Altar in the East. In plain fact, we are not even trying to copy the supposed ancient practice, and the two procedures cannot be reconciled.

I have never seen an interpretation of the 'Winding Stairs' in K.S.T. which proves that they rose clockwise or anti-clockwise, and although

Above: Tracing Board of the 2°, c. 1820 Winding Stairs, clockwise.

At Left: Tracing Board of the 2°, by Bro. Esmond Jefferies. Winding Stairs, anti-clockwise.

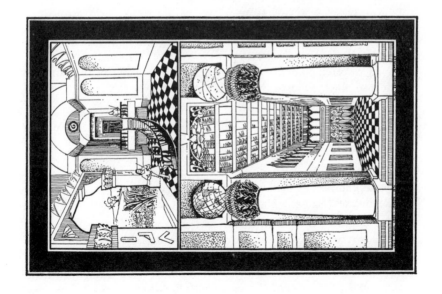

Lodge customs in such matters should not be changed lightly, the objection to the anti-clockwise approach would be removed if the Cand. were to *begin his journey from a point in the middle of the floor*, travelling clockwise towards the Altar. This procedure is practised in many overseas jurisdictions, especially in those which have their Altar in the centre of the lodge.

This question is closely connected with the illustrations of the Winding Stair on the Tracing Boards. A glance at the illustrations in Dring's famous paper on Tracing Boards (*AQC* 29) shows the vast majority of the Winding Stairs spring from left to right, i.e., anti-clockwise. But Figures 25, 34, 36 and 56 all show the stairs springing clockwise, from right to left. This is a problem that must have troubled many of the artists who designed the Boards, as well as the students who followed them, and the relevant verses in I Kings, vi, 5–10, do not throw any light on this point.

Reverting to the clockwise fetish; it probably had its origins in two quite separate sources:

    1. An interest in the movements of the sun (its rising, its meridian, and its setting) to be found in many of our earliest versions of the ritual. These themes continue in our ritual to this day and they certainly gave rise to our modern clockwise procedure.

    2. The custom of 'Drawing the Lodge' which led to the practice of 'squaring', as described in the preceding answer.

In the course of time, these two practices merged quite naturally, and our modern ceremonies are all the better for this degree of uniformity which is so much admired by our visitors from overseas.

---

18.   PENALTIES IN THE OBLIGATIONS

Q. What is the background to the penalties in the Obligations? Everyone knows that they were never inflicted, but they must terrify the Candidates. Can anything be done about them?

A. The question, as framed above, is a composite of questions and comments received, following the publication in *AQC* Vol. 74, (1961), pp. 129–133, of a paper by the present writer, 'The Obligation and its place in the ritual', which traced the evolution of the mason's Obligation, from the earliest hint of its existence, in *c.* 1390, down to 1730. A footnote to that paper made reference to some well-founded criticism of the Craft in relation to the penalties, and applauding some useful modifications, then recently introduced in Scotland with permission of their Grand Lodge. A number of comments came in, as usual, but the paper—which was not intended to be more than a historical account of the Obligation—did not arouse any unusual notice.

I shall try to deal, first, with the background to the penalties and then with the steps that have been taken by the United Grand Lodge of England in this matter.

It is not possible to discuss the penalties here in detail. They were apparently borrowed from treason penalties that were current in England in the 14th and 15th centuries and they seem to have been of rather late introduction into the Craft ritual. The earliest ritual documents, for example, 1696—*c*.1710, indicate that there was a penalty (or penal sn.,) for the E.A., but no others are mentioned. The *Dumfries No. 4 MS.*, *c*. 1710, adds several others, but it is not until 1730 that we find three lots of penalties all embodied in the E.A. Obligation.

Thirty years later, in 1760, we have the earliest examples of exposures containing separate Obligations for each degree, each of them with the penalties of their time.

There is no shred of evidence that the penalties were ever inflicted, though the Craft has often been attacked on the wholly unfounded assumption that they were.

As to what can be done about them, a great deal has been done in recent years, and that story—so far as English practice is concerned—forms an interesting stage in the history of our ritual.

The most interesting comment on the 'Obligation' paper noted above, was in a letter dated 1 September 1962, from the Grand Master of the Grand Lodge of Quebec, M.W. Bro. B. V. Atkinson, and it was reproduced in the Q.C. Lodge Summons for October 1962:

> Apropos of your comments on the *Obligation and its place in the Ritual* [*AQC* 74, p. 133], I thought you might be interested in a development in respect of the penalties, as adopted by our Grand Lodge at its meeting in June last. [See extract below.]
>
> You will note that we have placed the *physical* and *real* penalties in proper relation to each other, without eliminating the former from the obligation. Herein we are following what I believe is the practice under the Irish Constitution.
>
> I am extremely pleased that we have adopted this change in wording, for I have felt for a long time that calling on the name of God, and binding a solemn obligation in the terms of the physical penalty on the pages of the Holy Bible, was nothing less than sacrilege.
>
> I note that Scotland, too, has dealt with this matter, and basically on the same premises, though in a somewhat different manner.

[Extract relating to the E.A.]

These several points I solemnly swear to observe, without evasion, equivo-
cation, or mental reservation of any kind, and, while *bearing in mind* the
ancient symbolic penalty of etc., etc. (here the I.G. impresses the symbolic
penalty in the usual way), binding myself under the real penalty on the
violation of any of them, of being branded a wilfully perjured individual,
void of all moral worth, and totally unfit . . . etc.

[Note, the F.C. and the M.M. are instructed in similar fashion.]

Many years later, I heard that in 1955, in response to an invitation
from R.W. Bro. Sir Ernest Cooper, then President of the Board of
General Purposes, the Committee of the Emulation Lodge of Improvement had submitted drafts of several different forms in which the
Obligations might be revised, but the Board did not recommend any
action and there was no mention of the matter in the *Grand Lodge
Proceedings*. It seemed as though the subject had died a natural death.

About a year after the publication of my own paper on 'The Obligation . . .' we had a visit at Q.C. headquarters from one of our much
respected and senior Past Masters, Bro. J. R. Rylands, of Wakefield,
Yorks. He came into my office, threw a paper on my desk, and smiling,
said, 'There you are, Harry, and I dare you to print it'. I glanced at the
title, 'The Masonic Penalties' and skimmed a few paragraphs and said,
'I'll not only print it; I am going to get you the biggest audience any
Q.C. paper ever had'. A date was fixed for the delivery of the paper in
the Q.C. Lodge, 3 January 1964, and a letter was sent to the Grand
Secretary asking permission for advance proofs to be sent to every
member of the Board of General Purposes and to all the Provincial
Grand Masters.

Permission was granted and, in due course, copies were posted to all
those distinguished Brethren, with a special invitation to each of them
to attend the January meeting but, in case they were unable to be
present, to send their comments on the paper, which would be printed
in full, with all the comments, in the 1964 volume of *AQC*.

The synopsis of the paper could not fail to attract the attention of
every Freemason and it gives a very good idea of the author's approach
to a difficult and delicate subject:

Synopsis to 'The Masonic Penalties' by Bro. J. R. Rylands: Open to
criticism; The legal position; Their unreality; Penalties on the V.S.L.;
Their 'antiquity'; Their *raison d'être*; Their present place in the ritual;
Symbolic significance; Practices elsewhere; Possible action.

The Q.C. meeting on 3 January 1964 was one of the best-attended and
most exciting within living memory. It was, as always, a distinguished

gathering, honoured on this occasion by the presence of three Provincial Grand Masters and three members of the Board of General Purposes. Despite ill-health, Bro. John Rylands attended and read the paper himself; his fine resonant voice and expert delivery were additional highlights to that memorable evening. The verbal comments that followed the paper were sufficient to show a deep gulf in opinions, which ranged from the traditional die-hard view that the penalties must not be touched, to the opposite extreme, urging their total abolition.

Written comments began to pour in. The original paper was quite a short piece of only 4000 words. The comments, which included valuable contributions from twelve Provincial Grand Masters, totalled 36,000 words! The paper had become a best-seller and it was actually reprinted three times *before* it appeared in its final form, in *AQC* Vol. 77. Several attempts had been made during the preceding decade to promote official action on the penalties, but, for one reason or another, they had all come to nothing. Bro. Rylands had designed his paper to side-track former difficulties, and to lay the points at issue before a world-wide Masonic audience.

Precise details of the events of the next few months are not available, but there was a major development in Grand Lodge, at the Quarterly Communication on 10 June 1964, when the M.W. Grand Master announced, before the close of business, that R.W. Bro. Bishop Herbert, Provincial Grand Master for Norfolk, wished to address Grand Lodge 'on a matter which has for some time been exercising both his mind and the minds of other experienced Masons'. The subject was the Masonic Penalties.

Bishop Herbert began his address with a generous tribute to the manner in which the Quatuor Coronati Lodge had very well illustrated the many aspects of the subject in its proceedings, and he gave notice that he was going to move a Resolution at a future Communication of the Grand Lodge. He then outlined the religious and ethical problems that were involved in the penalties, especially from the point of view of a Candidate for Initiation being called upon, 'suddenly, without warning, . . . to repeat certain statements about penalties which give him a moral shock . . .'. Underlining his theme that the prime objection to the penalties was 'a moral one, and, therefore deserving of our sympathy' he continued:

> I think that almost all of us would welcome a removal of this cause of stumbling which is, incidentally, as we know well, also a potent weapon in the hands of the adversary.

He then explained, briefly, his own objections to any drastic changes, which might cause controversy in the Craft, and suggested that a small alteration of only a few words would have the desired effect, to which change he would (in his Resolution) ask the Grand Lodge to give its approval as *a permissive variation*. He read the details of the proposed change, to be used in each of the three degrees, as follows:

> In place of the words 'under no less a penalty on the violation of any of them than that of having' the words 'ever bearing in mind the ancient penalty on the violation of them, that of having'.

The attendance that day was an average one, 1136 in all, because the subject of the Bishop's address was not on the *Paper of Business* and his speech, being simply advance notice of a future Resolution, could not be discussed that day. But the effect on the Brethren was electrifying, because this was no longer an academic question, but would be of immediate importance to all the 7000 lodges under English Constitution.

It proved impracticable for the Resolution to be put and discussed at the Quarterly Communication in September, because the majority of the English lodges having been in recess during the summer months, there had been no time for proper discussion, and at the Bishop's request it was deferred till 9 December 1964.

There was a 'packed house' attendance in Grand Lodge on that day, over 2100 in all (against an average of 1300). Every seat was occupied; Brethren were sitting on the stairs and standing in the gangways. Some 200 or more Brethren were left standing in the ante-room outside the Grand Temple, because there was no more room inside, and the main doors were left open so that they could hear the debate.

The M.W. Grand Master, the Rt. Hon. the Earl of Scarbrough, K.G., was in the Chair and, after preliminary business had been completed, he opened the Penalties Debate by outlining the order of procedure that he proposed to follow, indicating that after the leaders on the Resolution and on several Amendments had spoken, there were several members of Grand Lodge who had notified the Grand Secretary of their desire to speak, and they would be called in turn. After this, every Brother who wished to speak, would be given an opportunity to do so.

R.W. Bro. Bishop Herbert, in opening the discussion, said it was not necessary for him to repeat his former arguments, and he described, very briefly, the scope and limitations of his Resolution. He noted wide differences of views on the subject, ranging from those who found the penalties wholly repugnant, to those who insisted that not one word should be moved or altered. For the latter, he said that the Resolution was not intended for them and they need pay no attention to it. For all others who found serious objections to it, for whatever reason, he emphasized that the proposed changes of only a few words would remove a serious moral problem, leaving the penalties in the Obligation simply by way of allusion to them, but effectively excluding them from 'what the candidate so solemnly swears to'. He added that there would be some necessary consequential amendments, which could be settled easily, since they would not involve any questions of principle. Finally, for those who might feel that the Resolution did not go far enough, he said 'It's the first bite that counts'.

In the capacity of Secretary–Editor of the Q.C. Lodge, the present writer had been invited, some days before, to second the Resolution and his approach was from a different angle. Speaking of the fortunate situation of the Craft in England, where it is virtually immune from the scourge of anti-Masonry which has plagued the Freemasons in so many countries in Europe and the Americas, he urged that 'we dare not withhold from the Grand Lodge the ability to move in defence of the Craft, at a time when we all have to be on our guard'. He also asked that the adjective 'ancient' in the Bishop's Resolution, which might imply that the penalties had actually been used in the Craft in olden times, should be altered to 'traditional'; Bishop Herbert had already agreed to this change.

The first Amendment, relating to a legal question of authority, was proposed by the Grand Registrar, seconded by his Deputy, and carried; it did not affect the objects of the Resolution.

An Amendment was then put by Bro. Lt.-Col. J. W. Chitty, *M.B.E.*, P.S.G.D., who proposed that if the accepted wording was to be altered, the alternative should be:

> under a penalty no less than that of death, ever bearing in mind the ancient symbolic penalty of . . .

This was seconded; but among all the points that were discussed that day, this was the only instance of a desire to strengthen the standard wording; when a vote was taken, it was defeated by a large majority.

The debate continued for over two hours, covering literally every aspect of the subject. One noteworthy point was made in the suggestion that the whole matter should be referred to a committee, to be appointed by the Board of General Purposes 'to consider to what extent it is possible to delete from the Ritual the various references to physical penalties in the three Degrees, and to make appropriate recommendations to

Grand Lodge . . .'. The proposal found a seconder, but the President of the Board of General Purposes rose to say that

> never in the long course of its history has the Board of General Purposes touched Ritual in any shape or form . . . [and that he could find] . . . no authority in the *Book of Constitutions* whereby the Board of General Purposes can be compelled to accept responsibility for Ritual.

The proposal was defeated and the debate continued. There were sixteen speakers in all and when it became obvious that everyone who wished to speak had spoken and that all points had been covered, the M.W.G.M., before putting the Resolution, added a few words himself on the understanding that the whole question was a matter of conscience and that he did not want to influence anyone. He then described how often, in his travels in England and abroad, Brethren had approached him of their own accord to say that 'they wished something could be done about the penalties'. Then, with a few closing words, he put the Resolution and it was carried by an overwhelming majority.

Within the space of a few weeks the representatives of *Emulation, Logic* and *Stability* workings had examined the consequential amendments and agreed on the forms which were to be recommended for adoption (thereby avoiding the probability of hundreds of different 'home-made' versions). They were published in leaflet form and some 100,000 copies were distributed to lodges and individual Brethren by the Q.C. Lodge alone.

Another by-product of the 'Permissive Changes' was the establishment, almost immediately, of governing bodies for three extremely popular versions of the Ritual, namely, *Taylor's, Universal,* and *West End*, which had never previously enjoyed the advantage of having a controlling authority. All three of them subsequently published 'Authorized Versions' of their workings.

Writing now, some ten years after those events, it would have been pleasant to record that the 'Permissive Changes' have been widely adopted, but the truth is that we do not know. A large number of lodges, out of the 1700 in the London area, have certainly adopted the changes, but it seems likely that they represent only a fraction of the whole.

In the Provinces, it is impossible to gauge the extent of their adoption. One finds them being worked in all sorts of Lodges, large and small, in cities and in villages. Generally, one might expect that they would follow the views of their Provincial Grand Masters and there are one or two Provinces in which every lodge has adopted the changes, but there seems to be no overall pattern.

If they have not found a wider acceptance, it is almost certainly be-cause of official reluctance to prescribe the changes and there must be many Brethren today who wish that the Grand Lodge had ordered the changes instead of making them purely optional. [This report of the Penalties Debate is largely based on the *Grand Lodge Proceedings* for 9 December 1964, in which all the speeches were reported in full.]

---

19.   CONFIRMING MINUTES AND VOTING

THE MANNER OBSERVED AMONG MASONS

Q. What is the significance of the right hand stretched out at length, palm downwards, when voting for the confirmation of minutes, as being 'the manner observed among Masons'?

A. After discussion with several learned Brethren, I am still not sure of the answer. It is probably an act of ratification and, as such, it may bear some relationship to the position of the R.H. during the Ob. In that case I suggest that the outstretched hand alone is not enough, but that the thumb should be forming a square. We are taught that '. . . all squares, levels, etc. . . . are true and proper signs . . . etc.', and the early eighteenth century catechisms indicate that 'squares' and similar more-or-less unobtrusive modes of recognition were quite common practice (even to the point of writing the superscription of a letter in the form of a square).

So far as I know, the outstretched hand is customary all over England and in the Commonwealth.

But the problem has a different aspect if we distinguish between con-firming the minutes and voting in general. A regulation of the Grand Lodge on 6 April 1736 prescribed that the mode of voting should be by 'holding up one hand', and those same words appear in Rule 59 of our present-day *Book of Constitutions*. Clearly the regulation requires that the hand should be held up, not outstretched, and if we assume, as we must, that the Grand Lodge adheres to its own regulations, then 'holding *up* one hand' has been, for more than two centuries, 'the manner observed among Masons'. Yet, it must be admitted that even in Grand Lodge, when confirming the minutes and for ordinary voting, the vast majority of Brethren use the outstretched hand.

20. THE ST. JOHN'S CARD

Q. The St. John's Card—what does it mean and how did it arise?

A. It was introduced in Q.C. Lodge originally as a kind of annual greeting-card from the W.M. and Officers to all the members of the Lodge and Correspondence Circle. It was always dated 27 December, i.e., St. John's Day in Winter, and bound in the annual volume of Transactions (*Ars Quatuor Coronatorum*).

At its first appearance, in 1887, it consisted of an octavo card, printed in shades of rust, beige and blue, showing a well-known picture of the four Crowned Martyrs, with some other Masonic symbols. The 'Card' also contained a letter of greetings from the W.M. surveying the achievements of the Lodge during its first year. This was followed by a list of names and addresses of all members of the Lodge and the C.C., covering some nine pages, and a separate letter from the Secretary explaining the list and giving a four-page list of Abbreviations used for the ranks and titles of the members.

With the passing years, the artistic quality of the coloured 'Cards' (never of a high standard) grew steadily worse, and in 1896 they were mercifully abandoned, a quiet monochrome design being adopted in their place. This ran for several years until 1901, when the Card was set up without ornaments.

Meanwhile, the actual lists of members had grown steadily larger; in 1912 (Vol. 25) the St. John's Card occupied 107 full-size pages of the *Transactions*. The cost of printing the lists must have been an intolerable burden by this time, but it was not until December 1919 that the Lodge was forced to economize, and in Vol. 32, for the first time, the St. John's Card listed only those who had joined the Lodge during the preceding year. It was abandoned after Vol. 86 (1973) as an economy measure.

One word of warning about the St. John's Cards. The early volumes of the *Transactions* are exceedingly rare, and as collector's pieces they are fairly expensive. It is therefore worth noting that although the St. John's Cards are of no particular value to the Masonic student, the volumes, from the booksellers' and collectors' point of view, are considered faulty and incomplete if they lack the Cards.

21.   MASONIC RITUAL IN ENGLAND
                    AND U.S.A.

Q. What is the custom in England in regard to the distribution and maintenance of the standard forms of Masonic ritual? There are many variations of practice in the U.S.A. and we would like to know how you compare.

A. The United Grand Lodge of England does not publish, nor does it give its authorization to any specific form of ritual, either written, printed or spoken. For several years prior to the Union of the two rival Grand Lodges, in 1813, efforts were being made behind the scenes to bring them together. In 1809, the premier Grand Lodge (Moderns) took a major step in that direction by the formation of the Lodge of Promulgation, 1809–1811; its membership consisted of seven senior Grand Officers of the year, with a number of elected Brethren who were all deemed expert in ritual matters. Their task was to study the landmarks and esoteric practices, and to recommend the changes that were to be made in bringing the ritual to a form that would be acceptable to both sides.

On 7 December 1813, twenty days before the Union, the Lodge of Reconciliation was warranted by the Moderns, and a similar body was erected on the same day (by Dispensation) for the Antients. At the Union on 27 December 1813, the two bodies combined, their main duty being to teach and demonstrate the ceremonies which had been officially adopted. Apart from the Grand Master and other senior officers of the two Grand Lodges, the main membership now consisted of eighteen experts in the ritual and procedures, i.e., nine appointed by each side.

Surviving post-union documents indicate that the Reconciliation ritual was not identical with the Promulgation recommendations; some changes had been made, but no official copy of the newly-approved forms was issued. The Lodge of Reconciliation gave a series of demonstrations in London to large audiences representing London and Provincial Lodges, and it closed down in 1816.

Several of its expert members then undertook to demonstrate the new forms to Lodges in the London area, and in visits to the Provinces. This was, of course, a very slow process, and, considering that no official version had been issued as a basis for instruction, the numerous 'workings' in use all over England today have achieved a truly remarkable degree of standardization. There are, indeed, a few differences in phrasing, in the manner of communicating the signs, and some marked variations in the 'words' of the third degree.

In the north and west of England there are occasionally wider variations, largely due to the retention of ancient practices, e.g., 'The Bristol Working', but, with these exceptions, it may be said that the standard of uniformity is very high, especially so when we remember that the Grand Lodge does not interfere in these matters and exercises no official control.

The first post-Union ritual to appear in print was 'An Exposure of Freemasonry', by Richard Carlile, who was the printer and publisher of a weekly magazine, *The Republican*. He was a colourful character, a Freethinker and a great fighter for the freedom of the press. He had, above all, no respect for persons, and he served several terms of imprisonment for printing 'scandalous, impious, blasphemous and profane libels'. His ritual of the Craft degrees, with Lectures and his own commentaries, appeared in consecutive weekly parts of *The Republican*, beginning on 8 July 1825, at a time when he was still in prison. The text of his exposure was extremely interesting, but the series as a whole was a scurrilous attack on Freemasonry. His ritual, shorn of its anti-Masonic material, was published as *The Manual of Freemasonry* in 1831, 1836 and 1843, and it had a ready sale.

The first 'respectable' post-Union ritual was published by George Claret in 1838, without official approval, of course. He had attended at least six meetings of the Lodge of Reconciliation and had served as Candidate for the third degree at one of those demonstrations. Claret's Ritual (121 pages, 12mo.) was printed in clear language, with dashes and dots to indicate words and letters that were necessarily omitted. His book achieved numerous editions and it was undoubtedly the ancestor of most of the 'little blue books' in use in Britain today.

The two formularies which claim pride of place as being nearest to the forms adopted in 1813 are known as *Emulation* and *Stability*, and these, with many more modern versions, have appeared in print, all readily obtainable by Masons (and often by non-Masons) at the Craft outfitters. *The Emulation Ritual*, approved by its governing body, the Emulation Lodge of Improvement, was not published until 1969, though there were many unauthorized versions during the preceding century which claimed to be in accordance with strict Emulation working.

In the late 19th century and in more recent times the opinion was widely held that Emulation working was favoured by the Grand Lodge. This impression may have arisen because it is certainly one of the earliest forms that had its own governing body since 1823, but neither this nor any other working has any kind of official authorization. All are printed in plain language, with omissions at the appropriate points, and they usually exhibit only minor differences in phrasing and rubrication. Maintenance of the 'standard forms' is achieved largely by means of Lodges of Instruction which meet, usually once a week, for rehearsal purposes.

The Grand Lodge view in regard to ritual practices is not expressed precisely in the *Book of Constitutions*; indeed, the word 'ritual' does not appear there. Rule 155, however, runs:

> The members present at any Lodge duly summoned have an undoubted right to regulate their own proceedings, provided they are consistent with the general laws and regulations of the Craft;

The Regulation, as it stands, is somewhat obscure in regard to ritual practice, but its relevance was clarified in the *Year Book*, under Decisions of the Board of General Purposes on Points of Procedure:

> Q. Is a Master entitled to decide *what ritual* shall be practised during his year of office?
> A. Rule 155, *B. of C.*, lays it down that the majority of a Lodge shall regulate the proceedings.

The question was altered in the *Year Book* for 1966, so that it now reads:

> Q. Is the Master entitled to decide *what procedure* shall be practised during his year of office? [My italics.]

But the answer remains the same. In effect, ritual in the English lodges is treated, to all intents and purposes, as a purely domestic matter, although the Grand Lodge would undoubtedly intervene in the event of any undesirable innovations.

For the benefit of Brethren who are unacquainted with comparable practices in the U.S.A., the following notes are added.

The various Grand Lodges differ widely in their approach to the methods of instruction and dissemination. In Pennsylvania and California, all printed or MS. rituals are forbidden and instruction is purely from 'mouth to ear'. The would-be officer of a Lodge must attend at rehearsal until he attains proficiency by ear. In most jurisdictions, however, printed rituals (and so-called monitors) are permitted, being published by authority of the Grand Lodges and, of course, officially recognized. These productions vary considerably. A few, like our English rituals, are in plain language, with gaps. Others are in a two-letter code, i.e., the first two letters of every word. There are some in a one-letter code, i.e., the first letter of each word, and, needless to say, these codes present great difficulties to the *untrained eye and ear*. Another code, rather easier to read, usually gives the two or three main consonants of each word, e.g., *wt* for *what*. Several jurisdictions use this together with a kind of geometrical cipher, terrifying at first glance, though not nearly so difficult as it appears to be.

The Grand Lodge of Kansas prints a ritual containing most of the material in code and, in addition, distributes a monitor which contains *verbatim* much of the lectures and Scriptures, and this seems to be the practice of several of the Grand Lodges.

Uniformity of practice is ensured by the appointment of 'Grand Lecturers', each in charge of a 'manageable' group of Lodges. In England we might, perhaps, describe them as 'Grand Preceptors', because their main duty is not to give lectures, but to supervise the Lodges under their care and ensure that they do not deviate from the official working. This they do by means of 'Exemplifications', i.e., full-scale dress rehearsals in which all the officers of the Lodges participate. Occasionally the officers of a whole 'District' (varying from five to fifteen Lodges) will take part in an Exemplification, the first team doing a portion of the ceremony, and, after comments and corrections from the Grand Lecturer, the next team continues where the others left off.

Section 355 of the Regulations under the Grand Lodge of Massachusetts may be quoted as an example of normal procedure:

> It shall be the duty of each District Deputy Grand Master to convene the Lodges of his District at least once in two years for the purpose of holding a District Exemplification of the work and lectures under the supervision of one of the Grand Lecturers, unless excused, for cause, by the Grand Master.

It is noteworthy that in many jurisdictions the Grand Lecturers are 'compensated' for their services from funds provided by their Grand Lodges and by the Lodges under their supervision.

If uniformity of ritual practice is to be deemed a desirable end in itself, the methods adopted by the Masonic authorities in the U.S.A. to preserve their own particular forms are extremely effective. If uniformity is considered as a safeguard against the individual Lodges indulging in a riot of modified 'workings' that might easily lead to the introduction of all sorts of undesirable practices, then the zeal for uniformity would also seem to be fully justified.

In England, however, despite the generally high degree of standardization, the studious visitor to Lodges will often find stress laid on a particular word, or phrase or action; or he will see some little piece of time-honoured procedure conducted in a manner entirely different from that in his own Lodge. It is these variations which give a kind of local colour and character to the work that is always interesting and often admirable, and there can be little doubt that these are the best arguments against standardization.

---

22.   THE BIBLE IN MASONIC LITERATURE
                AND IN THE LODGE

WHEN DID THE LODGES TAKE ON A FORMAL SETTING?

Q. When did the word 'Bible' first appear in Masonic literature? When did the Bible first appear in a Masonic lodge; the name and location of the said lodge?
When did Masonic lodges first take on a formal setting, as distinct from informal gatherings or assemblies of masons?

A. If you insist on the word 'Bible', its first appearance in a Masonic context seems to be in the later 1600s.

No part of the Bible was printed in English until 1525, and the first complete Bible in English was not printed until 1535. At this date, therefore, one would hardly expect to find the Bible in general use anywhere outside a Church or Monastery, or in a really wealthy household, and this may well explain the absence of early references to the Bible in our oldest Masonic documents.

Many versions of the *MS. Constitutions* or *Old Charges* contain instructions, usually in Latin, prescribing the form of administering the oath. The earliest of these instructions appears in the *Grand Lodge No. 1 MS.*, dated 1583. It begins:

> *Tunc unus ex Senioribus tenerit librum . . .*, and the passage may be translated: Then one of the elders holds out a book and he or they (that are to be sworn) shall place their hands upon it and the following precepts shall be read.

Here the book might mean the 'Book of Charges' (i.e., the copy of the *Constitutions*), but the word 'book' is ambiguous, and a doubt remains.

In many of the later cases the reference to the book may safely be assumed to refer to the V.S.L., e.g., the *Harleian MS. No. 1942*, which is another version of the *Old Charges* belonging to the second half of the seventeenth century. It contains a form of the masons' oath of secrecy, in which the final words show clearly that the Holy Book was used for this purpose: '. . . soe helpe me god and the holy contents of this booke'.

Possibly the first clear reference to the Bible in this connection appears in the *Colne No. 1 MS.*, dated *c.* 1685:

> Heare followeth the worthy and godly Oath of Masons. One of the eldest taking the Bible shall hould it forth that he or the(y) which are to bee maid Masones, may Impoase and lay thear Right hand upon it and then the Charge shall bee read.

(Hughan, Old Charges, 1895, p. 72.)

The oldest Lodge Minutes in Scotland begin in 1598; they belonged to the now-dormant Lodge of Aitchison's Haven. Those of the Lodge of Edinburgh (Mary's Chapel), No. 1, begin in 1599; Lodge Mother Kilwinning, No. 0, in 1642, etc. All these ancient Lodge records, and many others, have been published, but a careful check of the earlier minutes reveals no hint of a Bible as part of the Lodge equipment. The same applies to the oldest English Lodge records (Alnwick, 1701, and Swalwell, 1725).

Yet, having regard to the deeply religious character of those days, it is probable that from the time when printed copies became readily available, the Bible was amongst the most constant items of Lodge equipment. At Lodge Mother Kilwinning, the minutes in 1646 record that Fellows were 'sworne to ye standart of ye said lodge *ad vitam*', and the Deacon swore his oath '*de fidelij administratione*'.

It is almost certain that a Bible would have been used, yet the earliest record of the purchase of a Bible was in 1766, when the Lodge ordered 'two song books' as well! (Carr, *Lodge Mother Kilwinning No. 0*, pp. 35, 257.)

An inventory of equipment of the Lodge of Peebles in 1726 shows: 'One Bible, the Constitutions of the Laws of the Haill Lodges in London', etc. (Lyon, *Hist. L. of Edinburgh*, p. 83.)

A schedule of property of the Old Dundee Lodge, Wapping, London, in December, 1744, records: 'A Bible . . . [valued at] 15.0'. Another was presented to the Lodge in 1749. (Heiron, *The Old Dundee Lodge*, p. 23.)

The Minutes of the Lodge of Antiquity, No. 2, for November, 1759, report that one of the members 'could not provide a proper Bible for ye Use of this Lodge . . . for less than 40/-, and ye Lodge ordered him to provide one and not to exceed that sum'. (W. H. Rylands, *Records of the Lodge of Antiquity*, vol. i, p. 203.)

But, of course, these random notes only appear in those cases where the lodge Clerks or Secretaries thought fit to record them, and very little early evidence has survived.

For the most interesting descriptions of the use of the Bible amongst Masons we have to go outside the normal lodge records, examining instead the early *aides-mémoire* and exposures which claim to describe the admission-procedures of their times, and in these sources there is ample material:

> *Edinburgh Register House MS.*, 1696.
> The Forme of Giveing the Mason Word
> Imprimis you are to take the person to take the word upon his knees, and after a great many ceremonies to frighten him you make him take up the bible and laying his right hand on it you are to conjure him to sec(r)ecie...
> (Knoop, Jones & Hamer, *The Early Masonic Catechisms*, p. 33.)

> *The Chetwode Crawley MS.*, c. 1700.
> Imp^r. you are to put the person, who is to get the word, upon his knees; And, after a great many Ceremonies, to frighten him, yow make him take up the Bible; and, laying his right hand upon it . . . (*Ibid.*, p. 35.)

> *A Mason's Confession*, 1755–6, describing Scots procedure in c. 1727.
> [From the candidate's preparation for the Obligation.]
> . . . and his bare elbow on the Bible with his hand lifted up . . . (*Ibid.*, p. 94.)

> *The Mystery of Freemasonry*, 1730.
> Q. What was you doing while the Oath was tendering?
> A. I was kneeling bare-knee'd betwixt the Bible and the Square, taking the solemn Oath of a Mason.
> (*Ibid.*, p. 106.)

> *Masonry Dissected*, 1730, by Samuel Prichard.
> [From the preparation for the Obligation.]
> . . . my naked Right Hand on the Holy Bible; there I took the Obligation (or Oath) of a Mason. (*Ibid.*, p. 111.)

Most difficult of all the questions is that relating to the Lodges adopting a 'formal setting', because, in the early days especially, so much of our knowledge is based upon inference. For example, among the earliest lodge minutes still in existence is a brief note, dated 27 November 1599, in the minutes of the Lodge of Edinburgh, ordaining that all Wardens (equivalent to the Masters of Lodges) were to be chosen on St. John's Day. This implies a high degree of formality, because it not merely prescribed the chief meeting-day for the Scottish Lodges, but also the principal item of business that was to be transacted.

The records of admission of members of the 'London Masons' Company', and others, into the Acception (which was a Mason Lodge that had evolved as a kind of off-shoot or branch of a masonic *trade*

organization) may be cited here. The early notes relating to the Acception in 1621, 1631, 1650, etc., are void of any evidence of 'formal
setting'. Yet, when we consider the parentage of the Acception, i.e., an
ancient Livery Company that had existed since 1375, it is fairly certain that some real degree of formality was already embodied in their
procedure.

The early Clerks, or Lodge Secretaries, in writing up their minutes,
tended to give only the bare facts of the work done, without descriptive
detail or elaboration, and that is our main difficulty. Yet, even in the
bare records that survive, we can discern the beginnings of 'formality'.
Perhaps the best early example, for our purpose, is in the Minutes of
Lodge Mother Kilwinning, which reveal the pattern of the meetings:

(1) 'Court lawfully affirmed' (i.e., the Lodge constituted and opened).
(2) Roll-call. Absentees fined.
(3) Admission of Entered Apprentices or Fellows of Craft.
(4) Election of Officers (at the Annual Meetings).
(5) Collection of fees, fines.
(6) The Lodge in judgment (as a Court) against offenders.
(7) Money-lending to members (upon security).

This pattern of procedure repeats itself fairly regularly from the
1640s onwards. The routine, furnishings and equipment may have been
very rough-and-ready, but it was from ancient Lodges like this one that
the old traditions stemmed, and when they began to acquire their special
character, with richer symbolism and furnishings, these were the Lodges
that laid the pattern of 'work' which later spread all over the world.

[For descriptions of Lodge furnishings and equipment, and for details
of the actual procedure of the ceremonies, all of which may well be
regarded as evidence of formality, useful information can be drawn from
two essays in *AQC* Vol. 75, 'Pillars & Globes, etc.' and 'Initiation Two
Hundred Years Ago'. The former is based largely upon Lodge records
and inventories; the latter is based on the eighteenth century exposures.]

---

23.   DULY CONSTITUTED, REGULARLY ASSEMBLED AND PROPERLY DEDICATED

Q. 'Duly constituted, regularly assembled and properly dedicated.'
What do those words mean, precisely?

A. These words are from the first sentence of the M.M. Obligation and
it is rather strange to see that the words 'duly constituted' do not appear
in the corresponding sentence for the E.A. and F.C.

E.A. . . . regularly assembled and properly dedicated . . .

F.C. . . . regularly held, assembled and properly dedicated . . .

It is difficult to find a logical explanation for the omission of the 'duly constituted' from those two degrees, because it is obvious that no lodge would have the power to confer the degrees unless it had been duly constituted. One is driven to the conclusion that in this instance—as in so many other cases—the variations were introduced simply to draw distinctions between the degrees. Now, to the questions:

Duly Constituted

The Book of Constitutions (Rule 97) requires that 'Every new lodge shall be solemnly constituted, according to antient usage, by the Grand Master or by some other Grand Officer or Master or Past Master of a Lodge appointed to act for him'. The act of constitution is pronounced by the Consecrating Officer at the end of the ceremony, when he says:

> In the name of the United Grand Lodge of England and by command of the M.W. The Grand Master, I constitute and form you, my good Brethren, into a Lodge of Antient, Free and Accepted Masons under the name or style of the . . . Lodge, No. . . .

Regularly Assembled

A lodge is made 'regular' by the Seal of the Grand Lodge on its Warrant. The word 'assembled' involves several other points, some of which are governed by the *Book of Constitutions*.

A lodge is 'regularly assembled' when it meets at the place and on the dates specified in its By-laws, and with a proper quorum, of course. These are the main requirements, but, surprisingly, the quorum is not defined in the *Book of Constitutions*. Many of us are familiar with the passage in our (English) Lecture on the Second Tracing Board, which runs 'Three rule a Lodge, five hold a Lodge, seven or more make it perfect . . .', but neither those words, nor any similar directive is to be found in the *B. of C.* The official ruling on this subject is in the 'Points of Procedure' (i.e., rulings of the Board of General Purposes) issued in *Information For The Guidance Of Members Of The Craft*:

> ### Quorum
> 1. How many Brethren must be present before a Lodge can be opened or a degree worked?
>
> Five (excluding the Tyler and the candidate for the degree in question): two must be members of the Lodge and one an Installed Master (see Rule 119 *B. of C.*)

2. How many Installed Masters must be present before a Board can be opened?

Three (excluding the Master Elect and the Tyler).

PROPERLY DEDICATED

In the Consecration Ceremony our Lodges (under English Constitution) are dedicated 'To God and His service . . . also to the memory of the Royal Solomon . . .'

---

24.   THE SECRETARY'S ANNUAL SUBSCRIPTION

Q. Rule 104 of the *Book of Constitutions* permits a Lodge, by its By-laws, to exempt its Secretary from paying the Annual Subscription while he serves in that office, his services being deemed equivalent to the appropriate sum. Is this a very ancient practice?

A. In its present form, the regulation quoted above is comparatively new It was introduced in 1940 as part of the rule prescribing the Officers of a Lodge. Before this date there was no mention of the subject under that heading, but in 1827 one of the regulations, under the heading 'Fund of Benevolence', shows, by implication, that secretarial exemption from payment of subscription was then quite customary:

> Secretaries who are by their lodges exempted from the payment of subscription shall not thereby be disqualified from obtaining assistance from the fund . . .

and this regulation reappeared regularly in the *Constitutions* from 1827 to 1873. In the 1884 edition of the *B. of Const.*, Rule 235 (under the heading of 'Board of Benevolence') said nothing about non-paying Secretaries being eligible for benefits, but categorically defined their status in regard to this exemption:

> 235. Secretaries who, by the by-laws of their lodges, are exempted from the payment of subscription, shall be considered in all respects as regular subscribing members of their lodges, their services being equivalent to subscription, provided their dues to the Grand Lodge have been paid.

The oldest Craft regulation governing the appointment of lodge secretaries is contained in the Schaw Statutes, dated 28 December 1599, addressed primarily to the Lodge of Kilwinning, although most of its provisions applied equally to all the Lodges in Scotland. The statute required the senior officers of the lodge to 'elect, choose and constitute *ane famous notar*' (i.e., a reputable notary or lawyer) to act as 'clerk and scribe', and he was to be responsible for drawing up all indentures and other documents relating to apprenticeship, as well as all other records belonging to the Lodge, so that no document was recognized as valid unless it had been 'made by the said clerk and subscribed with his hand'. The Clerk in those days had a modest income from his services; a Kilwinning regulation of December 1643, provided that every apprentice at his 'booking' in the Lodge, was to pay 40 pence (Scots money) to the Clerk. A regulation at Dunblane in December 1703, also enacted that prentices' indentures were to be written by the Clerk, and that they were to 'pay him therefor'.

The Lodge of Aberdeen regulations dated 27 December 1670, did not specify any such fees, but they afford useful indication as to the status of the Clerk:

> A Clerk is to be chosen everie yeire because wee allow no sallarie to him, it is only a piece of preferment.

It is evident that there was no uniformity of practice, but there can be little doubt that the fine collection of early Scottish Lodge minutes that have survived to this day would have been lost to us but for the old regulations relating to the appointment of Clerks.

Early English Lodge minutes are very scarce, and of those that survive there are few that afford evidence on the Secretary's Dues. The oldest minutes of the Lodge at the Queen's Arms, St. Paul's Church Yard (now Lodge of Antiquity, No. 2), go back to 1736, but the first mention of the election of a Secretary is in July 1737, when John Howes was 'chose'. The minutes for that day show that he paid his dues, and he paid them again a year later.

The records of the Lodge of Probity (now No. 61), Halifax, show that the Secretary paid his dues in 1762 and 1776, and the By-laws of the Lodge dated 1767 make no mention of exemption.

The By-laws of the Lodge of the Nine Muses, now No. 235, in 1807, and those of the Lodge of Antiquity in 1819, use precisely the same words on this subject:

> The annual Subscription of each Member of the Lodge (Secretary excepted) shall be . . ., etc.

This identity of expression is the more remarkable because the former was an Antients' Lodge, and its By-laws ante-date the Union of the rival Grand Lodges; the latter was a Moderns' Lodge, 'time immemorial', and the particular regulation quoted here was dated six years after the Union.

25.   WHAT IS THE AGE OF THE THIRD DEGREE?

Q. What is the earliest reference to the division of Freemasonry into three degrees?

A. The precise answer to this question depends on the significance of the word 'degrees'. It may well mean the grades, i.e. the different levels of status within the framework or organization of operative masonry. In this sense, it is certain that there were three 'grades', apprentice, fellow, and master, very well established in the mason trade in *c.* 1390, and perhaps a hundred years earlier.

In modern Masonic usage, the word 'degrees' relates to the actual ceremonies of admission into the Craft. In this sense, which is presumably the point of the question, the full set of three degrees did not make its appearance in Masonic practice until the third decade of the 18th century, full 300 years later than the earlier 'grades' usage.

Unfortunately, it is impossible to say exactly when the three-degree system came into practice. To answer that question with reasonable clarity, we have to go back to the beginnings. If we could find actual documents by which we might prove the nature of the earliest ceremony of admission into the Craft, it seems certain that we should find there was only one degree in the 1400s and it must have been for the fellow-craft, i.e., for the fully trained mason. There is a great deal of legal and other documentary evidence showing that, at that period, apprentices were the chattels of their masters and in those circumstances it is impossible that they can have had any status within the lodge. It was probably in the early 1500s that the two-degree system came into practice with the evolution of a ceremony for the apprentice which made him an 'entered apprentice' on his entry into the lodge. In 1599, we have lodge minutes (in Scotland) confirming this and showing the existence of a two-degree system, the first for the entered apprentice and the second for the fellow craft.

In 1696, we have the first of a set of three texts describing the ritual, all indicating that the second and highest degree then being worked in Scottish lodges was for the 'master or fellow craft'. *Within the lodge, both were of equal status*, i.e., fully trained masons. *Outside the lodge* the master could be an employer, but the F.C. was an employee. Although this was Scottish practice, there is useful evidence that a somewhat similar situation applied in England at the time when the first Grand Lodge was founded in 1717, i.e., only two degrees; and

Reg. xiii in the 1723 *Book of Constitutions* confirms that the second or senior degree of those days was 'Master and Fellow-Craft'.

Several of the earliest ritual texts, 1696—*c*.1714, confirm that the basic elements of that second degree consisted of an Oath or Obligation, an undescribed sign, and 'fyve points of fellowship' accompanied by an unspecified word. Thus, it can be proved that certain elements of what subsequently became the third degree were originally embodied in the second degree of the two-degree system. It can also be shown, from the same documents in conjunction with some later texts, that *the three-degree system was achieved by splitting the first degree into first and second, thereby promoting the original second degree into third place.*

Having outlined the manner of its development, the search for 'the age' of the third degree involves certain difficulties, because, while we know the dates of the earliest surviving records of its conferment, there are at least two texts which suggest that it may have been known, or practised, before those dates.

The first of these is the *Trinity College Dublin MS.*, dated 1711. It consists of a brief catechism, followed by a paragraph that might be described as a catalogue of the Masons' words and signs, allocating specific words and signs to the 'Masters', the 'fellow craftsman', and the 'Enterprentice'. The so-called 'Masters sign' is recognizable as a very debased version of the F.P.O.F., accompanied by a word—also much debased. Of course, this cannot be accepted as proof of three degrees in practice, but it certainly furnishes the supposedly esoteric material of three grades in 1711, full fourteen or fifteen years before the earliest actual records of the conferment of the third degree.

Another hint of a three-degree system appears in 'A Mason's Examination', the first printed exposure, which was published in a London newspaper in 1723. It contains a much enlarged catechism and a piece of doggerel rhyme which certainly seems to imply a threefold division of the Masons' secrets, though the details are not particularly impressive:

An enter'd Mason I have been,
Boaz and *Jachin* I have seen;
A Fellow I was sworn most rare,
And know the Astler, Diamond, and Square;
I know the Master's Part full well,
As honest *Maughbin* will you tell.

(*E.M.C.*, pp. 72–3.)

This text, like that of 1711, cannot be accepted as proof of three degrees in practice, but when we attempt to date the advent of the third degree, both texts have to be taken into account.

The earliest record of a third degree actually being conferred comes, rather surprisingly, not from a lodge, but from the minutes of a London society of gentlemen who were lovers of music and architecture, the *Philo-Musicae et Architecturae Societas Apollini*. Their story is an entertaining piece of English Masonic history.

The Musical Society was founded in February 1725 by eight Freemasons whose quality may be judged from the fact that each of them had his coat of arms emblazoned on one of the opening pages of the minute book. Seven of them were members of a lodge that met at the Queen's Head Tavern, 'near Temple Barr', only a few hundred yards from the present Freemasons' Hall. These men loved their Masonry and, in the course of an elaborate code of regulations, one of their rules was 'That no Person be admitted as a Visitor unless he be a Free Mason'. Their regulations did not prescribe Freemasonry as a qualification for membership, but it was their custom, if an elected Candidate was not already a Brother, to initiate him as a Mason before receiving him into their Society.

A complete analysis of the Musical Society's minutes would be unnecessary in this brief essay and it will suffice for our purpose if we follow the career of only one of the founders, Charles Cotton Esq. The preliminary pages of the minute book furnish the Masonic details for several of the founders and we read that on 22 December 1724 'Charles Cotton Esqr was made a Mason by the said Grand Master', His Grace the Duke of Richmond, who had 'constituted', i.e., opened the Lodge on that day, presumably acting as W.M. About two months later, on 18 February 1725, the same record continues:

> And before We Founded This Society A Lodge was held Consisting of Masters Sufficient for that purpose In Order to pass Charles Cotton Esqr [and two others] Fellow Crafts In the Performance of which Mr. William Gulston acted As Senior Warden Immediately after which Vizt the 18th Day of February A.D. 1724 [old style, i.e., 1725] He the said Mr Willm Gulston was Chosen President of the Said Society . . .

It must be emphasized that these records of the Lodge meetings on 22 December 1724 and 18 February 1725 belong to the period '*before We Founded This Society*', i.e., they are notes about two perfectly regular Lodge meetings at which Charles Cotton was 'made a Mason' and 'passed' F.C. The next record that concerns us is an actual minute of the Musical Society:

> The 12th day of May 1725—Our Beloved Brothers & Directors of this Right Worshipfull Societye whose Names are here Underwritten (Viz.)
> Brother Charles Cotton Esq^e.
> Broth^r Papillon Ball
> Were regularly passed Masters

There, in a nutshell, is the earliest record of the conferment of the third degree, but it had taken place in a Musical Society, not in a lodge, and Masonically it was obviously irregular! The proceedings attracted the attention of Grand Lodge and on 16 December 1725 the Society's minutes record the receipt of a letter from Bro. George Payne, Junior Grand Warden, enclosing a letter from the Duke of Richmond, Grand Master

> ... in which he Erroneously insists on and Assumes to himself a Pretended Authority to call Our R^t Worpfull and Highly Esteem'd Society to an account for making Masons irregularly ...

The Duke's letter was deemed impolite, because it had not been addressed directly to the Society and it was ordered 'That the Said Letters do lye on the Table', i.e., they were ignored. The last minute of the Society is dated 23 March 1727 and apparently it disappeared soon afterwards.

Gould, in a fine study of the records of this society (*AQC*, Vol. 16), while conceding that at *face-value* they certainly indicate the practice of the third degree, showed that they were open to wide interpretation, and he came to the conclusion that they do not necessarily prove that the third degree was being conferred. For a variety of reasons, unsuitable for inclusion in this short note, I cannot agree with this conclusion, and I believe that, in regard to this point at least, the records may be construed quite safely at their face-value. This is supported by the fact that incontestable records of the third degree in practice make their appearance within the next few years, starting in 1726.

The earliest Lodge record of a third degree belongs to Scotland. Lodge Dumbarton Kilwinning (No. 18, S.C.) was founded in 1726 and the minutes for 29 January 1726 state that there were present the Grand Master (i.e., the W.M.), with seven M.M.s, six F.C.s and three E.A.s. At the next meeting, on 25 March 1726,

> ... Gabrael Porterfield who appeared in the January meeting as a Fellow Craft, was unanimously admitted and received a Master of the Fraternity and renewed his oath and gave in his entry money ...

On 27 December 1728, Lodge Greenock Kilwinning (now No. 12, S.C.) prescribed separate fees for entering, passing, and raising.

In England it is noticeable that Masons were quite satisfied to be merely 'made masons', taking only the first grade, or the first and second together. This custom, combined with the scarcity of Lodge minutes, makes it difficult to trace early records of the third degree being conferred in an English Lodge. As an example, in the Lodge of Antiquity (founded before 1717) the earliest mention of the third degree is in April 1737, in a minute which states that 'Richard Reddall paid 5/- . . . for passing Master . . .'. In the same Lodge, in October 1739, it was '. . . Voted that the following Brethren be Raised Masters, vizt . . .' [six names], and at the Old Dundee Lodge, London, which was in existence in 1722, the earliest record of the third degree is in 1748.

To sum up; it would be safe to say that *the age* of the third degree goes back, in Scotland, to a time in the middle or late 1600s, when some of its essential elements formed a part of the senior degree in the two-degree system, the degree for 'Master and Fellow Craft'. The same would apply to England in *c.* 1700, as confirmed by the *Sloane MS.* There is a possibility that the three degree system was already known (in Ireland?) in 1711 and in England in 1723. It was certainly worked in London in May 1725 by the members of the Musical Society, who had doubtless acquired it from their 'mother' Lodge at the Queen's Head, in 1724. The three degree system was certainly in practice in Scotland from 1726 onwards and by the end of 1730, after the publication of Prichard's *Masonry Dissected*, it must have been widely known in England, though its adoption was rather slow.

So much for the documentary evidence and dates of the various stages in the evolution of the three-degree system. But it is important to emphasize that the Hiramic Legend did not come into the ritual all ready-made as we know it today. The modern Legend contains elements of at least two (and perhaps three) *separate streams of legend*, as is shown in the earliest record of a 'raising' in the *Graham MS.*, 1726.[1]

---

26.   DUES CARDS—GRAND LODGE CERTIFICATES
And Clearance Certificates

Q. What are Dues Cards and why are they forbidden to be used in Lodges under the Grand Lodge of England?

A. A Dues Card is a Lodge Certificate of membership, issued annually and much used in the United States and other Masonic jurisdictions overseas. It certifies that the holder is a member of his particular Lodge and has paid his Dues for the year ending . . . The cards are usually about the size of a railway season-ticket (approx. 3 × 2½ inches), often

---

[1] See Q. 4, p. 8, above; also Carr, 'The Relationship Between the Craft and the Royal Arch', *AQC* 86.

printed on special cheque-paper that is not easily copied. The card must always bear the owner's signature and in many jurisdictions it will also bear his photograph. They are indeed a handy means of identification, but open to abuses. In England, except for the various Certificates under Rule 175, outlined below, no Private Lodge is allowed to grant a Certificate of any kind to a Brother; that is why Dues Cards are banned.

GRAND LODGE CERTIFICATES

For the benefit of readers overseas, I must explain that the nearest equivalent, in England, to the Dues Card, is the Grand Lodge Certificate, an official document which certifies that the Brother named therein was regularly Initiated in the . . . Lodge No. . . . on . . . [date], duly Passed and Raised, and Registered in the books of the Grand Lodge. The modern design, first issued in 1819, is headed by the Arms of the M.W. Grand Master and the text is set out in the spaces between Three Pillars standing on a chequered floor, on which Masonic Tools and Emblems are displayed. The Certificate, when completed, will bear the owner's specimen signature, and this, together with a receipt for the annual Dues, would be accepted to establish 'regularity' and 'good standing'.

Some of our modern rituals, e.g., *Universal, Benefactum, New London*, etc., include a formal 'Address on the Presentation of the G.L. Certificate'. There are many versions and as they are easily obtainable it is not necessary to print it here.

CLEARANCE CERTIFICATES

The issue of Lodge 'Clearance' Certificates is governed by Rule 175, *B. of C.* They are of two kinds:

(a) A Certificate issued to a member of a Lodge, stating that he is a member and (if such be the case) that he is not indebted to the Lodge.

(b) A Certificate issued to a *former* member of a Lodge, giving the date and circumstances of his resignation or exclusion. It must also state whether he was at that time indebted to the Lodge, and if so, whether and at what time such indebtedness was discharged by him.

The opening lines of the regulation make it perfectly clear that the Lodge shall grant such a Certificate to a Brother *whenever required by him* in each of the above cases, and that is the answer to the question.

It is easy to imagine circumstances which might compel a Brother to ask for more than one certificate under these headings, e.g. he might be joining several lodges, and a Certificate issued on a given date might be out of date and therefore useless shortly after issue. So the Rule is quite clear; Certificates must be granted *when required*.

There is, however, the possibility that a Certificate might be put to some improper use. If there is any such fear, the Lodge Secretary, whose duty it is to issue the Certificate, should delay long enough to obtain guidance from the Grand Secretary (or the Prov. or Dist. Grand Secretary).

---

27.   ARCHITECTURE IN MASONRY

Q. Could you let me have some information of general interest on the subject of 'Architecture of Masonry'?

A. If we take the accepted definition of architecture as the study of the science, or art, of building, then the Architecture of Masonry would comprehend every development of the building craft since mankind ceased to live in caves. In the period of 'operative masonry', say, up to the late 1600s, the masons earned their livelihood in that craft, and their interest in architecture is no more surprising than the tailors' interest in clothes.

After a period of transition, which started apparently in the early 1600s, the character of the craft began to change very rapidly, and in the early years of the 1700s (say, from *c.* 1700 to *c.* 1740) the changes had so far accelerated that the lodges had lost all interest in the trade and trade-control, and had become social and benevolent societies, still practising the old ceremonies, but with a substantial membership of gentlemen and tradesmen who did not belong to the Craft and had no interest in it. These were the non-operative lodges which later acquired the speculative teachings and principles which are the basis of modern Freemasonry.

This period, *c.* 1700 to *c.* 1740, coincides very closely with the beginnings of what soon became generally known as the 'Grand Tour'. In those days it was part of the basic education for young men of culture to travel the principal cities of Europe, thereby promoting their appreciation of the arts in general and architecture in particular. There is useful evidence, in this same period, that Freemasons were also taking a lively interest in architecture. The following are a few items that spring readily to mind:

1. The first *Book of Constitutions*, by Dr. James Anderson, published in 1723, contained a so-called historical introduction of some forty-eight pages, designed to show how the great men of all time were interested in architecture.

A large part of this introduction would have been wasted if Anderson had not been sure of his readers' interest in the subject, and, incidentally, he showed his own preferences for the 'Augustan Stile', for Palladio and Inigo Jones.

2. In 1725, a Masonic musical and architectural society was founded in London and its minutes have already been discussed briefly (on pp. 60–1, above). The opening pages of the minute book contain a dissertation on the Seven Liberal Arts, and especially Geometry, Music and Architecture. The following is a short extract, which is apt to our present enquiry:

Musick and Architecture, the Happy produce of Geometry, have such Affinity, they Justly may be Stil'd TWIN SISTERS, and Inseperable; Constituting a perfect Harmony by Just Rules, Due Proportion, & Exact Symmetry, without which neither can arrive to any Degree of Perfection.

A Structure form'd according to the Nice Rules of Architecture, having all its parts dispos'd in a perfect & pleasing Harmony, Surprizes the Eye at every different View, Elates our Fancy's to Sublime Thoughts, & Imprints on our Imaginations Vast Ideas.

3. On 4 October 1723, the famous antiquary, Dr. William Stukeley, read a 'Discourse on the Roman Amphitheater at Dorchester' to the Lodge at the Fountain Tavern, in the Strand, London. This is the earliest record of its kind that has survived, but there must have been many more.

4. Calvert, in his *History of the Old King's Arms Lodge*, (pp. 13 and 75) recorded that on 1 August 1737 the Lodge passed a Resolution amending By-law viii so as to give Masters the right to order that 'a portion of Andrea Palladio's Architecture' be read at each meeting, *instead of the By-laws or Constitutions*. Palladio's 'First Book' had been recently presented to the Lodge, but the Lodge purchased the three remaining Books in 1739.

The King's Arms Lectures ranged very widely, over such subjects as Optics, Fermentation, Muscles, Magnetism, Watch-making, Welding, Truth, Friendship, etc., etc. Bro. W. K. Firminger's survey of their Lectures from 1732 to 1743 (*AQC*, Vol. 45, pp. 254–9) shows five evenings devoted to Architecture:

The Requirements of an Architect (1732)
Military Architecture (1733)
Civil Architecture (1733)
Rise and Progress of Architecture in Britain (1735)
Architecture and Masonry (1741)

Presumably these were all in addition to the readings from Palladio.

5. Bro. T. O. Haunch (in *AQC*, Vol. 77, p. 135) speaks of Batty Langley, a celebrated 18th century author of numerous works on Architecture, and he notes among the subscribers to *The Builder's Compleat Chest-Book*, 1737, the 'Sun Lodge of Free and Accepted Masons, in St. Paul's Church-Yard', and the 'Talbot Lodge of Free and Accepted Masons, at Stourbridge'.

6. Bro. C. D. Rotch, in his *History of the Lodge of Friendship, No. 6*, furnished a list of the twenty-eight Lectures given in the Lodge at the Shakespear's Head from 1738 to 1743. No fewer than eleven of these were on branches of building and architecture, including eight readings from Palladio, on Chimneys, on Roads and Streets, on Staircases, on Temples, on Decorum of Buildings, and on the Management of Foundations, etc.

Here we have ample evidence of a genuine interest in architecture, and it is noticeable, too, that within a few years after the formation of the first Grand Lodge, our ancient brethren were already putting into practice the idea of 'a daily advancement'. In the circumstances, it is not surprising that the 'Five Noble Orders of Architecture' have found a permanent place in the 'Explanation of the [Second Degree] Tracing Board', and in the Lectures.

---

28.   QUESTIONS AFTER RAISING

Q. The 'Questions after Raising' are printed in some Rituals (though not in *Emulation*). When should these questions be put?

A. For reasons which will soon be apparent, it is difficult to say when the 'Questions after Raising' should be put. They are a collection of some seventeen Questions and Answers, drawn mainly from sections of the 'Third Lecture of Freemasonry', and there are several versions, all very much alike, but not identical. Because of their general origin in the Third Lecture, they may be said to date back to the late 18th or early 19th century; but, as a block of selected questions to be used specifically as Questions after Raising, I believe that their earliest provable use was soon after the Union of the Grand Lodges.

The Lodge of Reconciliation was warranted in 1813, mainly to establish and demonstrate the ritual of the Craft Degrees, which they did, and their work on the degrees was finally demonstrated in Grand Lodge on 16 May 1816, and approved, after minor alterations in the third degree, on 5 June 1816.

The minutes of 4 August 1814 contain the first note relating to a Candidate who 'was *after proper examination* passed in due form to the second degree'. Several of the following minutes record that Brethren were passed or raised after 'due examination', or words to that effect.

On 6 September 1814, the W.M., Dr. Hemming, wrote to the Grand Master reporting the work that had been done on the Openings and Closings in all three degrees, 'and the ceremonies of making passing and raising, *together with a brief test or examination in each degree . . .*'. This *may have included an examination after raising*, but we cannot be certain of that at this stage.

During 1814 several second and third degrees were conferred without any mention of examinations, but at the meeting on 22 September 1814 the minutes record them again. There is no hint of an intermediate ceremony. *The examinations were apparently part of the degree which was being conferred.*

The earliest minute relating to the examination of a Candidate *after raising* occurs on 8 December 1814:

> Bro^r. John Milward was passed in due form to the third degree or that of a M.M.
>
> *The necessary examination was then gone thro' as to the qualification of being admitted to office.*

There are two similar minutes in the later records of procedure following the raising ceremonies:

> [On 10 December 1814.] The *Examination necessary previous to receiving Office was then gone through.*
>
> [On 12 December 1814.] The *further examination for Office was then made.*

After this there were a number of meetings at which the third degree was performed without any examination after raising, and it is not clear whether the practice had been abandoned or if the Secretary had merely failed to record it. (*AQC* 23, pp. 267–269. Author's italics.)

Thus, the examinations after raising were designed to determine the Master Mason's qualifications for office, but the particular office is not stated, and we cannot be sure whether this examination of the M.M. as a preliminary for office was invented by the Lodge of Reconciliation, or was based on an earlier tradition.

If we go back in search of possible sources for this examination, there are several documents that appear to be helpful. In the earliest description of the Installation ceremony (in Anderson's *Constitutions* of 1723), at a time when the three-degree system was not yet established, the first item of procedure runs:

> . . . the Grand Master shall ask his *Deputy* if he has examin'd them [i.e., the Master-designate and the Wardens] and finds the Candidate *Master* well skill'd in the *noble Science* . . .

More than fifty years later, long after the trigradal system was firmly established, Preston, in his *Illustrations of Masonry*, 1775, and in his later editions, opened the Installation ceremony with almost identical words, except that the Wardens were not mentioned in this context. There is no evidence of a standard set of questions for this 'examination' until 1814 and I have not been able to find any Lodge minutes before or after 1814 that confirm this kind of examination of prospective Masters and Wardens. It seems likely, therefore, that the practice had not been adopted widely, and that the Lodge of Reconciliation was trying to bring it back. Certainly, the wording of the 1814 minutes seems to imply the existence of a well-known set of questions, and we may fairly deduce that they were the earliest form of the 'Questions after Raising'.

Although the 'Questions after Raising' had made their first appearance in 1814 in an official body, the Lodge of Reconciliation, when we study the documents relating to the Installation ceremony and its stabilization in 1827, there is no evidence (in Grand Lodge or Private Lodge records) of the 'Questions' having been retained for that purpose. It is a pity that we have no similar form of examination for prospective Officers nowadays.

THE QUESTIONS AS A TEST FOR VISITORS

The first appearance, *in print*, of a set of Questions after Raising, seems to have been in the *Perfect Ceremonies*, 1874, where they had an entirely different purpose. They are headed:

Test Questions of the M.M. Degree

with a sub-heading:

Put to a M.M. who goes as a Visitor.

A catechism of this kind would make an excellent test for visitors, though rather severe for a stranger unaware of what was in store for him. That may have been the reason for the removal of the sub-heading in the later editions, which continued to appear regularly, without any explanation of their purpose. This was one of the most popular rituals from 1870 to 1970 and it claimed, without authority, to represent Emulation practice. The same set of Q. & A. appeared under the same heading in various editions of *The Lectures of the Three Degrees*, also claiming to be 'in strict accordance with Emulation Working', but still without any hint of when the test was to be applied.

The Test Questions do not appear in the four best known workings in the London area, *Taylor's, Universal, West End*, and the 1969 authorized edition of *Emulation*. This may suggest that they are virtually unused, or unknown, in the rest of England, but that is not so. The following note from Bro. Colin F. W. Dyer, Secretary of the Emulation Lodge of Improvement, is an interesting comment on the situation:

> During negotiations in about 1970 concerning the withdrawal from publication in England of *The Perfect Ceremonies*, on the issue of the present *Emulation Ritual* book, a number of objections were received to the fact that the new *Emulation* book did not include these Test Questions, as

they were used. The objections came mostly from the N.W. of England and from one or two places overseas.

Clearly, the Test Questions are still in use in some places and we return to the main questions, when and why?

As A Preliminary To The Royal Arch

Apart from the abandoned test for visiting Master Masons, the earliest ritual I have found that explains the purpose of the Test Questions and the manner in which they are used, is the *Sheffield Ritual*, as practised by the Britannia Lodge, No. 139, which was constituted in 1761. (The date of the ritual would be rather later than that.) At the end of the explanation of the Working Tools of the Third Degree, which is the end of the ceremony in most Craft workings, the W.M. in the Sheffield working continues without a break:

> Bro. —, a month must elapse before you can be exalted to the degree of Royal Arch Mason, a Chapter of which is attached to this Lodge. In the meantime it will be necessary for you to make yourself acquainted with the answers to certain questions, which for your instruction I will put to my S.D., who will give the proper answers.

There follows a set of eleven Q. & A., which are, in effect, a condensed version of the sets of Test Questions, but with an explanation of the F.P.O.F.

Another Provincial ritual, printed for the Lodge of Friendship, No. 202, Plymouth (warranted in 1771) has a lengthy 'Charge in the Third Degree', followed immediately by the introductory passage almost word-for-word as at Sheffield, above, with a set of ten Q. & A., in which the F.P.O.F. are moralized at somewhat greater length than in the Sheffield version.

It is hardly necessary to emphasize that both texts link these questions directly with the qualification for the Royal Arch Degree, and they are 'demonstrated' by the W.M. and S.D., *in both cases as part of the Raising ceremony*, the Candidate playing no part in them, except as a listener: moreover, there is no such heading as 'Test Questions after Raising', because they are actually *at the end of the Raising.*

I am reliably informed that there are several Royal Arch Chapters which require the Test Questions after Raising to be answered before Exaltation, and it seems possible that the use of the Q. & A. in this manner may be a relic from the time when the R.A. was regarded as a fourth Degree. The Sheffield and Plymouth rituals described here certainly lend support to this view.

BEFORE PRESENTATION OF THE GRAND LODGE CERTIFICATE

There are two comparatively modern rituals that use the 'Test Questions of the M.M. Degree' for an entirely different purpose, in no way connected with the Royal Arch. The *Logic Ritual*, in its edition of 1899, and again in its revised Coronation edition, 1937, included the Test Questions, without any explanation of their purpose, but the *Logic Ritual, Revised Edition*, 1972, added a sub-title to that heading:

Prior to Presentation of Certificate.

(For the benefit of our readers overseas, this refers to the Grand Lodge Certificate, which is presented to every Master Mason shortly after he has been raised. It is an ornamental parchment, headed by the Arms of the Grand Master, and it certifies that the holder has been regularly Initiated, Passed and Raised in the . . . Lodge, No. . . ., all duly recorded in the Grand Lodge Register. It requires the holder's signature, for purposes of identification, and for that reason the signature must never vary. The presentation of the Certificate is prefaced by a brief address explaining its origin, purpose and symbolism, the ceremony usually being performed by a senior P.M. of the Lodge, or a visiting Grand Officer.)

Another working, *The Benefactum Ritual*, which was specially compiled for the Benefactum Lodge, No. 5231, London, in the 1930s, by the late Bro. R. H. B. Cawdron, also prints the 'Test Questions of a Master Freemason' as a preliminary to its 'Address on the Presentation of a Master Freemason's Grand Lodge Certificate'. The Test Questions are answered by the Candidate while the Lodge is Open in the Third Degree and the Certificate is presented later, in the First Degree, during the 'First Rising', after the Report on the Proceedings of the Grand Lodge has been read.

This practice, providing as it does, a useful additional lesson for the Candidate on the essentials of the Third Degree, is obviously praiseworthy, but it is all-too-rarely witnessed in the English Lodges. Generally, we are content to pass our Candidates to the Second Degree after answering only eleven questions; to the Third, after only nine questions, and although the test for Master Masons may be in use for various purposes in some parts of England, the Grand Lodge does not prescribe it and its existence is virtually unknown.

To sum up, there appear to be four distinct uses for the 'Questions after Raising':

1. As a preliminary for Office in the Lodge. (No longer practised.)
2. As a test for Visitors.
3. As a preliminary to the Royal Arch.
4. As a preliminary to the presentation of the Grand Lodge Certificate.

IN THE U.S.A.

It is interesting to compare our procedure with that which is followed in most of the U.S.A. jurisdictions, where the Candidate must pass his 'Proficiency Test' in the M.M. Degree before he actually becomes a member of the Lodge.

There, the examinations between degrees constitute a complete résumé of the preceding ceremony, in Question and Answer, and they require a *memorized repetition of the Obligation, too.* This would be a sufficiently difficult test even if the texts were supplied to the Candidates in clear language. But the whole procedure is made infinitely more difficult in the numerous cases where these inordinately long Question Cards are printed in the ciphers which are customary in the U.S.A.

The following extracts from a recent letter from the Grand Secretary for Rhode Island, R.W.Bro. A. R. Cole, will serve to explain the procedure:

> In Rhode Island the Senior or Junior Deacon acts as Teacher or Instructor for the whole of the year that he holds the office. Candidates are examined in open Lodge on their proficiency after each degree.
>
> The Instructors hold enough rehearsals until they are satisfied. This generally occurs between the Stated Communication dates [i.e., Regular Meetings]. The questions propounded, and the answers, are both given from memory.
>
> Generally speaking, there are more than one candidate to be examined, and they take turns answering the questions—but all give the obligation together. The candidates being found satisfactorily proficient, *after being examined in the Master Mason Degree in open Lodge, then are eligible to sign the register and become members of the Lodge, in this Jurisdiction.* [My italics. H.C.]

The *General Laws of the Grand Lodge of Iowa* also reflect the importance attached to the proficiency test following the Third Degree:

> Section 168. (Amended in 1932.)
> ... A Master Mason must become proficient in the Third Degree before he can vote, hold office or demit from his lodge, or before he can be permitted to petition for degrees for membership in such Masonic bodies as are recognized ... by this Grand Lodge.
>
> A brother who has not passed his examination in the third degree is not eligible to sit on a committee whether it be of investigation or otherwise.
>
> Until a Master Mason has been examined, and his proficiency entered of record, he has no right to object to a person being made a mason.

A final example from the *Book of Constitutions of the Grand Lodge of Massachusetts*:

> ... no candidate shall be in good standing in the Lodge to which he is elected until he has signed the By-Laws, and he shall not be permitted to sign the By-Laws until he shall have attained suitable proficiency, and shall have received the required instruction, in all three degrees.

This jurisdiction has seventy Q. and A. for the E.A., thirty-nine for the F.C., forty-nine for the M.M. Rhode Island has nearly as many!

Undoubtedly the system has great advantages, for it ensures that the brethren acquire a useful knowledge of the nature and contents of the ceremonies, and a better understanding of their symbolism and principles, before they may enjoy all the privileges of membership.

---

29.   PUBLIC GRAND HONOURS

Q. One frequently reads in old minutes that 'the Grand Honours were given', when ladies and non-Masons are known to have been present. Is anything known of the nature of these Grand Honours?

A. The following is extracted from the *Constitutions & Ceremonies of the Grand Lodge of California*, 10th Edn. (1923), a copy of which was recently presented to the Q.C. Library by Bro. O. E. Wightman, of Vallejo, California, U.S.A.

> The public Grand Honors of Masonry are given thus: Cross the arms upon the breast, the left arm outermost, the hands being open and palms inward; then raise them above the head, the palms of the hands striking each other; and then let them fall sharply upon the thighs, the head being bowed. This will be thrice done at funerals and the action will be accompanied with the following ejaculation: 'The will of God is accomplished—So mote it be—Amen'. The private Grand Honors are the signs of the several degrees given in a manner and upon occasions known only to Master Masons.

Mackey, in his *Encyclopedia*, edition of 1921, describes the public Grand Honours exactly as given above, but the procedure has been changed since that time, and Bro. Wightman writes:

> I, personally, have never seen the public Gr. Honors as described above. They are given nowadays as follows: Extend the left hand in front of the body at about chest height, palm up, and on the call 'The brothers will join with me in giving the public grand honors of Masonry by three times three', strike (in unison with the leader) the left hand with the right, at the third stroke reverse the position of the hands so that the right is now the lower one, strike the right with the left three times, reverse again so that the hands

are in the original position, strike the left with the right three times, making nine times in all. The honors are always given standing.

I haven't been too successful in tracing when they were changed, but the consensus of several Past Masters is that the change came about in 1936. I do know that they were given as they are now in the jurisdiction of the State of Illinois, because I saw them given at the laying of a school cornerstone long before I ever thought of becoming a Master Mason . . .

The 'Public Grand Honors' are just that—given in public where honors are to be bestowed, at public installations, cornerstone layings, and all occasions where anybody can be present.

We add a note, below, from Bro. T. O. Haunch. His final paragraph indicates that the American practices described above were certainly known in England during the nineteenth century.

'Grand Honours'. This expression occurs also in the ceremony to be observed at a Masonic Funeral given in Preston's *Illustrations of Masonry*.

Preston seems to draw a distinction between 'Grand Honours' to be given in that part of the ceremony taking place in the lodge opened in the Third Degree *at the deceased's house*, and the 'usual honours' given in public at the graveside.

With regard to other public use of 'Grand Honours' as referred to in the original Query, could not this have been the equivalent of 'firing'? In lengthy nineteenth century newspaper accounts of masonic banquets at which non-masons and ladies were often present (the latter as spectators!), one finds references to 'masonic honours', 'masonic firing', etc., after toasts. It is possible also that 'firing' was to be observed by non-masons at functions other than banquets.

It is only necessary to add that although 'Public Grand Honours' may have been common in England in Preston's day, no such practices would be permitted in public nowadays.

---

30.   BREAST, HAND, BADGE

Q. What is the origin and symbolism of the F.C.'s 'Breast, Hand, Badge', and why was it discarded in favour of the present sign, except during the Installation Ceremony?

A. The B.H.B. procedure in the Installation is a *salutation; it is not a sign and there is no evidence that it was ever used as a substitute for the F.C. sign.* That sign was described in two of our oldest ritual documents, dated *c.* 1700 and 1711. In those days it only partially resembled our modern F.C. sign, which is a much expanded version.

The salutation to which you refer made its first appearance in print in the 1760s, when it was described as The Fellow-Craft's 'Clap'. It was probably used as part of the 'Toasting' routine, though it *may also* have been used as a 'salutation' at the 'Instalment of a Master'. It seems that the procedure was never standardized and there are several different versions in use in England to this day. It may therefore be interesting to compare the usage of the 1760s with the practice in your own Lodge. I quote from *Three Distinct Knocks*, 1760; *J. & B.*, 1762, is almost identical:

> ... holding your Left-hand up, keeping it square; then clap with your Right-hand and Left together, and from thence strike your Left-Breast with your Right-hand; then strike your Apron, and your Right-foot going at the same Time. This is done altogether as one Clap ...

Why in the Installation and not elsewhere? I suggest that it is because the F.C. was, from time immemorial, the *essential degree* during Installation. Masters were chosen 'from the Fellow Craft' in the days when only two degrees were known, and long before the Installation Ceremony had come into general practice, and to this day the M.Elect takes his M.Elect's Obligation in the F.C. Degree.

As to symbolism, I suggest that the Craftsmen are pledging their Hearts (i.e., their thoughts) and their Hands (i.e., their actions) for the welfare of the Craft (i.e., the Badge = Apron). This is my own view; I have never seen an expert interpretation.

THE CORRECT SEQUENCE OF THE BREAST, HAND, BADGE

Q. What is the correct sequence of the 'B—H—B' as given for the salutation of the newly installed W.M.? In my Lodge, where we work *Emulation* with some alterations, the practice has arisen of describing the salute as H . . . t, A . . . n, and Glove. This is different to the normal sequence and it seems as though the original working has been changed at some time. Will you please comment.

A. In response to enquiries made on this matter, I find that the sequence 'Heart, Apron and Glove' (virtually unknown in London) is the general practice throughout the West Riding of Yorkshire. This serves to strengthen my long-held theory that the further one goes away from London the more likelihood there is of finding old practices that have somehow survived and continue to make our procedures far more interesting than they would be under strict standardization.

The vast majority of the Lodges I have visited use the 'B—H—B' sequence, finishing up with the hand on the Apron. In one provincial Lodge I distinctly remember seeing an unusual sequence which ran H—B— and B—, i.e., starting at the top and working downwards, still finishing with the hand on the Apron; this is the practice in the Province of Bristol.

We have already found three different sequences in the course of this and the preceding note and a moment's thought will show that there are six possible variations. Over the length and breadth of England there is little doubt that one might find every possible version in use, but nobody can say that any particular procedure is 'correct' and that others are wrong.

The sequence which you have described finishes in mid-air and I suggest that this seems to be rather an unattractive and uncomfortable procedure. For that reason alone I dislike it. Incidentally your Lodge is supposed to be working '*Emulation*, with some alterations', but you do not follow their ruling in this case, which is 'b., h. bdge'. One likes to see old 'local' practices preserved and this human failing of introducing 'alterations' is perhaps a very natural one; it certainly happens in many other workings too. But it can become dangerous, because it feeds on itself and, once started, there seems to be no limit.

Finally, on the question of 'correct sequence', in 1827, the M.W. Grand Master, H.R.H. The Duke of Sussex, set up a special 'Lodge or Board of Installed Masters', to revise and standardize the Installation ceremony, which had not been stabilized at the time of the Union of the Grand Lodges in 1813. There is a single-page minute in the Grand Lodge Library, dated 24 February 1827, which gives a much-abbreviated summary of their work. The portion relevant to our present question reads:

Sal : 5 Br : ha : Ba;

This should be the final word on the subject, but there are so many variations still in use today as to raise a doubt whether this ruling was ever promulgated outside London.

---

31. GAUNTLETS

Q. When did gauntlets come into use in the Craft, and have they any symbolical significance? (I do not refer to the gloves worn by operative masons in the course of their work.)

A. The word 'gauntlet' has undergone several stages of meaning. The *O.E.D.*, for its earliest definition, *c.* 1420, says:

A glove worn as part of mediaeval armour, usually made of leather, covered with plates of steel.

Later:

In recent use, a stout glove covering part of the arm as well as the hand, used in driving or riding, fencing . . .

In modern usage, it becomes 'The part of a glove, intended to cover the wrist', but it is still *a part of the glove*, not a separate piece of apparel.

In our modern Masonic usage we may safely regard gauntlets as a legacy from early operative times, because the operative masons all wore sturdy gauntlets as a necessary part of their protective clothing.

The frontispiece to Anderson's *Constitutions*, 1723, shows a Tyler (?) carrying aprons and a pair of gauntlet gloves, and a hundred years later gauntlets were still *a part* of the gloves. There is a portrait of William Williams, Provincial Grand Master for Dorset, 1812–1839, which shows him wearing a gauntlet attached to the glove, the glove being white, and the gauntlet of much the same colour as in use today.

Rural Philanthropic Lodge, No. 291, owns a set of gauntlets, all of white linen (now much discoloured), bearing emblems of the various offices, and made to tie round the wrist with tapes.

In an old Lodge at Blandford, the members all wore white leather gloves *with gauntlet extensions*, like modern motoring gloves. The gauntlets, originally, had no special significance, i.e., in the eighteenth century days, when almost all gloves for dress occasions were made with gauntlets, any member of a Lodge would have worn such gloves as a matter of course.

The Lodge of Unanimity and Sincerity, No. 261, on 24 September 1817, required the Treasurer 'to provide Gloves and Gauntlets for each member of the Lodge conformable to the pattern pair approved of by the Provincial Grand Master . . .' Note: They were to be provided *for each member*; this was a voluntary adoption of a fashion proposed by the Prov. G.M., and it had no Grand Lodge authorization.

Gauntlets did not become prescribed Regalia until 1884, when the *Book of Constitutions* added a new paragraph to the list of Regalia, under the heading 'Gauntlets'. It prescribed garter-blue for Grand, Past Grand, Provincial and District Grand Officers, as obligatory, but for Private Lodges, '. . . gauntlets of light blue silk with silver embroidery *may be worn* by the Officers . . .'. In June 1971, the Grand Lodge resolved that gauntlets are no longer obligatory for Grand Officers wearing full dress regalia; they are also optional for Officers of Private Lodges.

Finally, gloves as such have a range of symbolical meanings, but the loose gauntlets are regalia, and they have no special symbolical significance.

---

32.   LEWIS

Q. What is the definition and origin of the Masonic term 'Lewis', and what are his privileges, if any?

A. Lewis: 'An iron contrivance for raising heavy blocks of stone' (*O.E.D.*). Three metal parts (i.e., two wedge-shaped side pieces and a straight central piece), which are set into a prepared hole in a stone. When bolted into position the metal parts form a dovetail grip inside the stone, and a metal eye or shackle, attached at the exposed end, enables the block to be easily hoisted.

The origin of the term 'lewis' is obscure. It appears in mediaeval architectural usage as *lowes* and *lowys*, but several notable authorities have examined the possibility that our form is derived from the French word *louve* [= she-wolf] and *louveteau* [= wolf-cub], both of which can be traced in French usage in 1611 and 1676, where they have the same architectural meaning as the English word 'lewis'.

It is perhaps more than a mere coincidence that the word *louveteau* appears in French Masonic usage, in the 1740s, to describe the son of a Mason, at about the same time as the English word 'Lewis' acquires a similar significance.

The above is a very brief summary of the points in question. For a more detailed study, see *The Wilkinson MS.* (pp. 40–45), by Knoop, Jones and Hamer, and *The Freemasons' Guide and Compendium* (pp. 414–419), by Bernard E. Jones.

In Speculative Masonic usage, 'A Lewis is the uninitiated son of a Mason' (Bd. of Gen. Purposes; Points of Procedure), and the word has had this meaning in the Craft since 1738, if not earlier.

There is a fuller definition in an official directive, issued by the Grand Lodge (Enquiry Office) and it is also very explicit on the privileges of a Lewis:

A Lewis is the uninitiated son of a Mason, irrespective of the date of his birth, i.e., it matters not whether he was born before or after his father became a Mason.

A Lewis has no special privileges other than should there be more than one candidate on the day of his initiation he can claim to be the senior for the purpose of the ceremony. He cannot claim precedence over candidates proposed previously to himself and must take his place in the usual rotation on any waiting list of applicants that there may be.

LEWISES & THE 'TENUE BLANCHE'

(A note from Bro. Walter F. Knight, New York, U.S.A.)

The notes on the word Lewis in the Mar. 1963 Summons were of particular interest as I am a member of La Sincerité Lodge No. 373 (N.Y., U.S.A.), a French Lodge formed in 1805. We recognize the son of a Brother officially (when requested by the Brother) by receiving the son in Lodge during a very impressive ceremony we like to call a Baptism. The reception may be during a regular meeting but generally it is done in a *tenue blanche* (i.e., an untiled assembly, which non-Masons and ladies may attend) to which the mother and other guests are invited. The *louveton* has no other rights in our lodge than those mentioned in your Lodge communication. We do open a savings account for him, to be paid out to him at age 21, again at a *tenue blanche*, unless he has become a brother himself, when it would be presented to him during his official reception. At present there are three *louvetons* listed in our roster; the newest addition was in 1962 when I was Master of the Lodge. The *louveton* was nine months of age and took the whole thing in with great gusto.

---

33.   DARKNESS VISIBLE

Q. What is the origin of the phrase 'darkness visible'?

A. It appears in Milton's *Paradise Lost* (Bk. 1, 1. 63):

> A dungeon horrible on all sides round
> As one great furnace flam'd, yet from those flames
> No light, but rather darkness visible
> Serv'd only to discover sights of woe . . .

This great work was begun in 1658, when Milton was already blind, and the sombre gloom of these lines may well be contrasted with the many beautiful passages in which the poet was able to conjure up his visions of light, in words which seem to acquire a greater strength and majesty because of the perpetual darkness in which he lived.

The same phrase, 'darkness visible', was used, far less effectively, by Alexander Pope, in the *Dunciad* (Bk. iv, 1, 3), and by Gilbert White, in his *Natural History of Selborne* (Letter xxvi).

---

34.   THE POINTS OF MY ENTRANCE

Q. What is the origin and meaning of 'the points of my entrance'? Why do those words appear in the course of the examination of the E.A., before he is passed to the Second Degree? The 'points of entrance' are mentioned in answer to one of the 'Questions Leading to the Second Degree', but the answer seems to be vague, or incomplete; if this is a survival of early ritual, have we lost something en route?

A. These are three questions that underline a defect in our 'proficiency test' for the E.A. The 'points of entrance' arise in the vast majority of English workings, but for the benefit of Brethren (mainly overseas) to whom they may be unknown, I quote the relevant Question and Answer. The W.M. asks the Candidate:

> Q. How do you demonstrate the proof of your being a Freemason to others?
> A. By Sns., Tns., and the perfect points of my entrance.

None of the modern rituals offers any definition of the 'points of entrance' and that part of the answer remains unexplained; hence the regular flow of questions on this subject. The *modern* explanation does appear in the course of five Q. and A. in the 'First Lecture, First Section' which is only rarely heard nowadays and it would be fair to say that, even there, the explanation is far from clear or complete.

ORIGIN

The 'points of entrance' are a part of the earliest known ritual belonging to the Craft and they made their first appearance in the *Edinburgh Register House MS.*, 1696, which contains the oldest description of the E.A. ceremony, with the catechism that followed it, under the heading:

> SOME QUESTIONES THAT MASONS USE TO PUT TO THOSE WHO HAVE Y^E WORD BEFORE THEY WILL ACKNOWLEDGE THEM

and the questions were probably rehearsed after the E.A. admission ceremony. The first questions in the *E.R.H. MS.* run:

> Q. Are you a mason.
> A. yes.
> Q. How shall I know it?
> A. you shall know it in time and place convenient.

A note follows this answer and it contains a kind of warning:

> Remark the fors^d answer is only to be made when there is company present who are not masons. But if there be no such company by, you should answer *by signes tokens and other points of my entrie*

It is clear, therefore, that these test Questions were designed for use *both inside and outside the lodge*. The 'points of entry' were to be discussed only among Masons and (as we shall see when we deal with the next question) they could provide a very adequate test of whether a stranger was, or was not, a Mason.

There is, moreover, a mass of evidence to show that the questions involving the 'points of entry' were widely used in England and Scotland at that period. They appear in almost identical terms in the *Chetwode Crawley MS., c.* 1700, and in the *Kevan MS., c.* 1714, both sister texts to the *E.R.H. MS..* quoted above, and all of Scottish origin. The earliest version that shows English influence is the *Sloane MS., c.* 1700, a vastly different text, but on the 'points of entrance', its answers are very similar to the Scottish texts:

(Quest^n)   are you a mason
(Answ^{er})   yes I am a freemason
(Q)   how shall I know that
(A)   by perfect signes and tokens and the first poynts of my Ent^{er}ance

As regards origins, the test questions relating to the 'points of entrance' can be traced back in Craft usage to late operative times; they were widely known in England and Scotland in *c.* 1700, and probably a hundred years before that.

THE MEANING OF THE POINTS OF ENTRANCE

In the course of the century that followed the appearance of the 'points' in our early ritual documents their meaning was altered considerably, as a result of natural expansion and interpretation of the ritual. Here, our main concern is what they meant at their first appearance and for that purpose we must examine the third question in the set of three relating to the test. The *E.R.H. MS.* and its sister-texts continue with the questions, as follows:

Q. 3. What is the first point?
A. Tell me the first point ile tell you the second,

The remainder of this sentence seems to be an instruction on the procedure that is to be followed:

. . ., The first is to heill and conceall, second, under no less pain [= penalty], which is then cutting of your throat, For you most make that sign when you say that

The *Sloane MS.* uses much the same materials at this stage, but there are some changes:

(Q) which is the first signe or token shew me the first and I will shew you the second

(A) the first is heal and Conceal or Conceal and keep secrett by no less paine than cutting my tongue from my throat

The 'points of entrance' appear again (in a debased version) in the *Dumfries No. 4 MS.*, *c.* 1710, in the *Trinity College, Dublin MS.*, 1711, and in the 'Mason's Examination', the first newspaper exposure, dated 1723, but in these three texts, as in *Sloane* above, *there is no reference to making any particular sign.*

It is noteworthy that in all seven of the earliest ritual texts, quoted above, the 'points' always appear at the very beginning of the catechisms, and this may well be taken as evidence of the importance attaching to them. They reappear regularly in all nine subsequent exposures up to *c.* 1740, in somewhat abbreviated form and without reference to an accompanying sign.

The instructional answers to Q. 2 and Q. 3 in the three Scottish texts confirm that the 'points of entry' consisted of the cautionary catchphrase, 'heal and conceal', together with an examination on the modes of recognition of those days, plus 'other points' which were not specified. The object of this little group of Q. and A., was to give Candidates a ready means of identifying themselves as Masons; also, to teach them how to interrogate anyone, *outside the lodge*, who might claim to be a Mason. If a man, under examination, was able to produce the requisite sign or token, that might normally have been sufficient to satisfy the questioner. If any doubts remained, the examiner would presumably ask about the 'other points' of entrance. Yet, apart from the catchphrase 'heal and conceal' our texts are completely silent on the 'other points'. It seems likely that there could have been several optional questions, relevant to the initiation, that might have been added, but there is no evidence, at this stage, of a standard form of further questions, or of any further explanation of what the 'points of entrance' really were.

The precise nature of those 'other points' remains a matter of pure speculation. Almost certainly they embodied items of procedure in the admission ceremony which could not have been known to anyone outside the Craft. This view is confirmed in one of the best of the early French exposures, 1745, where the 'perfect Points of my Entrance' are rendered as '*the circumstances of my Reception*'. (*E.F.E.*, p. 259.)

In *c.* 1727, the *Wilkinson MS.*, contained a new Q. and A. following immediately after its answer to Q. 2:

A. by Signs, tokens, & perfect Poynts of Entrance
Q.[3] What are Signs
A. All Square, Levells & perpendiculars

Masonry Dissected, 1730, in answer to the same question, says:

A. All Squares, Angles and Perpendiculars.[1]

As a definition of 'Signs', it seems likely that these answers are directly related to the 'points of entrance', in which case they represent the earliest attempt to explain them. Several of the earlier texts had indicated that 'squares', in one form or another, may have been used as modes of recognition, but the two full answers given here are the earliest known versions of the words which form a preliminary to our modern method of entrusting the E.A.

There were no new revelations of English ritual between 1730 and 1760; when the English exposures begin to appear again in a steady stream from 1760 onwards, the questions on the 'points of entrance' seem to have gone out of use and there is no longer any trace of them in the documents of that time.

LATER DEVELOPMENTS

The 'points', after what may have been a long period of neglect, came back into use in the last quarter of the 18th century. That was the time when the great interpreters of the ritual, Wellins Calcott, William Hutchinson and, notably, William Preston, had begun their work and it is in Preston's 'Lecture of the First Degree' that we find what appears to be the first real attempt to enumerate and explain the 'points of entrance':

First Degree, Section I, Clause II

Are you a Mason?
    I am so taken and received by Brn. and Fellows.
How do you know yourself to be a Mason?
    By the regularity of my initiation, by repeated trials and approbations and by my readiness to undergo the same when duly called on.
How do you make yourself known as a Mason to others?
    By signs, by tokens and by perfect points of entrance.
What are signs? . . .
What are tokens? . . .
Give the perfect points of entrance.
    These are secrets I am bound to conceal.
What is their number?
    They are innumerable but three are generally known.

---

[1] All the English texts mentioned hitherto are reproduced in *Early Masonic Catechisms*, 2nd edition, 1963, publ. by the Q.C. Lodge.

Name those three.
  With you reciprocally I have no objection.
Begin.
  Off – at – on [*sic*].
Why are they called perfect points?
  Because they include the whole ceremony of initiation.
What does the first include?
  The ceremony of preparation.
What does the second include?
  The ceremony of admission.
What does the third include?
  The ceremony of the obligation.[1]

The opening questions confirm that the 'points of entrance' were intended to serve a Mason as a ready means of identification. The catchword answer 'Off – at – on' would present problems to anyone who was unable to enlarge on them, or explain them; but the three answers that follow those words state that they relate to three parts of the ceremony, 'preparation, admission and obligation'. This suggests that there might have been further questions on those three themes.

There is an extended version of the same Lecture, by William Preston, which has three different answers following the 'Off – at – on', as follows[2]:

Off what?
  In respect to apparel.
At what?
  The door of the Lodge
On what?
  The l*** k*** b***

These three answers supplement the somewhat obscure references to 'preparation, admission and obligation' in a most useful manner, especially when we combine them, thus:

The ceremony of preparation—In respect to apparel
The . . . ceremony of admission—[At] The door of the Lodge
The ceremony of the obligation—[On] The l*** k*** b***

The answers presented in this form leave no doubt as to Preston's views on 'the points of entrance'. They may also throw light on another question that has arisen frequently on the word 'entrance' in relation to

---

[1] Quoted from *AQC*, Vol. 82, pp. 117–18, in which the late Bro. P. R. James produced an invaluable synthesis of Preston's 'First Lecture of Free Masonry' from manuscripts and prints in the Grand Lodge Library.
[2] Bro. James listed it as the 'F' version. (ibid p. 118)

the 'points'. Does it mean the precise moment of entrance into the Lodge, or does it relate to the whole ceremony of admission? The latter is clearly implied in Preston's threefold answer. If all his questions and answers (in the extracts quoted above) had survived into our present-day ritual, the question would not arise, but there have been several changes in the interpretation of the 'Off – at – on' since Preston's day.

John Browne, in his *Master Key*, 1798, was completely different:

> A. Of, At, and On.
> Q. Of, At, and On what?
> A. Of my own free will and accord, At the door of the L***e, and On the point of a sharp I********* extended to my n**** l*** b*****.

Finch, *A Masonic Treatise*, 1802 gives:

> A. Of my free will, At the door of the L, and ON the point of a s[****] or some sharp i*********.

Carlile, in the *Republican*, 15 July 1825, gave the same answers as in Preston's extended version, i.e., 'In respect to apparel' etc.

Claret's answers (in 1838) were like those in Browne's *Master Key*, 1798, with the word 'presented' in place of 'extended'.

The *Perfect Ceremonies*, 1872, followed Claret precisely and, although the questions leading up to the final answer vary slightly, the answer is as given in most of the 'workings' which use the Q. and A. 'Lectures' today. It is evident that at some stage between Preston in c. 1780–90 and Browne in 1798, there was a substantial change in the interpretation of the 'points of entrance'. Preston's definitions indicated that he equated 'entrance' with the whole ceremony of admission into the Craft, i.e., preparation, the moment of entrance, and the moment of taking the obligation. Browne's interpretation—in use today—finishes at the moment when the Candidate is about to pass through the door of the Lodge.

I am inclined to believe that when Preston produced (or perhaps reproduced) the three-point interpretation of the 'points of entrance', the intention was to give the Candidate, within the span of a single catchword phrase, a reference to three incidents that would prove— quite apart from word and sign—that he had undergone a 'perfect' and proper initiation. It may appear that we have neglected the word 'perfect' in the 'perfect points of my entrance' and it seems possible that the word 'perfect' belongs directly to the three points outlined by Preston. It might also refer to three in the sense of 'the perfect number', though one hesitates to engage in this kind of symbolism.

Why Do The Points Appear In The E.A. Examination Before Passing?

Originally, as shown above, they formed part of the catechism *within the E.A. ceremony* and they were clearly designed for test purposes. When the Passwords came into use in the first half of the 18th century, there is ample evidence that they were conferred *during* the E.A. and F.C. ceremonies, to furnish candidates with an additional safeguard, either in proving themselves or in testing strangers. In effect, the Candidate, in those early days, received during each degree what later became a separate intermediate ceremony of Test Questions and Entrusting, as a preliminary to the next degree.

The questions leading to the next degree, i.e. the 'proficiency tests' were not standardized, and were apparently not in general use until after the union of the rival Grand Lodges. The earliest *official* record I have been able to trace of our modern procedure of *the separate intermediate ceremony before the next degree*, is in the minutes of the Lodge of Promulgation, which was created in 1809 to prepare the ground for the Union. On 9 February 1810, Bro. Robson, acting as candidate for the second degree

> . . . having answered the questions put to him satisfactorily, was invited by the R.W.M. to repair to the extremity of the East, where, unobserved by the rest of the Lodge, he at the Master's command was entrusted by the W. Past Master with . . .

after which the appropriate ceremony was performed. (*AQC*, Vol. 23, pp. 41/2.)

One week later, the Lodge of Promulgation resolved that this procedure should be followed in future (but on this occasion they were dealing with the third degree).

So the answer to this question is that the practice of examining the E.A. on the 'points of Entrance' immediately before the second degree became official at the Union, though it may have been in use, in some cases, before that time.

Have We Lost Something En Route?

As to whether we have lost something en route, that is rather difficult to answer. If we are justified in assuming that the 'other points of entrie' in 1696 implied items that might have led to further (unspecified) test questions, then apparently we have lost something since 1696. Indeed, it may well be that Preston's 'Off – At – On' was an attempt to fill the gap, and even in his day there seems to have been some real doubt as to how the 'catchword' answer should be interpreted, i.e., with two distinct 'Preston' versions and an entirely different one from Browne in 1798.

Nowadays, Browne's version seems to be widely favoured in those 'Workings' which use the 'Lectures'; but the 'Off – At – On' has disappeared from the Questions, etc., leading to the Second Degree, which contain a mention of 'the perfect points of my entrance' without the least attempt to explain them; and that is a great pity.

---

35.   COWANS

Q. What are 'cowans' and why were they excluded from the Craft?

A. The *O.E.D.* definition is: 'One who builds dry stone walls (i.e., without mortar); a dry-stone-diker; applied derogatorily to one who does the work of a mason, but who has not been regularly apprenticed or bred to the trade'.

Cowan is an essentially Scottish trade term, and it belongs to the time when lodges, as trade-controlling bodies, put restrictions against the employment of cowans, in order to protect the fully-trained men of the Craft from competition by unskilled labour. The earliest official ban against cowans appeared in the Schaw Statutes in 1598:

> Item, that no master or fellow of craft receive any cowans to work in his society or company nor send any of his servants to work with cowans, under the penalty of twenty pounds so often any person offends hereunder.

The first record of a breach of this rule is the oldest surviving minute of the Lodge of Edinburgh (Mary's Chapel) dated 31 July 1599; [word for word, in modern spelling]:

> George Patoun, mason, granted and confessed that he had offended against the Deacon and Masters for placing of a cowan to work at a chimney-head for two days and a half . . .

He made 'humble submission' offering to pay whatever fine might be imposed. Having regard to 'his estait' the offence was pardoned, but with a strict warning to all future offenders. The minutes suggest that the Edinburgh masons were very well behaved in this respect, perhaps because of the limited and clearly-defined area under the control of the Lodge. At Kilwinning, where the Lodge had jurisdiction over a very wide territory, with consequent difficulties of proper supervision, a large number of breaches were recorded and substantial fines were paid in each case. Cowans also appear regularly in the minutes of several other old Scottish Lodges.

Nevertheless, there are several records for Edinburgh Castle, in 1616 and 1626, where cowans were permitted to work, apparently on certain special duties and *when no masons were employed in the same weeks.* Some of these unspecified jobs must have been exceptional, because 'One cowan received 16*s.* 8*d.* a day, one 13*s.*, one 12*s.*, one 10*s.*, and two 6*s.*, as compared with a mason's normal rate of 12*s.* a day on the same building operations. (Knoop and Jones, *The Scottish Mason and the Mason Word*, pp. 28–9. Manchester Univ. Press, 1939.)

In the Burgh of the Canongate, adjoining Edinburgh, cowans were able to attain to a higher status and the minutes of the Incorporation of Wrights, Coopers and Masons &c. show how readily the ban against cowans could be lifted when trade conditions (or local circumstances) permitted. On 27 May 1636, John McCoull was admitted to the Freedom 'during his lyftyme to work as a cowan any work with stone and clay only and without lime'. For this privilege, he was to pay £4 a year to the Craft or the boxmaster (i.e. treasurer) in four instalments, with a doubled fine if he failed to pay. On 30 May 1649 Williame Reull was admitted

. . . during his lifetime to work as a cowan any work with stone and clay only without lime except only to cast with lime timber doors cheeks and timber windows and clay chimney heads . . . within the Canongate and whole Regality of Broughton . . .

Reull was to pay £6 a year, again in four instalments and with doubled penalties for any failure. There are altogether some fifteen records of 'cowaners' admitted to work in the Canongate, including several men from neighbouring areas, and several records of penalties levied for infringement of the rules when they dared to undertake work that was not permitted to them. (A. A. A. Murray, 'Freeman and Cowan with Special Reference to the Records of Lodge Canongate Kilwinning'. *AQC*, Vol. 21, pp. 198–9.)

In 1705, the minutes of Lodge Mother Kilwinning indicate that although there were still some restrictions, the employment of cowans was occasionally to be permitted in the territory under its jurisdiction, but always depending on the availability of labour. The Lodge resolved:

. . . that no man shall employ a cowan, which is to say without the word [i.e., the Mason word] to work; *if there be one mason to be found within fifteen miles* he is not to employ a cowan under the penalty of forty shillings, Scots.

(Author's italics; all quotations word-for-word but in modern spelling.)

Cowans And Intruders

Q. 'Cowans and Intruders' or 'Cowans and Eavesdroppers'. When was the wording changed and which is correct?

A. There is no evidence that the words were ever changed and the question of which is correct does not really arise, because the words are used synonymously, despite their widely different meanings. The *O.E.D.* traces the use of the word 'eavesdropper' in the *Borough Records of Nottingham* as early as 1487, and it means 'One who listens secretly to conversation'. The same authority quotes the word 'entrewder' (= intruder) in an Act of Henry VIII, in 1534. So far as the Craft is concerned, to intrude means 'to thrust oneself in without warrant or leave; to enter or come where one is uninvited or unwelcome'.

In our modern practice, both words are used. In the 'Opening' ceremony, most workings speak of 'intruders', but in the Investiture of the Tyler, *Stability, Logic, Universal, West End*, and most of the other widely used versions prefer 'eavesdroppers'. *Emulation*, however, speaks of 'intruders' in both places.

Instead of asking 'which is correct?' it seems that we may arrive at a better solution if we try to ascertain which word is more appropriate to the circumstances of the Craft. For example, a cowan, in operative times, was certainly an intruder—from the trade point of view; he could not have learned very much of the trade if he merely listened under the eaves. In Speculative Masonry, it is likely that the eavesdropper, the secret listener, would be the greater source of danger. So it is not surprising, perhaps, that when the relevant words begin to appear in our ritual documents, *c.* 1710–1730, the eavesdropper forms come first.

The first hint of that word in the ritual is in the *Dumfries No. 4 MS.* of *c.* 1710, where there is a question:

'is ye house cleen' [i.e., is the room tiled?], and if the answer is 'it is dropie or ill-thatched . . . you are to be sillent'. The word 'dropie', here, is part of the word 'eavesdroppers'.

In 'A Mason's Confession' of *c.* 1727, there is a note to one of the questions:

. . . the secrets of the Lodge are hid from the *drop*; that is, from the unentered prentice, or any others not of their society, whom they call *drops*.

The earliest appearance of our 'cowans and eavesdroppers' is in Prichard's *Masonry Dissected,* 1730:

Q. Where stands the Junior Enter'd 'Prentice?
A. In the North.
Q. What is his Business?
A. To keep off all Cowans and Evesdroppers.

Another question followed, implying that our Brethren in those days were very willing to let the punishment fit the crime:

Q. If a Cowan (or Listner) is catch'd, how is he to be punished?
A. To be plac'd under the Eves of the Houses (in rainy Weather) till the Water runs in at his Shoulders and out at his Shoos.

Incidentally, the phrase 'cowans and intruders' does not appear in our ritual until the late 1700s.

---

36.   DECLARING ALL OFFICES VACANT

Q. One often hears the outgoing Master, at the beginning of the Installation ceremony, '. . . declare all offices vacant'. Is this correct?

A. One would hesitate to describe a purely local Masonic procedure that is not governed by the *Book of Constitutions* as being correct or incorrect, but it seems that the W.M. has no such powers. It is his right and his duty to appoint the Officers, but he has no right to remove them, or to declare the offices vacant (except in the special conditions governed by Rule 120 of the *B. of C.*, when he must lay '. . . a complaint before the Lodge . . .').

As a matter of convenience, the Wardens and other Officers at an Installation meeting may vacate their seats or hand over their Collars a few minutes before the new Officers are appointed, but the Officers, like the W.M., are appointed for the ensuing year, and their tenure of office terminates at the moment when their successors are appointed. For these reasons, the W.M. should not 'declare all offices vacant'.

Another point arises in this connection. During the Investiture one often hears the new Master announce: 'Bro. A.B. . . . appointing you my Senior Warden' (or any other office). The officers are officers of the Lodge, not of the Master, and it always seems to me, simply out of politeness, or a proper respect for my colleagues, that the word 'my' is out of place in this context.

Against this view, it could be argued that Rule 104 of the current *Book of Constitutions* speaks of 'the Master and his two Wardens' and the first *B. of C.*, in 1723, also referred to 'the Master and his Wardens' and several modern English rituals use the same words. Of course one cannot quarrel with these authorities, but I can never suppress a feeling of embarrassment when I hear the expression 'my Senior Warden' etc., because of the somehow patronizing sense of ownership which it conveys. These are purely personal views, but I believe that the only Brethren who really have the right to use the word 'my' in this connexion are those eminent Grand Officers, e.g., Grand Masters, Princes of the Blood Royal, etc. who are empowered, by the *B. of C.*, to appoint a Deputy; needless to say, they invariably speak of 'The Deputy . . .'.

---

37.   REPLACEMENT OF DECEASED OFFICERS

Q. When an Officer dies, should the W.M. appoint an acting-officer to finish the year? I have been told that the deceased Officer's name should remain on the Lodge Summons as the holder of the office, while the acting officer discharges the duties until the next Installation.

A. Dealing, first of all, with the list of Officers printed on Lodge Summonses, it is not generally known, perhaps, that such lists are purely optional and there are hundreds of Lodges that never print a complete list. Many give only the name of the W.M., with the names and addresses of the Treasurer and Secretary.

As to the main question; under English Constitution the Officers of the Lodge are divided into two classes, i.e., *Regular Officers who must be appointed or elected*; they form the minimum team and the list of Officers would be legally incomplete without them. Three of these, the W.M., Treasurer and Tyler are elected. The Master, at his discretion, may also appoint a number of *Additional* Officers, but these are not obligatory. Rule 104 (a) of the *B. of C.*, runs:

> The *regular* Officers of a Lodge shall be the Master and his two Wardens, a Treasurer, a Secretary, two Deacons, an Inner Guard and a Tyler. The Master may also appoint as *additional* officers a Chaplain, a Director of Ceremonies, an Assistant Director of Ceremonies, a Charity Steward, an Almoner, an Organist, an Assistant Secretary and a Steward or Stewards but no others. No Brother can hold more than one *regular* office in the Lodge at one and the same time, but the Master may appoint a Brother who is holding a *regular* office to one *additional* office also.

When a *Regular* officer dies, it is the W.M.'s duty to replace him as soon as possible. In the case of the Treasurer, it is essential for the signing of the documents, etc. In the case of Secretary, it is essential , not merely for the business of the Lodge, but also to maintain proper contact with the Grand Lodge. Of course, an 'acting secretary' might complete the year's work equally well, but the Office carries heavy responsibilities; it must be filled and the new holder automatically becomes a regular Officer. All this is plain common-sense, but Rule 121 of the *B. of C.* covers the question and leaves no room for doubt:

> If a vacancy shall occur in a regular office other than that of Master, such office shall be filled for the remainder of the year by the election or appointment (according to the normal method of filling the office) of a member not serving a regular office in the Lodge at the time the vacancy occurred. If an election be required, due notice thereof shall appear on the summons.

As regards *Additional* officers, the W.M. might invite a Brother to 'act', but an acting officer is neither a *Regular* officer nor an *Additional* officer, so that he would have no real status. Indeed, the *B. of C.* makes no provision for acting officers. In effect, an acting officer is simply a deputy, discharging a duty temporarily, in the absence of the Brother for whom he serves.

Finally, the idea that two men cannot be appointed to the same Office in one year, and that the first (deceased) officer remains the 'official' holder until the next election, is plain nonsense.

---

38.   DEACONS AS 'FLOOR OFFICERS'

Q. When did Deacons become 'Floor-Officers' in the Lodge, discharging their present-day duties?

A. The principal duty associated with the office of Deacon nowadays, i.e., the conducting of Candidates during the ceremonies, was originally discharged by the Wardens of the Lodge. In the first well-detailed description of the ceremonies, Prichard's *Masonry Dissected*, 1730, it is evident that the J.W. received the Candidate (as the I.G. does today) and, after some kind of perambulation, the Cand. was handed over to the S.W., who 'presented' him and showed him how to advance towards the Master by three steps.

This work was an exposure and there is no proof that the procedure described in it was correct, but it finds support in later documents of the same class.

Le Secret des Francs-Maçons, of 1742, gives a useful description of the 'floor-work' in the admission ceremony of that period, and in this text, after the report, the W.M. orders the Cand. to be admitted

'. . . and the Wardens [*Surveillants*] place themselves on either side of him to conduct him'.

Another French exposure, *L'Ordre des Francs-Maçons Trahi*, 1745, gives interesting details of the Wardens' duties in the M.M. degree. 'One man alone keeps guard inside the door of the Lodge, with a drawn sword in each hand'. After the report, etc., the Second Warden (i.e., the J.W.) goes to the Guard, takes one sword from him and admits the Cand., with the sword pointing to his L.B. After three perambulations at sword-point, the Cand. is placed facing the W.M. and flanked by the Wardens. The J.W. strikes '. . . three times three on the shoulder of the First Warden [the S.W.], passing his hand behind the Candidate . . .', and the ceremony proceeds.

Several of the later English exposures of the 1760s show that the Wardens were discharging the duties which we associate nowadays with the Deacons, and under the first Grand Lodge, the Moderns, the office of Deacon was extremely rare, though not altogether unknown. The 1743 minutes of the Royal Oak Lodge, Chester, record the election of a Master's Deacon and a Warden's Deacon, and they were regularly appointed until 1758, when they were superseded by Senior and Junior Stewards. (*Misc. Lat.*, vol. 23, p. 114.)

Deacons were known in Bristol in 1758 and were appointed for the first time in the Lodge of Probity, Halifax, now No. 61, on 24 June 1763. Deacons were recorded at Darlington, No. 263, and at Barnard Castle, No. 406, in 1772, both Moderns' Lodges. (*Ibid.*) Two Deacons were also mentioned in the minutes of the Lodge of Antiquity in December, 1778.

Bro. Waples, of Sunderland, has sent a note quoting the By-Laws of the Marquis of Granby Lodge, No. 124, in 1775, where it was ordered that two E.A.s be appointed annually. The senior, seated in the N.E., was to carry 'messuages' from the Master to the S.W. The junior was to stand inside the door, to welcome strange Brethren and 'to carry messuages from the Right Worshipful to the Tyler'. There is no mention of their performing any Deacon's duties in the course of the ceremonies, but probably, in 1775, they did.

The appointment of Stewards was fairly common, and there is reason to believe that it was customary for them to discharge the duties of the modern Deacons. A further note from Bro. Waples mentions that, at the Swalwell Lodge, Durham, in 1734, the Officers included S.W., J.W., and also 'Senior Deacon (or Steward), Junior Deacon (or Steward)', and two Deacons were appointed in 1732, but, he says, there was no further mention of Deacons in their records until 1818.

There appears to be no trace of any early eighteenth century appointments of Deacons as floor officers in Scotland. There, it was customary to appoint Stewards, usually two or more, and occasional references to Stewards' wands suggest that their duties were not confined to refreshment.

The early references to the appointment of Deacons in the modern sense seem to come most consistently from Ireland. They are named in the famous St. John's Day procession at Youghal in January, 1743-4. They appear in the 1744 minutes of the Lodge of Lurgan, and in Dassigny's funeral processional in the following year.

Dermott, the Grand Secretary of the Antients, stated that he had served the offices of J.D. and S.D. (as well as the Wardens' offices) prior to his Installation as Master of No. 26 in Ireland in 1746, and it was probably from Ireland that the Antients' Grand Lodge adopted the practice of appointing Deacons. They are mentioned in the Antients' minutes in July, 1753, and in the records of Lodge No. 37, Antients, in 1754, and their appointment was a regular feature of Antient practice.

On 13 December 1809, the Lodge of Promulgation, in preparation for the Union of the rival Grand Lodges, resolved '. . . that Deacons (being proved on due investigation to be not only Ancient but useful and necessary Officers) be recommended'. This was only one of several measures for standardization that were taken at that time, and a nice example of the effect of this new regulation on the Moderns' lodges appears in the minutes of the Old Dundee Lodge, No. 18, dated 8 February 1810: 'The Master reported that 2 New Officers are necessary to carry the new alterations into effect, and they are to be named "Deacons" and the R.W. Master then appointed . . .' a S.D. and a J.D., and he then ordered jewels for them in the old design, i.e., Mercury, the messenger of the gods, not the modern 'Dove and olive branch'.

---

39. THREE STEPS AND THE FIRST REGULAR STEP

Q. What is the origin and significance of the Three Steps and the First Regular Step?

A. The use of three steps in the course of the ceremonies, or for advancing to the W.M. or to the Altar, is very old practice, but the manner in which the steps were taken is not described in the early texts. In the

Grand Mystery of Free-Masons Discover'd, of 1724, and in its twin, the *Institution of Free Masons*, of *c*. 1725, there is a question:

Q. How many Steps belong to a right Mason?
A. Three.

But these two documents have nothing more on the subject.

A Mason's Confession, which is supposed to represent lodge practice of *c*. 1727 (but was published in 1755-6), speaks of three chalk lines drawn on the lodge floor, and reproduces a rough diagram showing the lines with a set of three right-angles, indicating that the 'advance' was by three steps, the feet being placed in the form of a right-angle at each step, and, if the diagram is to be trusted, it seems that the Candidate advanced sideways, i.e., with his left shoulder towards the W.M., but, although the steps are described very clearly, they are not explained in any way.

The *Wilkinson MS.*, *c*. 1727, and Prichard's *Masonry Dissected*, 1730, both mention that the Candidates of their day took three steps towards the Master, as a preliminary to the Obligation.

Thus it seems fairly certain that the three steps were in use before 1730, and although we do not know how many there were for each degree, or how they were taken, it would appear that only three steps were known.

By this time a certain amount of symbolism was already making its appearance in the ritual and it seems rather strange that the significance of the steps was never explained.

In 1745 the European exposures, French and German, give good evidence that the steps in the third degree had been expanded into something approaching modern practice and they are shown in diagram as three zig-zag steps. Note, there were then only three steps, but they still remained without verbal or written explanation or symbolism.

An English exposure of 1760, *Three Distinct Knocks*, which is supposed to represent the practice of the Antients, indicates that their Cands. took only one step in the 1°, two in the 2° and three in the 3°, and this may indeed have been Antient practice, but we cannot be certain. Laurence Dermott, their Grand Secretary, in the 1778 edition of *Ahiman Rezon* (their Book of Constitutions), derided the various steps used by the Moderns, and, if we read between the lines of his criticism, it looks as though Moderns' practice in this respect was by this time approaching our present-day custom.

After many years' observations on those ingenious methods of walking up to a brother &c., I conclude, that the first was invented by a Man grievously afflicted with the Sciatica. The Second by a Sailor, much accustomed to the rolling of a Ship. And the third by a man, who for recreation or through excess of strong liquors, was wont to dance the drunken Peasant.

(*Ahiman Rezon*, 1778 Edn., Footnote to p. xxxviii.)

Dermott, of course, was being malicious, but two noteworthy points emerge from all this. First, that the Moderns' Grand Lodge, the older foundation, had adopted substantial changes in practice. Secondly, that practices were by no means uniform in regard to the steps.

The extraordinary thing is that even at this late date there seems to have been no explanation or symbolism attaching to the various methods of 'advancing', and this leads to the conclusion that any interpretation offered on this point nowadays is a comparatively modern introduction.

John Coustos, in his confession to the Inquisition at Lisbon in 1742, spoke of three steps (and seven steps), the first of them always 'heel to heel', and apparently they were all 'heel to heel'. The modern practice of a particular place for the R.H. seems to have been unknown in the eighteenth century.

The Pilgrim Lodge, No. 238, London, take only three steps in all degrees, and this serves to emphasize that the variations in practice that existed in the eighteenth century still exist to this day.

THE FIRST REGULAR STEP

The step (feet forming a square) goes back to *c.* 1700. In the *Sloane MS.* of that date, we find:

> Another signe is placing their right heel to the inside of their left in forme of a square so walk a few steps backward and forward and at every third step make a Little Stand placeing their feet Squre as aforesd.

Are we safe in drawing a distinction between 'heel to heel' and 'inside of their left [heel]'? Undoubtedly, the step, however it was made, was already a means of recognition, and in the next thirty years or so we begin to find evidence of three steps. In 1730 there were still three steps prior to the Obligation and entrusting. In the 1760s the E.A. was 'taught' to take only one step as a preliminary to the Obligation and the entrusting that followed it. The F.C. took two steps, and the M.M. took first the one E.A. step, then the two F.C. steps, and finally three M.M. steps. Note: all these steps were *before the Obligation*. There is no record, so far as I know, of additional steps before the entrusting.

In Browne's *Master Key*, of 1802 (one of the last major works on ritual to appear before the Union in 1813), the E.A. advanced 'by three regular steps' to the Master for the Obligation, and no step is mentioned for the 'entrusting'. The three steps are symbolically explained as follows:

> What do they morally teach us?
> Upright lives and well squared intentions.

Later, in the N.E., the Candidate stood with his feet forming a square, symbol of 'a just and upright man and Mason'.

I quote these only to show how practices were developing during the eighteenth century. They were standardized at the Union. On the symbology, I have little to offer, because none of the *early* records explains the symbolism of the steps. We work that out for ourselves (the simpler the better), and Browne's explanation, above, is certainly adequate.

---

40. ST. BARBARA AS A PATRON SAINT OF MASONS

Q. What is the supposed connection between St. Barbara and the Masons?

A. Reference was made in *AQC*, Vol. 75, p. 77, to Santa Barbara as a Patroness of the Masons' Guild at Rotterdam, *c.* 1491, and some doubt was evinced as to the reason why the Masons should have consecrated a chapel to her.

Saint Barbara was a virgin martyr who died *c.* 235. She was a Saint of the Roman Catholic and Orthodox Eastern Churches, and the place of her death is uncertain, being variously given as Heliopolis, a town in Tuscany, and Nicomedia, Bithynia. Her father, a heathen, on discovering that she professed Christianity, had her tortured and beheaded by order of the prefect of the province, and the father himself carried out the final act of the sentence.

Retribution was swift, and he was struck by lightning on his way home. This seems to be the reason why she was adopted as a patron Saint in thunderstorms, and as protectress of artillerymen and miners. Her immediate connection with masons and the mason craft would have seemed to be rather vague, but we are indebted to Bro. Gault MacGowan, of Heidelberg, who points out that St. Barbara was invoked for protection against *lightning*. In the days before the invention of lightning-conductors, many fine buildings were destroyed by lightning, and this explains why the operative masons sued for her protection.

When lightning-conductors came into general use her assistance was no longer required, and she gradually disappeared from the list of Saints associated with the mason craft.

---

41.   SPONSORING A NEW LODGE

Q. Why is it necessary for those wishing to form a new lodge to obtain the recommendation of an existing one?

A. The first and obvious answer to this question is, of course, that the *Book of Constitutions* so requires it. Rule 94, which lays down the procedure for petitioning for a warrant to hold a new lodge, states:

> ... To every such petition must be added a recommendation, signed in open Lodge, by the Master and Wardens of a regular Lodge under the Grand Lodge ...

In seeking, however, the reason behind this regulation, one might meet question with question. Why is it necessary for a candidate for Freemasonry to have sponsors? The analogy is not perfect: the candidate is a stranger to the Craft, whereas a new lodge is formed of brethren already within it; but the uncontrolled formation of new lodges would be just as undesirable as a too free and unguarded recommendation of candidates for initiation. We charge the candidate, after his initiation, to exemplify his fidelity by, among other things, 'refraining from recommending ... unless ... he will ultimately reflect honour on your choice'. Is it not just as important that we should guard against a new lodge being brought into being unless we are assured that there is a need for it, and we have strong grounds for believing that the brethren who seek to form it do so from the highest Masonic motives and are worthy of our support? Otherwise we are indirectly surrendering our trust and, perhaps, even sowing the seeds of decay from within.

It is possible that without any control over the formation of new lodges, and without a procedure for scrutinizing the initial make-up of a lodge, and for sponsoring it if found worthy—without this guarantee we might open the door to undesirable elements and disunity might arise. New lodges might be formed, for instance, by groups of brethren disgruntled at some grievance, real or imaginary, against their own lodges. Taking the argument a step further, if the grievance was against higher authority, the position might conceivably be reached where rival grand lodges might come into being, just as they did in the past for this very reason (e.g., the 'Wigan Grand Lodge').

It is only prudent, therefore, that the petition for a warrant must be accompanied by this recommendation from an existing regular lodge (and also by the observations of the Provincial or District Grand Master in the regions outside the London area).

Perhaps an instance of what happened in Halifax, Yorkshire, two centuries ago, will give point to what has been said above. The Bacchus Lodge, meeting there, 'had a doubtful reputation . . .' It had been warranted by the Moderns in 1769, on the recommendation of 'two very respectable Lodges in London'. The Brethren of the existing Halifax Lodge had grave doubts about the founders of the new Lodge, and went so far as to describe them in a letter to Grand Lodge as 'a number of loose fellows'. It appears from what eventually came to light that certain frequenters of the Bacchus Inn, some of whom were Masons, had determined to form a Lodge as the basis of a secret society of coiners and counterfeiters, and no doubt plied their criminal but profitable activities behind tyled doors and under the obligations of Masonry.

> . . . They kept up appearances remarkably well; they sent up regular Charity subscriptions to London—as they could well afford to do—and no doubt attended such masonic functions of a semi-public character as could be made to serve their purpose.
> . . . The counterfeiters were ultimately caught and justice dealt out to them; a number of the Brethren were sentenced to transportation for life.
>   (*AQC*, Vol. 56, pp. 251–2.)

The Lodge itself was erased from the List in 1783.

Whilst agreeing that such an affair could not happen today—or so we trust!—the lesson remains.

One last point which might be made is that Freemasonry is not alone in requiring the backing of an existing group for the formation of a new one. Other organizations and societies, religious and secular, require the new offshoot to be sponsored by a parent body, and this is, after all, a very natural process of propagation and regeneration.

We are indebted to Bro. T. O. Haunch for the answer, above, to this question. It may be useful, however, to add that the rule requiring that the petition for a new Lodge should be recommended by the Master and Wardens of a sponsoring Lodge is of comparatively modern introduction. It is certain that no such requirement existed in the operative Lodges in Britain, because there was no governing body to exercise that kind of control.

In 1598, William Schaw, Master of Works to the Crown of Scotland and Warden General of the Mason Craft, issued a code of regulations,

'The Schaw Statutes', which may be taken as the first official attempt at some kind of nation-wide control of the Craft in Scotland. (No comparable regulations are known for England.) They were 'to be observed by all master masons within this realm' and, although they contained some twenty-two regulations relating to Lodge and trade practices, and the word 'lodge' is mentioned in five of them, the only rule relating to the Lodge itself was one requiring the Masters, i.e., Master Masons, to vote and choose a Warden (i.e., presiding officer or master) each year, whose name was to be notified to the Warden General. The Lodges in those days were self-governing bodies, formed by inherent right, and there was no hint as yet of Petition, or Recommendation, or Warrant, as necessary preliminaries to their formation.

In England, Dr. Anderson's *Book of Constitutions*, 1723, provided the first code of regulations for the then recently established Grand Lodge. It contained a section describing the 'Manner of constituting a New Lodge', but that dealt only with the ceremony, and with the Officers who were empowered to conduct it. In Rule viii, however, there was a requirement that if any Brothers separated themselves from their Lodge they must immediately join another,

> or else they must obtain the *Grand-Master's* Warrant to join in forming a *new Lodge*.

This was the first English rule requiring the Warrant as a prerequisite to the formation of a new Lodge.

New Lodges were now coming into existence quite frequently, but there were still no rules relating to formal Petition or Recommendation. The first indication of the necessity for some kind of approval or recommendation for the establishment of a new Lodge is implicit in the Grand Lodge minutes of June 1741, when it was resolved

> That no new Lodge should for the future be Constituted within the Bills of Mortality [i.e., the parishes in a given area in and around London] without the Consent of the Brethren assembled in Quarterly Communication first obtained for that purpose.

Six months later, on 12 January 1742, an objection was raised to the new rule, on the grounds that it was 'derogatory to the Prerogative of the R^t Worshipful the G:M.', but upon the Grand Master

> Expressing his satisfaction of the Expediency of that Law The same was on the Question put Agreed to.

The rival Grand Lodge, the Antients', was founded in 1751 and a very comprehensive code of 'Rules and Orders' was 'agreed and settled' on 17 July 1751. Their 8th Regulation was the first Masonic law in

England that embodied the three requirements, Petition, Attestation (or Recommendation) and Warrant:

> NO Admission or Warrant shall be granted to any Brothers to hold a Lodge until such time they have first form'd a Lodge of Ancient Masons and sitt Regularly in a Credible House and then to Apply by Petition and such Petition to be Attested by the Masters of three Regular Lodges who shall make a Proper Report of them.

There seems to be no record of a similar regulation in the practice of the premier Grand Lodge. In the first edition of his *Illustrations of Masonry*, 1772, William Preston devoted a chapter to 'The Manner of Constituting a Lodge . . .', in which he printed a form of Petition, and continued:

> This petition, being properly signed, and recommended by three Masters of regular Lodges, must be delivered to the Grand Secretary . . .

It may be assumed that 'recommendation by three Masters of Lodges' was being practised in Moderns' Lodges by this time.

Following the union of the rival Grand Lodges in 1813, the new *Book of Constitutions* of the United Grand Lodge was published in 1815. The section headed 'Of Constituting a New Lodge' began:

> EVERY application for a warrant to hold a new lodge must be by petition to the grand master . . . The petition must be recommended by the officers of some regular lodge and be transmitted to the grand secretary . . .

The 'three Lodge' or 'three Masters' requirement had disappeared; the officers of one regular lodge were now sufficient for the recommendation; but the rule in its present form prescribing that the recommendation *must be signed in open Lodge by the Master and Wardens* did not come into existence until 3 December 1913.

---

42.   THE BEEHIVE

Q. What is the significance of the beehive in Freemasonry?

A. The date of its introduction into Masonic symbolism is obscure. In a Masonic skit, 'A Letter from the Grand Mistress . . .' dated 1724, and attributed erroneously to Jonathan Swift, we find:

> A Bee hath in all Ages and Nations been the Grand Hieroglyphick of Masonry, because it excels all other living Creatures in the Contrivance and Commodiousness of its Habitation . . . (*E.M.C.*, p. 233).

The text rambles and the remaining references to the beehive have neither literary merit nor Masonic interest.

The beehive was always an emblem of industry, and it appears often in the second half of the eighteenth century on Tracing Boards, Lodge certificates, jewels, glass and pottery.

The Lodge of Emulation, No. 21 (founded in 1723), has had the beehive as its emblem for nearly 200 years at least, and it is depicted on drinking vessels presented to the Lodge in 1776, and on their firing-glasses of the same period.

Dring, in his great study of the evolution of the Tracing Boards (*AQC* 29), reproduced a large number of pictures of early Lodge 'Cloths' and Boards, and the beehive appears regularly in almost every set. By the time it had achieved such a degree of prominence in Lodge symbolism, there can be no doubt that it was also being featured in the explanatory work, or Lectures, and the eighteenth century ritual of the Royal Cumberland Lodge, No. 41, Bath, contains the following in its Third Degree Lecture:

> The Beehive teaches us that we are born into the world rational and intelligent beings, so ought we also to be industrious ones, and not stand idly by or gaze with listless indifference on even the meanest of our fellow creatures in a state of distress if it is in our power to help them without detriment to ourselves or connections; the constant practice of this virtue is enjoined on all created beings, from the highest seraph in heaven to the meanest reptile that crawls in the dust.
>
> (From G. W. Bullamore, 'The Beehive and Freemasonry', *AQC*, Vol. 36, p. 222.)

At the Union of the rival Grand Lodges in 1813, many of the old symbols that had formerly adorned the Tracing Boards were abandoned; among them were the Hour-glass, the Scythe, the Ark and the Beehive. The explanation of these symbols disappeared from English practice. But many modern American rituals, which owe their origins to English pre-Union sources, have preserved the explanations that we discarded. To cite only one example, the Royal Cumberland quotation, above, appears almost word-for-word in the third degree *Trestle-Board* published by the Grand Lodge of Massachusetts in 1928.

The symbols listed here, including the beehive, owe their survival in the American 'monitorial' workings to Thomas Smith Webb, a prominent Masonic ritualist and lecturer (b. 1771; d. 1819), who may well be described as the William Preston of American Masonry. He was still a young man in his early twenties when he became acquainted with John Hanmer, an Englishman, well versed in English ritual and especially in Preston's system. With Hanmer's help, Webb published the first edition of *The Freemason's Monitor: or Illustrations of Masonry,* in 1797. Its main section was a substantial reproduction of Preston's *Illustrations*, although Webb forgot to mention that. There were at least six further editions in Webb's lifetime, all 'enlarged and improved', and the work became very popular. The edition of 1802 contained his interpretation of the symbolism of the beehive and it is probably the most widely known explanation in use today. It is reproduced here, in full:

THE BEE HIVE

Is an emblem of industry, and recommends the practice of that virtue to all created beings, from the highest seraph in heaven, to the lowest reptile of the dust. It teaches us, that as we came into the world rational and intelligent beings, so we should ever be industrious ones; never sitting down contented while our fellow-creatures around us are in want, when it is in our power to relieve them, without inconvenience to ourselves.

When we take a survey of nature, we view man, in his infancy, more helpless and indigent than the brutal creation: he lies languishing for days, months, and years, totally incapable of providing sustenance for himself, of guarding against the attack of the wild beasts of the field, or sheltering himself from the inclemencies of the weather. It might have pleased the Great Creator of heaven and earth, to have made man independent of all other beings; but, as dependence is one of the strongest bands [sic] of society, mankind were made dependent on each other for protection and security, as they thereby enjoy better opportunities of fulfilling the duties of reciprocal love and friendship. Thus was man formed for social and active life, the noblest part of the work of God; and he that will so demean himself, as not to be endeavouring to add to the common stock of knowledge and understanding, may be deemed a *drone* in the *hive* of nature, a useless member of society, and unworthy our protection as masons.

There is something of a mystery here. In England, despite the numerous appearances of the beehive in 18th century Masonic Jewels, Certificates, Tracing Boards, and furnishings, it has proved impossible to trace any *relics of 18th century ritual or commentary relating to the bee, or the beehive as Masonic symbols*, except the extract quoted above from the Third Degree Lecture used in the Royal Cumberland Lodge, No. 41. That Lodge was in existence in 1733 and it would not be surprising to find isolated items of early ritual practices surviving there; but Bro. P. R. James, who was a member of that Lodge for many years (and whose scholarly work on Preston's *Lectures* commands the highest respect), held that the 'beehive note' in the English Lecture was 19th century material. It is quite clearly related to Webb's 'Bee Hive' and the problem is whether Royal Cumberland borrowed from Webb, or was it originally English material—adopted and elaborated by Webb?

Another point of interest is the question of which degree contained the beehive? In the early English T.B.s it invariably appears in the first, but sometimes in a 'combined' first and second. In the Royal Cumberland working it appeared in the third Lecture, and the Massachusetts working states that all the symbols listed above, including the beehive, belong to the third degree.

---

43. FELLOWCRAFTS AND THE MIDDLE CHAMBER

Q. The Lecture on the Second Tracing Board states that '. . . the F.C.s received their wages in the Middle Chamber of King Solomon's Temple'. Later, we are told that it contained 'certain Hebrew characters', from which we may assume that the Chamber must have been completed.

If the men to be paid were actually engaged on the building of the Temple, where were they paid while the room was being built, or before the work had begun on that portion of the building?

A. I appreciate the questioner's difficulty, but it is impossible to provide a satisfactory factual answer to a question that arises from the statements made in a legend. The description of the Middle Chamber in 1 Kings VI, verse 8, is not at all clear and, wherever F.C.s were paid when that room was built, they were paid elsewhere before that time, but the Old Testament affords no information on this point.

There are, however, several other interesting problems that arise out of the Lecture on the Second T.B. We all accept that Solomon built the Temple and, as already indicated, the Biblical accounts in Kings and Chronicles are so complicated that they furnish endless difficulties in themselves. To make matters worse, the compilers of the ritual overlaid and embroidered the original story with masses of invented detail. No doubt they meant well; they were simply trying to arrange various items of ritual and procedure against a Biblical background, creating a kind of Masonic allegory: but allegory, in this case, is a very polite euphemism.

To understand how much embroidery was added, one needs to compare the relevant details in the Lecture on the Second Tracing Board with the story as given in 1 Kings, chapters V to VII, and II Chronicles, chapters II to IV. In fairness to the later expounders and embellishers who were certainly responsible for some of the subsequent 'improvements', the prime culprit in this case was Samuel Prichard, who published in his *Masonry Dissected*, 1730, the first exposure of a three-degree system, which contained the earliest known version of the Fellow Craft's Degree in that system. (*E.M.C.*, pp. 165–7.)

The F.C. 'ceremony' is presented in the course of some thirty-three Questions and Answers, which probably represent the essentials of the ritual of their day, but without any details of 'floorwork' or procedure. The brief synopsis that follows will suffice to show that, despite numerous changes in the intervening years, it is the direct source of much of the Middle Chamber material in use today.

In the course of his answers the Candidate (in 1730) said that he was made F.C. 'For the sake of the Letter G' which means 'Geometry, or the fifth Science'. He travelled 'East and West' and worked 'in the Building of the Temple'. There, 'he received his Wages . . .' in the middle Chamber. He came there 'By a winding Pair of Stairs, Seven or more'. When he 'came to the Door of the middle Chamber . . . he saw a Warden' who demanded 'Three Things' . . . i.e., 'Sign, Token and a Word'. [Described in detail.] When he 'came into the middle' [of the middle Chamber?] he saw the 'Resemblance of the Letter G' which denotes 'The Grand Architect and Contriver of the Universe, or He that was taken up to the top of the Pinnacle of the Holy Temple' [i.e., Jesus Christ].

It is noteworthy that in this version the letter G had at least two meanings, i.e., Geometry and the Grand Architect . . . of the Universe. We cannot but wonder at the mentality of the ritual compiler who believed that the Middle Chamber in Solomon's Temple could have contained a symbolic reference to Christ, several hundred years B.C. Unfortunately there are no means of ascertaining where Prichard obtained his material, or whether he wrote some of it himself.

The study of Prichard's catechism also reveals some confusion arising from a series of questions which embody two completely separate themes:

(a) The making or passing of a F.C., with the symbolism of the G for Geometry, which was its earliest meaning.

(b) The legendary place of the F.C. in the construction of the Temple, i.e., work, wages, and admission to the Middle Chamber.

The following Q. and A. are all from Prichard's second degree, but they are tabulated to show the line of argument as to the two themes:

The 'PASSING' theme

Q. Why was you made a Fellow-Craft?

A. For the sake of the Letter G.

Q. What does that G denote?

A. Geometry, or the fifth Science.

[Note: I would take this to be part of the 'early-type' catechism, relating to the actual ceremony. But see how it links up, later, with the Q. and A. in the next column.]

The 'WORK-WAGES' symbolical theme

Q. Did you ever work?

A. Yes, in the building of the Temple.

Q. Where did you receive your Wages?

A. In the middle Chamber.
[Several other questions relating to the Porch, Pillars, their ornamentation, etc.]

Q. When you came into the middle [Chamber], what did you see?

A. The Resemblance of the Letter G.
[Several Q. and A. have been omitted, but note that the G now has a new significance, i.e.]

Q. Who doth that G denote? . . .

A. . . . The Grand Architect and Contriver of the Universe, or He that was taken up to the . . . Pinnacle . . .

The Q. and A. in the right-hand column may be taken as the beginnings of Speculative expansion on the beauty and meaning of the Temple; here are the various 'strands' of the material which ultimately became the Lecture on the Second T.B. None of our early documents made any attempt to separate the two themes. The 'G' for Geometry disappeared from modern workings. Within the Middle Chamber (in English practice) it became the four letters of the Tetragrammaton, J.H.V.H., or their Hebrew equivalents and nowadays we have two Wardens on guard at the Winding Stairs, with two tests, instead of only one Warden and one test, as in Prichard's day.

One further example of the zeal with which our ritual compilers embellished their materials may be taken from William Preston's 'Second Lecture of Free Masonry':

Where did our Brn. go to receive their wages?

The E.A. in the Outer Chamber, the F.C. in the Middle Chamber, the Master in the Inner Chamber of the Temple. (*AQC*, Vol. 83, p. 203.)

The outer and inner chambers were mercifully abandoned toward the end of the 18th century; Browne, in his *Master Key*, 1802, retained only the middle one. So, we are able to see how the ritual grows.

44.   THE MASTER'S HAT

Q.1. In ancient practice, where the Master wore a hat, did he enter the lodge hatted, or did he ceremonially don the hat when the lodge was declared open and remove it when the lodge was closed, or 'untiled'?

2. Is there any ground for associating 'hat practices' with operative masonry, or were they introduced in the speculative period?

3. Is there any evidence to support the suggestion that hat practices are linked with the slang word 'tile' = hat; i.e., that the Master symbolized the lodge, and that, when he was hatted, this meant that the lodge was tiled?

4. Are there any other explanations of hat practices?

A. The answers to your questions must be made with reservations, because there is no authoritative evidence for any of the procedures under discussion, i.e., there is no mention in Grand Lodge minutes, or Regulations, of any 'hat customs', so that practically our only information is from unofficial (and sometimes unreliable) documents.

The following is a brief survey of some of the 'hat' evidence bearing on your questions:

(a) In the Bristol and Bath area, records of a Foundation Stone ceremony, Dedication of a Masonic Hall, and at a funeral, at all of which the Brethren were required to wear cocked hats. To this day the W.M.s under the Prov. G. Lodge of Bristol all wear a kind of cocked hat on entering and retiring from the Lodge, but not during the Lodge session. (See *AQC*, Vol. 74, pp. 154–5.)

(b) *Calliope*, an English eighteenth century song-book, has an illustration to a Masonic song, dated 1738. It depicts a group of seven Masons in the costume of that day, three of them being the W.M. and Wardens, wearing their aprons and jewels. They stand round a table with three lighted candles on it, and the Letter G is displayed above, i.e., it is a lodge-room. All seven have wine-glasses in their hands. None of them wears a hat, and no hats are visible.

(c) The frontispiece of *Hiram*, an English exposure of 1765, illustrates an Initiation ceremony. The plate exists in two states—one with the Candidate, the other without. In both plates, only the W.M. wears a tricorn hat.

(d) In the well-known series of English 'Palser Prints', 1809–1812, illustrating the ceremonies, the W.M. wears a hat in some pictures and is hatless in others. Palser's work was based on some of the French *Assemblée* prints of *c.* 1745 (noted below), but presumably he was depicting English practices, for the English market.

(e) The *Ordre des Francs-Maçons Trahi*, a famous French exposure of 1745, contains two well-known pictures of the first and third degrees in progress. In each case, all the Brn., excepting the Candidate, are wearing hats. (See illustrations, pp. 190, 195.)

(f) In the *Assemblée des Francs Maçons*, a very interesting series of prints dated *c*. 1745, there is one which depicts the Ob. in an Initiation ceremony. Only the W.M. wears a tricorn. All others are hatless. (See illustration on p. ii.)

(g) In the same *Assemblée* series relating to the third degree, one print shows the W.M. with hat, and another without. All other Brn. are hatless.

From the evidence adduced above, it may be stated firmly that even in those places where hats were worn there was no uniformity of practice, and that is why it is impossible 'to lay down the law' or even to answer all questions on the subject with any degree of certainty. Nevertheless, the following may be helpful:

Q.1 Where the W.M. alone or all the Brn. wore hats, it is probable that they were worn throughout the meetings. It is not good argument to cite modern practices in an attempt to deduce ancient customs, but the present-day practice in U.S.A. may be relevant. Only the W.M. wears a hat throughout the meeting, and he removes it only during Prayers, Obligations and when welcoming visitors. In the Pilgrim Lodge, No. 238 (a German-speaking Lodge in London), all present wear hats throughout the meeting, except the Candidates, and hats are only removed at the moments when the Name of God is mentioned. (See also the Bristol custom in (a) above, which dates back to the late eighteenth century.)

Q.2 There is no evidence for the wearing of hats in operative practice.

Q.3 There cannot be any association between the slang word 'tile' and the Tyling of the Lodge. The *O.E.D.* date, 1823, for the slang word, would preclude any link with practices which were common in 1738, 1745, etc., as shown above.

Q.4 The Pilgrim Lodge practice, based on the Schroeder (German) ritual of *c*. 1790, makes the hat a symbol of freedom or equality, and the Cand. is hatless until the end of his ceremony, when his hat is formally returned to him. The Lodge adopted this ritual in *c*. 1850.

In all those cases where the W.M. alone wears the hat, the symbolism is clearly reversed, because the hat, in those cases, is a symbol of leadership, rule or power.

45.   ON MASONIC VISITING

Q. Could you give us any information on the origin of Masonic visiting?

A. The practice of visiting is one of the oldest customs in the Craft, dating back to the earliest days of operative Masonry. Practically every version of our *Old Charges*, from 1583 onwards, contains a rule on the subject. The following is from the *Beaumont MS.*, of 1690 (I quote this version because the English is easy to read, but all the texts are very much alike on this point):

> And also yt every Mason receive and cherish every strang[e] Mason when they come to their country and sett them to Worke as the mannor is ... if he have mould stones in ye place, he shall sett him a fortnight at least to worke & give him his pay, & if he have no stones he shall refresh him wth mony to ye next Lodg.

In effect, every lodge attached to a large building job became a visiting centre for masons in search of employment, in the sure knowledge that they would find work, if available, or else get hospitality and help towards their next call.

Later, when operative trade-controls began to break down, the lodges gradually acquired the character of social and benevolent clubs, and now the visiting took on a more convivial aspect.

It is interesting to see that the newly-erected Grand Lodge, in the first *Book of Constitutions*, 1723, made a regulation strongly advocating the practice of inter-lodge visiting:

> [Reg.] XI. All *particular Lodges* are to observe the same *Usages* as much as possible; in order to which, and for cultivating a good Understanding among *Free-Masons*, some Members out of *every Lodge* shall be deputed to visit the *other Lodges* as often as shall be thought convenient.

As late as 1919, the *Constitutions* still contained Rule 149, almost in the same terms as the above, but the modern rule 'enjoined' only the Master and Wardens to visit.

In the early eighteenth century we begin to find lodge minutes and occasional by-laws and regulations governing the custom of visiting, and it is from these old records that we trace how most of our modern practices have developed.

The proper precautions regarding visitors to lodges must have been rather slack in the early years of the Grand Lodge, and with the publication, in 1730, of Prichard's famous exposure, *Masonry Dissected*, Grand Lodge was compelled to take action. The minute of 15 December

1730 was the first official step towards a proper control of visiting, and it was also the first official regulation relating to the present-day Signature Book:

> Proposed till otherwise Ordered by the Grand Lodge, that no Person whatsoever should be admitted into Lodges unless some Member of the Lodge then present would vouch for such visiting Brothers being a regular Mason, and the Member's name to be entred against the Visitor's Name in the Lodge Book, which Proposal was unanimously agreed to.

A nice example of the manner in which this regulation was observed appears in the By-Laws of the Lodge held at the 'Shakespear's head in little Marlborough Street St. James' (now the Lodge of Friendship, No. 6):

> Ordain'd Augt. 7, 1736 . . .
> To prevent at all Times ye Admission of Persons not Masons, into ye Lodge, no Visitor shall be admitted, unless some one of ye Brethren present is able to avouch yt . . . he is a worthy Brother, or unless such ample Satisfaction be by him giv'n to those Deputed to receive him, as shall put that Matter beyond all Dispute. The so recommending Bror, shall withdraw and see if he do personally know any Visitor thus offering before he can be admitted into ye Lodge. He must certifie it to the Brethren present and then, with Leave from ye Chair, he may be introduced.

In the Lodge of Antiquity (now No. 2), in 1736, a minute records that there were five visitors, who paid one shilling each for their evening's entertainment. Three of them were from 'named lodges', and two are recorded as 'St. Johns', i.e., they were unattached Masons.

At the Lodge at the Swan and Rummer, in Finch Lane, London, there was a By-Law in 1726 requiring all visitors to pay one shilling, and the names of their lodges were to be entered in the Lodge Book, '. . . the Better to give us an opportunity of Returning their visits'. This is probably one of the earliest records of the practice of a regular exchange of visits, a custom which became extremely popular later on.

In the same code of By-Laws there is record of the W.M. having the right to invite two guests (gratis?) on Initiation nights, and the Wardens were allowed one guest apiece. (*Records of the L. of Antiquity, No. 2*, vol. i, p. 41.)

At the Old King's Arms Lodge, No. 28, the W.M. read a letter on 17 November 1735, announcing a general 'Invitation from the Stewards Lodge', which gave the dates of their four meetings annually, '. . . where the Visit of the Master Masons belonging to this Society [i.e., to Lodge No. 28] would be always acceptable'. At the same Lodge, in 1743, the Dining Fee was fixed at 2*s*. 6*d*. and members were allowed to 'introduce

any other Brother belonging to a regular Lodge on paying 2*s*. 6*d*. . . .'.
Apparently, this was only the price of the dinner, because the subscription for a visitor was raised (at the same time) from 1*s*. to 2*s*., which
doubtless paid for more potent refreshment.

The minutes of the Lodge of Emulation, No. 21, show that the practice of 'Public Visits' (i.e., exchange visiting) had developed quite
strongly in the last quarter of the eighteenth century:

> March 9th, 1778.
> . . . proposed that a Public Visit be return'd in form to the Tuscan Lodge,
> which was agreed to unanimously.

The record of a return visit six weeks later shows that the visitors comprised a full team, 'Masters, Wardens, and Officers of the Tuscan Lodge'.
Emulation had some wealthy men amongst its members, and the
visitor's fee was fixed, in 1809, at 10*s*. 6*d*., which was a lot of money in
those days. A more realistic minute appears in the records of the Union
Lodge, No. 52, Norwich, in May 1810, when it was resolved that
'. . . visiting Brethren be charged the price of a Bottle of Wine'. This
was more akin to the old Scottish lodge custom of 'paying the club',
which involved each man present contributing a fixed amount at the
beginning of the evening's entertainment or sharing the cost equally at
the end.

---

46.   VISITING OF LODGES
                  BY 'UNATTACHED' BRETHREN

Q. There seems to be some ambiguity in Rule 127 (ii) in the *Book of
Constitutions* as to the rights of visiting pertaining to an unattached
Brother. Does it mean that a Brother who resigns from his Lodge may
visit only one Lodge once, or any Lodge once?

A. The rule is actually quite clear but, perhaps because it seems to be
over-generous, there is a tendency to misinterpret it. Rule 127 (i) deals
with Brethren *excluded* under rules 148 or 181. A Brother so *excluded*
is barred from attending any Lodge or Lodge of Instruction until he
again becomes a subscribing member of a Lodge.

B. of C. Rule 127 (ii) says:

> (ii) In any other case [i.e. if he simply resigns from his Lodge or Lodges]
> he shall not be permitted to attend any one Lodge more than once until he
> again becomes a subscribing member of a Lodge . . .

This means he may visit *any or every Lodge under English Constitution once, and once only*; but he must sign the Attendance-book appending the word 'unattached', and giving the name and number of the Lodge of which he was last a subscribing member.

---

47.   THE NETWORK OVER THE PILLARS

Q. The explanations of the Second Tracing Board in many different workings describe the Pillars enriched with network, lily-work, etc. Later they say:

They [i.e. the Pillars] were considered finished when the network or canopy was thrown over them.

Two questions arise out of this passage:

(1) What does the final word 'them' refer to?
    (a) The two pillars complete, *in toto*, or
    (b) The globes with which the pillars were adorned?

(2) Do the two references to network relate to the same thing or to different things? In replying to this, will you consider the Biblical references, and also the suggestion (in the *Trans. of the Leics. L. of Research*, 1956–7, p. 39) that they were simply designed as protection against birds?

A. Your questions are more difficult than you imagine. But, first, let it be clear that the *ritual quotation is not Biblical*; it is a piece of ritual embroidery expressing only the ideas of the author of that part of the ritual. It follows that we are not bound to explain the Biblical text to suit the quotation, but only according to the words of Holy Writ.

Unfortunately, the latter are somewhat obscure and the renderings into English are not always precise. The relevant passages are in I Kings, VII, verses 17–20, 41, 42, and in Jeremiah LII, verses 22, 23. I have already indicated (in the article on 'Pillars and Globes', etc., *AQC* 75, pp. 206–7) that we cannot be entirely sure, from the text, whether the pillars were surmounted only with bowl-shaped chapiters, or whether they had additional bowls or globes *above* the chapiters. Generally, I believe that the accepted view is that the pillars were surmounted by two 'features', (a) chapiters, and (b) 'globes or bowls'. (The reasons for reopening this part of the problem will appear below.)

Now let us turn to your Q.2. There was only one kind of 'Network' (which should not be confused with the seven festoons of 'chains' on each pillar). What the 'Networks' were intended for is a puzzle, but Hebrew scholars, ancient and modern, are agreed that their purpose was decorative; there is no suggestion of a utilitarian purpose. (I have seen them drawn as rigid metal 'grilles', such as might be used to protect a jeweller's window!)

The Hebrew word has several meanings, all suggestive of 'interlacing', i.e., network, lattice-work, grille or grating, chequer-work or mesh. Rashi and Kimchi, two famous medieval commentators, agreed that the chequer-work was formed 'like palm-branches', implying a kind of angular mesh or trellis-work; and the Geneva Bible speaks of 'grates', suggesting flat, rigid grilles. Rashi adds that they were 'shaped like a ball', which also implies a rigid grille designed to enclose the globe completely.

Dr. Herz, the late Chief Rabbi, who was a great scholar, stated in his commentary that 'the capitals were decorated with tracery', and he identifies the 'Networks' with tracery. The Geneva Bible (I Kings, vii, 17) says 'Hee made grates like networke, . . .' and shows an illustration of one of the pillars surmounted by a globe, which is covered with interlaced metal strap-work or chequer-work, so as to appear almost as though the patterns had been carved in low relief. This would seem to agree with Rashi's idea of a net or grille fitting closely over the 'globe'.

Now you may see why I reopened the 'bowls or globes' question at the beginning of this long and complex problem. The nature of the 'Networks' would depend very much on the objects they were intended to cover. If the crown of the pillar was a bowl, it could be covered with a rigid grate, or a pliable 'Network'. If it was a globe, any kind of rigid grille would have had to be attached, either to the pillar or to the globe itself; but a pliable mesh might have been used without any such fixing.[1]

I do not believe anyone can be sure of the answer to these questions. My own view is that the 'Networks' were of some sort of pliable mesh, and this is largely based on the details of the rows of pomegranate decorations which were attached to them. I think we are all agreed that the 'Networks' or 'grilles', whatever they were, were designed *only as a decoration for the upper part of the pillars*, and that they did not cover the pillars down to the ground. The Leicester suggestion, that the 'Networks' were simply a protection from birds, may be a valid one, but I am inclined to doubt it.

---

[1] See 'Nets' hanging from 'Bowls' in illustration on p. 273.

48.   'WILL YOU BE OFF OR FROM?'

Q. 'Will you be off or from?' Is this a test-question or a 'catch-question'? Please explain.

A. This is *not* a catch-question. It is a question in what is known, in Scottish working, as the 'short method' of passing or raising the Lodge from one degree to another. Let us assume that the Lodge is in the first degree and the next item of business is 'to pass Brother N. to the Second Degree'.

> The Master orders the Lodge to be proved tyled in the usual manner, and the Brethren all stand to order 'while the Lodge is being passed'. The Master then asks the Senior Warden: 'Will you be off or from?' The S.W. replies: 'From' (if the Lodge is going *up* to the degree). The Master then says: 'From what to what?' The S.W. says: 'From the Degree of E.A. to that of Fellowcraft'. The Master then says: 'By virtue of the Authority vested in me as Master of this Lodge, I declare it closed in the E.A. Degree' (gives knocks of E.A. Degree) 'and opened in the Degree of Fellowcraft' (gives knocks of F.C. Degree). And that is that! Very simple and very quick—as opposed to all the usual questions about squares, etc. Note: If the Lodge is coming *down*, the S.W. will answer 'Off' instead of 'From'—to be followed, of course, by the Master asking: 'Off what to what?'

This method of getting the Lodge up and down from one degree to another is quite popular and is much used by the Scottish country Lodges. It is also used in all Lodges when coming down from M.M. at the end of a raising—unless there is no more Business, when the Lodge is closed *finally* on the third (by the Wardens giving the substituted secrets, etc.). The Scottish working also allows the Lodge being *finally* closed on the second.

When this question came in, in 1963, I was under the impression that the 'Off or From' was purely Scottish practice. I therefore sent it to Bro. G. S. Draffen, *M.B.E.*, then S.G.W. of the Grand Lodge of Scotland. He, very kindly, furnished the answer printed above, which, I hasten to add, is perfectly correct. Scottish influence in Craft customs has always been so strong that one would expect to find similar practices in use overseas and soon after the Summons was issued, a number of letters came in, from Brethren in England and overseas, pointing out that the answer was incomplete. In particular, a note that the 'Short Method' is used in Derbyshire started me on a search for early English usage. I found that it was in print, in the two most important English exposures of the 1760s, when it was used in the course of testing Candidates and Visitors, but not as a 'Short Method' of raising or lowering the Lodge from one degree to another. The following is from the Master's Part Catechism, in *Three Distinct Knocks*, 1760:

Mas. Will you be of [*sic*] or from?
Ans. From.
Mas. From what, Brother?
Ans. From an enter'd Apprentice to a Fellow-Craft.
Mas. Pass, Brother.

This was followed by the (then customary) P.G. and P.W. leading to the 2° and further questions embodying the Tn. and Wd. of the F.C. The same text also contained a chapter describing the examination of a visitor 'at the Door of a Free-Mason's Lodge', in which the 'Of or From' appears twice, once with the word 'Of and once as 'Off'.

In Ireland, Scotland, certain Canadian jurisdictions, California, Texas, and doubtless in many other places too, the question 'Will you be off or from?' is still used as part of the 'Entrusting' and subsequent testing of candidates, i.e., for passing from the grip of one degree to the one immediately above, and also from the pass-grips to the second and third to the proper grips of these degrees. The interrogator poses the question, 'Will you be off or from?' and the interrogated *always* answers, 'From'. The former then says, 'From what to what?' and the latter replies, for example, 'FROM the grip of an E.A. Mason to the pass-grip of a F.C. Mason', or 'From the pass-grip of a F.C. Mason to the grip of the same', or 'From the grip of a F.C. Mason to the pass-grip of a M.M.', etc., etc., as the case may be. The answer to the original question is *never* 'Off'.

Bro. J. Pendrill, Prov. G. Secretary, Warwicks., writes to say that the 'Off or From' questions are also used in Scotland for testing visitors to Lodges.

Bro. B. Kelham, Secretary of Lodge No. 278, Gibraltar, says that the questions are also used in Derbyshire, and possibly in other English Provinces, as the 'Short Method of Raising (or Reducing) the Lodge'.

Bro. C. R. J. Donnithorne, Dist. G. Secretary of the District Grand Lodge of the Far East, writes from Hong Kong:

In Scottish Lodges here it is the Junior Warden who gives the answers when the Lodge is 'going up' from first to second degree and 'coming down' again. The Senior Warden replies to the questions when moving to the third degree and coming down again. Lodges here also close finally in the third degree in the manner mentioned in your notice, and this means that 'any other business' after the conferment of a degree is always dealt with before the degree working.

49.   LONDON GRAND RANK

Q. I have to propose a Toast to the 'Holders of London Grand Rank'. Could you please give me some factual information on the subject?

A. It began on 4 December 1907, when, as reported in the Grand Lodge *Proceedings,* the Grand Master, H.R.H. Prince Arthur, Duke of Connaught, feeling

> '. . . that special merit on the part of London Brethren is not and cannot at present be adequately recognized in the Metropolis as it is in the respective Provinces and Districts, is desirous that power should be given to confer upon a certain number of Past Masters of London Lodges a distinction for long and meritorious service, equivalent to what is known as Provincial or District Grand Rank.'

At first, there was to be a limit of 150 awards annually; nowadays there are approximately 600 per annum. At its inception the distinction was known as London Rank, and the first awards were made in 1908.

It was not until June, 1939, that the title was altered so as to bring it into line with Provincial honours, and the new title became 'London Grank Rank', but without any actual change in its status.

The distinction is awarded 'for long and meritorious services' *to a London Lodge.* Recommendations can come only from London Lodges, and all Past Masters, *of and in the Lodge,* must be invited to the nominating meeting, or Selection Committee, which is specially convened for that purpose. A Brother must be a P.M. of five years standing before he is eligible for recommendation.

There are some 1700 Lodges in the London area, and, on average, one Lodge in every three is invited to nominate a P.M. Thus, every London Lodge has the opportunity to nominate a Brother at roughly three-year intervals.

It is a reward to the recipient for services rendered, and, indirectly, to the recommending Lodge. Those modest Brethren who say they do not know what it is, or why they received it, ought to know better, or they should be quietly ashamed of their ignorance.

L.G.R. is rank without Office; the recipient has no duties to perform in connection with his new rank, but he has responsibilities, because he was selected by his Lodge for that honour—responsibilities to serve, to guide, to help and advise.

The London Grand Rank Association is the organization through which the holders of L.G.R. exercise their corporate functions as a society of responsible members of the Craft. The L.G.R.A. is not an official body, though its usefulness is recognized and esteemed by the authorities of the Grand Lodge. But the holders of L.G.R. join it voluntarily; they are not obliged to join.

In the London area, L.G.R. has precedence over Provincial or District Grand Rank, but L.G.R. has no special status in the Provinces, where the holder rates simply as a P.M.

Provincial Grand Rank (or Office) takes its proper seniority only in its own Province, i.e., a Prov. G. Officer of Essex is, strictly speaking, only a P.M. when visiting a Lodge in Kent, though he would, of course, receive the usual courtesies.

---

50.   ROSETTES

Q. What is the 'symbolism' or purpose of the three rosettes on the M.M. apron?

A. The rosettes originally must have been pure decoration, and there are numerous early 18th century illustrations, etc., which show rosettes used purely in that form. With the standardization of the regalia at the Union, the two rosettes were adopted for the F.C. apron, and three rosettes for the M.M. It is, of course, possible to draw a symbolism from all this, but my own opinion is that the rosettes are used exactly in the same way as two or three 'stripes' are used in the Army.

---

51.   THE KNOB, OR BUTTON, ON A P.M.'S COLLAR

Q. The projecting knob or button on a P.M.'s Collar; does it represent the 'Beehive'?

A. For those readers who are unfamiliar with our regalia, it should be explained that under English Constitution the Master and Officers of the Lodge wear collars of light blue ribbon, four inches wide. They are shaped to fit snugly on the shoulders and they come down to a V at the front. There is a vertical seam at the join, where the ribbon forms the V, and that is usually covered by a strip of silver braid with a dome-shaped braid button at the centre. The Past Master's collar is the same, but it has a central band of silver braid a quarter of an inch wide all round the collar, finishing at the centre front, under the button.

The Beehive, depicted on many of the early Tracing Boards, had virtually disappeared from English usage at the time of the Union in

1813. The domed button was never intended to represent the Beehive, but was probably designed as a convenient means of hiding the raw ends of the braid that meet on the seam of the collar.

There is useful evidence that the dome button was not introduced until some time after the standardization of regalia in the *Book of Constitutions* of 1815. Before that date, there are numerous portraits of prominent 18th century Masons wearing collars of ribbon or cloth, with a metal or braid ring encircling the front of the collar, or stitched to it, thereby providing a loop or hook, from which the jewels were suspended. In these portraits there is no trace of a button, either flat or domed.

---

52.   THE LADDER AND ITS SYMBOLS IN THE FIRST TRACING BOARD

Q. Can you give me any information concerning the symbols on the Ladder in the First Tracing Board. Should there be only three, or seven symbols, and how many rungs in the Ladder?

A. The emblems on the 'Jacob's Ladder' in the First T.B. are by no means uniform, and it is fairly certain they are mid or late eighteenth century introductions, because there is no trace of them in the earlier rituals. An examination of the early T.B.s on which the emblems appear shows several points of interest:

(1) On Craft T.Bs., the Ladders are sometimes drawn with only three rungs, but they are usually longer, and some have three extra thick rungs, representing the three religious virtues. Most of the well known designs show the Ladders with their heads disappearing in the clouds. The Ladder, however, is not purely a Craft symbol; it is to be found in several of the additional degrees.

The story of Jacob's dream and 'the Ladder, the top of which reached to the Heavens' appears in the Lecture on the First Tracing Board and in the Fourth Section of the First Lecture, where the Ladder is said to have 'many staves or rounds, which point out as many moral virtues; but three principal ones, which are, Faith, Hope and Charity'.

Those three virtues are described and interpreted at length, and we are told that the Ladder rests on the V.S.L. (as it does in most illustrations of the First T.B.) because

> . . . by the doctrines contained in that Holy Book, we are taught to believe in the dispensation of Divine Providence; which belief strengthens our Faith, and enables us to ascend the first step . . .

(2) The early designs indicated the three virtues, Faith, Hope and Charity, by the initial letters, F., H., and C., between the rungs. Bro. T. O. Haunch (in *AQC*, Vol. 75, pp. 190, 194) believes that the initial letters came first and that Josiah Bowring, a famous designer of Tracing Boards, *c.* 1785–1830, introduced three female figures to replace them. They appear in many Tracing Boards nowadays, the first holding a Bible, the second with an Anchor, and the third with children nestling at her skirts.

Several drawings of the 1870s and later omit the figures, but show a Cross, an Anchor, and a Chalice with a pointing Hand. Presumably the Chalice and Hand are meant to represent Charity, but they are probably illustrations of a piece of religious mythology, depicting the Holy Grail which was snatched up to Heaven by God's Hand.

There are many different versions of the symbols and their arrangement, but most of the Boards that contain the three figures also depict the angels of Jacob's dream, ascending and descending the Ladder.

(3) If seven virtues were to be symbolized, I assume that the additional four would be the Cardinal Virtues, and although I have examined a great number of early T.B.s I cannot recall any in which the four Cardinal Virtues are symbolized in addition to the other three.

(4) Apart from the three virtues, there is one more symbol which appears regularly on or near the Ladder, and that is the 'Key'. Bowring, for very good reason, showed it hanging from one of the rungs. It is one of the old symbols of Masonry, and it is mentioned in our earliest ritual documents, i.e., the *Edinburgh Register House MS.*, 1696, and its sister texts:

> Q. Which is the key of your lodge
> A. a weel hung tongue

Many of the early texts expanded the 'Key—Tongue' symbolism, saying that it was lodged in 'the bone box' (i.e., the mouth) and that it is the key to the Mason's secrets. But one of the best answers on this point is in the *Sloane MS.*, *c.* 1700, which was the earliest ritual document that contained the words 'the tongue of good report', which have survived in our ritual to this day:

> Q. wt is the Keys of your Lodge Doore made of?
> A. it is not made of Wood Stone Iron or steel or any sort of mettle but the tongue of a good report behind a brothers back as well as before his face.

Ladder Symbols Including the Key
By courtesy of The Association for Taylor's
Working and The Logic Ritual Association

Ladder Symbols
First Degree Tracing Board by Bro. Esmond
Jefferies. By courtesy of the Logic Ritual
Association

53.   SYMBOLISM AND REMOVAL OF GLOVES

Q. Does the wearing of White Gloves have a symbolic meaning? Opinions seem to vary as to whether they should be removed, by W.M., Wardens and Candidates for communicating the 'tokens' and when taking the Obligations. Is this a matter in which opinions may rightly differ, or is one way or the other irregular?

A. It would not be difficult to find a whole series of reasons for the removal of one or both gloves at particular stages in the ceremonies, but the Grand Lodge regulation is quite specific on this point:

> As laid down by the Grand Lodge in June 1950, it is left to the discretion of the Master of each Lodge to decide, after considering the interests of the members generally, whether to request that they be worn.
>
> (a) The Board considers that when such a request is made it should cover all present, and not, as sometimes occurs, the Officers only.
>
> (b) The Board recommends the Grand Lodge to rule that if gloves are worn they should be worn at all times except
>   (i) By candidates for the three degrees.
>   (ii) By the Master Elect when actually taking his Obligations on the V.S.L.
>
> Gloves would thus not be removed by the Master (or Wardens or temporary occupant of their Chairs or by any Brother assisting them) in the course of entrusting or examining candidates, or when investing Officers.
>
> (c) The Board sees no objection to Entered Apprentices and Fellow Crafts wearing gloves when not actually being passed or raised.
>
> (Extract from Report of Board of General Purposes adopted 10 June 1964.)

White gloves are worn in most of the Lodges under English Constitution, but it is the W.M. who decides this, and the note 'White Gloves' is usually printed on the Lodge Summons. As to the removal of gloves, the rulings under paragraph (b) above, give a clear answer: gloves are not to be worn by candidates for all three degrees, and must be removed by the Master Elect when taking his Obligations. There is evidence for the antiquity of the candidate's ungloved hand in one of the earliest descriptions of the 'posture' during the Obligation, in Prichard's *Masonry Dissected*, 1730, where the Candidates speaks of '. . . my naked Right Hand on the Holy Bible . . .'.

As to symbolism, I am inclined to believe that gloves came into Speculative usage, like the aprons, as a direct heritage from operative practice, both aprons and gloves being essential items in a mason's working apparel. This would suggest that the prime symbolism of gloves (and aprons) is to emphasize the operative origins of Speculative Masonry.

Gloves have had a wide ranging symbolism since the middle ages, in legal, military, and liturgical use. Our custom of wearing white gloves, as with our aprons of white lambskin, is probably associated with the idea of purity. (See also Q. 147, p. 319.)

---

54.   THE RISINGS

Q. What is the derivation and purpose of the words spoken by the W.M. on the Risings, when he asks if '. . . any brother has aught to propose for the good of Freemasonry in general . . .', etc.?

A. Essentially, the Risings are a part of the formalities of Closing the lodge, and it is in that portion of lodge-work that we should look for early evidence of the procedure. Formal 'Opening' and 'Closing' of the lodge was established in the Continental lodges *c.* 1742–1760, and did not make its appearance (in print) in English practice until the 1760s.

Le Maçon Démasqué, a French exposure of 1751, in its description of the preliminaries before closing the lodge, states that the Master, addressing the Warden, asked:

> has no one . . . any representations to make upon the matters in which we have worked? Speak brothers.

These words were incorporated in the first English translation of that work, *Solomon in all his Glory*, 1766, and this is the earliest evidence I have been able to trace of anything approaching the purpose of the Risings. But, apart from this, there seems to be no evidence in early eighteenth century practice of anything resembling the Risings. Nor can I trace any hint of such procedure in the important later works of Preston, Browne, etc. Preston, for example, has a brief chapter on the 'Ceremony of opening and closing a Lodge', which must have been established procedure at that time (1775), but there is no trace of anything resembling the Risings. Nor is there anything on the subject in Browne's *Master Key*, 1798, where the full ritual and procedural detail would lead us to expect some indications of Rising practices.

I am, therefore, of the opinion that Risings were probably introduced at the Union of the Grand Lodges, 1813, or soon afterwards, as a result of the work of the Lodge of Reconciliation.

THE PURPOSE OF THE RISINGS

I believe they were linked, in some way, with the Senior Warden's duty 'to see that every Brother has had his due'—itself a link with the *Old Charges*. (See *AQC*, Vol. 74, p. 151.) The Risings were designed, primarily, to ensure that every Brother in the lodge would have a proper opportunity of making proposals, or initiating discussion, on matters of interest to the lodge and the craft.

Why three Risings? The threefold Risings are to be compared, in origin, to the threefold proclamation of the new W.M., or to public proclamations which were thrice repeated in order to ensure that they were heard by all.

This necessarily leads to the conclusion that the threefold Risings were not at first intended as three separate opportunities for three different types of communication, which is the present-day practice.

THE RISINGS IN MODERN PRACTICE

The wording of the formula in which the W.M. asks '. . . if any Brother has aught to propose . . .' seems to imply that every Brother has the right to answer, i.e., the First Rising was not originally reserved to the lodge Secretary for reading communications from the Grand Lodge, as it is nowadays.

Clearly, a standardization of practice in regard to the Risings must be a great advantage and, although they are not mentioned in the *Book of Constitutions*, or in the Points of Procedure in the *Masonic Year Book*, the Grand Lodge does, in fact, recommend the following procedure:

In London:

1. First Rising—Communications from the Grand Lodge.
2. Second Rising—Propositions for new and joining members; notices of motion.
3. Third Rising—General communications; apologies for absence, and other matters properly raised by members of the lodge.

In Provincial lodges:

First Rising—As No. 1 above.
Second Rising—Communications from the Prov. Grand Lodge.
Third Rising—A combination of Nos. 2 and 3 above.

Emergency meetings. The Risings are omitted at emergency meetings because lodges are not empowered to deal with any business other than that printed on the lodge summons.

55. EMULATION WORKING

Q. 'Emulation' working. Is it the original or the oldest form now worked in England? Is it the form now practised by the majority of Lodges in England? Are figures available on this point?

A. *Emulation* is one of the oldest post-Union workings. It may well be the oldest, but in view of rival claims and in the absence of complete proof, this question cannot be answered with certainty.

There are two points about *Emulation* that seem to put it into a class of its own:

(a) As a Lodge of Instruction, it goes back to 1823, with continuous existence since then.

(b) It is today the best organized of all the 'named' rituals, having had a governing body to 'protect' it throughout its history, and in that respect, I believe, it far outstrips all other 'named' forms.

Bro. C. F. W. Dyer, in his *Emulation—A Ritual To Remember*, which is the standard history of the Emulation Lodge of Improvement, published in connection with its sesqui-centennial in 1973, shows that the founders experienced difficulties in its formation, because Lodges of Instruction at that time had to be sponsored by a Lodge. The Emulation founders had decided that their Lodge of Instruction was to be *for Master Masons only* (as it is today), and the Lodges which were invited to act as sponsor were not ready to accept that restriction. Eventually, the Emulation Lodge of Instruction was sponsored, on 27 November 1823, by the Lodge of Hope, then No. 7, whose Master, Joseph Dennis, was one of Emulation's original members.

Is *Emulation* 'the original or oldest form now worked in England?' It is certainly one of the oldest, but it would be impossible to say whether it is the 'original'. As Bro. Dyer explains:

No *official* record has ever been found of the Lodge of Reconciliation Ritual that was approved by the Grand Lodge. (*op. cit.* p. 22.)

Emulation is probably as near to the forms then prescribed as any of the workings surviving from that period. Its principal virtue is that it has enjoyed a proper continuity of control of its forms ever since its foundation.

Are figures available? Outside the London area, our Grand Lodge does not keep records of the particular forms of ritual worked by all the Lodges on its Roll; hence no figures for each working are available.

We tend to think in terms of the older and best known versions, *Emulation, Stability, Bristol, Oxford, Humber, Taylor's, Logic, Universal, West End*, etc., etc., but there are countless other forms. *Emulation* has achieved a widespread popularity and has played a great part as the basis for many workings that have stemmed from it. Perhaps the best answer to this question is from the dust-jacket of Bro. Dyer's book:

> The work of well over half the lodges under the English Constitution and the standard work of several overseas Constitutions is based on the Emulation method.

During the past century there have been printed rituals which claimed (or were believed) to represent the *Emulation* working, 'but none of these has had any authorization from the Emulation Lodge of Improvement', which has firmly resisted the temptation to compile, sponsor, or authorize a printed ritual.

> However, times change, and it now seems to the Committee that reasons once cogent have progressively become less so. They feel that the time has arrived when a change of policy may be of advantage to those Lodges which prefer to work the Emulation system of ritual. This book is the result.

These words are from Bro. Oskar Klagge's Introduction to the *Emulation Ritual*, published in 1969, the first officially authorized edition 'Compiled by and published with the approval of the Committee of the Emulation Lodge of Improvement' and, despite the many publications that appeared in the second half of the 19th century claiming to give the Lectures 'As taught in ... the Emulation Lodge of Improvement' (e.g. The *Perfect Ceremonies, The Lectures of the Three Degrees*, etc.), the first version of the Lectures authorized by the governing body of Emulation did not appear in print until 1975. (See Dyer, *Emulation, A Ritual to Remember*, 1973, pp. 76–7, 108–9, 212–5.)

---

56.   MASONIC 'FIRE'

Q. What is the origin and the correct method of Masonic 'Fire' after toasts?

A. The 'Fire' seems to have been adapted from the military custom of firing guns or muskets after toasts. The records of the Preston Gild Merchant describe an annual procession by the Mayor, with an escort of soldiers and representatives of the Trade Companies, to each of the city gates, at which toasts were drunk, each health being followed by a 'volley of shott from the musketiers attending'. One of the earliest descriptions of Masonic 'Fire' appears in *Le Secret des Francs-Maçons,* a French exposure of 1742, from which the following extracts are drawn:[1]

> All the terms they use in drinking are borrowed from the Artillery . . . The Bottle is called Barrel· . . . Wine is called red Powder, & [Water] white Powder . . . The Routine which they observe in drinking does not permit the use of glasses, for there would not be a whole glass left after they had finished: they use only goblets, which they call Cannon. When they drink in ceremony, the order is given: *Take your Powder*; everybody rises, & the Worshipful says: *Charge.* Then each of them fills his goblet. The commands follow: *Present Arms: Take Aim. Fire. Grand Fire.* . . . On the first they stretch their hands to the goblet; on the second, they raise them as though presenting arms, & on the last, they drink . . . they all watch the Worshipful so that they keep perfect time throughout. When taking up their goblets they carry them forwards a little at first, then to the left breast & across to the right: then, in three movements, they replace their goblets on the Table clap their hands three times & every member cries out three times *Vivat* . . . there is no Military Academy where the drill is performed with greater exactitude, precision, pomp, & majesty . . . you will see no Stragglers. . . . The noise as they place their goblets on the table is quite considerable . . . a clear & uniform stroke, hard enough to shatter any but the strongest vessels . . .

Many different versions of the 'Fire' appeared in print in the following centuries and there is still enormous variety in present-day English procedure. Moreover, there is no authority that would justify the description of any particular procedure as 'correct'. In the London area, where there are some 1700 lodges, the 'Fire' forms a series of seven triads, their rhythm being set by the W.M. (or the Brother giving the toast) as he calls the orders:

P . . ., L . . ., R . . .; P . . ., L . . ., R . . .; P . . ., L . . ., R . . .;
One, Two, [Gavel = Three].[2] 1–2–3; 1–2–3; 1–2–3.

Finally, in answer to many correspondents who have asked 'Why must the dining-room be tyled during the Firing-routine?', it is perhaps necessary to explain that *the modern P.L.R.* is only a kind of airy triangle drawn with the finger-tip, but it was not always thus. Despite the numerous variations that have appeared since those days, the careful reader may find the answer in the quotation from 1742, above.

---

[1] *The Early French Exposures*, pp. 62–3. Publ. by the Q.C. Lodge; it contains a collection of twelve of the earliest texts, all in English translation.

[2] Up to this point, the W.M. has been speaking; now the assembled Brethren take over, by clapping 'three times three'.

THE KNOCKS IN CRAFT 'FIRE'

Q. What is the significance of the twenty-one knocks in Craft Fire and why are they usually given in the time (or rhythm) of the F.C. knocks?

A. They are not twenty-one 'knocks'. The first three sets of P.L.R. were *ab origine* signs, or a substitute for signs. The next three 'moves' (usually given as 'One, Two, Bang!') are merely rhythm-makers, rather like a starter's gun. Whatever the preliminaries were and are, the actual knocks, in firing, are the 'three times three' at the end, whether they are made by hand-claps or with firing glasses.

But it is almost impossible to explain all the different versions of the 'Fire' in this way. Outside London, many curious variations are practised. In one of our Midlands' Provinces they start with 'P.L.R. Bang!' thrice repeated, and then continue with the 'One, Two', etc., as above.

One Australian visitor to Q.C. Lodge demonstrated five different versions practised in his country, each with its own peculiar name and purpose, and several of them requiring a good deal of physical agility. But the 'Three times three' appears to be the standard practice, generally used wherever the Craft 'Fire' is given.

I can find no trace of the F.C. rhythm being used; so far as I am aware, only the E.A. knocks are used, at great or lesser speed, according to taste, or to local custom.

I have indeed noticed that the 'caller' sometimes announces the P.L.R. with a pause at the wrong moment, which would seem to suggest the F.C. rhythm, but I believe this is simply a quirk of the 'caller'. *It would surely be improper to give the 'Fire' in the F.C. rhythm, when E.A.s are likely to be present at Table.*

'SILENT FIRE'—WHEN AND WHY IS IT USED?

A. This is usually given in the normal rhythm, but, instead of 'clapping', the right hand taps lightly on the left forearm. Our Grand Lodge has no 'official' view or ruling on the practice, which appears to be largely a matter of local custom.

In some places it is used at the end of a toast to 'Absent Brethren'; elsewhere, as a salute to 'Departed Brethren'. I discussed the question with Bro. E. Newton, formerly Assistant Librarian of the Grand Lodge, and we have both seen the 'Silent Fire' used for both purposes.

His view is that the Fire, when given properly, is intended as a hearty, enthusiastic (and noisy) salute, and should be given with the proper zest. 'Silent Fire' is a contradiction in terms, an anomaly, and it is perhaps just as well that the practice is gradually dying out.

With all due deference to old established customs, I agree readily with this view.

WHEN IS THE 'FIRE' OMITTED?

Q. Is it correct to omit the 'Fire' when there is no responder to a toast?

A. I know that this omission is usual in certain Provinces and in some Lodges, but the question 'correct or not' does not really apply. Apart from the general prohibition, when non-Masons or ladies are present, the 'Fire' is a matter of custom, not law, and local customs should be respected. The following notes are therefore no more than my personal views, based mainly on London practices.

Regardless of whether there is a responder to the toast, or not, with the one exception noted under 'Silent Fire', above, I can find no reason for omitting the 'Fire'. The 'Fire' is the completion of the toast and, by long-standing custom, it is actually a part of the honours accorded to whoever is the subject of the toast. There are numerous long lists of Masonic toasts (going back more than 200 years) including many to the ladies, all of which were drunk, *with 'Fire'*, thus transforming them into *Masonic* toasts.

---

57.   HOLINESS TO THE LORD

Q. What is the translation and significance of the words inscribed around the 'Porchway' of the Third Degree Tracing Board?

A. For the sake of many thousands of Brethren who have never seen the words you refer to, and are wondering what all this means, I must point out that they do not appear in the majority of Third Degree Tracing Boards. There is, however, one design which does usually incorporate 'the words' nowadays, though they did not appear in the artist's original sketches.

The Grand Lodge Library possesses two very similar Third Degree T.B. designs in colour, both by John Harris, one dated 1820 and the other 1825. Each of them displays, in the centre of the 'coffin' outline, a black-and-white chequered pavement leading to an arched porch with its curtains slightly parted to reveal the *Sanctum Sanctorum*. The semi-circular arch in both sketches is purely ornamental, i.e., there are no words on it. (One of these designs is illustrated in *AQC* 75, p. 196.)

Harris was a famous facsimilist in his day, a painter of miniatures and an architectural draughtsman. Soon after his initiation in 1818, he began to draw, engrave and publish designs for Tracing Boards. His work became deservedly popular and a set of three, submitted in a competition in 1845, were officially adopted by the Emulation Lodge of Improvement, and are in use to this day.

In the 1870s, when printed rituals began to make their appearance with some regularity, they usually contained pictures of the Tracing Boards, in engraved line drawings, and it is in the *Text Book of Freemasonry*, 1870, and in editions of the *Perfect Ceremonies* from *c.* 1870 onwards, that we find the Third Degree T.B., based directly on a composite of Harris's two boards of 1820 and 1825, but now drawn with 'the words' in very defective Hebrew characters, but fortunately recognizable. Whether Harris was responsible for their introduction is uncertain.

The words, when you find them, are in Hebrew (i.e., reading from right to left), *Kodesh la-Adonai,* and are translated 'Holiness to the Lord'. They are the same two words which form the Hebrew motto above the Ark of the Covenant in the coat-of-arms of the United Grand Lodge. (See illustration on p. 19 above.)

The words would be invisible in any normal vest-pocket ritual, and, in fact, there are very few of the large printed rituals that show them. I have been unable to trace a single version of the ritual in which the words are mentioned or explained in such a manner as to demand their being included in the Illustration of the 3rd T.B.

The modern T.B.s in use in our Grand Lodge Temples do not show the words, and I examined many really old Boards in the store-rooms of the Grand Lodge Museum, without success. It is obvious that 'the words' are not an essential part of the Third T.B., and we may accept their inclusion in the Harris design as a simple piece of artistic exuberance, either by Harris himself, or by some later 'improver'.

As to the question of symbolism, I would suggest you read Exodus, Chap. xxviii, vv. 36–38, which describe how Moses was commanded to prepare a plate of gold, with those two words engraved upon it, to be worn '. . . upon the forefront of the mitre . . .' of the High Priest. This is one of the instances in which the symbolism is explained in clear and unmistakable language: '. . . it shall be always upon his forehead, that they [the children of Israel] *may be accepted before the Lord*'. In this sense every Mason symbolically wears the badge of 'Holiness to the Lord'.

58.   WEARING TWO COLLARS

Q. In Lodge, a Brother should wear the regalia of the highest Craft rank that he holds. If appointed to carry out an office in the Lodge, should he wear the collar of that office over the other collar?

A. The general answer is Yes, especially for an 'appointed or elected' office where the Brother will serve in that office for a whole year. For example, a Grand Officer serving his Lodge as Treasurer or Secretary, would wear the light-blue collar above his dark-blue. Even in the case of a Grand Officer deputizing *temporarily* for an absent Officer, e.g., acting as Deacon, he should wear the Deacon's collar over his own dark-blue. This is the procedure recommended by our Grand Lodge and it applies equally to Provincial and District Grand Officers and to holders of London Grand Rank.

An exception arises when the W.M. vacates the Chair to enable a Past Master, or a Brother of higher rank, to conduct a ceremony. The rule is that the W.M. retains his collar and 'the P.M. must be clothed according to his rank'. (See, 'Points of Procedure—Board of General Purposes' in the 1974 *Year Book*, p. 833.)

In the English Installation ceremony, it is customary to invite three senior Brethren to act as S.W., J.W., and I.G., during a portion of the work. I believe that there is no need for those three Brn. to wear the collars of their temporary offices, and in my experience, that is the general practice, probably because the collars are required so soon afterwards, for the Investiture of Officers. But I would not press this view against established Lodge custom, or where it conflicts with the rubric of a particular working.

In recent years, there seems to be a growing practice, where two collars would be called for, of wearing only the senior collar, but with two jewels; or wearing one collar with the jewel which should be worn with a different collar, e.g., a Provincial Grand Chaplain's jewel on the collar of a Past Asst. Grand Chaplain. My own view is that these practices are to be deprecated.

---

59.   IMPROPER SOLICITATION

Q. Why are we forbidden to solicit Candidates? How did the rule arise? Is there a distinction to be drawn between 'solicitation' and *improper solicitation*?

A. Let us first be clear about the rule. There is *no rule* on the subject of soliciting, either in the *Book of Constitutions* or in the Points of Procedure listed in the *Grand Lodge Year Book*. The prohibition against the soliciting of Candidates is *implicit* in two documents which the Candidate must sign before his Initiation. The first is in the Candidate's portion of the Proposal Form, in which he declares:

My application is entirely voluntary.

The second appears in Rule 162 of the *Book of Constitutions*, which prescribes the form of Declaration that must be signed by every Candidate before his Initiation:

I . . ., being a free man, and of the full age of twenty-one years, do declare that, *unbiassed by the improper solicitation of friends*,[1] and uninfluenced by mercenary or other unworthy motive, *I do freely and voluntarily offer myself* a candidate . . .

There is no 'rule' and, therefore, no specific penalty. The ban against soliciting arises out of this requirement that the Candidate shall declare that he comes voluntarily and without improper solicitation. The words in italics above are the crux of the answer to the first question.

How did the 'rule' arise? It cannot have been old operative practice. When a lad was bound apprentice, probably by (or to) his father, it may be assumed that there was no improper solicitation. When he ultimately took his freedom, that was certainly voluntary, and all the information we have relating to oaths, in the *Old Charges* and in craft Gild practice, show that they were simple oaths of fidelity to the appropriate authorities, i.e., the King, the Master, the Craft, the Gild, or the municipality. But for operative masons, so long as a lad was apprenticed, he would automatically join the lodge to become E.A., and then F.C. or Master, because these were essential stages in his trade career. The questions of voluntary application or improper solicitation simply did not enter into the operative system.

Early non-operative and speculative records are curiously silent on these matters; there is no evidence on them in the early exposures, or in any of our oldest lodge minutes. There is, however, some possibility that the 'rule' had its roots in the clandestine and improper admissions of Masons, which became a serious problem in England in the 1730s. Even so, there is no textual evidence of a ban against improper solicitation, either in the 1723 or the 1738 *Constitutions*, or in any of the English exposures of that era.

---

[1] Author's italics throughout this piece.

In trying to trace the source of our present regulation on voluntary application and improper solicitation it is essential to view the two ideas as one, which indeed they are, the latter being a natural though strict corollary to the insistence on 'voluntary application'; and our earliest evidence on the subject is concerned with this *voluntary* approach. It appears first in a Q. and A. in the *Wilkinson MS.*, c. 1727:

Q. How Came you to be Made a Mason
A. *By my own Desire* & ye Recomendat^n of a friend

A better example appeared in a French exposure, known as the *Hérault Letter*, of 1737, which was reprinted in several English translations at that period. I quote from the opening lines, with my own free translation:

Réception d'un Frey-Maçon [The *Hérault Letter*], 1737

Le Récipiendaire est conduit par le Proposeur (qui devient son Parrain) dans une Chambre (de la Loge) ou il n'y a pas de Lumière; Là on lui demande s'il a la Vocation pour être Reçu.	The Candidate is conducted by the Proposer (who becomes his Sponsor) into one of the Rooms of the Lodge where there is no Light; There he is asked if he has a Vocation [i.e., a calling] to be Received.

The crux of the matter lies in the word vocation, or calling, i.e., a personal and almost spiritual inner desire to join the Craft. The question was considered so important in 1737–8 that it was actually repeated twice more, inside the Lodge, before the Candidate took his Obligation, and always with this same word, *Vocation*.

In the period 1738 to 1745 there was a spate of exposures printed in France and Germany, exhibiting the rapid expansion of the ceremonies at that time. To avoid overloading these notes with too much repetition I will merely summarize by saying that, apart from a few trivial publications which were mere catchpennies, every one of the Continental exposures that described the Initiation reproduced this same question (or one in similar terms), and there is no doubt at all that this was the origin of our own well-known phrase 'of my own free will and accord'.

No useful new exposures were published in England between 1730 and 1760; only a long series of re-issues of Prichard's work of 1730, and this gap in our English documents makes the foreign productions doubly interesting. But, starting in 1760 we have the first of a whole new series of English exposures, all containing a great deal of Prichard's and earlier material, but all exhibiting some of the expansions that had come into practice in the intervening years.

The first, and one of the best of the series, was *Three Distinct Knocks*, published in 1760. The preliminaries to Initiation are not described very well in this text, and the first item that has a bearing on our study appears in the opening words of the Obligation, where we read (for the first time, in print):

I . . . Of my own free Will and Accord . . .

J. & B., one of the most popular works in the whole series (it was reprinted many times), was first published in 1762. It contains much more detail, and after the opening ceremony the Candidate

. . . proposed last Lodge-Night . . . is in another Room, which is totally dark;

The Wardens come to prepare him and he is

'then asked whether he is conscious of having the Vocation necessary to be received?'

The admission procedure is described in detail, and after three per-ambulations the Master asks the Candidate again

'Whether you have a desire to become a Mason? And if it is of your own free Will and Choice?'

and the Obligation begins, 'I—A.B., of my own Free Will and Accord . . .'

Mahhabone and *Hiram*, both of 1766, are almost word-for-word identical with the above. *Shibboleth*, of 1765, shows a new variation:

Having obtained from him [the Candidate] a frank declaration of his desire of being a Mason . . .

This is the earliest use of the word 'declaration' in this connection; the Obligation begins, 'I, C.D., of my own voluntary choice . . .'

From 1772 until the early years of the nineteenth century the out-standing figure in the study and literature of Masonic philosophy and ritual was William Preston, and the next evidence on the development of these themes of 'voluntary application' and 'improper solicitation' comes from Preston's *Illustrations of Masonry*, first published in 1772, a work which was greatly enlarged and frequently reprinted in many editions from 1775 onwards.

In the 1772 edition we find (so far as I am aware) the first version of the Declaration which is required to be made by every Candidate now-adays, and which is prescribed in our Rule 162 of the *B. of C.* I quote only the first few lines of Preston's version:

A DECLARATION

To be subscribed, or assented to, by every Candidate for Masonry previous to his Initiation.

'I. A.B. do seriously declare, upon my honor, that unbiassed by friends and
'uninfluenced by mercenary motives, I freely and voluntarily offer myself a
'candidate for the mysteries of masonry;'

(1772 edn., pp. 210–211.)

Preston's 1775 edition did not mention a *signed* declaration:

A Declaration to be assented to by every Candidate, previous to his being
proposed.

Do you seriously declare, upon your honour, before these gentlemen The
Stewards of the Lodge, that unbiassed by friends and uninfluenced by
mercenary motives, you freely and voluntarily offer yourself . . .

(1775 edn., p. 59.)

It is possible that the signed declaration was already in use by this
time, but it was not prescribed in the contemporary *Constitutions*. The
first *B. of C.* of the United Grand Lodge was published in 1815, and
there we have the earliest version of the Declaration, as an Official
requirement; this is the earliest version which contains the words
'improper solicitation':

I, . . . being free by birth,[1] and of the full age of twenty-one years, do
declare that, unbiassed by the improper solicitation of friends, and uninfluenced by mercenary or other unworthy motive, I freely and voluntary[2]
offer myself a candidate for the mysteries of masonry.

(*B. of C.*, 1815, pp. 90–91.)

And so we come to the last of our questions: 'Is there a distinction
to be drawn between solicitation and "improper solicitation"?' This
is a most difficult question, largely because the answers will usually
depend entirely upon the particular circumstances of each case.

Assuming that some close friend, or a relative, were to open the
subject and express some interest it would be quite proper to tell him
all that may be told and to give him a leaflet[3] describing the Craft and
its objects. In the case of a really suitable person, the next conversation
might easily contain an element of 'solicitation', especially if he were to
say, 'Do you think I ought to join?' Broadly, I am convinced that unless
a man *has expressed a proper interest in the Craft, asking the kind of*
questions fully indicative of his interest, any suggestion that he ought to
join would be improper solicitation.

---

[1] The present version says '. . . being a free man . . .'.

[2] The word appears thus in one of our copies in the Q.C. library. Misspellings in
the *Constitutions* are rare; this word should be, of course, 'voluntarily'.

[3] e.g., The G.L. of Scotland pamphlet, 'The Candidate', in *AQC*, Vol. 76, p. 121
or Bro. John Dashwood's paper, 'What shall we tell the Candidate?'

As a piece of general guidance, I suggest three rules to be followed:

1. The prospective Candidate must have opened the discussion himself.
2. Do not make it easy for him. After he has read and heard all the information that you may properly give him, do not offer to propose him until you have full evidence of his interest and intention.
3. If you have the slightest grounds to suspect his reasons for wanting to join the Craft, any kind of help would be 'improper solicitation'.

These rules, used as guiding principles, should be a sufficient safeguard, and I trust that the foregoing may indicate my views on the distinction between proper and 'improper' solicitation. I believe that such a distinction can and may be drawn, and this view is confirmed by Bro. the Rev. J. T. Lawrence in his *Masonic Jurisprudence* (1912 edn., p. 148).

One final note, which may serve to show how far Masonic ideas can differ. I am informed, by a well-known Masonic writer and student, that in the American State of Vermont it is customary for groups of Brethren to hold 'Invitation Evenings', when selected local businessmen and professional-men, all non-Masons, are invited to attend Lectures on Freemasonry and its objects, followed by dinner or refreshment, at which the guests can meet and talk to some of the Masons in their locality.

The motives may be wholly praiseworthy, the proceedings and their environment may be completely dignified and respectable, yet, to our English way of thinking, this must surely be the most flagrant kind of 'improper solicitation'.

---

60.   BIBLE OPENINGS

Q. Can you tell me what are the proper page-openings for the V.S.L. in the three degrees, and are there any official rules on the subject?

A. Customs vary considerably in different parts of the country, and the following notes are designed to show some of the best-known procedures. I have added a brief note, in each case, indicating the essential Masonic significance of the passages quoted.

The earliest French exposure of the ceremonies, *Reception d'un Frey-Maçon*, states that the E.A. took his Obligation with his right hand on the Gospel of St. John, and this is confirmed by the next-oldest French version, *Le Secret des Francs-Maçons*, of 1742. Several later documents of this period indicate that the V.S.L. was usually opened at St. John, i, v. 1, 'In the beginning was the Word . . .'

Three Distinct Knocks, an English exposure of 1760, gave different pages for all three degrees:

1° The Second Epistle of Peter (with its references to brotherly kindness and charity).
2° The story from Judges, xii, of the test of the Ephraimites.
3° I Kings, chap. vii. The final details of Solomon's Pillars.

Cartwright, in his *Commentary on the Freemasonic Ritual*, cites the procedure in old Yorkshire Lodges where the following is customary:

1° Psalm 133. 'Behold how good . . . it is for brethren to dwell together in unity.'
2° Amos, vii, v. 7. '. . . the Lord stood upon a wall made by a plumbline, with a plumbline in his hand.'
3° Ecclesiastes, xii. 'Then the dust shall return to the earth as it was: and the spirit shall return unto God who gave it.'

The Bristol working is unusual in that the Master actually quotes—during the three Opening Cermonies—the texts from the pages on which the V.S.L. has to be opened, i.e.:

1° Ruth, ii, v. 19. The story of Ruth and Boaz.
2° Judges, xii, vv. 5, 6. The test of the Ephraimites.
3° Gen., iv, v. 22. The birth of Jabal and Jubal, who are mentioned in the *Old Charges*, from *c.* 1400 onwards.

Of course, there is no official Grand Lodge ruling on this question, and few of the 'named' rituals prescribe any particular page-openings for the three degrees.

Cartwright states that the *Perfect Ceremonies*, in their editions from 1918 onwards, specify II Chron., chap vi, as a standard 'opening' for all degrees; it deals with Solomon's prayer at the consecration of the Temple. Generally, Cartwright agrees with the widespread practice in English Lodges, where a haphazard opening of the V.S.L. suffices, but if a particular page is to stay open through all degrees, he favours II Chron., ii, which is prescribed in the *English Ritual*. That passage deals with the preliminaries to the building of the Temple, and of Solomon's first embassage to Hiram, King of Tyre, asking for timber, etc., and a 'man cunning to work in gold, and in silver, and in brass . . .', etc.

A German correspondent writes to say that many Lodges in his country use the following:

For the 1°: John, i, 1. 'In the beginning was the Word . . .'
For the 2°: Matt. xxii, 39. 'Thou shalt love thy neighbour as thyself'.
For the 3°: II Chron. vi. Solomon's dedication of the Temple.

My own favourite passage is in I Kings, vii, vv. 13–21, which deals with the design, casting, erection and naming of the pillars.

---

61. THE LION'S PAW OR EAGLE'S CLAW

Q. What is the origin and the symbolism of the 'Lion's Paw' or the 'Eagle's Claw'?

A. Whenever this kind of question crops up, I always like to look at the earliest-known rituals to see how the words appeared there. We have, in fact, several early descriptions of the F.P.O.F. from 1696 onwards, also the 'story' of a raising, dated 1726, and the first description of the Third Degree in 1730. The procedure you mention does not appear in any of the earliest texts, but a form of it does appear in the 1730 version, though without any reference to lions or eagles:

> ... spreading the Right Hand and placing the middle Finger to the Wrist, clasping the Fore-finger and the Fourth to the Sides of the Wrist ...
>
> (*E.M.C.*, p. 169.)

This is from Prichard's *Masonry Dissected*, dated 1730, the earliest description of the actual procedure of a 'Raising Ceremony'.

It is not necessary for me to emphasize that our procedure is different nowadays, and even in modern practice there are numerous variations, so that one would hesitate to assert that a particular manner of executing the movement is 'correct'! I do not believe, moreover, that there is any symbolism attached to the G . . .; it was made different from the others to suit a special purpose, and it is, of course, particularly suitable for the 'lifting' job.

The earliest use of the word 'Claw' that I am able to trace in describing this particular grip comes from *Le Catéchisme des Francs-Maçons*, a French exposure of 1744, which gives a particularly good account of the 3° as it was in those days. In the description of the actual raising it says (my translation):

> Then he takes him by the wrist, applying his four fingers separated & bent claw-fashion at the joint of the wrist, above the palm of the other's hand, his thumb between the thumb and index [finger] of the Candidate . . . & holding him by this claw-grip, he orders him . . . (*E.F.E.*, p. 103.)

Note that, even here, there is no mention of Lion's-Paw or Eagle's Claw, and although some modern rituals describe the grip in those terms, I have never been able to trace either of those titles in the earlier eighteenth century rituals.

In London Lodges, the Lion's Paw and Eagle's Claw are virtually unknown; these curiosities of nomenclature seem to belong to particular localities, and flourish there, often far from London headquarters. After a search I found the Lion's Paw in at least one version of Scottish ritual, and both terms in use in an English Lodge, i.e., the Lodge of Friendship No. 202, Plymouth. There, at the proper moment, the W.M. says:

> . . . there yet remains a third method, known as the Lion's Paw or Eagle's Claw, which is by taking a . . .

Apparently this refers to one particular G . . . that has two titles.

---

62.   A MODERNIZED RITUAL?

Q. In order to facilitate understanding of meaning, it has been thought well to translate the Bible into English that is 'as clear and natural to the modern reader as the subject matter will allow'. Would not similar benefits arise from the re-writing of our ritual in twentieth century English?

A. There is no true analogy here between the Bible and the Masonic ritual. The former, in its original Hebrew, is full of complex passages which had to be interpreted even for those to whom Hebrew was their native tongue. And the interpretations, in many instances, show quite extraordinary variations. (As an example, the architectural drawings of Solomon's Temple, all based on the same 'technical' descriptions in the Old Testament.)

When, after a while, the Bible became the Holy Book for a large part of the civilized world, it had to be translated, and with some truly excellent results, but the various interpretations still remain.

With the ritual we do not have the same problems. More than 99 per cent of it is in simple and beautiful English, and practically all of it is readily comprehensible even to simple folk. I agree that there are perhaps two or three passages which would lend themselves to further interpretation (a notable example is the speech at 'the grave', but even this lovely piece can be readily understood, and a little thought will reveal most of its inner meaning).

The standard rituals have, of course, been translated into many anguages, but I doubt if a *modernized* version is really needed, and, personally, I would oppose its adoption. We would lose far too much and gain little or nothing.

Reluctantly, it must be admitted that there are several passages (especially in the Lectures) that I would like to see removed entirely. They are mainly items of miscellaneous detail that have no symbolical or allegorical value, i.e., mere verbal padding that add nothing to our teachings and simply cause doubt or confusion. (See 'Inaccuracies in the Ritual', Q. 178, p. 368.)

---

63.   THE LEFT-HAND PILLAR

Q. The October, 1944, issue of the *Masonic Record* contains an illustration of King Solomon's Temple, showing the J. Pillar at left of the Porch, when viewed looking towards the building. This appears to contradict the customary ritual explanation which places B. on the left. Which is correct?

A. It would be difficult to answer this question without numerous quotations from Old Testament which, taken together, indicate that the 'left-hand' and 'right-hand' pillars are to be understood as though *they are being described by someone standing inside the Temple, looking out towards the entrance in the East.* Perhaps the simplest explanation is Whiston's note, in his edition of Josephus, *Antiquities of the Jews,* Book VIII, Chap. iii, Section 4. I quote first the passage from Josephus, followed by Whiston's note:

> the one of these pillars he set at the entrance of the porch on the right hand, and called it Jachin, and the other at the left hand, and called it Booz [sic]

Whiston's footnote:

> Here Josephus gives us a key to his own language, of right and left hand in the tabernacle and temple, that by the right hand he means what is against our left, when we suppose ourselves going up from the east gates of the courts towards the . . . temple, and so vice versa; whence it follows that the pillar Jachin, on the right hand of the temple, was on the south against our left hand, and Booz on the north against our right hand.

Thus the *Masonic Record* is correct; our ritual is at fault, only because it lacks the very necessary explanation.

---

64.   THE VALLEY OF JEHOSHAPHAT

Q. In answer to one of the questions in the Fifth Section, First Lecture, a reference is made to the Valley of Jehoshaphat. This place is mentioned twice in the Bible (Joel, iii, vv. 2 and 12), but the context gives no indication as to why this particular site may have been selected for mention in the Masonic ritual. Can you explain?

A. The strong emphasis on isolation and solitude as a necessary feature in the situation of the Lodge, is reflected in the 'Laws and Statutes' of the Lodge of Aberdeen, 1670:

> . . . Wee ordaine lykwayes that no lodge be holden within a dwelling house wher ther is people living in it but in the open fieldes except it be ill weather, and then Let ther be a house chosen that no person shall heir nor see ws . . .

The idea of Masons meeting in the open air, but yet in some quiet secret place, is to be found in our earliest Masonic catechisms e.g., the *Edinburgh Register House MS.*, 1696, *Chetwode Crawley MS.*, c. 1700, and *Kevan MS.*, c. 1714, all speak of:

> A dayes Journey from a burroughs town without bark of dog or crow of cock.

Sloane MS., c. 1700, and *Dumfries No. 4 MS.*, c. 1710, use similar phrases, but none of these earliest texts mentions the valley of Jehoshaphat. The first Masonic reference to that specific place is in 'A Mason's Examination', of 1723, and by coincidence that was the very first *printed exposure*, i.e., it was published in a newspaper, for entertainment, profit, or spite. I quote the relevant question and answer:

> Q. Where was you made? A. In the Valley of *Jehoshaphat*, behind a Rush-bush, where a Dog was never heard to bark, or Cock to crow, or elsewhere.

The answer (to which you refer) in our modern Lecture, is almost a paraphrase of the corresponding passage in *Masonry Dissected*, 1730:

> . . . the highest Hill or lowest Vale, or in the Vale of *Jehosaphat*, or any other secret Place. [*E.M.C.*, p. 162.]

From this time onwards the place-name appears quite regularly in the eighteenth century exposures, and it is certain that these words formed a part of the ritual *before* the Union of the Grand Lodges in 1813.

All this confirms ancient practice and the desire for solitude, but it does not explain the 'valley of Jehoshaphat', which still remains a problem. The name Jehoshaphat means 'whom Jehovah judges' (i.e., whose cause He pleads) and the valley of that name, according to the Book of Joel, is where the Almighty 'will gather all the nations' and especially the 'heathen', who have scattered His people, Israel, and driven them from their land.

Hastings's *Dictionary of the Bible* says that in Moslem and Jewish tradition it was the valley east of Jerusalem, the scene of the Last Judgement. 'It was a place of burial in pre-exilic times', and, by implication, a quiet, deserted place.

---

65.   APRONS: FLAP UP, CORNER UP, ETC.

Q. In many jurisdictions the E.A. Apron is worn with the flap up. Some Lodges have a practice of turning up the corner of the apron. Is there any symbolic significance in these matters, and why did the practices arise?

A. In non-operative or speculative Masonry these practices owe their origin to the time when all Freemasons wore a plain white apron, so that the 'flap up', or 'corner up', was used to indicate the Masonic grade of the wearer. Two of the early exposures, *A Mason's Examination*, of 1723, and Prichard's *Masonry Dissected*, of 1730, both mention the apron given to the Candidate, but make no reference to distinctive ways of wearing it—for the different grades of Masons.

The earliest documents that offer information on the subject are the French exposures. *Le Catéchisme des Francs-Maçons*, of 1744, says: 'Fellow-crafts wear the apron "point up", while Masters allow the flap to fall.' The English exposure, *Solomon in all his Glory*, published in 1768, is a translation of *Le Maçon Démasqué*, 1751, and it says that the Apprentice ties his apron with 'the flap on the inside'. The F.C. is entitled to wear the flap outside 'and fixed to one of my waistcoat buttons' (i.e., flap up) . . . the Master is 'at liberty to let it fall down'. Here, within a space of seven years, we find new details of the E.A. method of wearing the apron. Both texts are agreed that F.C.s wear the 'flap up' and M.M.s wear 'flap down'.

We may assume that in England variations persisted throughout the eighteenth century, until aprons were standardized after the Union, and many examples of early aprons are to be found (e.g., in the Grand Lodge Museum) with a button-hole in the flap. With the introduction of two rosettes for the F.C. and three for the M.M., there was no longer the

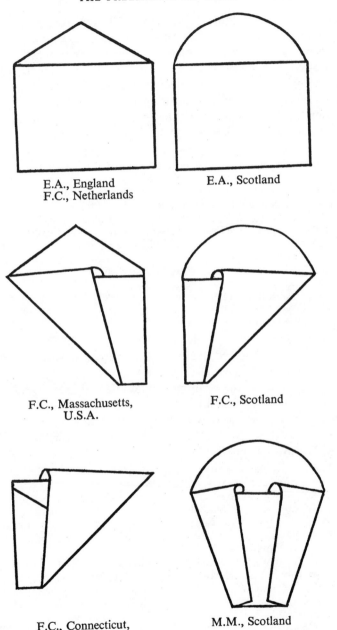

E.A., England
F.C., Netherlands

E.A., Scotland

F.C., Massachusetts,
U.S.A.

F.C., Scotland

F.C., Connecticut,
U.S.A.

M.M., Scotland

need for any other means of distinguishing the grade of the wearer, but the 'point up' for the E.A. has persisted in many cases to this day.

In some jurisdictions, however, it is still customary for all Brethren and visitors to a Lodge to wear a plain white apron. Only the Officers wear decorated aprons in those countries, and there the need remains for some means of distinguishing the grade of the wearer. I quote first from a letter from Bro. Conrad Hahn, Secretary of the Masonic Service Association of the U.S.A.:

> In answer to your questions about aprons and apron-wearing in the States: every initiate receives his personal white lambskin apron (without any decoration or distinguishing mark) when he is initiated. He carries it home, puts it away carefully, and leaves it there until his death. It is then brought out and put on his body and interred with him. At lodge he wears a cloth apron (usually all white, but sometimes emborbered in blue, and sometimes bearing the lodge name and number on the flap) taken from a supply of such aprons furnished by the lodge and kept in a pile near the Tiler's station.
>
> In Connecticut, where I hold Masonic membership, we are taught to wear the apron as follows:
>
> E.A. 'with the bib (flap) turned up'.
> F.C. 'with the bib turned down, and the left-hand corner of the apron brought up and tucked in'.
> M.M. 'with the bib turned down, and the apron spread'.

Bro. Dwight W. Robb confirms similar practice in Massachusetts for the E.A. and M.M., but there the F.C. wears the *'flap up'* and the *right-hand* corner of the apron tucked into the string at the waist.

Lodges under the Grand Lodge of Scotland also use the plain white apron, and their practices are described in the following note from Bro. George Draffen of Newington, M.B.E., R.W. Depute Grand Master of the Grand Lodge of Scotland:

> It is impossible to say what percentage of the Scottish Lodges use what, for want of a better term, I shall refer to as the 'English System', and what number use the old Scottish custom. At a guess, I'd say that the bulk of the country Lodges use the old system and most, but not all, of the City Lodges use the English system. (The regulations allow for the English system by laying down sealed patterns of aprons for Entered Apprentice, Fellow Craft and M.M.)
>
> In those Lodges where the old custom is still in use, the practice is to wear the apron in the E.A. Degree with the flap UP, covering the chest. The apron is plain white and, when worn with the flap UP, presents the appearance of a square with a semi-circle on one side. (*Note: The flap on all Scottish aprons is semi-circular in shape and NOT triangular as in England.*) In the F.C. Degree the flap is still up, but the lower left-hand corner (left-hand as viewed from the wearer's point of view) is tucked up and held in position by the

apron-string. The shape now is a triangle with a semi-circular shape on one side.

In the M.M. Degree, both corners are tucked up, but so that the bottom of the apron has a little short flat bit between the turn-ups. The shape now is meant to be reminiscent of a coffin!

Bro. I. H. Peters, of Loge Rosa Alba, Eindhoven, Holland, furnishes details of present-day practice under the Grand East of the Netherlands. The Candidate gets his own apron for all three Degrees, and it is the normal Lodge apron, i.e., edged with the Lodge 'colours'. (Each of the Dutch Lodges, as in Scotland, has its own distinctive colours.) The E.A. wears his apron with the flap tucked inside, i.e., invisible. The F.C. wears his apron with the flap 'point up'; the M.M. wears it with the flap down.

From our correspondents listed above, I have quoted only four current variations; of course, there must be many more.

The Scottish practice of the 3° apron resembling a coffin is perhaps the only instance in which some sort of symbolism is involved. In all other cases the practices are simply to distinguish the grade of the wearer and nothing more.

---

66.   SIGNS GIVEN SEATED

Q. In the Emulation system of Lectures, at the end of the various Sections, in the 1st and 2nd degrees, the rubric says: '3 E.A. Sns., seated', or 'B.H.B. five times, seated'.

The question is:

(a) Why seated?
(b) What authority is there for this practice?
(c) When was it introduced?

A. The Q. & A. 'Lectures', which were introduced in the first half of the eighteenth century, were usually rehearsed after the ceremony (if any), i.e., when the assembled Brethren were seated at table. Early references to the subject indicate that the 'lectures went round', i.e., the questions and answers went in rotation right round the table, with frequent interruptions for refreshment and 'toasting'.

In these circumstances, it is not surprising that when the Brethren arrived at the end of a Section they gave the Sn. (or the B.H.B.) seated. After a long session, with several bottles, it was easier to remain seated, and this is the best explanation I can offer for a practice which I have not found elsewhere.

What authority? The rubric in the Emulation Lecture is (so far as I know) the sole authority, and, for Brn. who follow that working, the Emulation Lodge of Improvement is the authority. I am indebted to their Secretary, Bro. C. F. W. Dyer, for his confirmation of the views outlined in the first two paragraphs of the answer, above.

As to the separate question whether it is proper to give those salutations or signs seated, it is my view that the E.A. sign requires a step and is incomplete without it. The W.M., during the 'Entrusting', says, '. . . it is in this position . . .', etc., and the position is now a part of the sign.

In the course of visits to many Lodges, especially in the midlands and northern Provinces, I have often noticed that floor-officers give the proper sign to the W.M. as they pass his Chair, and *he usually replies with the same sign, seated*. Similarly, one sees the W.M. responding to the salute of a late-coming visitor by giving the sign *seated*. These practices are to be deprecated. The B.H.B. is a salutation, not a sign, but since it begins with the posture for the 'threefold Sn.', it should begin with a step and be given standing.

An interesting note on the method of Masonic teaching by question and answer appears in *Le Secret des Francs-Maçons*, published in 1742. It says that the catechism was used for training

'a newly-made Brother. If he is unable to answer, he places his hand in the form of a square, on his breast, and bows, which means that he begs to be excused from answering. Then the W.M. will address an older Brother . . .', etc.

Could the E.A. have bowed while seated?

The Lectures in the English exposures of the 18th century yield *no evidence on signs to be given seated* and the same applies to Browne's *Master Key*, 1798, Carlile's *Republican*, 1825, and Claret's Craft rituals from 1838 onwards. Preston, in his remarkable Lectures in the late 18th and early 19th century, gives the word 'Salutation' or 'Salute' at various points, but never a word about their being given seated. As a rubric in the Lectures, this *Sn. seated* must have been a very late introduction.

---

67. WHAT DO WE PUT ON THE V.S.L.?

Q. My Lodge works in the *Nigerian Ritual*, which claims to be that which is taught by the Emulation Lodge of Improvement. At our last Installation, a visiting Grand Officer was extremely critical of the fact that the Tyler, while being invested, placed his sword diagonally across the V.S.L. The *Nigerian Ritual* expressly requires that this should be done, but several eminent Brethren say that it is wrong. Is there any ruling on the matter?

A. The only ruling is the rubric in your own particular ritual, e.g., the official *Emulation* working, published in 1969, also prescribes that the Tyler, on arriving at the Master's pedestal for his investiture 'places Swd. diagonally across the V.S.L.' I would quote two other workings, chosen at random, *Universal* and *New London*, both of which direct the Tyler to lay the sword

> ... in a convenient position at the side of the pedestal (never on the V. of S.L.)

In my own Lodges (*Logic* working) and in most of the English Lodges that I have visited, we count it a Masonic 'crime' to put anything on the V.S.L., except the Square and Compasses, and the Candidate's hands (which must be without gloves, under the Grand Lodge ruling).

The Grand Lodge has not made a ruling upon your question, but I can assure you that it is the opinion of some eminent Grand Officers that nothing is laid upon the V.S.L., except as indicated above.

To preserve a proper sense of the universality of Freemasonry, I should add that there are several regular workings in Europe and overseas that have a sword on the V.S.L. throughout all the degrees. In problems of this kind, the ever-recurring question of what is right, or wrong, simply cannot be answered. A procedure which is perfectly correct in one working, will be absolutely taboo in another; a sensible tolerance is the best answer and that is always right. If your Lodge works *Nigerian*, the 'Swd. placed diagonally across the V.S.L.' is correct in your Lodge.

Incidentally, the title *Nigerian Ritual* is something of a misnomer. It was compiled, *c.* 1939, by Bro. C. M. Browne, Dep. Dist. G.M. of Nigeria, claiming to be Emulation working, but with the addition of explicitly detailed rubrics to facilitate the teaching of the ceremonial procedures in that country and in others far removed from the seat of authority. It achieved great popularity for that reason, but it was not used officially in the Emulation Lodge of Improvement.

---

68.   THREE, FIVE AND SEVEN YEARS OLD

Q. In the Netherlandic ceremony of the first degree the candidate is told that his Masonic age is now three years and in the second and third degrees it is respectively five and seven years; an explanation of this symbolism will be appreciated.

A. Your practice, in this respect, dates back to an old question in the early 18th century catechisms. The first version that I could trace is in the *Wilkinson MS. c.* 1727:

> Whats the Age of a Mason
> Three times seven
> When you are Asked how Old you are
> When an Apprentice under Seven:—
> fellow Craft under 14;
> When a Master, three times Seven

The *Wilkinson MS.* is the only version that gives these numbers. *The Mystery of Freemasonry*, published in 1730, says:

> Q. How old are you?
> A. Under 5, or under 7, which you will. N.B.—When you are first made a Mason, you are only entered Apprentice; and till you are made a Master, or, as they call it pass'd the Master's Part, you are only an enter'd Apprentice and consequently must answer under 7, for if you say above, they will expect the Master's Word and Signs.

These extracts are an exact transcript of the relevant words and you will notice that the 'age three' did not come into the answers at that date, nor did 'age three' appear in any of the early exposures. A French exposure, *La Désolation des Entrepreneurs Modernes . . .*, of 1747, gives the respective ages as 'Under seven years for the Apprentice; Seven years for the Fellow; Seven years and more for the M.M.'

It should be noted that the idea of seniority expressed in the Mason's supposed age is also expressed—rather similarly—in the number of steps allocated to each, i.e., in England, three, five and seven respectively.

It seems to me that your Netherlandic working is simply a natural development or expansion of those earlier questions. The symbolism is probably based on the supposedly magical properties of those numbers.

Very soon after the above answer was published (in the Q.C. Summons for March 1965) a very useful example of this 'natural development' was received in the course of a letter from Bro. K. L. Jacobs, the

Secretary of Lodge *Nos Vinxit Libertas*, No. 69, also in the Netherlandic Constitution. He wrote:

On our 'tableau' or tracing-board for the first and second degree a door appears, which is said to lead to the inner chamber and which can be reached by a staircase of seven steps An entered apprentice is told that he has climbed three of them only, a fellow craft five and a master mason all seven. These are also their Masonic ages. We use these ages in 'tiling,' the answer giving the degree of the visitor.

These steps are equal to the ritual steps which, with you, are taught to the candidates, but which have, to my great regret, disappeared in our rituals. The entered apprentice makes three of them, the fellow craft two more and the master mason all seven.

When candidates for the Royal Arch are prepared these steps are shown to them and they are requested to repeat them as a mark of proficiency in the Craft.

Here is excellent evidence of the way in which the idea of the candidate's 'age' has been correlated to the number of 'steps', not only in the three Craft degrees, but right up to the moment of preparation for the Royal Arch. We are able to see the ritual growing and being shaped to reflect the ideas of its interpreters.

One problem that seems to defy solution is the wide variation in the three answers, quoted above, from the English and French exposures. I am prompted to quote one more, from *Masonry Dissected*, 1730:

Q. How old are you?
A. Under Seven (*Denoting he has not pass'd Master*).

This is in the E.A. catechism, but the answer appears to be wholly unrelated to the E.A. When all these variations are taken together (and they all belong to the period *c.* 1727–1747) they would seem to suggest that the 'age' question had no particular ritual significance. For all these reasons I am inclined to believe that *originally* this 'age' question was simply a 'trap' question, requiring a particular answer in the candidate's own Lodge, though the answer might have been different in different localities or in different Lodges.

---

69. ORIGIN OF THE WORD 'SKIRRET'

WHY IS IT NOT DEPICTED IN THE GRAND LODGE CERTIFICATE?

Q. What is the origin of the word Skirret; is it connected with the word skewer, i.e., 'skewer-it'?

Why is the Skirret omitted from the Tools which are illustrated on the Master Mason's Grand Lodge Certificate?

A. As to origin, the *O.E.D.* lends no support to 'skewer' as a root. It provides much information on the roots of skirret, as a perennial plant, but for the Masonic word Skirret it quotes Oliver (*Dict. of Symb. Masonry*) and Mackenzie (*Roy. Mas. Cyclop.*) giving their definitions, which are virtually the same words that we use in the ritual; but *O.E.D.* gives no hint of the source of the word, nor the date of its first appearance in its Masonic sense.

The earliest known use of the word in that sense is in a letter dated 24 September 1816, from Philip Broadfoot to a member of the Lodge of Probity, No. 61, Halifax, and the relevant passage runs:

> The Schivit Line represents the strict and undeviating line of duty marked out for our pursuit in the Volume of the Sacred Law.[1]

Broadfoot was a member of the Lodge of Reconciliation, which was created to promulgate the newly approved forms of the ritual at the time of the Union of the rival Grand Lodges. It was, almost certainly, one of the bodies responsible for the introduction of the Skirret as a Working Tool of the third degree. It is therefore surprising to find the Tool described as 'Schivit' by one of the leading members of that Lodge, and this is not the only instance.

Bro. T. O. Haunch, in his important paper on 'English Craft Certificates', records the earliest pictorial representations of the Skirret on Tracing Boards from 1817 onwards. Later in the same paper he also mentions his recent discovery of another instance of the early use of the word Skirret in print, and I quote him:

> It occurs in *The Free Masons' Melody*, a collection of Masonic songs etc. published at Bury, Lancashire, in 1818. In the section 'Masonic Toasts and Sentiments' in this book is 'May a master mason never forego the use of the skivet, pencil, and compasses'. This, incidentally, reflects the early confusion over the spelling of this, then new, Masonic term.[2]

These two examples, 'Schivit' and 'skivet', create further doubts as to the source of the word, especially as *O.E.D.* contains no trace of either of those two forms. Richard Carlile, in his *Republican*, 1825, printed the word 'skirret'; George Claret favoured the spelling 'Skirrit', and since then the printed rituals all use one or other of those two forms.

For all these reasons and because I believe that the word 'skewer' (mentioned by the questioner) has no connexion with our 'skirret', I suggest another root-word 'skirr', which may furnish a solution. The following extracts are from *O.E.D.*:

---

[1] T. W. Hanson, *History of the Lodge of Probity No. 61, 1738–1938*, p. 210.
[2] T. O. Haunch, 'English Craft Certificates', *AQC*, Vol. 82, pp. 215 and 253.

Skirr—(Doubtful origin, possibly Old French). A sound of a grating, rasping, or whirring character . . .
To move . . . rapidly . . . sometimes implying a whirring sound accompanying the movement. To throw with a rapid skimming motion.
(1652) . . . as a Man hurles a Die or Skirrs a Card.
(19th cent.) See me skirr this stone.

Note that the last two quotations imply a rotating motion with a whirring sound, almost precisely describing the sound and movement of a skirret in use. In the absence of a better explanation, I suggest that this may be the origin.
Another suggestion comes from Bro. Dr. G. Malcolm Dyson:

The Old Norse 'skyrta' gives rise to the verb 'to skirt'—'to go along or round or past the edge of' as in 'skirting board', 'on the skirts (or outskirts) of Leicester'; I suggest that skirret is a variant of 'skirt' in this sense; it is a more probable derivation than the 'skirr' root, above, being derived from a fundamental use, rather than from a sound which would scarcely ever be heard from a practical full-scale tool.
The skirret has two modern uses and one interesting older, but obsolete use: the modern uses are to mark out circular beds in landscape gardening and to set out borders and parallel lines of plants. The older use was to lay out rectangles and squares, using a simple construction for obtaining a right angle now, of course, familiar to every schoolboy. . . . Modern instruments and methods have, of course, completely displaced such a system. The tool as sold today for horticultural purposes is exactly similar to the miniatures seen in our lodges.

Bro. Dyson's 'practical' suggestion seems to indicate a very probable source for the name of the Skirret.

*   *   *   *   *   *

As to the reason for the omission of the Skirret from the Grand Lodge Certificate, that may have been because the Skirret is not, strictly speaking, a mason's tool. It is an implement for marking-out ground, not stone, and when we moralize it we lay stress on the 'straight and undeviating line', rather than on the tool itself.
In the paper on 'Grand Lodge Certificates', mentioned above, Bro. Haunch deals with the omission question at some length. On the basis of William Preston's reference (in *Illustrations* . . . 1792) to 'the Line' with its symbolism, Bro. Haunch infers that it was originally 'a simple length of cord'. He then goes on to show that *the Skirret was not depicted on two Third Degree Tracing Boards painted in* 1810 *and* 1812, just before the Union. He agrees that the Skirret was apparently introduced by the Lodge of Reconciliation and 'must already have been

known . . . as a Masonic emblem when the design of the Pillars Certificate was under consideration' and concludes that 'its omission must
therefore have been deliberate'.

The crux of his explanation for the 'non-inclusion' of the Skirret is
that the illustrations at the foot of the Certificate represent the Furniture
and Jewels of the Lodge, not the 'Working Tools'; and this also explains
why they are not displayed in 'clusters', in the manner that is customary
for pictures of the Tools.

The whole article is extremely useful and should be read by all who
are interested in this problem. The Skirret, unknown in the workings of
several overseas jurisdictions, appears in miniature, resting on the
Master's Board in the illustration of the Third Tracing Board, on p.
325.

---

70.   THE QUEEN AND THE CRAFT

Q. I am told that it is wrong to toast 'The Queen and the Craft'. It
seems illogical to couple a lady with a Masonic toast. What is the rule?

A. When this toast is given, the Lodge is not bestowing Masonic
honours on a lady, but displaying its proper and loyal duty to the
Crown. In mediaeval times the *Old Charges* required masons, at every
grade in their careers, to swear loyalty to the King. The toast 'the King
and the Craft' is given with 'Fire', quite properly, even if the King is not
a Mason; and it is given to the 'Queen and the Craft' when there is no
King.

---

71.   CALLING OFF—IN WHICH DEGREE?

Q. In which Degree should a Lodge be 'called off'? May it be left to
the Master's discretion, to do as he wishes? Of course, he could not call
off in the middle of a ceremony.

A. The Board of General Purposes has ruled (8 March 1961) and
'recommends that the Master of a Lodge should be permitted to make
a short break in the proceedings at a suitable time during a meeting,
provided that the Lodge is properly "called off" and "called on" again'.

It is noteworthy that no particular Degree is specified in the recommendation. Generally, it would be advisable to resume in the First
Degree prior to 'calling off', as this avoids the possibility of confusion

on re-entering. The Master certainly has discretionary powers, but in this instance he would be well-advised to adhere to this practice.

There is, however, an exception to this question of 'which Degree', and it arises during the Installation ceremonies, where many Lodges make a short break after the Inner Working. In such cases, the Lodge *must be 'called off'*, and that is done in the Third Degree. (The possibility of confusion is avoided here because, on re-entry, none below the rank of M.M. may enter.)

I am informed that in Lodges overseas that suffer very hot climate, it may become necessary to call off several times during a single ceremony, because the temperature, in a confined space, becomes intolerable. In such cases, it would be the W.M.'s duty to select the appropriate moments when the ceremony can be interrupted without impairing its solemnity. In temperate climates, however, the Lodge would not be called off in the middle of a ceremony, except in the event of some serious mishap (e.g., if the Candidate or one of the Officers had a sudden heart attack).

---

72.   SIR WINSTON SPENCER CHURCHILL

Q. Was Sir Winston Churchill a Freemason?

A. Yes. Brother Winston S. Churchill was initiated in the United Studholme Lodge No. 1591, London, on 24 May 1901; Passed on 19 July 1901; Raised on 25 March 1902. The modern style Proposal Forms did not come into use until World War I, and the names of his Proposer and Seconder are now unknown.

He joined the army in 1895 and had seen active service in the Malakand Field Force (1897) and the Tirah Expeditionary Force (1898), giving him the material for two important books. During the South African War he was correspondent for *The Morning Post*, was taken prisoner by the Boers and had escaped from Pretoria Jail. He returned to England already famous as an author, journalist and soldier, and he was soon in great demand as a speaker on political platforms.

Three months before his Initiation he had taken his first seat in Parliament as the Conservative member for Oldham, Lancs., and had made a brilliant 'maiden speech' within his first week.

In 1901, at age twenty-seven, a great and busy career was opening up for him, but he continued as a member of the Craft until July 1912 when, as First Lord of the Admiralty, he was charged by Asquith, the

Prime Minister, to 'put the fleet into a state of instant and constant readiness for war, in case we were attacked by Germany'.

---

73.   WILLIAM PRESTON
        AND THE 'PRESTONIAN LECTURES'

Q. What are the 'Prestonian Lectures' and are they obtainable in print?

A. William Preston died in the year 1818, aged 76, after a lifetime of service to the Craft, devoted largely to the study and perfection of the Masonic Lectures. They were designed, primarily, to furnish instruction and explanation of the procedure and symbolism of the ceremonies, by means of Question and Answer, and Preston—perhaps more than any other single individual—may be credited with the best of the English language that is preserved in our present-day Ritual.

By his Will he left various legacies to Masonic charities, and an additional sum of £300 in Consols to the Grand Lodge, with the direction that the income from it was to be applied as a fee

'to some well-informed Mason to deliver annually a lecture on the First, Second or Third Degree of the Order of Masonry according to the system practised in the Lodge of Antiquity during his Mastership.'

In 1819 United Grand Lodge endorsed the opinion of the Grand Master that insistence on uniformity in regard to the Lectures was not desirable in the interests of Masonry, but Preston's Lectures were delivered each year, with occasional intermissions, from 1820 until 1862, when they were discontinued. Until that time the Lectures were mainly in Question and Answer form, as Preston had designed them, but surviving records show that some of them were rearranged and delivered in narrative form.

In 1924 the Prestonian Lectureship was revived with substantial modifications to the original scheme, *the Lecturer now submitting a Masonic subject of his own selection*, and (with the exception of the years 1940–1946) regular appointments have been made annually since 1924 to the present day.

The foregoing notes may suffice to show the distinction between Preston's Lectures and the Prestonian Lectures since 1924. Nowadays, the Prestonian Lecturer is chosen by a special committee of the Grand Lodge and he has to deliver three 'Official' Lectures to Lodges applying for that honour. The 'Official' deliveries are usually allocated to one selected Lodge in London and two in the provinces. In addition to these

BROTHER WILLIAM PRESTON

three, the Lecturer generally delivers the same lecture, unofficially, to other Lodges all over the country, and it is customary for printed copies of the Lecture to be sold—in vast numbers—for the benefit of one of the Masonic charities selected by the author.

The Prestonian Lectures have the unique distinction that they are the only Lectures given 'with the authority of the Grand Lodge'. There are also two unusual financial aspects attaching to them. Firstly that the Lecturer is paid for his services, though the modest fee is not nearly so important as the honour of the appointment.

Secondly, the Lodges which are honoured with the Official deliveries of the Lectures are expected to take special measures for assembling a large audience and, for that reason, they are permitted—on that occasion only—to make a small nominal charge for admission.

Prints of the earlier 'Prestonian Lectures' are now very scarce, but the *Collected Prestonian Lectures, 1925–1960,* have been published by the Quatuor Coronati Lodge (twenty-seven Lectures in one volume) and that is available to members of the Q.C. Correspondence Circle.

---

74.   THE HIRAMIC LEGEND AS A DRAMA

Q. (From Canada)—Thomas Smith Webb, according to Mackey, became 'the inventor and founder of a system of work which, under the appropriate name of the American Rite, is universally practised in the United States'. It replaced the rituals of the 'Antients' and 'Moderns' of England and those of the Grand Lodges of Ireland and Scotland which were in use until *c.* 1800.

The Hiramic legend, complete with cast, costumes and dialogue, is played as a drama in the American Rite and is one of the principal differences between it and the Canadian work, which is based on English *Emulation.* Is it possible to confirm when the 'dramatic' form arose and whether it came from British sources or from Webb's inventive mind?

A. In problems of this kind, precise dating is virtually impossible. It may well be that Thomas Smith Webb was responsible for the *American version of the 'dramatic' presentation,* but if so, he came on the scene rather late. He was born in 1771, and initiated in Rising Sun Lodge, at Keene, New Hampshire, in 1790, aged only nineteen. His main Masonic work was *The Freemason's Monitor: or Illustrations of Masonry: in Two Parts,* first published in 1797. The work was '. . . a substantial reproduction of Preston's first book . . . Webb, however, neglected to give Preston credit for the material'. (Herbert T. Leyland, *Thomas Smith Webb,* pp. 431–2, The Otterbein Press, Dayton, Ohio.) These notes are helpful as to dating, but they are of little use as regards ritual, because both Preston's *Illustrations* and Webb's version of it were purely 'monitorial'. They did not deal with ceremonial details and certainly contained no guidance on esoteric procedures or on the 'drama'.

The search for sources in the British Isles is promising. Prichard's *Masonry Dissected,* 1730, gave the earliest known version of the legend, all in the form of question and answer but omitting the names of the three villains.

In the absence of reliable documents we are compelled to make use of the evidence of exposures, often well finished pieces which have at least the appearance of completeness and authenticity. Broadly, it may be assumed that the authors of all the printed exposures were eager to divulge all that they knew on the subject and, in those texts which appear to be complete any important omissions would imply:

(a) that those missing items were unknown to the authors, or
(b) that they had not yet come into existence.

Both points might apply to Prichard's work. In 1744 and 1745, two important French exposures appeared, *Le Catéchisme des Francs-Maçons* and *L'Ordre des Francs-Maçons Trahi*, which contained quite remarkable versions of the Hiramic legend, *still without any trace of those three names*, I believe we are forced to the conclusion that those names had not yet appeared in the ritual. The same applies to the many other exposures which were published in France, Germany and other European countries, up to 1760. Whether in the narrative sections, or in the catechisms, the three names do not appear and there is never any hint of 'drama'.

During the thirty years that followed the publication of *Masonry Dissected*, it was reprinted frequently and it was not until 1760 that a new exposure made its appearance, entitled *Three Distinct Knocks*. It contained, as might be expected, many items that had not previously appeared in documents of this class, e.g., new details of clothing, equipment, etc., and much information relating to the ceremonies. There was a full legend of Hiram Abif, *with the names of his assassins,* the story of the search, their capture, and the penalties meted out to each of them. All this was told in the form of question and answer with some lengthy narrative passages, virtually all the materials for the 'drama', but still without 'stage directions'.

Three Distinct Knocks claimed to be Antients' practice, but there seems to be no evidence that they ever worked the Degree as a 'drama'. History has shown that there was more than a tenuous link between Ireland and the Antients. Indeed, a high proportion of their founders, in 1751, were of Irish origin and although it would be impossible to say when the 'drama' form was first used in Ireland *it appears to have been Irish practice since time immemorial.*

In England, there is only one small Province that could attempt to make a similar claim, and that is Bristol. It has a unique form of

Masonic ritual, one of the oldest workings in England, and the only one that uses the 'drama' form. Where did they find it? If one had to hazard a guess as to how the 'drama' came to Bristol the answer would be, almost certainly, via Ireland; of all the ports in Britain, Bristol is the one that has the oldest links with the Emerald Isle.

ILLOGICALITIES IN THE THIRD DEGREE

Q. On the subject of Masonic Penalties does anyone know how a Fellow Craft—assisting in 'the drama of the Third Degree'—quotes the penalty of the Master Mason Degree? (From Bro. J. G. Wolff, Providence, Rhode Island, U.S.A.).

A. In the 'drama' form of the ceremony, when the three assassins are discovered in hiding, they are heard bemoaning their crime:

> The first cries that he would rather have suffered . . . (the 'E.A. penalty') than consent to the death of H.A.; another would sooner have undergone . . . (the 'F.C. penalty') than be concerned in it; and the third, who struck the final blow, says he would rather have suffered . . . (the 'penalty of the Third Degree') 'ere he had been the cause of our Master's death.

All this is strange to English ears, but, as shown in the preceding answer, it dates back to English exposures of the 1760s.

On the question 'How could a F.C. quote the M.M. penalty?' it may be helpful to observe that *Masonry Dissected*, 1730, gave an elaborate *E.A. Obligation which embodied all three penalties* (which were presumably customary in the ritual of that day). This implies that the E.A. in 1730, could have known of a penalty which was to appear thirty years later in the M.M. degree.

Now, as to the question; it is always difficult to provide a logical and factual answer to an allegorical question. I would explain at the outset that the rendering of the Third Degree is (though one may not have realized it) the story of the supposed evolution of the Third Degree, so that when we recite or display the legend of H.A. we are actually telling the story of how the Degree arose, with its signs, words, etc.

This emphasizes the fact that until *c.* 1724–5, when the Third Degree first came into practice in Britain, only two Degrees were known, one for the Entered Apprentice, and the other for the Fellow Craft. (In Scotland he was called 'Master or Fellow Craft'.)

It is certain that *in 1696 the F.P.O.F. were already in existence as part of the F.C. ceremony, and the word of the M.M. was also known to F.C.s long before the three-degree system had come into practice.* At the dates (1696–*c.* 1700) when we have textual proof of these two statements *we still have no details of the remaining contents of the F.C. ceremony.* It is possible that they had the legend of H.A. in the Second Degree, but it is extremely unlikely that they had all the signs and other details.

When, around 1725, the three-degree system was evolved by a splitting of the First Degree into two parts, the material described above, *previously part of the Second Degree,* automatically became the Third Degree and, although there was a splendid version of the legend in print by 1730, I believe we must assume that some of its minor details (which were apparently unknown in the earlier two-degree system) were invented or 'produced' to make the narrative complete.

Thus, according to the legend as it was narrated in *Three Distinct Knocks,* in 1760, the three Fellowcrafts who were responsible for the death of H.A. knew the penalties of all three degrees, and the F.C. searchers who discovered the corpse knew the F.P.O.F. The same texts continue the legend by saying that, after the F.C.s had reported to Solomon, he decreed [prophetically] that:

... for the future, the first occasion'd Sign and Word that is spoke at his raising, shall be his [i.e., the M.M.'s] ever after.

In this way, they were, all unwittingly, responsible for the 'Master's Word' and for the 'grand Sign of a Master-Mason'.

These are all minor illogicalities, evidence of stages in evolution, and I doubt if there can be a certain answer to the many points that arise in the question. I have merely stated the evidence, based on reliable manuscripts of 1696–*c.* 1700, in conjunction with details in *Masonry Dissected,* 1730, and especially in two very popular exposures of 1760 and 1762. Needless to say, our modern working of the Third Degree in the English system, bears little or no resemblance to the procedures of those days.

I must add, however, that the earliest French versions of the same Hiramic legend are much more logical than ours. In four separate texts dated 1744, 1745, 1747 and 1751, Solomn sent 'nine Masters' to search for H.A. (not fifteen F.C.s as the story goes nowadays) and in those versions the question would not arise. (See *E.F.E.*, pp. 97, 257, 331, 454.)

---

75. ORIENTATION OF THE LETTER G

Q. Should the letter G be 'readable' from the East or West?

A. I hold that in those Lodges where the G is displayed it should be one of the most prominent items viewed on entering the Lodge, and it should therefore be readable from the West.

The oldest references to its position all suggest that it was 'in the centre'. In the early 1700s it was usually on the floor in the middle of a Tracing Board, either drawn in chalk or laid out in templates. In such cases it would certainly have been laid on the floor so as to be readable from the West.

It is perhaps necessary to add that there is no uniformity of practice in relation to the use of the G, or the 'Blazing Star' (with or without the G at its centre), which has the same significance. Many Temples do not have it at all. In the English Provinces it usually hangs from the ceiling in the centre of the Lodge, arranged so as to be read from the West. In many U.S.A. jurisdictions and quite often in England, it is displayed in the East, over the Master's Chair. That is perhaps the surest guide as to how it should be placed, because, in that position, it can only be read from the West.

Nevertheless, there are some European jurisdictions in which the G appears high up *on the western wall* of the Lodge.

---

76.   PASSWORDS

Q. What is the real purpose of the passwords between the Degrees? In England we give them to the Candidates just before they take their degrees, actually within moments of their being asked for them; in any case they are usually prompted in the answers! Why, passwords?

A. There are no 'official' records, i.e., Grand Lodge Minutes, which would indicate the *reasons for the introduction of the passwords*, and these notes are based very largely upon the evidence surrounding their earliest appearance.

We know, from our Grand Lodge Minutes, that from 1730 onwards the Craft was greatly troubled by the publication of exposures and by the growth of clandestine and irregular makings of Masons, and it seems that around that period the Grand Lodge took action by reversing the order of certain words of the First and Second degrees. But those measures were not recorded at the time, and the only general and imprecise confirmation we have of this theory comes from a pre-Union minute of April 1809 which stated that it was no longer necessary 'to continue in force those Measures which were resorted to in or about the year 1739 respecting irregular Masons . . .'. But those measures, so far as we know, had nothing to do with the introduction of passwords, and there is no *English* textual evidence of the use of passwords until the 1760s.

In France, however, starting in 1737, there began a whole flood of exposures, several of them worthless, but others that were—at least—interesting, and some of their compilers seem to have been confident that they were stirring up trouble.

The Abbé Perau, author of *Le Secret des Francs-Maçons*, 1742, wrote:

When this important work is ended it will become necessary, as you are well aware, to acquire new signs; it would be of little use merely to add something to the old ones, for you would always be liable to error: and moreover why be niggardly in a matter which costs so little?

Similar ideas were expressed in some of the texts that followed during the next three years. In 1745, there appeared a new work, *L'Ordre des Francs-Maçons Trahi* by an unknown author, largely made up of materials that had already appeared in earlier works. But there were several new items in this work and some of them of particular interest. Among these novelties, we find the first reference to passwords. They appear in the course of a Catechism, i.e.:

Q. What is the Password of an Apprentice?
A. . . . .
Q. That of a Fellow?
A. . . . .
Q. And that of a Master [= M.M.]?
A. . . . .

It is not possible to discuss the Answers here. Though they would be familiar to Brethren of the requisite grades, they are not the same as those in use in present-day English practice. The writer adds an interesting footnote which explains why they were introduced, indicating that they were a novelty, not yet widely adopted:

These three Passwords are scarcely used, except in France, and at Frankfurt on Main. They are in the nature of Watchwords, introduced as a surer safeguard, [when dealing] with Brethren whom they do not know.

This 'Password' material appeared for the first time *in print* in 1745 and, until recently, there was no evidence to suggest that they were in use much before that time. In March 1971, however, Bro. Dr. S. Vatcher read a paper in the Quatuor Coronati Lodge, 'A Lodge of Irishmen in Lisbon in 1738' (*AQC*, Vol. 84) which contained a lengthy report of the examination by the Portuguese Inquisition authorities of the members of that Lodge, in 1738. The Inquisition records give full details of the witnesses' replies. One of the members, a Cavalry Lieutenant in the Alcantara Regiment, but a native of Newtown, Ireland, in the course of one of his answers listed a series of words and names, including one that might well have been a 'password', though he did not describe it as such. We may therefore envisage the possibility that in Ireland, or in some parts of Europe, the passwords may already have been in use in 1738, seven years before their first appearance in print.

One word more; although the passwords make their first appearance in print in France, it is highly probable that they were in use in England at about the same time, if not earlier, but this is pure speculation at present, because there is no evidence of their use in English practice until the exposures from 1760 onwards.

Our modern system of entrusting the Candidate with pass-grip and password in a kind of intermediate ceremony, immediately before he takes his next degree, was probably established at the Union of the Grand Lodges, but it was not always like that, and it gives rise to another question:

> Q. After answering the requisite questions (i.e., the English equivalent of the 'proficiency test') the Candidate gets the P.G. and P.W. *before* he has taken his Obligation for the 2° or 3°. This seems wrong; can you explain?

The early documents which show the introduction of passwords in the course of the ceremonies are extremely vague as to the moment when they were actually conferred. *L'Ordre des Francs-Maçons Trahi*, 1745, has a long section headed 'Signs, Grips and Words . . .' and at the end of its chapter headed 'For Apprentices' we read that 'The Password for Apprentices is . . .'; at the end of the chapter headed 'For Fellows', 'The Password is . . .'. It seems reasonable to assume that the password for each degree was conferred in the course of that ceremony, probably after the entrusting with the other secrets. (See *E.F.E.*, pp. 272–4.)

In *La Désolation des Entrepreneurs . . .*, 1747, there are separate catechisms for each of the three degrees and, in the E.A. catechism, the Candidate, after lettering the 'word' and explaining its meaning, is asked:

> Q. What is the password of the Apprentices?

He gives the appropriate answer, and there is similar procedure for the F.C. password. There can be no doubt that the E.A. received his password *during* the E.A. ceremony, and the Fellow received his password *during* the second degree. (*E.F.E.*, pp. 344, 352.)

Le Maçon Démasqué, 1751, contains a long and interesting narrative description of the E.A. ceremony. After the entrusting, the Candidate goes round the Lodge and is tested by the Officers. He returns to the Master who addresses him as follows:

> We have found out, my dear Brother, that the word **** has come to the knowledge of the Profane by the perfidy, or by the carelessness of some Brother, & Masonry always anxious to hide its profound mysteries from the Profane, has overcome this difficulty by the ingenious invention of a password, with which to reinforce its secret. This word is ****

Here, in the earliest detailed description of the password being conferred during the ceremony, we also have the reason for the introduction of the passwords, and the Lodge of Apprentices is closed immediately after this. The Fellow's password is similarly conferred in the second degree. (*E.F.E.*, pp. 434, 443.)

When the passwords make their first appearance in our English texts, the evidence is not so clear. *Three Distinct Knocks*, 1760, and *J. & B.*, 1762, do not mention passwords in their descriptions of the E.A. proceedings, and their '*Fellow-Craft's Part*' describes that ceremony all in the form of Question and Answer. Question 7, at the beginning of the F.C. ceremony, asks:

> Q. How do you expect to attain it [this Degree]?
> A. By the Benefit of a Pass-word.

and the Candidate gives the password. It is noteworthy that later in the ceremony *the p.w. is mentioned again and is described as 'The Pass-word of a Craft'*. This is an important change, since it implies that the 'Password of an Apprentice' had become the 'Password of a Craft', and suggests some doubt as to when it had been, or when it should be, conferred. We can only guess when the E.A. received it but, as there is no evidence of an intermediate ceremony, it seems likely that it was conferred at the beginning of the F.C. degree. Incidentally, these two texts are the earliest that contain English details of pass-grips as well as pass-words.

Browne, in his *Master Key*, 1798, showed the F.C. Candidate receiving the secrets of the second degree at their usual place in the ceremony, followed immediately by *the former E.A. password etc.*, now described as '*the pass grip and pass word of a Fellow Craft*'. This procedure probably represents the general practice in England at that time.

The first official hint of what later became the intermediate ceremony, appears in the minutes of the Lodge of Promulgation on 28 December 1810, in a complicated resolution which ended:

> . . . and the making of the pass-words *between* one Degree and another, instead of *in* the Degree.

(*AQC* 23, p. 46.)

Nevertheless, some doubt seems to have remained as to when the 'entrusting' (i.e., the intermediate ceremony) should take place, and the minutes of the Lodge of Reconciliation relating to their demonstrations show conflicting procedures. Several of the earlier records say that the Lodge was opened in the second degree and after 'examination', or after answering 'probationary questions', the Candidate was passed F.C. But the later entries, and by far the majority of them, show that the Candidate was examined (and presumably entrusted) in the first degree. Then the Lodge was opened in the second degree and he was passed F.C. This was the arrangement which set the pattern for our intermediate ceremony of 'Questions leading to the Second Degree' followed by the entrusting with the p.g. and p.w., with similar procedure, of course, between the second and third degrees.

I have developed this theme at some length, partly to show the various stages in the evolution of our entrusting procedures, but mainly to demonstrate that *originally* the passwords were given to the E.A. and F.C., *during their respective ceremonies*. That explains why they were conferred without an additional Obligation, and why we confer them today before the Candidates take their next Obligation.

Fundamentally, there is no need for the Candidate to be called upon to take a further Obligation before the entrusting, because his first E.A. Ob. binds him to keep secret the things . . . that may now, *or at any future time* . . . be communicated to him.

---

77.   'WITH GRATITUDE TO OUR MASTER . . .'

Q. In the Third Degree Closing, we respond, 'With gratitude to our Master we bend'. To whom does this refer? Does the W.M. also bend?

A. A difficult problem upon which I can find no ruling, so that the following notes are simply a statement of my own opinions.

I cannot accept the view that, when we say those words, we are thanking the W.M. for 'ratifying and confirming' the sub. s . . . 'with his sanction and approval . . .'. Our ritual is singularly free from any such mass expressions of gratitude and I believe that, if any expressions of thanks were really intended, they would probably have been introduced at the moment when the Candidate is r . . . . . d with the assistance of the Wardens. They might also have been introduced, quite logically, in the Openings in all three Degrees, after the W.M. acknowledges 'the correctness of the s . . .'. But the ritual never requires us to 'bend' to the W.M.; we simply give him the prescribed salutations.

It seems to me that when we bend before 'our Master' in the Third Degree Closing we acknowledge our indebtedness to the Most High. My reasons are briefly as follows. Each of the Openings and Closings in all three Degrees concludes with a short prayer, invocation, or religious exhortation. In the Opening of the Third Degree the W.M. promises to assist in repairing 'that loss, and may Heaven aid our united endeavours'. In the Third Degree Closing, after the W.M. has '. . . confirmed . . . etc.', we bend in gratitude to the 'Most High—our Master' for his help.

Thus the words 'With gratitude . . . All glory to the Most High', are not a reply to the W.M.'s ratification, etc., but the completion of the brief prayer in the Opening, when we asked for Heavenly aid.

So, my own answer to the second question, above, is that the W.M. also 'bends' with all the other Brethren. But in those Lodges where it is held that the words are an expression of gratitude to the W.M., he would not 'bend'.

I posed the question to Bro. Roy Wells, and he made a suggestion that had not occurred to me, i.e., that we bend in gratitude to our Master, King Solomon, who ordained (in the terms of our legend) that the sub. s . . . '. . . should designate all Master Masons throughout the universe . . .'.

It is true that Solomon's Temple forms the scenic, spiritual and symbolical background to all our Craft ceremonies, and that suggests that we might well express our gratitude to him in all three degrees, not only at one point in the third. I am inclined to doubt whether we do, in fact, bend with gratitude to King Solomon; but the conflicting views will make a useful subject for debate.

---

78.   THE ORIGIN OF THE COLLAR

Q. Where did the Masters' (and Officers') Collars originate, and why?

A. By a resolution of Grand Lodge on 24 June 1727 the Master and Wardens of all private lodges were ordered to wear '. . . the jewels of Masonry hanging to a white ribbon'. This may be taken as the first regulation relating to what afterwards became the Master's, Wardens' and Officers' Collars. On 17 March 1731 white leather aprons lined with white silk were also specified for the W.M. and Wardens.

At this time, the 'ribbons' of the Grand Officers were blue, and those of the Grand Stewards were red, and their aprons were lined to match.

The word ribbon seems to have been interpreted rather loosely—perhaps because no particular width was specified, and early illustrations of Brethren wearing Masonic clothing seem to confirm that the ribbon was always quite narrow, sometimes no wider than a silken cord. Generally it seems that the ribbons (apart from the distinctions of colour, mentioned above), were strictly utilitarian, i.e., they were not at first intended as decoration in themselves, but simply as a means of hanging the respective jewels.

The first hint of the Collars as properly 'tailored' articles of clothing appears in *Le Secret des Francs-Maçons*, 1742, by the Abbé G. L. C. Perau, in which he describes the clothing of the Officers, as follows (My own translation):

> On Initiation days, the Worshipful [Master], the two Wardens, the Secretary, & the Treasurer of the Order, wear a blue Ribbon round their necks, *cut in the shape of a triangle* . . . [My Italics]. At the base of the Master's Ribbon there hang a Square and Compasses . . . The Wardens and other Officers wear only the Compasses.

Perau uses the word 'Cordon' which may be translated as 'cord' or 'ribbon', but his phrase '*taillé en triangle*' [cut in the shape of a triangle] confirms the interpretation that this was a 'Collar', tailored approximately to the same shape as we use nowadays. As though to confirm his intention, he adds a footnote:

> It is not absolutely necessary that the Ribbon should be of the shape described here. I have seen them being worn like the Cordon [of the Order] of the Golden Fleece; that always forms a sort of triangle but it is not so exact as the one which I have described.

Obviously, there was no rule—and indeed no strict fashion—that was to be observed in this matter, but Perau's description in 1742 may be taken as the earliest evidence of the beginning of the Collar in its modern shape.

---

79.   THE 'WORKING TOOLS'

Q. How did the 'Working Tools' come into our ceremonies? Were all our present-day Tools used and moralized from the earliest times, or were they introduced gradually?

A. Before we discuss the appearance of 'Working Tools' in our early ritual documents, it may be interesting to list some of the principal tools used by the operative masons, as recorded in the Fabric Rolls and similar sources. An inventory in the *York Fabric Rolls* of the tools stored in the masons' lodge at the end of the year 1399, listed inter alia:

> 69 stone axes, 96 iron chisels, 24 mallets, 1 hatchet, 1 big gavel, 1 compass, 2 tracing boards . . . etc.

A broader survey shows that stone-hammers and stone-axes were used, in a large variety of shapes and weights. We read of setting-hammers with hollow heads, for the hard-hewers; scappling-hammers for the rough layers, for making flat unsmoothed surfaces; hammers with one vertical edge; hammers with one horizontal edge; hammers with both vertical and horizontal edges.

There were hammer-axes, brick-axes, pickaxes, chisels and trowels; hatchets and mattocks; crowbars, levers and wedges; 'points', puncheons and augers; mallets and mauls. The cutting edges of iron tools were usually 'steeled' and on large undertakings the smiths were kept very busy sharpening and repairing them.

The principal wooden tools were, of course, squares, rules, levels and plumb-rules, all usually made from cask-staves. There are frequent references to string or 'packthread', used for 'lines' (ancestor of the 'skirret'?) and for plumb-lines.[1]

It is clear that our Speculative forebears had a wide range of tools from which to select those that were to be 'moralized' in the ritual.

Although there are ample records of the mason's tools as such, there are no really early records of the tools *which were used in the course of the lodge ceremonies*. In all the old *MS. Constitutions* until the 1650s the admission ceremony seems to have consisted of no more than a reading of the Charges and an oath of fidelity. A text of *c.* 1650 gives a form of the Obligation containing a reference to secret 'words & signes', implying that there had been a substantial expansion of the contents of the ceremonies, but the 'Working Tools' are not mentioned. The earliest reference to 'Tools', in what might be described as a non-operative context, is in the *Academie of Armory*, 1688, by Randle Holme, the third distinguished member of that family bearing the same name, all associated with the city of Chester. Holme was a Herald and a Gentleman-Mason, and in a brief passage in his book, relating to the Free-Masons, he said 'I have observed the use of these severall Tools

---

[1] The foregoing details on masons' tools, listed in modern spelling, are based on the relevant chapters in *Building in England down to 1540*, by L. F. Salzman, Oxford Univ. Press, 1967, and *The Mediaeval Mason*, by D. Knoop and G. P. Jones, Manchester Univ. Press, 1949.

amongst them'. He then listed a series of tools, e.g., shovel, hand-hammer, chisel, pick and punch, all belonging to operative masonry, adding that some of the tools are borne in Coats of Arms. He did not say that all or any of these tools were actually used or mentioned in the course of the ceremonies, and we cannot be sure if they were. Incidentally, the *c.* 1650 version of the *Old Charges*, noted above, which contains the secret 'words & signes' Obligation (*Harleian MS., No.* 2054) is almost entirely in his handwriting.

The earliest evidence as to the tools in the Masonic ceremonies comes, as might be expected, in the early catechisms and the later exposures. It so happens that the oldest texts that have survived are all in manuscript, which may be taken, generally, as having been laboriously written out to serve as aides-mémoire. The printed pieces, which begin with a newspaper item in 1723, were generally published from motives of profit, curiosity, or spite. This distinction between the prints and the manuscripts is worth noting, therefore, because it implies that a greater degree of trust can be placed upon the *MSS.*, though all of them must be viewed with caution.

The first evidence comes from the *Edinburgh Register House MS.* of 1696, with two later versions, almost identical, of *c.* 1700 and *c.* 1714. They contain only one passage which mentions tools. It occurs in the course of the candidate's greeting to the Brethren on his re-entering the lodge:

> . . . as I am sworn by God, St. John by the Square and compass, and common judge . . .

The 'common judge' was a gauge or templet. A templet, described as a *jadge,* is pictured among the tools in the *Mark Book of the Lodge of Aberdeen.*

None of the other texts furnishes any more information on tools until April, 1723, when a newspaper *The Flying Post or Post-Master* published a Masonic catechism without a title, but now known as 'A Mason's Examination'. It contains the same three tools mentioned above, and elsewhere in the text the Astler and Diamond are mentioned with the Square or Common Square. There are several French exposures of a later period *c.* 1744–51 which suggest that the ashlar may have been used as a stone on which tools were sharpened, but it is unlikely that it was a tool in itself. The 'Diamond' may have been a diamond-hammer, used for broaching hewn-work. (*O.E.D.*)

In the following year, 1724, *The Grand Mystery of Free-Masons Discover'd,* in reply to a question on how the lodge is governed, has the answer 'Of Square and Rule', possibly the first reference to what is now the '24 inch gauge'. (It also repeats the Diamond, Asher [*sic*.] and Square.) A later text of 1725 has the answer 'Of Square Plumb and Rule'.

In a manuscript catechism dated 1724, *The Whole Institution of Masonry*, there is a question on the number of Lights in a Lodge, with the answer:

Twelve . . . Father. Son. Holy Ghost. Sun. Moon. Master Mason. Square. Rule. Plum. Line. Mell and Chizzel.

Here was a great advance, although it is of course not certain that all these tools were actually being used in the ceremonies. Another question in the same text brings the answer 'with Square and Compass at my Breast', a detail that appears regularly in later texts. It is certain that those two were being used; but the others were at least being talked about. The level, surprisingly, had not yet made its appearance!

So, in 1725, we have a large collection of tools including several not previously mentioned, e.g., the Rule, which may now safely be construed as the forerunner of the 24 inch gauge; the Mell, i.e., the maul or gavel and the 'Chizzel'. It should be noted that the 'Plum' and Line are given here as two separate tools; it is possible that the 'Line' is to be read as an early version of the skirret; but it may be a reference to the cable-tow; the Candidate in the *Dumfries No. 4 MS.*, *c.* 1710, in reply to one of its questions, says that he was brought into the lodge

'sham[e]fully w^t a rope about my neck'

The 1724 set of 'Twelve Lights' as they are called, appeared again in two other texts *The Whole Institutions of Free-Masons Opened* of 1725, a printed broadsheet, and in the far more interesting *Graham MS.* of 1726.

Another text of 1726, *The Grand Mystery Laid Open*, contains a disproportionate amount of nonsensical material, but one of its questions on the Tools requisite for a Free-Mason brings the answer 'The Hammer and Trowel . . .' and later it appears that the Candidate holds the Trowel in his right hand and the Hammer in his left during the Obligation. These details did not reappear in later texts.

A Mason's Confession of *c.* 1727, gives the square, level, plumb-rule, hand-rule, and the 'gage' [*sic*] and the latter still appeared in *The Mystery of Freemasonry* in 1730, but (so far as I can ascertain) it then disappeared. This was apparently the first appearance of the level.

And so we come to Prichard's *Masonry Dissected*, 1730, the most detailed exposure until that time. It mentioned the Candidate kneeling within the Square, with the Compass at his n.l.b., and the 'Moveable Jewels', i.e., Square, Level and Plumb-Rule, which were also the Master's and Wardens' Emblems. In its description of the murder of H.A., the ruffians use 'Setting Maul, Setting Tool and Setting Beadle', but we need not pursue them further.

A Dialogue between Simon and Philip, of *c*. 1740, adds only one item to our list, i.e., a 'Quadrant', a 90 degree segment of a circle in which the curved edge is marked to show degrees, but that likewise failed to reappear.

Prichard's text was probably the earliest of the whole series to explain at least some of the Tools in something approaching the modern manner. In reply to a question on the uses of the Square, Level and Plumb-Rule, he says:

> Square to lay down True and Right Lines, Level to try all Horizontals, and the Plumb-Rule to try all Uprights.

The *Wilkinson MS.*, a parallel but fragmentary text of the same period, says:

> the Square to see y^t Corner Stones are laid square; the Levell that they are laid Levell And ye Plumb to Raise Perpendiculars.

This is even nearer to our present-day style of explanation, but early explanations in regard to the other tools are non-existent.

In *Le Catéchisme des Francs-Maçons*, 1744, the 'floor-drawing' for a 'Lodge of Apprentice-Fellows' (i.e., First and Second Degrees combined), contained, among other symbols, the following tools:

> Square, Compasses, Level, Plumb-Rule, Trowel, and a Mason's Hammer (i.e., not a normal Gavel).

In 1760 we have the first of a new English series of exposures beginning with *Three Distinct Knocks* and now we begin to find several familiar explanations of some of the tools, but not all of them, because the explanations seem to have been confined to the E.A. ceremony, e.g.:

> The Bible, to rule and govern our Faith; the Square, to Square our Actions; the Compasses is to keep us within Bounds with all Men, particularly with a Brother.

Later the working tools of an Entered-Apprentice are explained as follows:

> Mas. What are their Uses?
> Ans. The Square to square my Work, the 24 Inch Gauge to measure my Work, the common Gavel to knock off all superfluous Matters, whereby the Square may set easy and just.

Mas. Brother, as we are not all working Masons, we apply them to our Morals, which we call spiritualizing; explain them?

Ans. The 24 Inch Gauge represents the 24 Hours of the Day.

Mas. How do you spend them Brother?

Ans. Six Hours to work in, Six Hours to serve God, and Six to serve a Friend or a Brother, as far as lies in my Power, without being detrimental to myself or Family: and Six Hours to Sleep in.

There are no explanations of tools for the F.C. or M.M. but in the Hiramic legend the ruffians now use the 24 Inch Gauge, the Square and the Gavel or Setting Maul.

The main period of the development in the elaboration of our ritual was in the last quarter of the 18th century, which was its most fruitful period. In 1801, Preston, in his Installation ceremony, listed the Rule, Line, Trowel, Chisel, Plumb, Level, Square, Compasses and Mallet, in that order, and 'moralized' each of them very briefly, in words which would be very familiar to us today. The best of that material was brought into our ritual at the time of the Union of the Grand Lodges in 1813 and shortly afterwards.

---

80. TUBAL-CAIN

Q. Why does Tubal-cain, an artificer in metals, play such a prominent part in our ritual? Why was not a builder chosen—or at least someone connected with the art of building?

A. For a full answer to this question, we have to go back to the oldest documents of the Craft, the *MS. Constitutions*, but first we should glance at the Biblical background to the story, which appears in Gen. IV, vv. 16–22.

The Bible tells how Cain, having murdered his brother, escaped from Eden to Nod, where his wife bore him a son, Enoch. Cain then built, or started to build, a city and, knowing himself to be accursed, he named it after his son Enoch. The succeeding verses then recount the birth of Enoch's grandson, Lamech, with the story of Lamech's two wives, and their four children:

Jabal, the father, or the originator, of the science of tending flocks. (Abel had been a shepherd, but Jabal had widened the class of animals that could be domesticated.)

Jubal, founder of the art of music.

Tubal-cain, inventor of the forge, skilled in brass and ironwork and in cutting instruments.

Naamah. The O.T. text simply names her as Lamech's daughter, but a Jewish tradition arose, and was well established among historians in the middle ages, that she was the inventor of the arts of weaving and other related skills.

So much for the background, amplified slightly with notes from the early commentaries. The story, in so far as it concerns our present ritual, is derived from the earliest pillar legend incorporated in the historical portion of the *MS. Constitutions*, our *Old Charges*. It tells how the four children of Lamech, fearing that the world was to be destroyed by fire or flood, 'took counsel together' and decided to inscribe 'all the sciences' that they had founded, upon two pillars, one of marble and the other of 'lacerus' (clay-brick), because the one would not burn and the other would not sink in water.

There is no need to discuss the 'accuracy' of the legend. Josephus gave one version of it in his *Antiquities*, and the story reappears in the writings of many of the medieval historians. The earliest 'Masonic' version appears in the *Cooke MS.* of *c.* 1410, where the compiler had clearly attempted to reconcile several conflicting accounts, but the *Cooke MS.* legend was repeated regularly (with variations) in all subsequent versions of the *MS. Constitutions*.

These two pillars, *not Solomon's*, were the earliest pillars in the legendary history of the Craft and our story then goes on to recount how the world was saved in Noah's flood and how the science of masonry travelled from the east through Egypt into Europe and was finally established in England.

Why was not a builder chosen? Doubtless because the first builder of a city, according to the O.T., was Cain, a murderer.

Why Tubal-cain? I would say, because he was the forerunner of H.A.; indeed the O.T. (Gen. IV, v. 22, and I Kings VII, v. 14) uses precisely the same two Hebrew words in describing their craft, [*choreish nechosheth*] 'a worker in brass'. Tubal-cain was the founder of the craft in which H.A., above all, excelled and he was the direct link between the two earliest pillars and those of Solomon's Temple.

Although the name Tubal-cain appears regularly in all our *Old Charges*, it should be noted that the name did not come into our *ritual* until a comparatively late date, *c.* 1745; there is no printed evidence of that name *in the Masonic ritual* earlier than 1745, but recently discovered transcripts of evidence given to the Portuguese Inquisition authorities suggest that the name was in use in a Lodge of Irishmen at Lisbon as early as 1738. (*AQC* 84, p. 93.)

---

81.   CROSSING THE FEET

Q. In many workings of the Sublime Degree, the Candidate is required to cross the feet. Is there any particular reason for this? It makes the subsequent movements very difficult.

A. This is, indeed, a most curious practice for which, after many enquiries, no satisfactory reason can be found. There are two so-called explanations, one practical, the other symbolical, but neither of them is really convincing.

The 'practical' explanation argues that the unbalanced posture of the Candidate makes it easier for the Wardens to manoeuvre him during the subsequent 'movements'. This is simply not true. There are only three 'movements' in this part of the ceremony; if the Candidate has his feet crossed, the first of them is very awkward and uncomfortable—and the second is quite impossible. The unbalanced posture may perhaps make it easier to carry out the third 'movement'; but with an experienced officer on either side of the Candidate, he could surely be guided to play his part by a whispered command, as he does in other parts of the ceremonies.

The symbolical 'explanation' is that the Candidate during those moments in the ceremony, represents Christ on the Cross. There may be grounds for believing that this was the position of the feet for crucifixion—I do not know—but whether it was or not, to require the Candidate to adopt the posture *for that reason* is a near approach to blasphemy. Moreover, if this is indeed a piece of Christian symbolism, it is contrary to the principle—adopted for the best of reasons—that the Masonic ritual must be strictly non-sectarian.

On the basis that the 'crossed feet' may have a Christian significance, that practice has been abandoned in several English Lodges that have a mainly Jewish membership.

There have been other tentative suggestions as to why the feet are crossed, e.g., it may derive from the view held by Lessing that the ancients depicted Death by the figure of a man outstretched, with his feet crossed. Even if this were so, there is surely no need for the Can-

didate to cross his feet several minutes too early. Other students have
noted that statues on many Crusader tombs depict their occupants with
the feet crossed; doubtless this is another Christian symbol, but our
Candidates are not Crusaders—and Crusaders did not habitually *stand*
with their feet crossed, however they were buried!

None of these 'suggestions' seems adequate to explain why the standing Candidate should be required to cross his feet.

A search through the early English and French exposures has failed
to reveal the slightest hint of anything in their texts which would have
made this posture necessary. One French exposure alone suggests some
peculiar arrangement of the feet while the Candidate was laying outstretched on the floor. This note appears in *Le Maçon Démasqué* (1751).
It was translated into English as *Solomon In All His Glory*, and published in London in 1766 with several subsequent English, Scottish and
Irish editions. In those days the Candidate was *not* required to cross his
feet but the text says that after he was 'thrown', his right foot was placed
upon his left knee so as to form a square.

> . . . & *mon pied droit posé sur le genou gauche pour former une équerre.*

It may be noted that even here the Candidate did not actually *cross* the
feet and a study of other texts which describe the subsequent raising
indicates, almost certainly, that the foot was placed in this curious position to facilitate the actual raising.

An examination of numerous modern rituals has also failed to reveal
any ritualistic reason why the Candidate should be kept in this uncomfortable posture and, although many modern rituals contain the
rubric 'The Candidate is directed to c . . . . his f . . .', it is interesting
to notice that Claret's ritual contained no such note and the same
applies to Carlile's exposure.

It has been suggested that the rubric really means that the Candidate
is to 'calm his fears'. An ingenious solution, but I do not believe it for
one moment and, if the Candidate at this late stage has to be told to
calm his fears, I would assume that the Deacons have been doing their
job very badly up to that point.

Finally, I join in the opinions of Bros. E. H. Cartwright and W. B.
Hextall that the practice of crossing the feet, at any stage in the
ceremony, is most objectionable and completely unnecessary.

82.   THE MASTER'S LIGHT

Q. I have heard of an old regulation that the Master's Light must never be extinguished, shaded or obscured, and that no lanthorn or substitute device is permitted. Does that rule still apply? All our lighting is by electricity and we shade the Master's Light in the Third Degree.

A. The rule was made in 1816, and was subsequently confirmed in a letter in 1839 from the then Grand Secretary, William H. White. The Grand Lodge reprinted that letter recently as an answer to a similar question, and extracts are reproduced here by kind permission of the Board of General Purposes.

FREEMASONS' HALL,
7th December, 1839.

DEAR SIR AND BROTHER,

In reply to your questions as to the propriety of extinguishing the Master's Light, and if extinguished, of introducing a Lanthorn with a Star, &c., I feel no difficulty of stating that such extinguishment is not only improper, but positively in violation of a most maturely considered and unequivocal direction of the Grand Lodge, and that the introduction of a Lanthorn, &c., is equally against the order.

In the Lodge of Reconciliation, the extinguishment had been proposed, and occasioned much dissatisfaction; in order, therefore, to settle that, and some other points, . . . a Special Grand Lodge was convened on the 20th May, 1816, to witness the ceremonies proposed by the Lodge of Reconciliation. These concluded, the several points were discussed; amongst others, the Lights in the third degree: and decisions were come to upon them. But . . . to leave the subject without a possiblity of objection, another Special Grand Lodge was holden on the 5th June following, to approve and confirm what had been done on the 20th May. . . .

The decision was, that the Master's Light was never to be extinguished while the Lodge was open, nor was it by any means to be shaded or obscured, and that no Lanthorn or other device was to be permitted as a substitute.

One of the reasons is, that one of the Lights represents the Master, who is always present while the Lodge is open, if not actually in his own person, yet by a Brother who represents him (and without the Master or his representative the Lodge cannot be open), so his Light cannot be extinguished until the Lodge is closed; the two other lights figuratively represent luminaries, which, at periods, are visible—at other times, not so. . . .

[Signed William H. White, G.S.]

At the time when this ruling was confirmed, electric lighting was unheard of and even gas was not in general use. Apparently the 'Lanthorn' was introduced as part of the business of arranging for a flood of light to appear at the moment when the W.M. made reference to the 'Bright (and) Morning Star'. Indeed, we have received several letters from elderly Brethren, who, in their Masonic youth, were charged with the duty of exposing the full brilliance of the 'Lanthorn' at the requisite moment.

Nothing could have been more surely designed to ruin the ceremony at the moment of its greatest solemnity, and it is good to know that this wholly deplorable practice has largely disappeared nowadays.

The old ruling still holds and, since the essence of the ceremony requires minimum illumination by a glimmering ray, arrangements can perhaps be made so that the W.M.'s Light—a lighted candle—be installed, when a Third Degree is to be conferred.

---

83.   MASONIC AFTER-PROCEEDINGS
          TOASTING PRACTICES IN THE LONDON AREA

INTRODUCTION

The following article is primarily the result of dozens of questions on individual points of procedure, which were always answered by letter. But there were also several requests for a more detailed description and two recent letters from Germany and the U.S.A., asking for the complete programme, prompted me to undertake a full-length paper, in the hope that it would satisfy our inquirers and prove a useful guide for prospective Masters of Lodges.

It must be emphasized, however, that the whole article is the result of personal experience *mainly in the London area* and, since our practices are not uniform, there will be many items that do not agree with well-established customs in some Lodges. I would not wish to change them, but I make no apology for expressing my own opinions because that is what I was invited to do.

In the U.S.A. and in several European countries, our English 'After-proceedings' are usually known as the 'Table Lodge' or the 'White Table' and they may sometimes include a Masonic catechism at Table, in the manner that was customary in the 18th century. No kind of Masonic ritual or catechism is permitted at Table in English Craft practice.

Experience as a Preceptor has shown that, although most of the Officers and Members of English Lodges are familiar with 'Table-procedure', they are usually all at sea when the time comes at last to handle the gavel at Table, and for many years past I have made it a practice to devote several hours of private tuition to each Master-elect, so that he arrives at the top Table adequately prepared for his duties and responsibilities. Any Officer who is anxious to do so can easily master the Lodge Ritual and procedure because, for years before he reaches the Chair, he actually takes part in the work. But it is far more difficult, without proper training, to conduct the Table proceedings with dignity and with proper attention to all the formalities and courtesies which are the distinguishing mark of a real Master. It is to those Brethren almost within reach of the Chair that my notes are mainly addressed, in the hope that they may prove a practical guide to the things that should be done and, even more important, to the pitfalls that should be avoided.

SEATING

The preparations for the Table work actually begin after the first or second rising in Lodge when the Stewards ask permission to retire in order to prepare for the comfort of the Brethren. This procedure is heartily recommended, especially at important meetings when it is necessary to see that seating etc. has been properly arranged for the principal guests.

The Tables on these occasions are usually arranged in the form of a top Table with sprigs, and the recommended seating at top Table is as follows:[1]

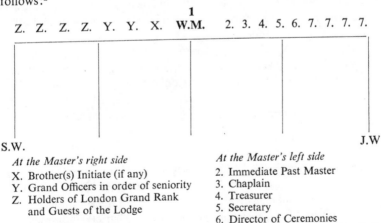

1

Z. Z. Z. Z. Y. Y. X. **W.M.**   2. 3. 4. 5. 6. 7. 7. 7. 7.

S.W.   J.W

At the Master's right side   *At the Master's left side*
X. Brother(s) Initiate (if any)   2. Immediate Past Master
Y. Grand Officers in order of seniority   3. Chaplain
Z. Holders of London Grand Rank   4. Treasurer
   and Guests of the Lodge   5. Secretary
                                      6. Director of Ceremonies
                                      7. Past Masters in order of seniority

[1] All seating is described as viewed by the Master from his place at the centre of the top Table.

The Senior Warden is seated at the head of the extreme right-hand sprig, i.e., farthest away on the right of the W.M. The Junior Warden is placed correspondingly, farthest away on the left of the W.M. The head places of the central sprigs are usually occupied by the Steward and Senior Past Masters, or Officers, if so desired.

RECEIVING THE W.M.

In the course of my travels in the Provinces I have noticed that the D.C. plays an important part in the Table procedure, i.e., in calling for order, announcing the speakers, and often conducting the 'Fire', etc. In London, however, this work is generally divided between the Master and the I.P.M. With nearly 1700 Lodges in the London area alone, it is obvious that there will be occasional variations in practice. These notes are intended to portray the customs generally in use in the London area; they do not lay down the law, nor is it claimed that these practices are 'right' and others 'wrong'. At best it is hoped that they will serve as a guide to procedure in the absence of any previously-established practice.

After leaving the Temple, the Brethren generally spend a few minutes at refreshment and, at the proper moment, the D.C. will ask them to take their places at Table. The Master waits until the D.C. announces 'To order Brethren to receive the Worshipful Master' and the Brethren applaud as he escorts the W.M. to his chair. In this connection, the funereal slow clapping, which is often heard at some Lodge banquets is, in my opinion, a practice to be avoided; it is a very dismal affair and I can find no authority for it.

In my youth it was customary for the Brethren to dine in full Masonic clothing; this rule was later relaxed, and Officers (and others so entitled) were permitted to wear their Collars only. Since World War II it has become customary to wear no Masonic regalia at Table, but for large gatherings it is sometimes helpful if the Stewards wear their Collars.

GRACE

Arrived at his chair, the W.M. sounds the gavel, one knock only, and says, 'Brethren, pray silence for Grace by Brother Chaplain'. If the Lodge has no Chaplain, the Master will say Grace himself, and it should consist of a short and simple formula, strictly non-sectarian. The following is a familiar example:

> For what we are about to receive may the GAOTU give us grateful hearts and keep us ever mindful of the needs of others.

The Gavel

This is perhaps the proper moment to add a note on the use of the gavel at Table. It will be sounded at intervals throughout the evening, usually with a single knock and, if order is to be maintained, the sound of the gavel must be respected. There should be a hardwood striking block for the gavel, so that it makes a sharp 'click'. A gavel sounded on a table-cloth is muffled and this causes the Master to strike much harder than is necessary. When there is a very large gathering, or if the Brethren are inclined to be boisterous, it is very helpful if the D.C. walks round the various tables with a quiet word to ensure proper attention, and the Brethren seated at the heads of the sprigs can also play their part. *It should never be necessary for the Master or I.P.M., or the D.C. to remind the Brethren aloud that they must respect the gavel.*

Another point, no less important; the amount of attention that the Master gets does not depend on the amount of noise he makes. The Brethren will be silent out of respect to him and the W.M. who makes the china bounce every time he uses his 'emblem of power' is not only deafening his friends and neighbours; he is admitting—publicly—that he does not know how to keep order. When the Master, or I.P.M., stands, there should be silence; experience will teach them not to attempt to speak above a din, but to wait a moment until the Brethren are attentive. But it is a good rule—as far as possible—to avoid the use (or abuse) of the gavel. (Wardens always 'reply' to the W.M.'s gavel, one knock each.)

'Taking Wine'

In some Lodges it is customary, soon after the meal has begun, for the W.M. to rise, sound his gavel, and ask,

> 'Bro. Wardens, how do you report your respective Columns'?
> The S.W replies, 'All charged in the West, W.M.'
> The J.W. replies, 'All charged in the South, W.M.'

If, however, the glasses are *not* 'all charged', this occasions some delay, and it seems preferable that the D.C. or Steward should signal to the W.M., as soon as the glasses are charged, and thus avoid disturbing the assembly with unnecessary 'procedure'.

During the meal, i.e., between courses, it is customary for the Master to take wine with the Wardens, the Grand Officers, and all the Brethren. The announcements are made by the I.P.M., in a single sentence, e.g.:

'Brethren, the W.M. will take wine with the Wardens' or 'Brethren, the W.M. will be pleased to take wine with you all, and requests that you remain seated'.

Unfortunately this pleasant practice has somehow grown out of hand in recent years and these little courtesies have become a series of constant and noisy interruptions to the dinner, serving also as a brake on pleasant conversation. I have seen 'Take Wine' lists running into more than twenty items, an unbearable chore for the Master, the I.P.M., and for the Brethren who have to endure them.

Nowadays, the official view is that these 'Take Wines' *should be kept to the minimum*. In addition to the three items mentioned above, the Master *on Installation night* might take wine with the Installing Master; *on initiation nights*, with the new Initiate, and if one of the members of the Lodge has been honoured—since the last meeting—by promotion to Grand or London Grand Rank, that would be a good reason for adding one more item. But it is fatally easy to extend the list to maddening lengths, and every effort should be made to spare the Brethren this readily avoidable nuisance. I would recommend that *never more than four or five of the items be used in any one evening*, and it is often possible to combine two or three items at one rising.

Smoking is not permitted at English Masonic banquets until after the final Grace has been said and the first two Toasts have been honoured. To avoid undue hardship for those Brethren who are eager to light up, it is customary to call for Grace before coffee is served. For this purpose the waiters and waitresses are asked to retire and the Tyler ensures that the doors are closed. (The 'Take Wine' list is used only *during* dinner and none are taken after the final Grace has been given.)

GRACE AFTER MEALS

The Dining-room is Tyled and the W.M. gavels and calls 'Brethren, pray silence for Grace'. All rise. If the Grace is sung, the Organist strikes the first signal-note; but usually the Master or Chaplain says the customary words, roughly as follows:

For what we have received may the **GAOTU** give us grateful hearts.

The keynote should be simplicity and brevity and this implies a warning that only the expert should dare 'to be different'.

THE LOYAL TOAST, THE TOAST LIST AND FIRE

(I) Grace being ended, the Brethren are seated and the W.M. rises again for the first Toast. In many London Lodges it is customary for the Wardens to rise at the same time as the Master to honour the Toast, i.e., *the three principal Officers of the Lodge are standing while the Toast is proposed*, and the Wardens stand for all Toasts up to, and including, the 'Toast to the Worshipful Master'. (They are seated, of course, during the replies.) I do not know the original reason for this practice which—in my own Lodges—is an inherited custom, but I am sure that the three dominant standing figures help to keep order and add a degree of importance and dignity to the Master's words.

The W.M. gavels, and S.W. and J.W. reply with a single knock each. W.M. 'Brethren, I give you [pause] "The Queen and the Craft".' All rise and drink. The W.M. continues, 'Good Fire, Brethren,[1] and take the time from me'. He recites at a smart pace, marking time with his finger (in the air) 'P.L.R., P.L.R., P.L.R., One, Two!' and the Brethren complete the triad with a clap and then three times three.[2] At this moment the organist strikes the signal note for 'God save the Queen', after which the Brethren are seated. (See Q. 94.)

It should be noted that the whole object of the Master's verbal introduction to the 'Fire' is to create the proper rhythm. Some Masters prefer to wave the gavel instead of a finger-tip, and in that case the 'One, Two'—is given as 'One, Two, Bang!' At most, the W.M. should never sound the gavel more than once during the Fire, and if he makes a good clear rhythm with the P.L.R.s, giving the word 'Two' smartly *on a higher note than the 'One'*, the timing is by then so well established that the Brethren will complete the exercise without need for the sound of the gavel. A couple of private rehearsals of the 'Fire'-procedure with the Master-Elect are well worth while, because they give him the requisite self-assurance and command of his audience. (Serving-staff and non-Masons are excluded during the 'Fire'. All doors are closed, and the room is Tyled, but the Tyler usually remains inside.)

The Loyal Toast is always given *tout simple*, with a minimum of words. It is not necessary to make a speech extolling the royal virtues, and any such embroidery is considered to be improper. The same rule applies to the next Toast which is likwise given only by the W.M.

(II) Brethren, I give you the Toast to the Most Worshipful The Grand Master, His Royal Highness The Duke of Kent, G.C.M.G., G.C.V.O. A.D.C.[3] [The Brethren rise and drink, and the W.M. continues:] 'Good Fire, Brethren, and take the time from me', etc.

---

[1] Some say 'Quick Fire', but 'Good Fire' is preferable.
[2] This is a description of the Fire as given in London. In the Provinces and in the Commonwealth there are many and substantial variations. (See pp. 125–6.)
[3] Generally, only the principal title is recited, in full, i.e., not initials.

The printed Toast Lists often show several of the Grand Master's titles and honours, usually ending with &c., &c., &c., &c., and one sometimes hears inexperienced Masters reciting them all, including the four 'et ceteras'. This is quite unnecessary and it verges on the absurd; only the senior title need be used, and when the fire is finished the W.M. rises and gives the Brethren permission to smoke. Coffee is served and it gives the gathering a welcome opportunity for conversation.

This is perhaps the best moment to emphasize that the Brethren are assembled primarily for the pleasures of companionship and not for an interminable series of speeches, which are all too often repetitious and boring. The W.M., in conjunction with the Secretary or D.C., should arrange the programme so as to get the best possible speakers *for the minimum number of Toasts*. All avoidable Toasts should be omitted and, in those which call for a response, only one good speaker should be chosen for that honour. If this practice is followed, the Brethren are able to enjoy the speeches, and will not be doomed to sit silent throughout the evening. A well-managed programme must allow time for intervals between the Toasts.

> (III) The third Toast is to: The M.W. The Pro Grand Master, The Rt. Hon. The Earl Cadogan, *M.C., D.L.*, the R.W. The Deputy Grand Master, Maj.-Gen. Sir Allan Adair, Bt., *K.C.V.O., C.B., D.S.O., M.C., D.L.*, the R.W. The Assistant Grand Master, The Hon. Fiennes Cornwallis, *O.B.E.*, with the rest of the Grand Officers Present and Past.[1]

If there are no Grand Officers present, this will be followed by the 'Fire', and there will be no reply to the Toast. If one or more are present, the W.M. would add a few words to the Toast, roughly as follows:

> Brethren, we are honoured this evening by the presence of eminent and distinguished Grand Officers, and I have much pleasure in coupling with

---

[1] For the benefit of our foreign readers, I hasten to explain that the word 'Past' does not refer to Grand Officers who are deceased, but to those who hold *Past* Grand Rank. They are made up of two distinct groups:

(a) Brethren who have served in *active* Office within the Grand Lodge, and have completed their terms, now retain their title with the additional word 'Past', e.g., a Junior Grand Deacon becomes Past Junior Grand Deacon, and an Assistant Grand Director of Ceremonies becomes Past Assistant Grand Director of Ceremonies.

(b) Because it is impossible to provide active Office for all the Brethren who qualify for promotion, it has been customary for more than 150 years for the Grand Masters to confer Past Grand Rank on the vast majority of Grand Officers; they hold Grand *rank* in recognition of their general services to the Craft, but they have *not served any Office* within the Grand Lodge.

this toast the name of Worshipful Brother . . . (adding details of his Grand Rank in full, NOT initial letters). Good Fire, Brethren, etc., etc.

Note, the rule is that *there is only one reply to this Toast*, and that honour *must be offered to the senior Grand Officer present.* It would be an affront to him if anyone else is asked to reply. Occasionally the senior Grand Officer may ask to be excused and then—and only then—is it permissible to couple with the Toast the name of a Grand Officer of lower rank. If the Master wishes to have two Grand Officers replying to Toasts, the junior must be coupled with the Toast to the Guests.

The first three Toasts detailed above are the obligatory Toasts. On Initiation night, the 'Toast to the Initiate' is an essential courtesy, but all other Toasts are purely optional—at the Master's discretion.

On Installation nights, there will often be a Grand Officer present who comes as a representative of one of the Masonic Institutions, specifically for the purpose of launching the Master's appeal. If he is the senior Grand Officer in attendance, he will automatically reply for Grand Lodge and make his appeal in that reply. If he is not the senior, it is advisable to insert, later in the programme, a special Toast 'To the Masonic Charities', and to couple the representative of the Institution with that Toast.

[In the Provinces, there would now follow a series of Toasts to the Provincial Grand Master and the Provincial Grand Officers, but these need not concern us here.]

(IV) The next Toast on a London programme is to The Holders of London Grand Rank (and the Provincial and District Grand Officers).

The portion in brackets is a courtesy which may be included or omitted at the Master's pleasure. On evenings when there is a long list of speeches, it is highly advisable that there should be no reply to this Toast. Indeed, I suggest that it is a useful general rule that the only time when there should be a reply, is when one of the members of the Lodge has been recently honoured by promotion to London Grand Rank. This gives the W.M. the opportunity—in proposing the Toast— to thank the Brother for his services to the Lodge; and the Brother, in replying, is thus enabled to thank the Lodge for having nominated him, and for the Regalia which has doubtless been presented to him that evening.

By long-standing custom, all the Toasts, hitherto, will have been proposed by the W.M. The first and second are always given by the Master, but in some Lodges, the subsequent Toasts are entrusted to senior Past Masters.

THE TOAST TO THE W.M.

Now it is the turn of the I.P.M. who gavels and rises (with the Wardens) to propose the health of the W.M., and here—as always—brevity is the soul of wit. In the course of the year, the I.P.M. will have to give the Toast five or six times in London (and even more often in the Provinces) and, except on Installation night, a single sentence made up of well-chosen words is far more suitable than an oration. In this connection, two speeches I recall which, following a flood of oratory, almost brought the house down, consisted of

> I.P.M. 'Brethren, the Master' (Fire).
> W M. 'Brethren—I thank you'.

On Installation night, however, this principle does not apply, since it is the I.P.M.'s duty to convey the good wishes of the Brethren to the new W.M. Still, brevity and sincerity should be the keynote and a touch of good humour makes excellent seasoning.

In many London Lodges it is customary, *on Installation night only*, to sing the Master's song 'Here's to his health in a Song', and this is done immediately after the Toast, and before the W.M. replies. The three verses are usually sung by a professional singer (or a competent member of the Lodge). *The Brethren should remain seated throughout*, except when *they rise to sing the final chorus*. For the benefit of our foreign readers, the procedure is as follows. The leading singer stands at the head of the sprig facing the W.M., and begins the song. About halfway through the first verse, he walks, glass in hand to the J.W., who rises, and their glasses touch as the singer gives the first chorus 'Here's to his health . . .' The singer returns to his position at the centre-sprig for the second verse, but this time he touches glasses with the S.W. For the third verse and before he reaches the chorus, he walks alongside the centre sprig, right up to the W.M., and both Wardens (walking round the tables towards the W.M., by the shortest route) join the W.M. so that they form a sort of triangle round the W.M.; for the refrain, all the Brethren rise, lift their glasses, join in the chorus, and call 'Worshipful Master' before drinking his health. It is indeed a most impressive and often moving ceremony, and a quite unforgettable experience for the Master.

The Master in his reply should confine himself to the items of Lodge business that need to be mentioned, and the proper courtesies suitable to the occasion. When he has covered those points, and without sitting down, he continues, 'And now . . .' and goes on to give the Toast to

The Immediate Past and Installing Master.

This Toast is given only once in the year, on Installation night. It should be brief and sincere; a few 'golden words' are far better than a long eulogy, and the Brethren are always more responsive when their endurance is not taxed!

TOAST TO THE INITIATE

On Initiation nights, the next Toast in order of seniority and importance is The Toast to the Initiate. By long-standing custom this Toast is given by one of the senior Past Masters and now the brevity rule may well be relaxed. Of all the Toasts on a normal Masonic programme, this is the one that most needs and deserves proper preparation and brings the greatest benefits, both to the Initiate and to the Lodge. It is an honour that should be entrusted only into mature and competent hands.

TO 'OUR GUESTS' OR 'THE VISITING BRETHREN'

For the next Toast 'Our Guests', or 'The Visiting Brethren', the mood changes, and it is often given in light-hearted fashion. Here again, a competent speaker should be chosen to propose the Toast, and skill rather than seniority should be the qualification. In the years of my Masonic youth, it was customary to have three or four Brethren reply to this Toast, a hardship to the listeners as well as to the third and fourth speakers, whose thunder had invariably been stolen by earlier responders. Nowadays, one reply is considered sufficient (or two at the most, and then only for compelling reasons).

TO ABSENT BRETHREN

The Toast to 'Absent Brethren' is followed by the 'Fire'. It is usually given at 9 o'clock (but that is custom, not law). This Toast is simply a means of maintaining a fraternal and spiritual link with the Brethren who cannot be present.

THE TYLER'S TOAST

This would complete the normal after-proceedings for the majority of full-length Masonic banquets, and the W.M. with two rapid knocks calls for the Tyler's Toast.

The Tyler standing behind the W.M. pronounces the time-honoured words:

Brethren, By command of the W.M. I give you the Tyler's Toast: To all poor and distressed Freemasons wherever scattered over the face of land or sea; wishing them a speedy relief from all their sufferings and a safe return to their native land if they so desire.

The Brethren rise and drink to the Toast and the Tyler leads the 'Fire'.

A few words of advice in conclusion. It is often said that the English take their pleasures sadly and, Heaven knows, they do! But it is the duty of the W.M. and his advisers to ensure that the Table-procedure is interesting, entertaining and instructive, and a well-managed evening can be made very pleasant indeed. It is a golden rule to cut unnecessary speeches; the time thus saved may well be used for a ten-minute talk on some subject of Masonic interest given by a Brother who can command attention.

Our Table customs, the fruits of age-old traditions, are an example to Masons under all jurisdictions. They show at their best when kept within due bounds.

---

84.   SEPULCHRE OR SEPULTURE?

Q. In the Traditional History in the third degree, we use the word 'Sepulture', but I gather that other workings say 'Sepulchre'. Will you please comment?

A. The word appears in our rituals always as a noun, e.g., '. . . to such a sepulchre [sepulture] as became his exalted rank and talents . . .' Both forms are rarely used nowadays, except, as the *Oxford English Dictionary* says, in a rhetorical or historical context, defining the words as follows:

> Sepulchre = A tomb or burial place, a building, vault, or excavation made for the interment of a human body.
>
> Sepulture = A burial place, grave, or tomb.

Thus far, the two words have virtually identical meanings and they both refer to a *place or structure* used for interment. (*O.E.D.* also shows that both words may be used as verbs, to denote *the action* of burying or interment; but this usage need not concern us here, because our context indicates that we only use the noun.)

But the word 'sepulture' has yet another extended meaning (which is not borne by 'sepulchre'), and the former may also be used to denote *interment or burial*. Thus, both words mean a *place* of burial, but 'sepulture' also means the actual *ceremony or procedure of a burial*, and the *Pocket Oxford Dictionary* gives the definition, *a burying*.

Here is a very substantial difference in meaning between the two words and it is impossible to say which is to be preferred, because we do not know precisely what was in the minds of those who introduced the term. We can test this by reading the relevant passage in the ritual, using the definitions in place of the original words:

> Solomon ordered the body of our Master '. . . to be raised to such a tomb [or burial place] as became his exalted rank and talents . . .' or, 'to be raised to such a [ceremonial] interment as became his . . .'

Thus, though the meanings are different, both 'sepulchre' and 'sepulture' would make sense, and it is not possible to say that either form is wrong.

The question has prompted me to try to ascertain the earliest use of either of those words in English Masonic Ritual, and the following brief details will show, as one might expect, that they are a comparatively modern introduction.

Masonry Dissected, 1730, the earliest description of a Raising, says that Solomon ordered H.A. to be 'decently buried', and he was interred in the Sanctum Sanctorum.

The principal exposures of the late 18th century, i.e., *Three Distinct Knocks, J. and B., Hiram,* and *Mahhabone,* all say that he was buried '. . . in the Sanctum Sanctorum . . .' and it is remarkable that this absurd blunder was never rectified even in the much-used *J. and B.* Only one text, *Solomon in all his Glory,* itself a translation from a French text of 1751, omits the Sanctum Sanctorum, and says that H.A. was buried with '. . . magnificent obsequies . . . [and] great funereal pomp . . .'

Preston, in his 'Third Lecture of Free Masonry', (*AQC* 85, p. 93) was unusually reticent in his description of Hiram's interment. He did not use the words 'sepulchre' or 'sepulture', nor did he give any dimensions for the grave; but he did avoid the blunder about the Sanctum Sanctorum:

> Solomon then commanded the necessary preparations . . . for the pompous interment of H . . . A . . ., which took place as near the sanctum sanctorum as the Jewish law would admit.

Masonry Dissected seems to be the earliest text, 1730, that gave measurements for the grave, '6 Foot East, 6 West, and 6 Foot perpendicular', but this was a 'handsome Grave' in which the assassins had buried H.A. There are no such details for his final burial.

The first text I can find using the word 'sepulchre' is Carlile's *Republican* of 29 July 1825:

'. . . to such a sepulchre as became his rank and exalted talents . . . He was not buried in the S . . . S . . . because . . .' etc., and the measurements are now '. . . three feet East, three feet West . . .' etc.

It seems certain that our present-day forms of this portion of the ritual did not come into use until after the Union, in 1813.

---

85.   THE W.M.'S SIGN DURING THE OBLIGATIONS

Q. (1) Does the W.M. remove his sign during the Ob.?

(2) When does he remove it after the Ob.?

(3) Which sign should he use?

A. (1) He removes his sign during the Ob., while the Candidate utters the words '. . . hereby and hereon . . .' and his r . . . h . . ., rests momentarily on the Candidate's fingers and on the V.S.L. (I prefer that his hand remains during the next few words until '. . . swear'). He then resumes his sign until the end of the Ob.

(2) He removes the sign after the Candidate has sealed the Ob. (Note, the Ob. is not finished until it has been sealed.)

(3) Some Lodges use the Sn. of Fidelity; others use the 'Stand to order' sign of the degree that is being conferred.

Lodge practices differ considerably on all these points, and it would not be difficult to find good arguments to justify the various usages. There is no official directive on the subject and the practice of individual Lodges is usually based on the rubrics (if any) in the printed rituals that they follow. Unfortunately, the rubrics are often inadequate, or insufficiently clear.

On Q. 3, experience suggests that the most popular usage over the length and breadth of England is the Sn. of Fidelity for all three Obligations, and I favour this practice, primarily, for its suitability, since it implies that all the Brethren participate in the Obligations.

Arising from the three replies given above several letters were received from Brethren using the *Emulation Ritual*, who protested, more or less forcibly, that the answer was wrong according to their teachings, and that Emulation practice should have been quoted as well.

There is a simple answer to this, and it is perhaps necessary to emphasize that all the questions answered in the Q.C. Summonses and in the *AQC* Supplements during my term as Editor were genuine questions that came from Brethren in many different parts of the world, and they related to an untold number of different 'workings'.

In *c.* 1965, I made a survey of Grand Lodge records of the Ritual 'workings' used in Lodges of Instruction *in the London area alone* and I found some eighteen different 'named workings' plus nine Lodges that claimed to be using 'their own working', i.e., twenty-seven different versions in the London area. There are many more in the Provinces, where it seems that every large centre claims to work its own peculiar forms, e.g., York, Sussex, Bristol, Oxford, Exeter, Humber, etc. This multiplicity of 'workings' was bound to govern our practice in dealing with questions of this kind, especially as 'catalogue' answers covering only a selection of the best-known rituals would have become unbearably dull.

Generally, when an enquirer asked about the procedure under a 'named working', every effort would be made to furnish the precise information required; but, where no specific Ritual was mentioned, it would have been idle to quote *Emulation*, or any other 'named working', each of which is usually deemed to be the most important of all by its adherents. In such cases, our answers, whether by letter or in print, were based mainly on study and experience.

Finally, and despite my own views, I am glad to quote the *Emulation* practice in relation to Q. 3, above:

1° Ob. All stand with Sp. and E.A. Sn.
2° Ob. All stand with Sp. and Sn. of F.
3° Ob. All rise with Sp. and M.M. P.Sn.

It is hoped that this will satisfy the Brethren who feel that they have been neglected.

---

86. DEACONS AS MESSENGERS

Q. In the Opening of the Lodge in the first degree—and in the Investiture of the Deacons—we are told that their duties are, *inter alia*, 'to carry messages and communications' to the J.W., or 'to bear messages and commands to the S.W.'. In fact, they never discharge any such duties. Why did those words come into the Ritual?

A. By long standing tradition, the Deacons are the 'Messengers' of the Lodge, and the earliest versions of the Deacon's Jewel or Badge consisted of a 'winged Mercury', the messenger of the gods. (Incidentally there are some beautiful examples in the Grand Lodge Museum, and several of our old Lodges still use them, in place of the 'dove'.)

It is certain that from *c.* 1760 onwards the Deacons—in English practice—actually performed some of these duties, i.e., there were certain portions of the ceremonies in which the W.M. sent a whispered message by the S.D. to the S.W., and the latter passed it on by the J.D. to the J.W. We have a perfect example of this in *Three Distinct Knocks*, an exposure of 1760, where the practice was in use for 'Calling On' and 'Calling Off'. (It was subsequently repeated in the popular *J. & B.*)

> The Master whispers to the senior Deacon at his Right-hand, and says, 'tis my Will and Pleasure that this Lodge is called off from Work to Refreshment during Pleasure'; then the senior Deacon carries it to the senior Warden, and whispers the same Words in his Ear, and he whispers it in the Ear of the junior Deacon at his Right-hand, and he carries it to the junior Warden, and whispers the same to him, who declares it with a loud Voice, . . .

The words have survived in the ritual, though the practice has disappeared from the majority of our English workings. It is likely, however, that some relics of it have survived in Europe and in the U.S.A. The present New York opening in the third degree contains the same duties for S.D. and J.D., and when the W.M. asks the S.W. if all present are M.M.s, the S.W. answers:

> 'I will ascertain *through my proper officer* and report.'

The S.W. then asks the J.D. the same question, a procedure which is clearly allied to the message-bearing duties.

Following the first appearance of the above notes several letters were received quoting instances in which communication between the W.M. and Wardens is still conducted *through the Deacons*, in accordance with the details given in the ceremony of Opening the Lodge.

The first is the case of a Lodge in which the W.M. and the Wardens all sign the Minutes. The S.D. carries the Minute-book to the W.M. and then to the S.W. After the S.W. has signed, the J.D. carries the book to the J.W. and after the latter has signed it, the J.D. takes it back to S.W. and the S.D. returns it to the Secretary's table.

Other instances arise under Rules 94 and 208(b) of the *Book of Constitutions*, when the W.M. and Wardens are required to sign their recommendation, in open Lodge, to the Petition for a Warrant for a new Lodge, or to Petitions addressed to the Board of Benevolence; but examples under these headings are comparatively rare.

87. THE EXPOSURES
How Can We Accept Such Evidence?

Q. I see frequent references to 'Exposures' which are quoted as a kind of authority for various Masonic practices. The word 'Exposures' has an unsavoury connotation. How is it possible that such documents can be accepted as evidence of early ritual or other Masonic practices?

A. This question arises in many different forms, and often in more forthright language. It is a very important question, moreover, because *it must be answered before we can justify the use of such dubious material as evidence of early ritual and procedure.* It would be much more satisfying, of course, in dealing with questions on the history of our modern usages, if we had a collection of officially-approved early rituals to provide the answers. Unfortunately, no such documents exist.

The first Grand Lodge, founded in 1717, and the Antients' Grand Lodge, founded in 1751, never published a ritual and never gave official approval to any such publication. In the circumstances we have to look for this early evidence wherever we can find it and until the last quarter of the 18th century our only detailed information on early ritual and Lodge practice is derived from two types of unauthorized documents, the manuscript catechisms and the printed exposures.

We know that, at some time before 1598, the two-grade system of admission into the Scottish lodges was already firmly established, although it is not until 1696 that we find actual details of the words and procedures relating to the ceremonies. They appear in a group of four manuscripts, three complete texts and a fragment, all of Scottish origin, and they form our main foundation for the study of the evolution of early Masonic ritual:

(1) The *Edinburgh Register House MS.*, dated 1696.
(2) The *Chetwode Crawley MS.*, c. 1700.
(3) The *Kevan MS.*, c. 1714.
(4) The *Haughfoot* 'fragment', dated 1702.

We refer to them collectively as the 'Edinburgh Group' of texts and, although they all stem from a common source, they exhibit differences in the arrangement of their contents, in phraseology and spelling, which show that they were not copied from each other, and suggest that they represent practices in vogue over a wide area. Of the four, the *E.R.H. MS.* is the most important because of its date, 1696, which makes it the oldest surviving description of the Masonic ceremonies of its day.

Illustration of the M.M. Degree
From *L'Ordre des Francs-Maçons Trahi*, 1745

Unlike the later printed versions, *these texts were not compiled from motives of profit, or spite*; they were copied out laboriously by hand to serve as *aides-mémoire* and there is no reason to doubt the respectability of their origins.

Each of the three complete texts is divided into two parts, under separate headings:

(i) Some Questiones That Masons Use To Put To Those Who Have Yᵉ Word Before They Will Acknowledge Them.

(ii) The Forme Of Giveing The Mason Word.[1]

The latter portion is the earliest description of the actual procedure of two ceremonies, for entered apprentices and 'master mason or fellow craft'. The E.A. candidate was required to kneel, 'and after a great many ceremonies to frighten him' he took up the bible and repeated the oath as follows:

By god himself and you shall answer to god when you shall stand nakd before him, at the great day, you shall not reveal any pairt of what you shall hear or see at this time whither by word nor write nor put it in wryte at any time nor draw it with the point of a sword, or any other instrument upon the snow or sand, nor shall you speak of it but with an entered mason, so help you god.

Note the earliest version of our 'indite, carve, mark, engrave . . .' etc., and the Obligation, incidentally, contained no penalty clause; that appeared at a later stage in the proceedings.

The candidate was then 'removed out of the company, with the youngest mason', who, after a certain amount of horse-play, instructed him in the 'due guard', i.e., the sign, postures and 'words of his entrie', which included details of the penalty, with an appropriate sign. After this partial 'entrusting', the candidate returned to the lodge-room, made a 'ridiculous bow' and the sign, repeated the 'words of entrie' and gave the sign again. Then 'The Word' was whispered all round the lodge, from man to man, 'beginning at the youngest' until it reached the Master, who then gave the word to the new entered-apprentice; this was the completion of the 'entrusting', by a kind of rotational whisper. The sign is actually described in the texts and it was clearly related to a supposed penalty 'in case he break his word'. Two 'words' are mentioned, either directly, or by biblical reference, and it is clear that *in*

---

[1] Quoted from the *Edinburgh Register House MS*. The other two complete texts in this group have similar headings, but they transcribe the two sections in reverse order. All the texts mentioned in this essay are reproduced in full, in Knoop, Jones and Hamer, *The Early Masonic Catechisms*, 2nd edn., 1963. Published by the Quatuor Coronati Lodge.

those days the E.A. had two pillar words. (There is no mention of a token for the E.A. in any of these documents.)

The ceremony ended with a catechism of fifteen or sixteen questions, and answers that were doubtless dictated to the candidate; he had not had time to learn them. Some were test-questions, for use outside the Lodge if non-masons were present.

The senior grade, i.e., the 'M.M. or F.C.' ceremony began with the retirement of all E.A.s from the lodge room. The candidate, on his knees, repeated the former oath, and was taken out of the room by the 'youngest Master' to learn the words, postures, and 'signs of fellow-ship'. On his return, he repeated a modified form of the 'words of entrie', and that was followed by the 'rotational whisper', (as described for the E.A. above) with the Master of the lodge giving the 'word' to the candidate at the end of the procedure. The signs and words are not mentioned, but the posture is described in one of the test questions as 'fyve . . . points of the fellowship', with full details, 'hand to hand . . .' etc. (There is no trace of a 'Hiramic legend' in the ritual at this period.) Two (or four) test questions followed, and that was all.

Allowing that there are no comparable documents before 1696, the three complete texts summarized here would be simply marvellous material for our purpose, if we dared to place any reliance on them. Unfortunately, a serious difficulty arises in handling any such materials, and it can be stated in a single sentence. *The more they reveal, the less they are to be trusted!* The oath of secrecy, which forms the central theme of all Masonic ritual documents, implies that any written revelation of esoteric ritual is *prima facie* evidence of the breach of an oath, and that, of necessity, renders all such material suspect. However interesting our four texts might be, their contents must perforce have remained under an insuperable burden of mistrust, unless it were possible, by some extraordinary chance, to produce the evidence which would link them in some way with the actual lodge practice of their time.

That vital evidence was preserved, by a rare fluke, in the minute book of the Lodge at Haughfoot,[1] near Galashiels, which flourished from 1702 to 1763, and it makes a good story.

The Lodge was founded in 1702 by a small group of local lairds and gentry. At the end of the first meeting one of the founders was instructed to buy a 'Register book' before the next meeting, which he did. Into its

---

[1] The minute-book survives as a treasured possession of the Lodge of St. John, Selkirk, No. 32 (S.C.). A full-length study of the minutes and the history of the Lodge by the present author, is in *AQC*, Vols. 63 and 64.

opening pages he probably entered some notes relating to the foundation of the Lodge, and then he continued by copying out what must
have been a complete version of the two ceremonies described above.
At that stage, he had filled the first ten pages of the book, with the last
twenty-nine words of his ritual text occupying the top five lines on
page 11, leaving most of that page blank. But he had paid 'ffourteen
shillings Scotts' for that book, and the idea of wasting three-quarters of
a page by leaving it empty offended his native Scottish thrift; and so,
immediately below the five lines of ritual, he inserted a heading:

The same day

and then continued with the minutes of the first meeting of the Lodge.

The minutes were kept in excellent order by several 'Clerks' throughout the sixty years or so of the Lodge's existence. At some time during
that period, an over-zealous busybody (one of the new 'Clerks' perhaps)
must have opened the book and been horrified by the sight of the ritual,
written out in detail in the opening pages. Ritual in a minute-book!
That was too much for him and, convinced that it ought to be destroyed, he tore out the first ten pages; they no longer exist. He might,
indeed, have destroyed page 11 as well, but even he did not have the
heart to destroy the minutes of the first meeting of the Lodge. It was
those minutes which saved the twenty-nine words at the top of that
page. Those golden words, 'the Haughfoot-fragment', are virtually
identical with the corresponding portions of the three complete texts,
which describe the finale to the admission procedure for the 'master or
fellow-craft'.

The 'fragment' thus provides the all-important link which shows that
the 'Edinburgh Group' of documents are what they claim to be, i.e.,
descriptions of the ritual and admission procedures of their time, 1696
to c. 1714, and almost certainly for some hundred years before that time.

The three complete texts, now authenticated by the 'Haughfoot fragment', also provide a valuable starting point, a kind of yardstick, by
which it is possible to assess the reliability of later texts, and to observe
the variations and expansions as they occur in a whole stream of
manuscripts and prints which need not be discussed here.

The earliest printed Exposure appeared in a London newspaper in
1723, and it was followed by several publications of the same class,
including broadsheets and pamphlets. The culminating piece in this
series and the most important of this group was Prichard's *Masonry
Dissected*, which appeared in 1730, being the first Exposure that

purported to describe a ritual of three degrees, including a recognizable version of the Hiramic legend, the first of its kind.

Some of these pieces were mere catch-penny rubbish but, throughout the better texts (and many of them are very interesting indeed), it is possible to trace a nucleus of the early ritual, authenticated by the 'Haughfoot fragment', and to notice the expansions and the changes that were creeping in.

Prichard's exposure was much fuller than any of the earlier texts and immeasurably superior in its contents. But, for some unknown reason, *he had framed the whole of his material in the form of question and answer*, so that—apart from a few brief hints in the first degree—*his account of the ceremonies was virtually devoid of information on the 'floorwork', i.e., the actual procedure of the ceremonies.*

Nevertheless, the work proved so deservedly popular that it achieved a vast number of editions and it became *the only publication of its kind in Britain during the next thirty years.* Whatever developments there were from 1730 to 1760, and there must have been many, we know nothing about them: a great thirty-year gap!

The Craft was spreading widely in Britain and abroad during those years, with corresponding expansions in the ritual and ceremonial procedures, but *our first information on such matters comes from across the Channel, notably from France.*

THE FRENCH EXPOSURES

Freemasonry had been imported into France, from Britain, in *c.* 1725, and it began there as a kind of pastime for the nobility and gentry, who were more or less permanent Masters of the Lodges which they held in their own homes. During the next twelve years or so, the Craft achieved a wider popularity among merchants and tradesmen. France was politically very shaky at that time and fears arose in government circles that Lodges meeting in taverns and restaurants might be used as a cloak for political conspiracies. In 1737, an interdict was proclaimed at Paris prohibiting tavern and restaurant owners from giving accommodation to Masons' Lodges. A few establishments were closed down and their owners were punished by severe fines. This action seemed to have little effect and probably did no more than drive the Lodges back into private houses.

René Hérault, Lieutenant General of Police at Paris, decided that, if he could lay hands on a copy of the ritual, he would do far more damage to the Craft by publishing it and holding the Masons up to ridicule.

The Circle of Swords
From *L'Ordre des Francs-Maçons Trahi*, 1745

The story goes that he obtained his material via a certain Madame Carton, who is described as a dancer at the Paris opera, and it was published in 1737 under the title *Réception d'un Frey-Maçon*, the first French exposure, often described as the *'Hérault Letter'*. It was a trivial piece and rather badly confused, but it contained details of many practices of which there are no comparable records in England.

Le Secret des Francs-Maçons, 1742, gave an excellent description of the Initiation ceremony of its day, with much besides. Another text of 1744 contained, *inter alia*, the earliest description of the opening of a Master Masons' Lodge, with a fully detailed account of the third degree of that period; in 1745 we have the first printed version of passwords, with the reasons for their introduction and both texts contain a great deal of interesting material that had never appeared in the English texts.

There is one characteristic of the French documents which is particularly helpful, i.e., the attractive narrative style in which the ceremonies are described, often so clearly that we can reconstruct them almost to the last detail, and *their catechisms, based directly on Prichard's work*, contain symbolical expansions and explanations which show how the ritual was growing.

Of course we are fortunate in being able to assess the value of these documents, because we have the English texts which immediately preceded them, e.g., Prichard's *Masonry Dissected*, and those which immediately followed, e.g., *Three Distinct Knocks* and *J. and B.* These English texts give us an excellent means of testing the accuracy of the French Exposures and, once we are assured of the reliability of one or more of those French documents, they form a perfect bridge across the thirty-year gap. That is the real importance of the French Exposures; they provide us with so much marvellously detailed information for the period when it is most needed.

From 1772 onwards, a great deal of authentic English ritual and Lecture material has survived and the exposures are no longer needed; but for the study of early ritual and procedures, they remain of the utmost importance.

Finally, the innumerable quotations in this book, from those English and French documents, afford ample evidence of their importance in the study of the ritual in its evolutionary stages, and a careful examination of the four early French engravings which we have reproduced will show how much fascinating detail they yield on procedural matters as well. (See illustrations on pp. ii, 190, 195 and 197.)

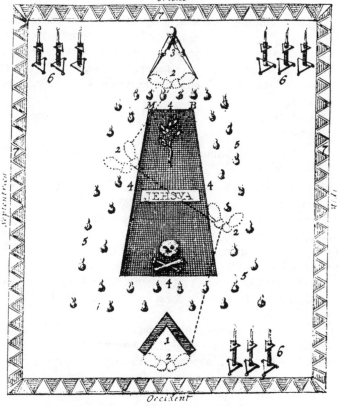

Floor-Drawing for the Third Degree
From *Le Maçon Démasqué*, 1751

88.   TITLES DURING INITIATION

Q. The Candidate for Initiation is generally introduced into the Lodge as 'Mr. John Brown, a poor candidate . . .', etc. But what should we say when the Candidate is a Doctor, or a naval officer, or a Lance-Corporal, or a nobleman?

A. On general principles, and because the Craft is a Fraternity or Brotherhood, connoting the idea of equality, my instinctive feeling is that for the Initiation every Candidate should be introduced by his Christian name(s) and surname alone, regardless of rank, or titles. We say that '. . . he who is on the lowest spoke of fortune's wheel, is equally entitled to our regard . . .', and it is an axiom that 'we meet on the Level'.

On the other hand, our ritual fully recognizes that some are more equal than others:

'. . . although distinctions amongst men are necessary to preserve subordination, yet . . .'[1]

With these somewhat conflicting quotations, the ritual offers little help on our question.

In the majority of Lodges, nowadays, Candidates serving in the Army or Navy are comparatively scarce and noblemen are indeed rare; so that the problem seldom arises except when the Candidate is a Doctor, and, in the absence of an official ruling, the Lodges tend to follow their own—somewhat haphazard—customs. In my own Lodges, we announce the Candidate as 'Mr. . . .', but for a Doctor, we omit the title and say plain 'John Brown'.

In discussing the question with a senior member of the Emulation Committee, he expressed the view that he would like to see a Candidate introduced 'with any title or rank that he had earned, e.g., Dr., Professor, etc., but omitting all hereditary titles'. But this raises the difficulty of where to stop. Would we introduce a Candidate as John Brown, M.A., or F.R.C.S., or A.M.I.Mech.E.?

In support of the view outlined above, I am told by an elderly Grand Officer who assisted at the Initiation of Earl Cadogan, who is now the Pro Grand Master, that he was introduced by his Christian names and surname, Cadogan, without any titles at all. Another high ranking

---

[1] An unhappy choice of words. I greatly prefer 'and although distinctions among men are inevitable, yet ought no eminence of situation . . .'.

Grand Officer tells me that in his day at Apollo University Lodge No. 357, it was the custom to introduce Candidates as '— Smith, — Jones, — Robinson, Viscount Montgomery, and — Thompson'.

Clearly procedures vary so much that it becomes necessary to obtain guidance from the best authority. I addressed a letter to the then Grand Director of Ceremonies, R.W. Bro. Frank W. R. Douglas, P.G.W., and I quote the relevant portion of his reply:

> I feel that a candidate should be introduced merely by his Christian and surname, without any preface such as Mr., Professor, Major, Doctor, or whatever it may be.
>
> On the other hand, a peer of the realm should be introduced by his Christian names, without the preface 'The Right Honourable', but should end with 'Baron "X" ', 'Earl of "Y" ', 'Duke of "Z" ', *etc.*
>
> I am sure that this overcomes all difficulties, especially in the case of peers, where very often the titles by which they are known are different from their actual surname.

The question may arise only on rare occasions, but when it does, there is no doubt that the views of the Grand D.C. represent the best guidance that can be had.

---

89.   CROSSING THE WANDS

Q. Why do the Deacons 'cross their wands' above the Candidate during Prayers and Obligations? If there is any particular significance in this procedure, should not the Candidate be made aware of it?

A. There are many answers and none of them certain. The use of the wand simply as an emblem of office goes back to ancient times, and there is little doubt that their introduction into the Craft was copied from the ceremonial use of wands in other spheres. As an example, the English exposure *Three Distinct Knocks*, of 1760, in its plan of the layout of the Lodge, has a note:

> The Master and his two Deacons have each of them a Black Rod in their Hands, about 7 Foot high, when they open the Lodge and close it.

but the text makes no mention at all of the wands being *used* in any way during the ceremonies. The Grand Stewards carried 'White Rods' in procession in 1721, but here, as with the Deacons' 'Black Rods', above, they were emblems of office having no practical purpose. This suggests that the 'crossing of wands' probably had a symbolical significance, and it is at this point that our difficulties begin.

One view is that the Deacons, during Prayers and Obligations, are forming a square with their wands above the Candidate's head. This may be directly related to an early exposure of 1730 which described the posture of the candidate at his initiation, kneeling, with his 'body within the square'. At that date, wands were not in general use *in lodges*, and the phrase 'within the square' has usually been interpreted as a large wooden square laid on the ground, or on a kneeling-stool.

Bernard Jones argued that the wands are arched nowadays to form 'a gateway, through which the Candidate passes to a new life'; and he quoted another view that the Deacons are forming a triangle—a symbol imbued with sacred qualities. But if so, where then is the base-line?

In some lodges it is customary, during the Obligation, for the D.C. standing behind the Candidate, to join his wand to those of the Deacons, forming a 'tripod' above the Candidate's head. Algernon Rose suggested that this procedure was to symbolize that the Candidate at this moment 'is in a state of suspense', rather like the smooth ashlar hanging on the tripod on the S.W.'s pedestal. This must surely be the most extraordinary piece of symbolical explanation I have ever read, and it only serves to emphasize the dangers of introducing inexplicable items of 'business' into our procedures, when they have no practical purpose.

Most of the writers on this topic have mentioned the arch of staves at a Scout's wedding, or of swords at a soldier's wedding; but I have never seen these references linked with Masonic practice. Yet there is a definite link that goes back over 200 years. The French exposure *Le Maçon Démasqué*, of 1751 (published in England in 1766 as *Solomon in all his Glory*), describes the admission of the candidate under an 'iron vault' later described as an arch of swords (*la voute ferrée . . . des épées croisées*). There are numerous illustrations of the French ceremonies from 1745 onwards, and wands were *not* used in those days, nor were they mentioned in any of the early texts.

This idea of an arch, or covering of some sort, goes back in all probability to pagan times, and relics of it have survived, especially in European country dances, in which many of the figures are executed under crossed or arched branches of blossom, or through an arch of joined hands.

The same idea had been brought into religious ceremonial, particularly at moments of solemn consecration. Thus, the Holy Sacrament is carried in Roman Catholic processions under a baldachin, and a canopy covers the altar in their churches. Jewish weddings are solemnized under a canopy in their Synagogues, and in Israel (where those ceremonies are often performed in the open air) a large 'tallith' or praying-shawl is held up by four congregants to form a canopy. The Hebrew word *'chupah'* meaning canopy or covering is linked with sanctity, 'for all glorious things shall be covered over (or protected)'. Isaiah IV, v. 5.

In Jewish religious practice, a boy is first called to the Reading of the Law at the age of thirteen to mark his acceptance of the responsibilities of manhood. Only once a year, at the 'Rejoicing of the Law' festival, all the boys in the Synagogue *under the age of thirteen* are called together for the Reading of the Law and when they are assembled on the Dais, a 'tallith' is held above them throughout the Reading, to symbolize the supreme religious significance of the occasion.

All this suggests that the canopy, the arch of swords, or staves, and the wands are directly associated with the idea of dedication, consecration, or a similar religious motive. A priest, when blessing his congregation, stretches forth his hands above them; an orthodox Jewish father, when he blesses his son on the eve of Sabbath, also holds his hands above the child's head, in benediction.

In Masonic usage, I have found several examples clearly linked with this practice. In the Inner Working of Preston's Third Lecture of Free Masonry, Section IX, Clause II, as reproduced from the *Turk MS.*, 1816, (*AQC* 85, p. 102):

> The candidate having given his assent is placed in due form for installation. He kneels on both knees, with two installed masters joining hands, & forming an arch over him . . .

In Claret's ritual (4th edn., *c.* 1847), for the Prayer at the Initiation ceremony, a footnote prescribes:

> While the Prayer is being given, the two Deacons *join hands over the head of the Candidate, holding their wands with the other.* (My italics.)

It should be emphasized, however, that the arching of the wands is not obligatory. It is a custom imported from outside the Craft, but now so well established as to be almost universal and the wands are only 'arched' *above a Candidate* (e.g., never above the Chaplain or W.M. for the Opening or Closing prayers).[1] For these reasons, I would suggest that he wands are raised at those vital moments in the ceremonies to symbolize the Candidate's dedication to the service of the Craft.

An interesting example of the arch of wands appears in an important manuscript in the Grand Lodge Library, known as *Henderson's Notebook, c.* 1835, p. 259. For the Obligation in the Inner Work:

---

[1] In some lodges the wands are 'arched' over the I.P.M., while he adjusts the 'Three Great Lights' for the Degrees and at Opening and Closing.

The Arch is formed [over the Master Elect]. (three is the proper number for forming it, but it may be formed by 2 if no more beside the Master be present).

This is an early example of the arch of three staves, mentioned above, but this procedure is comparatively rare in English practice. Incidentally the arched wands used in Lodge processions, before Opening and after Closing, are presumably a piece of showmanship, designed as a mark of respect to the W.M. and his Officers.

In fairness, I must add that on this question of an arch of wands, two great experts, the late Bros. W. B. Hextall and E. H. Cartwright, were of the opinion that this practice had 'passed into a custom, without any significance attaching to it'.

As to the question, 'Should not the Candidate be made aware of the significance of the raised wands?', I would say that so long as there is an *acceptable* symbolism, of course he should be made aware of it.

---

90. OPENING AND CLOSING
'IN THE NAME OF T.G.A.O.T.U.'

Q. During many years in the Craft, I have heard our Lodges being opened 'in the Name of the G.A.O.T.U.' and have accepted that formula as a matter of course. Recently a much-respected Brother voiced his objections to this procedure on several grounds. What are your views on it?

A. It is true that all too often we tend to accept inherited words and practices in the Craft without question. The objections in this instance are on two main grounds.

> (1) That the W.M. (in Opening), and the S.W. (in Closing), have no such authority from the Almighty.
> (2) That the phrase is irreverent because it involves a wholly unnecessary reference to the Name of God.

As regards the question of authorization, the objection would seem to be valid. An ordained priest may properly conduct a religious service 'in the Name of the G.A.O.T.U.' but a Lodge meeting, despite the Prayers at Opening and Closing and no matter how reverent and well-ordered, is not a religious service.

On the second objection, i.e., of taking the Sacred Name in vain, lightly or irreverently, I am not so sure, chiefly because we do not, in fact, pronounce the Name, but use a descriptive substitute, G.A.O.T.U., or Grand Geometrician, etc., and, if the use of the substitute is acceptable, then we have only the question of authorization to contend with. On that point, I would heartily endorse the phrasing of the *Benefactum Ritual*, in which the Lodges are opened and closed 'in the *presence* of the G.A.O.T.U.', with the customary alternatives in the other degrees. The *Oxford Ritual*, however, eliminates all objections: the Master says 'Brethren, I declare this Lodge duly opened for the purposes . . .' and the S.W., in Closing, also omits all reference to the Deity.

The 'religious' arguments outlined very briefly above need not be pursued further, but it may be interesting to try to ascertain how the practice arose. The students of our oldest Masonic documents, the *MS. Constitutions*, or *Old Charges*, are unanimous in the view that they were used (wholly or in part) at the admission of new men into the Craft. Nearly all of these texts begin with an opening prayer, which, in the 130 or so versions that now exist, appears in two main forms.

    (a) *A thanksgiving*. 'Thanked be God our glorious Father . . . for he made all things to be obedient and subject to man . . .'. (*Cooke MS. c.* 1410.)

    (b) *A prayer for guidance*. 'The might of the Father of Heaven . . . be with us at our beginning & give us grace so to govern us ourselves here in this life that we may come to his blessing . . .'. (*York No.* 1 *MS. c.* 1600.)

None of the *Old Charges*, so far as I am aware, uses the opening 'In the Name of . . .'.

The earliest evidence of actual *Lodge* ritual begins in 1696 and in a collection of some sixteen different texts that belong to the period 1696–1730 there is no evidence at all of any formal opening or closing of the Lodge, or details of any prayer that might have been used for those purposes.

The earliest description of a formal Opening of the Lodge in an English text is in *Three Distinct Knocks*, published in 1760, and the procedure then was very similar to that in use today. At the end of the series of Questions and Answers the Master declared:

This Lodge is open in the Name of God and Holy St. John, forbidding all cursing and swearing, whispering, and all profane Discourse whatsoever, under no less Penalty than what the majority shall think proper; not less than One Penny a Time, nor more than Six-pence.

This is supposed to have represented the Antients' practice; the 'Moderns' (according to *J. & B.* of 1762) opened simply 'in the name of Holy St. John' with the same ban on cursing, etc., except that the amounts of the fines were not specified.

It is clear, therefore, that the custom of opening 'in the Name of God . . .' is more than 200 years old in English practice, and I suspect that the real reason for the introduction of this phrase is indicated in the final words of the formula. The intention was to give or bring a kind of religious atmosphere into the proceedings, so as to eliminate cursing, swearing and profane Discourse; perhaps they were right.

---

91.   THE 'OPENING AND CLOSING' ODES

Q. When did the 'Opening and Closing' Odes, so well known in the London area, come into use? Who wrote and composed them?

A. The Odes to which you refer are doubtless:

'Hail Eternal . . .' for Opening, and
'Now the Evening Shadows . . .' for Closing.

They were written by W. Bro. Walter Clegg, M.R.C.S., P.P.G.W. (Lincs.) who was Master of the Lodge of Harmony, Boston, Lincs., in 1859. The music for both pieces was composed by Bro. Walter B. Gilbert, Mus. Doc., in 1869; he was, at that time, Organist of the same Lodge. All this happened roughly a hundred years ago, but the precise dates are uncertain.

At the ceremony of laying the Foundation Stone of the Temple, Main Ridge, Boston, Lincs., on 20 April 1860, a newspaper report says:

'. . . Ceremony, which was commenced by a hymn written by Dr. Clegg for the occasion' (*Stamford Mercury*, 27 April 1860).

This may have been the Opening Hymn (Hail Eternal), but that is not certain and there is some doubt also about the music, because the band was supposed to play 'the well-known tune, Martin Luther's hymn'— and Dr. Clegg voiced his disapproval of the band. (Did they play the wrong music, or the correct music, badly?)

The Dedication of the Temple at Main Ridge took place on 28 May 1863, and at the Lincolnshire Provincial Grand Lodge held on the same day at the Assembly Rooms, Boston, a newspaper report states that 'Hail Eternal . . .' by Dr. Clegg, was sung at the Opening (and the three verses are reproduced), with Bro. Keller, Prov. Grand Organist, at the piano, and the proceedings closed with 'Now the evening shadows closing', by the same author, and again the verses are reproduced in full.

So it is certain that the words of both odes were in existence in 1863.

But the music used on the latter occasion is not known and the tunes were apparently *not* those in use today. The Minutes of the same Lodge at Boston, Harmony No. 272, record that the composer of the present-day tunes, Bro. W. B. Gilbert, became a joining member of that Lodge on 11 February 1868, and was appointed Organist in December 1868.

On 12 January 1869, he was requested:

'to compose suitable and original music . . . for . . . the Closing Hymn . . .' [singular].

and on 8 June 1869, he was thanked in open Lodge

'. . . for the singularly able manner in which he has composed the tunes for the Lodge Hymns' [plural].

Thus, the best that can be said in reply to the questions is:

(a) The words were certainly in Masonic usage in 1863.
(b) The present melodies were composed in 1869.

A wall-plaque commemorating the author and composer was dedicated in Harmony Lodge No. 272 on 10 January 1967.

But the words and music, though widely used nowadays, are not obligatory. The Odes are sung to several different tunes and Bro. C. F. W. Dyer informs me that the tunes most generally used (St. Bees and St. Oswald) are both credited in *Hymns Ancient and Modern* to Rev. J. B. Dykes.

---

92.   'TOPPING-OUT' CEREMONIES

Q. I have a question which has puzzled all sections of the building industry, i.e., the origins of the 'topping out' ceremony which takes place on important new buildings when the construction has reached roof level. Usually these ceremonies are attended by the building owner, the architect, the main contractor and local dignitaries—including the Mayor. The building operatives are also represented at the ceremony on the roof, when the Union flag is raised. Similar ceremonies take place, I understand, at this stage of the construction of many buildings on the Continent. Nobody seems to be very clear about their origins.

Many years ago, I remember reading somewhere that it originated in Scandinavian countries where it was associated with the farming and agricultural industry; when the harvest was safely in, the farmer tied a wheatsheaf to his chimney stack and this was the sign for all his farm-workers and their families to join him in refreshment and celebration. I mention this in case it might help in any investigations you feel able to undertake.

As the number of important buildings seems likely to represent an even greater proportion of the total building programme, these 'topping out' ceremonies and the refreshment and conviviality which attends them seem bound to increase in popularity. Any help you may feel able to give in clearing up the mystery of how they originated would be of considerable assistance. (From Bro. W. B. Bryant, of the National Federation of Building Trades Employers.)

A. Nowadays, of course, the 'Topping-out' is simply a 'Completion ceremony' giving the contractors the opportunity for providing a suitable festivity for the men, in recognition of a job of work well done. There is no doubt that they are the modern equivalent of the Completion Sacrifices of pagan origin. You would find comparable customs even today, among uncivilized tribes who live in huts or shelters made of tree branches, etc. They fasten a dead animal or some other object to the roof to propitiate their gods, or to avert evil.

When we come to the days of real building, there arose related practices by way of Foundation sacrifices; there is indeed some evidence of human sacrifices for this purpose. Later, animals were used, and later still, only animal bones, or relics, were hidden in the foundations, or roof of a building.

It is the modern approach to such practices that prompts us nowadays to secrete coins and other objects in the foundations of large public monuments and other buildings.

To study the subject properly, one would need to take a fairly wide course of reading in folklore. There is a little pamphlet called *Builders' Rites and Ceremonies* (price 25p) which deals with some of these aspects of pre-Masonic history and the information given above is drawn from that work, which was written by Bro. G. W. Speth, the first Secretary of the Quatuor Coronati Lodge.

---

93.   'THIS GLIMMERING RAY'

Q. '. . . yet even by this glimmering ray, you may perceive that you stand . . .' The only illumination is the candle at the W.M.'s pedestal. Is that the glimmering ray?

A. The question really asks 'are we referring to a physical or a spiritual light?' There could be only two answers, the candle or the V.S.L. In our teaching, it would be impossible to refer to the Bible as a 'glimmering ray'. On the contrary, for us it is 'that Great Light . . .'. I have no doubt at all that this portion of the ritual actually refers to one of the 'three lesser lights', i.e., the W.M.'s candle.

---

94.   THE LOYAL TOAST

Q. Is it permissible to omit the Toast to 'The Queen and the Craft', or 'The Queen and Royal Arch Masonry' at Masonic banquets?

A. *Only if no Toasts are given at all.* Otherwise, at every Craft or R.A. meeting at which Toasts are given, the appropriate Loyal Toast must be given, and not simply 'The Queen', but linked with the Order, as stated in the question.

---

95.   THE ALTAR OF INCENSE—A DOUBLE-CUBE

Q. Bro. J. R. Clarke on 'The Ritual of the Royal Arch' (*AQC* 75, p. 231) mentioned the measurements of the Altar as given in Ezekiel (Chapter XLIII, 13–16) which are not those of a double-cube, and he added that he could not find a double-cube mentioned in the Bible. Where does it come from?

A. The Altar described in Ezekiel was a sacrificial Altar for 'burnt offerings'. Its measurements are not easy to follow in all the details, but the words 'twelve cubits long, and twelve broad' show that it would have been large enough to hold a 'young bullock' mentioned later in that Chapter.

The Altar in the R.A. is based on the Altar described in Exodus, XXX, vv. 1, 2, and that was specifically an Altar of Incense, which was to stand before the Ark, and on which Aaron, the High Priest, was to burn incense (i.e., sweet smelling spices), as a 'perpetual incense before the Lord'. For this purpose only a very small Altar was needed. It was made of wood, overlaid with pure gold, and verse 2 shows that it was indeed a double-cube:

A cubit *shall be* the length thereof, and a cubit the breadth thereof; four-square shall it be: and two cubits *shall be* the height thereof.

---

96.   LETTERING AND HALVING

Q. In *Emulation* working, when the Candidate is examined by the J.W., in the first and second degrees, he is instructed to say 'I will letter or halve it with you'. When, still under instruction, he letters the words with the J.W., he is also required to halve them. Is this correct and is there any reason for it?

A. The practices in different lodges in this respect vary quite widely. In the working with which I am most familiar we letter with the W.M., halve with the J.W., and letter with the S.W., but we do not give the Candidate any option; *he is told* to letter, halve, letter.

Emulation and some other workings apparently give the Candidate a choice, with the phrase 'Which you please, and begin'; but the *Emulation* rubric then requires the Deacon to instruct the Candidate to halve with the W.M., letter and halve with the J.W., and halve with the S.W., finishing each of the tests in both degrees by repeating the whole word. This seems to me to indicate a quite inexplicable preference for 'halving'; but I have no hesitation in saying that if you claim to work *Emulation*, you ought to follow the 'book', even in a matter which may not have a logical explanation.

Dr. Cartwright in his *Commentary on the Freemasonic Ritual* (2nd edn., p. 60) argued that the phrase 'Which you please . . .' appeared in the rituals 'merely by way of example' of what should be said at this point, and he was—I believe—quite unjustifiably rude to Masters and Wardens who use it as though 'no other formula is permissible'. Of course other words would do equally well, but for Brethren who adhere to a particular working, it is far safer to follow the 'book' than to try to interpret the words to suit their own ideas.

Cartwright preferred direct instructions to the Candidate instead of giving him a choice. He also added that, after the test by lettering or halving, the words *ought not to be repeated at length*, since the procedure is designed to teach the Candidate the proper method of testing *that might be used outside the lodge*. With these views I agree, heartily.

But now let us see how the practices arose. The earliest evidence on the subject is in the *Sloane MS.*, *c.* 1700 where the word which then accompanied the F.P.O.F. was 'halved'. (It was then in the 2°.) In *The Mystery of Freemasonry* and in *Masonry Dissected*, both of 1730, the two words referred to in the Question above were both lettered. Some of the earliest French Exposures lettered those words, and in 1744 *Le*

Catéchisme des Francs-Maçons also lettered the word of the third degree, a practice which became quite common in France. *L'Ordre des Francs-Maçons Trahi* of 1745 lettered and halved the first two words and repeated them 'whole'; I believe this is the earliest example of what later became the Emulation practice.

In the subsequent English Exposures, beginning in 1760, the 'lettering-halving' procedure seems to have been much neglected. *Three Distinct Knocks* halved its first word and apparently gave its second word at length; but at the end of the work, in describing the manner of answering examination at the door of the Lodge, it halved the first and lettered the second; *J. & B.* described similar practices, and both texts omitted the 'Which you please . . .'. Browne's *Master Key*, 1802, used the phrase 'Which you will, and begin' in the 1°, but its subsequent details are very hazy and tend to confirm that the lettering and halving were not rigorously practised and were by no means uniform.

The 'Which you will' or 'Which you please' seems to have gone out of fashion in modern ritual practice, especially in modern versions of popular workings, e.g., *Taylor's, Universal, West End, Logic*, etc., where the new-style detailed rubrics tend to prescribe specific procedures, without option.

It is generally agreed that the major steps to ensure uniformity of practice were taken at the time of the Union in 1813. The numerous variations that exist today—all stemming from the single ritual approved at that time—are a sad commentary on the fallibility of human memory.

---

97.   THE LIGHT OF A MASTER MASON

Q. What is the Light of a Master Mason?

A. This is a symbolical question to be answered with great diffidence, because I believe the best symbolism is that which the candidate (or the enquirer) will take the trouble to work out for himself. When he has pondered a question and has found an answer that satisfies *him*, he will have learned something far more valuable than anything he could get from a ready-made, 'slot-machine' answer. Yet, because this is the kind of question one would like to hear more often from our youngsters at Lodge of Instruction, I shall endeavour to give my own tentative views. The answer must, of course, be governed by the context:

'Let me now beg you to observe that the Light of a M.M. is but darkness visible serving only to express the gloom which rests on the prospect of futurity.

It is that mysterious veil which the eye of human reason cannot penetrate, unless assisted by THAT LIGHT which is from above. Yet even by this glimmering ray . . .'

As I see it, the 'light of a M.M.' is the dim light, as compared with that in the two earlier ceremonies. 'It is but darkness visible', i.e., it suffices only to show up the all-pervading gloom. Up to this point the explanation is (I believe) purely factual, not symbolical; but now we come to the spiritual lesson.

'. . . serving only to express the gloom which rests on the prospect of futurity.'

The faint glimmer of light is there to emphasize, by contrast, the darkness that it reveals, the darkness that symbolizes the incomprehensible mystery of the future that awaits us all. In relation to the essential teachings of the degree, concerning death and resurrection, the glimmering candle, representing life's brief and flickering span, reminds us that immediately outside its rays is the black curtain of darkness through which all must pass, and of the mystery of the transition to the everlasting life which lies beyond.

'It (the black curtain of death) is that mysterious veil which the eye of human reason cannot penetrate, unless assisted by THAT LIGHT, which is from above.'

The eye of man is not able to see beyond the veil, and the mind of man cannot penetrate it by plain reason or logic. True understanding of what lies beyond the veil is only vouchsafed to those who are assisted by 'THAT LIGHT, which is from above', the Light of pure Faith.

For me this passage emphasizes, more than anything else in our ceremonies, that it is only through the consolations of Faith that we can be reconciled to the loss of our loved ones; it is only the strength which comes to us through Faith that enables us to approach the veil secure in the knowledge that our mortal lives do not end in dust and waste.

Inevitably, the 'explanation' is inadequate; the question has so many aspects. Many readers will doubtless hold other views; so much the better. The object of these notes is not to lay down the law, but to stimulate Masonic discussion.

98.   MASONIC AND BIBLICAL DATES
                  AND CHRONOLOGY

Q. In *AQC*, Vol. 78, p. 46, Bro. G. Draffen dated a Knights Templar Charter as 3 December 1809, A.L. 5813. In England and U.S.A. we add 4000 to the calendar year so that 1809 should become 5809. Why does this Charter differ by four years?

A. The subject of Masonic chronology is a very difficult one. Our system is based on a tradition which (according to Hastings's *Dict. of the Bible*) goes back to pre-Christian times, that the Messiah (Christ) would be born 4000 years after the creation of the Universe.

Scientists have now been able to prove that the world is actually millions of years older than this, but that was not known in the 17th century, so that the calendar in those days counted the Creation (*Anno Lucis*) as 4000 B.C.

In 1611 the Irish Bishop James Usher published his famous *Chronology*, with the computation of 4004 years up to the beginning of the Christian era. This became so popular that certain editions of the Authorized Version of King James's Bible printed marginal dates for each page, according to Usher's work. I have found no trace of Usher's dating in Masonic documents of late operative times, but the speculative Craft adopted it in the 18th–19th centuries, generally adhering to the round figure of 4000 years, with consequent problems for the Masonic student. Bro. Draffen's date, above, is clearly based on Usher's 4004. I add a couplet which seems appropriate here:

> How strange it is for us to see
> That Christ was born in 4 B.C.

The Hebrew calendar counts the Creation as 3760 years before the Christian Era so that their dating for 1967 would be 5727. But because their New Year begins in September or October (a variable date according to the Gregorian calendar) the figure 3761 must be added after their New Year has begun.

Some of the additional degrees use different systems of dating:

ROYAL ARCH dating is from the commencement of the Second Temple 530 B.C., so that A.D. 1967 becomes *A. Inv.* (*Anno Inventionis* or the Year of Discovery) 2497.

ROYAL AND SELECT MASTERS date from the Year of Deposit (*Anno Depositionis*), that is the completion of Solomon's Temple, 1000 B.C. Hence A.D. 1967 becomes *A. Dep.* 2967.

KNIGHTS TEMPLAR usually date from the founding of the Medieval Order of the Temple, A.D. 1118. Hence they deduct 1118 from the present era and A.D. 1967 becomes *A.O. (Anno Ordinis)* 849.

THE ANCIENT AND ACCEPTED SCOTTISH RITE count from the Creation, *Anno Mundi*, and they use the Hebrew dating, as explained above, often with the prefix *A.H.* = *Anno Hebraico*.

---

99.   WHO INVENTED B.C., AND A.D.?

Q. The history of the invention of the term A.D. (Anno Domini) throughout most of the world is doubtless well known. Whose bright idea was it to coin 'B.C.' and when was it brought into use?

A. Obviously the inventor has to be one of the early Church historians after the birth of Christ. The most lucid answer I can give, is from the *Encyclopedia Britannica*, 14th Ed. ('Bible, New Testament, Chronology'):

> The date of the Nativity as fixed according to our common computation of Anno Domini (first put forward by Dionysius Exiguus at Rome early in the 6th century) has long been recognized to be too late. The fathers of the primitive church had been nearer the truth with the years 3 or 2 B.C. (See Irenaeus. . . . Clement of Alexandria . . . etc., [Modern research . . .] has pushed the date further back to 4 B.C., [and it is] probable that the true date is earlier still.

I think it is certain that Irenaeus, *c.* 130 to *c.* 200 A.D., and Clement of Alexandria, *c.* 150 to *c.* 215 A.D. (and perhaps others of their period), must have used the term B.C., or its Latin equivalent, in the course of their calculations. But it was Dionysius Exiguus, in the 6th century A.D., who first put forward the system B.C., and A.D., that is in use today.

---

100.   'DUE EXAMINATION' OF VISITORS

Q. Rule 125 of the *B. of C.* requires that visitors to a Lodge must be vouched for by one of the Brethren present. But if the visitor is unaccompanied, or if no Brother is able to vouch for him, the rule requires that 'he shall be well vouched for after due examination'. I cannot find a precise definition of 'due examination' and opinions on this point in our Lodge Committee vary considerably. Can you clarify the position for us?

A. The phrase 'due examination' has not been defined by Grand Lodge, and its interpretation is left to the discretion of the Brethren who conduct the examination. In the majority of Lodges visitors are vouched for by their hosts and, for that reason more than any other, examinations are extremely rare. Rule 125 says that 'He shall, *if required*, produce his Grand Lodge Certificate and proof of good standing in his Lodge'. The words, 'if required', indicate that the request is optional, implying that production of the G.L. Certificate is not essential. This may be taken as a useful guide to procedure, but I would urge that, in every case where there is the least doubt, 'due examination' must be strict.

Example: Bro. X, a Provincial Mason in London on business, is staying at the Right Royal Hotel where the notice board shows that a Lodge is meeting that evening. He presents himself, but without Grand Lodge Certificate or means of identification. The examining Officer would be fully entitled to refuse admission; but, assuming that he is willing to test the visitor, I would suggest the following:

1. Ask for the Signs, Tokens and Words of the three Degrees. The visitor may be hesitant, or not wholly correct in his answers. He may even be a non-Mason who has obtained his information from some irregular source. The examination should be extended to include one or two procedural questions relating to specific details *in the ceremonies.* But there is a useful additional check.

2. Ask the name and number of the visitor's Lodge with the place and dates of Meetings. (All these can be instantly checked in the *Masonic Year Book.*)

The examination should cover adequately all the Craft degrees that the visitor claims to hold. If the result is not wholly satisfactory, admission should be refused.

Responsibility for the admission of visitors is primarily with the Junior Warden, who is so directed at his investiture. But ultimate responsibility rests with the W.M., who undertakes, at his Installation, that no visitor shall be received 'without due examination, and producing proper Vouchers of his having been initiated in a regular Lodge'. If the J.W. is on duty in the Lodge, the W.M. may delegate the D.C., or one or more P.M.s to act as 'examiners', and it is they who become, in a sense, the 'proper Vouchers', when they are satisfied.

---

101. THE NAME 'HIRAM ABIF'

Q. Is Hiram Abif mentioned in the Bible, or in any other early record? I can find no mention of him *by that name* in the account of the building of the Temple in the Book of Kings. What does the Abif mean and where does it come from? The story does not say that he was a 'principal architect' or an operative mason; can you explain?

A. The story of the building of Solomon's Temple appears in the Old Testament in 1 Kings, chapters V–VII, and 2 Chronicles, chapters II–V, and the accounts differ in many respects. In 1 Kings VII.13 we read that 'Solomon sent and fetched Hiram out of Tyre': he was the son of 'a worker in brass'—[*choreish nechosheth* = an artificer in brass] but he was himself 'cunning to work all works in brass', wise and skilful indeed, but only brass is mentioned.

In 2 Chron. II.7, Solomon asked the King of Tyre for a man, cunning to work in gold, silver, brass, iron, purple, crimson and blue, and in graving. (This request does not appear in the Kings version.) Verses 13 and 14 contain the Tyrian King's answer:

> 2 Chron. II.13: And now I have sent a cunning man, endued with understanding, *Huram my father* [*le-Huram Avi*].
>
> 2 Chron. II.14: . . . skilful to work in gold, and in silver, in brass, in iron, in stone and in timber, in purple, in blue, and in fine linen, and in crimson: also to grave any manner of graving . . .

There is now a notable increase in the range of skills attributed to H.A., and the reference to stone and timber implies that he was a mason and builder. The words 'Huram my father' indicate that Hiram the craftsman was highly esteemed by the Tyrian King. The Hebrew word *Av* = father is frequently used in the *Old Testament* in the sense of 'teacher, counsellor, or master' as a mark of great esteem, e.g., Gen. xlv. 8, where Joseph says that 'God . . . hath made me a father to Pharaoh'.

Later, in 2 Chron. IV.16, in a catalogue of the Temple utensils and implements made by H.A., we find the original Hebrew words Huram Aviv, which are transliterated to form the name that we use in our ritual:

> 2 Chron. IV.16: . . . and all their instruments did *Huram his father* [*Huram Aviv*] make to King Solomon for the house of the Lord . . .

There is a marginal note to this passage in Robert Barker's Bible, 1616, which says 'Whom Solomon reverenced . . . as a father'.

It is not surprising, perhaps, that the Hebrew words Avi (= my father) and Aviv (= his father) posed difficulties for the early translators. Luther, in his translation of the Old Testament, 1533, gave the name as Huram Abif in both cases, i.e., in 2 Chron. II, 13, where it would have been more correct to say Abi, and in 2 Chron. IV, 16, where the original Hebrew does justify the word Aviv.

The *Revised Standard Version*, a truly modern Bible, gives the name as Huram Abi in both cases, also disregarding the differences in the original Hebrew text.

There is only one verse in the Old Testament that could give rise to our use of the name 'Hiram Abif' and that is in 2 Chron. IV, 16, and the correct *Hebrew* pronunciation would be *Huram Aviv*, or *Churam Aviv*.

Incidentally, neither of the two versions of the building of King Solomon's Temple describes H.A. as an architect, nor is there any mention at all of his death. Our legend of H.A. is pure legend.

---

102.   'TIME IMMEMORIAL' LODGES

Q. 'Time Immemorial' Lodges are mentioned in the report of the Especial Grand Lodge held for the Installation of H.R.H. The Duke of Kent as Grand Master, on 27 June 1967. Why 'Time Immemorial'?

A. They were the four original Lodges which combined to erect the first Grand Lodge, in 1717. The dates of their foundation are unknown, but they were already well established Lodges when they first met to discuss the project in 1716. There is no contemporary record of those events. The only reliable account was compiled and published by Dr. James Anderson in the second edition of his *Book of Constitutions*, in 1738, some twenty-two years after the events but, in essentials, this section of his work (apart from the reference to Sir Christopher Wren) is generally deemed trustworthy.

King GEORGE I. enter'd *London* most magnificently on 20 *Sept.* 1714, and after the Rebellion was over, *A.D.* 1716. the few Lodges at *London* finding themselves neglected by Sir *Christopher Wren*, thought fit to cement under a *Grand Master* as the Center of Union and Harmony, *viz.* the *Lodges* that met,

1. At the *Goose* and *Gridiron* Ale-house in St. *Paul's Church-Yard*.
2. At the *Crown* Ale-house in *Parker's-Lane*, near *Drury-Lane*.
3. At the *Apple-Tree* Tavern in *Charles-street, Covent-Garden*.
4. At the *Rummer* and *Grapes* Tavern in *Channel-Row, Westminster*.

They and some old Brothèrs met at the said *Apple-Tree*, and having put into the Chair the *oldest Master* Mason (now the Master of a Lodge) they constituted themselves a GRAND LODGE pro Tempore in *Due Form*, and forthwith revived the Quarterly *Communication* of the *Officers* of Lodges (call'd the Grand Lodge) resolv'd to hold the *Annual* Assembly and *Feast*, and then to chuse a GRAND MASTER from among themselves, till they should have the Honour of a *Noble Brother* at their Head.

Accordingly

On St. *John Baptist's* Day, in the 3d Year of King GEORGE I. *A.D.* 1717. the ASSEMBLY and *Feast* of the *Free and accepted Masons* was held at the foresaid *Goose and Gridiron* Ale-house. . . .

and the story continues with the election and investiture of the Grand Master and Grand Wardens.

The Lodge at the Crown in Parker's Lane made its last appearance in the Grand Lodge lists in 1736; an attempt at its revival in 1752 was unsuccessful and the Lodge disappeared. The three which survived the hazards of more than 250 years of eventful and turbulent history, after changes of name and amalgamations with other Lodges, are:

Original No. 1, at the Goose and Gridiron, now Lodge of Antiquity, No. 2.

Original No. 3, at the Apple Tree, now Lodge of Fortitude and Old Cumberland, No. 12.

Original No. 4, at the Rummer and Grapes, now the Royal Somerset House and Inverness Lodge, No. 4.

It is interesting to notice that No. 4 of the Founding Lodges (and still No. 4 to this day) was quite exceptional in the quality of its membership. The early Grand Lodge lists for the other three Lodges do not record a single member who rated the description of 'Esquire', i.e., they were apparently Lodges of artisans and tradesmen. In No. 4, the earliest list of members recorded in 1723 included two Dukes, two Earls, a Marquis, three Lords, a Baron, four Baronets or Knights, high ranking Military Officers, Ministers of Religion, and twenty-four Esquires. George Payne and Dr. J. T. Desaguliers, the second and third Grand Masters respectively, were members of No. 4, and so too was Dr. James Anderson.

As to the meaning of the term 'Time immemorial', the *O.E.D.* quotes a use of the term in 1602, with the definition 'ancient beyond memory or record'.

The Officers of 'Time Immemorial' Lodges enjoy the privilege of wearing Collars of a design which is confined only to those three Lodges, i.e., on the standard 'light blue ribbon four inches wide' they may 'wear a stripe of garter-blue one-third of its width in the centre of the collar'.

The same three Lodges also have particular privileges at the Installation of a new Grand Master, i.e., at the Especial Grand Lodge in 1967, after all the Brethren were seated and before the Grand Lodge was opened, they were permitted to furnish the 'Three Great Lights' and the Grand Master's Maul for the occasion. In solemn procession, the Master of No. 4 approached the Throne, and presented the V.S.L. The Master of No. 12 presented the Square and Compasses. The Master of No. 2 presented the 'Wren Maul', a treasured possession of the Lodge of Antiquity, which is believed to have belonged to Sir Christopher Wren.

---

103.   THE GREAT LIGHTS AND THE
              LESSER LIGHTS

Q. We speak nowadays of three 'Great Lights' and three 'Lesser Lights'. How did they come into our ritual?

A. In all the earliest ritual evidence that survives, there were only 'three lights', i.e., not 'three great lights' and 'three lesser lights', as we have them today.

The *Edinburgh* group of texts, 1696—*c.* 1714, all have three lights denoting the Master, Warden, and fellow-craft. (Spellings vary, but there is no doubt about what the words mean.)

The *Sloane MS.*, *c.* 1700, is the earliest that gives a new meaning 'three, the sun the master and the Square'.

Two texts of 1724 and 1725 say they represent 'The Three Persons, Father Son and Holy Ghost'.

Then there is a group of three texts of 1724, 1725 and 1726 which all give a set of twelve lights, as follows:

Father, Son, Holy Ghost, Sun, Moon, Master Mason, Square, Rule, Plum(b), Line, Mell [= Maul], Chizzel.

This collection of twelve items probably includes all the tools known or quoted at that time (1724–6) in the 'working' of a non-operative lodge. The list is given in answer to a double question:

Q. How many Lights in a Lodge.   A. Twelve.
Q. What are they? (Answer as shown above.)

Note also that, although the Square is mentioned, the V.S.L. and Compasses are omitted, and it is clear that the 'Three Great Lights', *in our modern sense of the term*, had not yet made their appearance *as part of the ritual*. But there is an interesting set of questions in the *Dumfries No. 4 MS., c.* 1710, which show that the V.S.L., Square and Compasses were in use, though they were not yet referred to as 'Lights':

Q. how many pillers is in your lodge.   A. three
Q. what are these   A. ye square the compas & ye bible

From the earliest days, i.e., 1696 onwards, there were questions about the *position* of the lights. The answers from 1696 to 1730 vary considerably but the majority favour 'East, South and West'; the earlier versions, when they discuss the *purpose* of the lights, generally state that they are to light the men to, at and from work. This is the most complete answer; some are not so detailed. When the question asks what the lights represent, the texts of *c.* 1730 (i.e., *Masonry Dissected* and the *Wilkinson MS.*) are agreed on the 'Sun, Moon and Master-Mason'. (*Masonry Dissected* adds they *'are three large Candles placed on high candlesticks'.*)

It is hardly necessary to point out that by 1730, when a period of some sort of standardization may be said to have started, only three lights were in general use, and they conform to our present-day 'Lesser Lights', *though they did not bear that title.* Our three 'Great Lights', even in 1730, were still unknown *as such.*

The English exposures are practically useless for any *further developments* in ritual practice in the period 1730 to 1760. In those thirty years there were many re-issues of Prichard's work of 1730 and very little apart from that, with nothing that throws any further light on our question.

A new and important series of exposures made their first appearance in 1760, with *Three Distinct Knocks*, and in 1762, with *J. & B.* Both became enormously popular and there is ample evidence that they were widely used, all over England, much as we use our little 'blue books' today. Both works were frequently reprinted, though their texts remained practically unchanged throughout.

On the subject in question, i.e., the 'Great Lights' and the 'Lesser Lights', the two versions are almost identical and I quote the relevant questions and answers from *Three Distinct Knocks* (1760 Edn.) to show how far the English ritual practice had advanced during those thirty years:

Mas. When you was thus brought to Light, what were the first Things you saw?

Ans. Bible, Square and Compass.

Mas. What was it they told you they signified?

Ans. Three great Lights in Masonry?

Mas. Explain them, Brother.

Ans. The Bible, to rule and govern our Faith; The Square, to square our Actions; the Compasses is to keep us within Bounds with all Men, particularly with a Brother.

Mas. What were the next things that were shewn to you?

Ans. Three Candles, which I was told were Three lesser Lights in Masonry.

Mas. What do they represent?
Ans. The Sun, Moon, and Master·Mason.
Mas. Why so, Brother?
Ans. There is the Sun to rule the Day . . . &c., &c.

So we may say with reasonable certainty that the three Candles some-times called the Three Great Lights (and later known as the 'Lesser Lights') were in use from the very earliest times. The Bible, Square and Compasses *may have been* in use quite early, but they did not acquire their status as the 'Three Great Lights' until some time between 1730 and 1760. I would hazard a guess that the dates should be between 1745 and 1760, because if they had been known in England before 1745 they would almost certainly have appeared in the great series of exposures that appeared in France from 1737–1745, which usually managed to incorporate (and sometimes to improve on) the best that was known in England. The various French texts to which I refer (1737–1745) afford no evidence on this question of Great and Lesser Lights; they merely refer to the three Candles, *called* 'Three Great Lights' and representing Sun, Moon and Master.

In short, the 'Lesser Lights' of today were originally the 'three lights'. It was not until the title 'Three Great Lights' came into general use that the term 'Lesser Lights' was introduced.

It is interesting to notice that the Lectures contain two separate descriptions of the Great Lights. In the First Lecture, Section 2, they are the V.S.L., Square and Compasses, defined as 'the three great though emblematical Lights . . .'. In Section 5, they are 'The V.S.L., Compasses and Square, defined as the "Furniture of the Lodge".'

---

104.   THE LESSER LIGHTS,
            SUN, MOON, AND MASTER
                WHICH IS WHICH?

Q. The following question was recently asked in a local Lodge:

'The lesser lights, in the East, South and West, are said to represent the Sun, Moon, and the Master of the Lodge. Which is which?'

The answer was given as follows:

We read them in the order stated, E., S., & W., but the interpretation is not given in that order. In my opinion, the W., is for the Moon, the E., for the Master, and the S., (at the meridian) for the Sun. There are perhaps other interpretations, but this seems to be the most logical.

Our correspondent continues:

Admittedly, this was a 'surprise' question, with little opportunity for prior study, but quite frankly the answer did not satisfy me and I think would be confusing to any candidate who—after his initiation—seriously studied the implication of the greater and lesser Lights.

In the Initiation ceremony, the candidate before receiving L. has gone through an impressive and meticulously prepared procedure, preceded by solemn prayer, and leading up to the great moment when, after his Ob., he for the first time sees L. in the Lodge. *Immediately* he receives L., his attention is directed to the three greater though emblematical L.s: the V.S.L.; the S.: the C.s. They are pointed out and named, and then *in their correct order*. their respective significance in each case is given. The V.S.L. to govern our faith; the Sq. to regulate our actions; the C. to keep us in due bounds . . . etc. There can be no possible mistake here, they are clearly interpreted in the same order in which they were first named.

Within a minute. the candidate has his attention next drawn to the three lesser L.s. Their position is given—E., S., and W. Following the procedure of the greater L.s, he is told that they (the lesser L.s) represent the Sun, the Moon. and the Master of the L. Surely there can be no doubt as to 'which is which?' The obvious interpretation to the candidate (especially bearing in mind the clearness of the description of the greater L.s) is that the lesser L. in the E. represents the Sun (to rule the day); that in the S., the Moon (to govern the night); and that in the W., the Master (to rule and direct his Lodge).

To a new candidate, the apparent contradiction must be noticeable and puzzling, for the W.M. is there in front of him in the E.—not in the West. And later, when closing, he hears the S.W. asked: 'What is your constant place . . .?' to which the answer is: 'In the West'. Here again the contradiction, for he was told earlier (the lesser L.s) that the W.M. is in the West. Yet the candidate can have no doubt in his mind that the W M. does indeed sit in the East, and rules and directs his Lodge from there.

The text and phraseology of our ritual has so stood the test of time that there can exist little or no possibility of an error. Therefore, if in their interpretation, the order of the three lesser L.s has been so obviously altered, it must be deliberate—presumably to stress some important point. It would seem that if our ritual, age-old as it is and yet unaltered, can lead—implicitly, if not explicitly—to puzzling a new candidate, there must be some strong reason involved. Is there an authoritative explanation . . . ? (From Bro. T. F. Pratt, Trevor Mold Lodge, No. 3293, E.C., Buenos Aires.)

A. Bro. Pratt says, 'E., S., & W. (for the lesser lights)', and continues, 'Surely there can be no doubt as to which is which . . .' And there's the rub. There is indeed grave doubt. He thinks, apparently, that they were always as we have them now, but when he reads how they were originally, and how greatly they varied in different practices, and at different times, he will begin to understand why there is no certain answer to his question.

Originally there were no 'greater & lesser lights', just three lights, and they may have been windows or candles. The earliest reference is in the *Edinburgh Reg. House MS.*, 1696. It has three lights, N.E., S.W., and 'Eastern Passage', and they represent the Master, Warden, and F.C.

The *Dumfries No. 4 MS., c.* 1710, has three; 'E., W., and Middle', representing Master, F.C., and Warden.

'A Mason's Confession', *c* 1727(?), has three; S.E., South, and S.W. *The Grand Mystery Discovered,* and *Institution of Freemasons,* 1724 & 1725, both give 'A Right East, South and West', and they represent 'Father, Son, and Holy Ghost'.

Prichard, in *Masonry Dissected,* 1730, said three lights, E., S., and W., representing 'Sun, Moon, and Master-Mason', with 'Sun to rule the Day, Moon the Night, and Master-Mason his Lodge'. *Three Distinct Knocks,* 1760, and *J. & B.,* 1762, followed Prichard, almost word for word.

William Preston, in his 'First Lecture of Free Masonry' was, I believe, the first writer who attempted to explain the E., S., and W. sequence, in his Section IV, Clause I (reproduced in *AQC* 81, p. 132):

How was he enabled to do this?
By the assistance of three great [sic] lights.
How are they situated?
In the east, south and west.
Why?
To represent the sun at its principal periods in its diurnal course, rising in the east, in its meridian in the south and in its setting in the west.
What moral inference do we draw from this?
That in the morning when we commence labour, at noon when we refresh, and in the evening when we close the fatigues of the day, that glorious emblem of God's goodness to man may always open to our view and we may be thence led to venerate the Source whence all blessings flow.
What do these great [sic] lights represent?
The sun, the moon and the Master of the Lodge.
What does the first represent?
The sun, as ruler of the day.
What does the second represent?
The moon, as ruler of the night.
What does the third represent?
The Master, as ruler of the Lodge.
Why is the Master compared with the sun and moon?
As it is by the influence of the sun and moon that we are as men to discharge the duties of social life, so it is by the assistance of the Master we are enabled to discharge, as Masons, the duties of the Craft.

It is hardly necessary to point out that although Preston did explain the E., S., and W. sequence, so long as they are given in that order, they will not agree with the situations of the three Officers whom they are said to represent. Certainly the E., S., and W. sequence seems to be the most popular, and the Brn. who helped to standardize the ritual in 1813 adopted it, without realizing the difficulties they were raising.

I am informed that, in several Provinces in the Midlands, at the moment when the W.M. recites this passage, the J.D., standing with the Candidate, points to the E., S., and W., and then to the J.W. (for the Sun), S.W. (for the Moon) and finally to the Master. That may clarify matters for the Candidate, but it still leaves one or other of the statements in the wrong sequence.

In my own Craft Lodges, 'Logic' working, we say 'S., W., and E.' which seems to solve the problem, but I would not dare to say that we are right and the others wrong. For those who adhere to the E., S., and W. sequence, it might be necessary to explain that we have three lights, *collectively representing* the Sun, Moon, and Master, without attempting to allocate each to each. This is only one of many instances which might prompt a desire to alter the ritual, in order to make it logical, and that is something to be avoided. The results might well be logically sound and literally deplorable.

Bro. Pratt says, 'The . . . phraseology of our Ritual has so stood the test of time . . . little or no possibility of error'. I believe this is an exaggeration. It may well be said that our Ritual, *since it was virtually standardized at the time of the Union of the Grand Lodges, in* 1813, has stood the test of time. But that arose largely out of the emphasis on standardization, and the evolution of 'named' workings, each with their own printed versions. If we go back to the earlier evidence of ritual development, it is obvious that the changes have been frequent throughout the 18th century, and the accretions and expansions throughout that period have been enormous. Yet, even after the standardization, there are still innumerable inconsistencies and illogicalities. Our ritual has stood the test, since 1813, because Brn. have not been unduly anxious to make it logical. When they are, it will need to be altered at so many points that it will become almost a new ritual. Heaven forbid!

---

105.   'INSTRUCTION AND IMPROVEMENT OF
        CRAFTSMEN'. WHY ONLY CRAFTSMEN?

Q. Certain of the Brethren here have observed that the ritual used in opening the Lodge in the first and third degrees states that *the Lodge is* *open for the purposes of Freemasonry in those degrees*; while the second degree opening states that *the Lodge is open for the instruction and improvement of Craftsmen.*

Hence the view is expressed that Lectures and work involving the dissemination of Masonic knowledge other than the conferring of degrees would more properly be done while the Lodge is working in the second degree, and not in the first degree as we now operate. Your views on this would be most gratefully appreciated.

A. Your enquiry really involves two separate questions, and I fear that you are drawing too strong a conclusion from something that was never intended to bear that kind of reasoning.

Why is the second degree treated differently from the other two? Our ceremonies nowadays owe their form very largely to the pattern laid down and approved at the Union of the rival Grand Lodges ('Antients' and 'Moderns') in 1813.

At that time certain practices were approved which seem to have been solely for the purpose of drawing distinctions between degrees, e.g., left foot, right foot; left knee, right knee; or,

1°. . . . regularly assembled and properly dedicated . . .
2°. . . . regularly held, assembled and properly dedicated . . .
3°. . . . duly constituted, regularly assembled and properly dedicated
    or
1°. So help me God . . .
2°. So help me Almighty God . . .
3°. So help me the Most High . . .

There are many such items and it must be obvious that they are purely for purposes of distinction, no matter what symbolism may have been added to them subsequently. In furtherance of this argument, it must be obvious that the Master's duty '. . . to employ and instruct the Brn. in Freemasonry' is one which applies to all three degrees, and not merely to the second.

The second question that arises here is, 'Why instruction and improvement only for Craftsmen?' I believe this goes back to the time when the second degree in our three-degree system arose by a splitting of the first degree into two parts (so that the original second degree with its 'Five Points of Fellowship' became the third).

The *Old Charges*, including the oldest version, the *Regius MS.*, of *c.* 1390, imply very strongly that some reference to the seven liberal arts and sciences, with special emphasis on the fifth science, Geometry, may have formed some part of the early admission ceremonies in medieval times, and it survived into some of our early ritual documents.

In 1730, on the appearance of the first exposure of a three-degree system, the second degree dealt with the Middle Chamber, and the Letter G, meaning both Geometry and the Grand Architect, but it made only casual references to sciences (plural) without naming them. All 'Seven Liberal Arts and Sciences' made their appearance, with very brief explanations of their uses, in *Three Distinct Knocks*, and in *J. & B.*, in 1760 and 1762, but they were there embodied in the E.A. catechisms.

In the 'interpretational period' of English ritual development, *c.* 1769 to *c.* 1810, the seven Liberal Arts and Sciences were brought back into the second degree, with a lengthy explanation of their uses. Indeed, William Preston printed the whole explanation in his 1775 edition of the *Illustrations of Masonry*, very much as it appears today in the 'long' explanation of the Second Tracing Board.

I believe that it was this move which lent a new 'instruction idea' to the second degree, that had not really been there before.

---

106.   SO MOTE IT BE

Q. What is the origin of the words 'So mote it be' which we use at the end of our Opening and Closing odes, etc.

A. From the Masonic point of view, they came into our usage in the 14th century, and our two earliest versions of the *Old Charges* both include the phrase in their closing words, which I render in modern spelling, as follows:

> The *Regius MS.*, *c.* 1390, after a closing prayer adds
> 'Amen, amen, so mote it be
> Say we so all, for charity'.
> The *Cooke MS.*, *c.* 1410, has 'Amen so mote it be'.

The phrase means literally 'So be it' and it was used in the middle ages in England as a pious finale to prayers or blessings. It should be noted that the medieval formula began with the Hebrew word 'Amen', nowadays often omitted from Masonic usage. The word 'Amen' has a range of meanings all related to fidelity, constancy, sureness, trust, and when used at the end of Hebrew prayers and blessings it was a formula of acquiescence and confirmation, as though to say 'Truly, we believe that it is [or will be] so'.

Thus, although the 'Amen', and the 'So mote it be', do not have the same *original meanings*, they have virtually acquired the same meaning in the course of centuries, and that possibly explains the modern omission of the Amen. (Privately, I prefer to use the response 'Amen' to 'Grace' at table, and keep 'So mote it be' for use in Lodge.)

---

107.   YOUR RESPECTIVE COLUMNS

Q. In our Lodge, before opening into a higher degree, the W.M. asks all Brn. below the rank of so-and-so to retire for a while. Then he asks the Wardens in turn:

Bro. S.W. (or J.W.) do you vouch for your column?

The Warden looks round the Lodge and replies 'I do, Worshipful Master', or possibly, 'To the best of my knowledge and belief, Worshipful Master', after which it is understood that only Masons of the required rank are present. Question: which part of the Lodge is covered by the word 'column' in relation to each Warden?

VOUCHING WITHIN THE LODGE

A. I believe this question harks back to early 18th century usage, when both Wardens sat in the West (J.W. in the South-West corner, S.W. in the North-West corner), both facing the Master. Thus, the J.W., without even turning his head, could vouch for the whole of the South column, in front of him, and the S.W. for the whole of the North column. As all Brn. in the East would be Masters or Past Masters, the assurance from the Wardens would cover the whole gathering. This seems to be the most satisfying explanation.

In the English practice, with which I am most familiar, the procedure is different. The W.M., addressing the J.W., asks: 'With the exception of the Cand. for Passing, are all present F.C. Freemasons?' The J.W. repeats the question to the whole Lodge and turns to the W.M., saying, 'Worshipful Master, with the exception of the Candidate(s) standing, silence implies assent'.

IN THE REFECTORY

Q. What is the origin of the expressions used in the Refectory, 'How do you report your respective columns?', or 'See your columns charged'. Has it anything to do with the fact that the Junior Warden is officially in charge of the Refectory proceedings and that his column is raised when the lodge is at refreshment?

A. At the dinner table, *this question is addressed to both Wardens*, only to ascertain that Brethren in the respective sprigs (or columns) have been served with beverages. Neither of these questions has anything to do with the Wardens' Columns, as portable emblems of their office; *they refer only to the the rows of Brethren under their care.*

Thus, the arrangement of Brethren in lodge would be roughly as though they were sitting at a U-shaped table, with a Warden at the head of each sprig, and within the lodge each sprig, or column, was under the supervision of a Warden. During the 18th century, a large part of the work was conducted at table, and the same procedure was carried on (even though there was probably no specific seating arrangement for the different grades of Brethren).

The main point is that all this was long before we have evidence of the Wardens' Columns on their pedestals, and it would seem that our present-day questions at table are a relic of the 1740s, when the different grades of Masons were ranged in their proper columns, inside the lodge.

---

108.   THE 'HALF-LETTER'
                 OR 'SPLIT-LETTER' SYSTEM

Q. In the course of correspondence with a Masonic friend in the U.S.A. I was asked to arrange to identify myself by the 'half-letter' system. What is it?

A. Briefly, the system is a means of identifying a Brother, or a Lodge visitor, without a verbal test. It is often used in the U.S.A. for Masonic identification purposes, especially when a lodge in one jurisdiction is going to confer degrees on a Brother from a different jurisdiction, and the procedure is simple.

. The lodge Secretary writes to his counterpart in the lodge to which the Brother is going (either as a visitor, or as a prospective candidate for a degree). He cuts the letter in half, *through the lodge seal.* He sends half to the Secretary of the other lodge, and the unknown Brother brings along the other half. They are duly matched, and all is well.

There are at least eight Grand Lodges in the U.S.A. that permit the 'Half-Letter' or the 'Split-Letter' system, as a proper means of identification.

---

109. USING THE V.S.L.
AT LODGE OF INSTRUCTION

Q. I would very much appreciate your views on a point which has been raised by a P.M. in our Lodge of Instruction. This Brother is very much concerned at the fact that at our meetings we use the open V.S.L.

We go through the ritual of one of the three Degrees with a Brother (usually fairly well up the ladder) acting as W.M. Another Brother acts as Candidate, and there are other Brethren acting as the other Officers; the I.P.M. and D.C. are always P.M.s.

The question is really as to 'whether it is proper to have the *acting* Candidate taking the Obligation on the V.S.L.?' The Brother who has raised this point argues that the V.S.L. should not be used when the Obligation is not being taken seriously. He considers it Masonically and morally wrong for a Brother, however sincere and competent, to administer an Obligation on the V.S.L. when he himself is not an Installed Master, and has not taken the Obligation of an Installed Master, and, in fact, may not be qualified to be elected as such by having served the office of Warden. Further, he fails to see how the absence of the V.S.L. makes the Lodge any less realistic or affects its solemnity.

A. The following is only a provisional answer, because I want to check the religious aspects of the question with a minister of religion; I believe the question lies very largely in that field.

Two questions are involved here. First, 'Is it Masonically correct for the Degree Obligations to be administered by a Brother who is not an Installed Master?' In lodge, there could be no doubt at all. Under *B. of C.* Rule 119, only an Installed Master or a Past Master may confer Degrees. At Lodge of Instruction, where Brethren who have not yet attained the Chair *are being trained and prepared for that Office*, it seems reasonable to permit them to rehearse the ceremonies in full, since the Lodge of Instruction is the only means they have for such training.

The second question arising here involves personal religious convictions and it is, for that reason, more difficult to answer. 'Is it proper for an acting Candidate to take the Ob. on the V.S.L.?' He is, in fact, repeating former Obligations previously taken in the full solemnity of his own admission and it seems to me that there could be no objection to the act of repetition, as such. The objections, if any, can only arise from what might be deemed unnecessary repetitions of the names of the Deity, and of the Oaths themselves.

My own view is that, for the purposes of training, all this is perfectly
proper so long as the work is conducted with due decorum. Indeed, I
think there might be a tendency towards carelessness if some other
book were used at L. of I., in place of the V.S.L. I sympathize with the
questioner's point of view and, if the proceedings at L. of I. were conducted with levity, he might have a strong case. It is really the spirit that
matters and this leads me to the strongest argument of all in replying
to the question, i.e., Clause 6 in the 'Basic Principles for Grand Lodge
Recognition':

> That the Three Great Lights of Freemasonry (namely, the Volume of the
> Sacred Law, the Square, and the Compasses) shall always be exhibited
> when the Grand Lodge or its subordinate Lodges are at work, the chief of
> these being the Volume of the Sacred Law.

Lodges of Instruction have a properly recognized status under the
control of the Grand Lodge (*B. of C.* Rules 127, 132–135) and I feel
that they should exhibit and use the V.S.L. in exactly the same way as
the regular Lodges do.

Since writing the above, I have had a reply from a much-loved Past
Grand Chaplain to whom both question and answer were submitted.
He fully approves the answer, and adds:

> ... If the V.S.L. is not used in the L. of I., the way will be open for other
> omissions. But the most necessary point, which I think it is important to
> make in answer to this matter, is that the acting candidate is not taking an
> Obligation at all. He is merely rehearsing and no degree is being conferred.

---

110.   THE LODGE ON HOLY GROUND

Q. Why do we give three reasons (in the First Lecture, Sect. IV) for
the Lodge standing on Holy Ground; how did this come into the ritual?

A. The three reasons, as given in the Lectures, apparently came in at a
fairly late date. *Masonry Dissected*, 1730, says that the Lodge stands
'Upon Holy Ground' but gives no reasons. The principal English exposures of the second half of the 18th century mention 'Holy Ground',
but there is no reference to three reasons. They deal with the matter
entirely in a single question and answer, in the catechism following the
Raising Ceremony, which they call 'The Master's Lecture', thus:

> **Q.** Why was both your Shoes taken from off your Feet?
> **A.** Because the Place I stood on when I was made a Mason was Holy
> Ground.

> (From *J. & B.*, 1762 and subsequent edns.)

Three Distinct Knocks (1760 and subsequent edns.) adds, by way of explanation:

> ... for the Lord said unto Moses, pull off thy Shoes, for the Place whereon thou standest is holy Ground.

It seems probable that the wider explanations were the work of the later interpreters of the ritual, Preston, Browne etc., in the last decades of the 18th century.

Preston dealt with this theme in several different ways, in his 'First Lecture of Free Masonry' (*c.* 1790):

> Why slipshod? Because the ground we are about to tread is holy.
> What rendered that ground holy? The Name of God impressed on it, Who has declared—where my Name is there I am—and therefore it must be holy.
> To what does this allude? To a custom observed in the east of throwing off the sandals from the feet when they enter the Holy Temple.
> To what does it farther allude? To a circumstance mentioned in Holy Writing ... when the angel of the Lord appeared to Moses in the burning bush a voice was heard to utter this word—Slip thy shoes from off thy feet for the ground upon which you tread is holy. What God commands must be obeyed.
>
> (From Section II, Clause I, Middle Chamber.)

But all this was much too simple for Preston and he took the question up again in Section IV, Clause III:

> On what ground is the Masonic mansion raised? On holy ground.
> Why? For two reasons:
> First reason. Because the Name of God must be thereon impressed.
> Second reason. Because the ground on which the first regular Lodge under the royal sanction was formed was peculiarly sacred.
> What rendered that ground holy? Three grand offerings were on that spot presented which met with divine approbation:
>
> First Offering   The act of Abraham.
> Second Offering   The act of King David.
> Third Offering   The act of King Solomon.
>
> What do these offerings exemplify? Three singular instances of divine mercy and of unparalleled virtue.[1]

There now follow three verbose paragraphs, explaining the 'offerings', typical of Preston at his worst. Among the surviving copies of his 'First Lecture' there are two other versions of this theme, in somewhat condensed form, but the precise dates of the individual texts are unknown.

---

[1] The whole 'First Lecture' is reproduced in *AQC*, Vol. 82, in an invaluable study by the late Bro. P. R. James. The paragraphs explaining the 'three offerings' and the two 'condensed versions' are on p. 133.

The version that gives the three reasons almost word-for-word identical with those in the modern 'First Lecture', Sect. IV, is in Browne's *Master Key*, of 1802, pp. 18–19. His reasons are the same as Preston's 'three offerings'.

Browne does not explain why those three particular reasons are given and not others, and if one were to ask the question, it seems likely that the answer is a matter of personal interpretation. I suggest:

(a) Abraham's complete and unflinching faith in the Almighty.
(b) David's whole-hearted dependence on Prayer.
(c) Solomon's immeasurable gratitude to God, upon the completion of the great work of his life, i.e., the Temple.

All three were expressions of faith, all different and for different reasons, and all utterly complete without reservations.

This 'Holy Ground' idea appears again in the Royal Arch ritual, in the Historical Lecture, but there the subject is overlaid with complications. One must confess that all this is quite unduly difficult for the Brother who really wants to understand the ritual. So far as the present writer is concerned, our Lodges stand on holy ground because, in the words of our Consecration Ceremony:

'To God and His Service we dedicate this Lodge . . .'
and if we mean that, could there be a better reason?

---

111.   THE MEANING OF THE WORD 'PASSING'

Q. What is the meaning of the word 'Passing' as we use it in the second degree? Has it something to do with passing up the Winding Stair?

A. The earliest minutes from which I quote, 1598–9, are from 'Operative' Lodges, (Aitchison's Haven Lodge and the Lodge of Edinburgh, Mary's Chapel) and they show that Apprentices were always 'entered' and 'Fellows of Craft' were usually 'made'. There is a rare case in the Edinburgh minutes, 1609, where a Fellow-Craft was 'exceptit' = accepted, but the usual formula was 'made', though we often get the phrase 'admitted and received'.

In England, around 1700 to 1730, after the Lodges had lost their operative character, the two degrees were frequently conferred in a single session and that was called 'making'. I have not been able to find an early record (under the two-degree system) of the word 'passing' being used for the Fellow-Craft's degree.

There is an interesting use of the word 'passing' in the minutes of the 'Philo Musicae', founded in 1725. They were a Masonic society for lovers of Music and Architecture, *not* a regular lodge; but, in those early days under the first Grand Lodge, controls were rather lax and those music-lovers certainly conferred Masonic degrees without any authority. Indeed, they are credited with having conferred the earliest recorded third degree in England, though it was hopelessly irregular, of course. Their minutes contain numerous instances of Brethren who were 'regularly passed Fellow Craft'. Unfortunately, we cannot give too much attention to the word 'passed' in this case, because they used exactly the same word for the third degree, e.g., on 12 May 1725, two gentlemen who had been passed Fellow Crafts some three months before, 'Were regularly passed Masters'. (See Q. 25, p. 60.)

Perhaps the earliest record of all, which uses the words 'passing and raising' as we use them in Masonry today, is in an extraordinary passage in the *Graham MS.*, of 1726, an extremely valuable ritual document. It speaks of a Mason '. . . being entered passed and raised and Conformed by 3 severall Lodges . . .'.

This is a clear English hint of the existence of a three degree system, although at that time there is no definite proof yet of three degrees being worked *in any regular English Lodge*. (Three degrees were already known in Scotland from 1726 onwards.)

There is a minute of the Old King's Arms Lodge (now No. 28), dated 17 November 1735, which refers to '. . . a Jewel for the use of the Master at the passing of Masters' (= M.M.s), and the Lodge of Antiquity, now No. 2, in its earliest record of the third degree, 5 April 1737, shows that Bro. Reddall paid five shillings 'for passing Master'. Prichard, in his *Masonry Dissected*, 1730, had mentioned the 'middle Chamber' and the 'winding Pair of Stairs' in his second degree, but his only reference to passing is in a question on his third degree, 'Where was you pass'd Master?'

After much searching through early Lodge minutes, the first Lodge record I can find which uses the words 'passing' and 'raising' in our modern sense, is in the minutes of the Lodge Greenock Kilwinning, now No. 12 (S.C.). It was founded in 1728, eight years before the Grand Lodge of Scotland. Immediately after the election of the Master and appointment of Officers at its first meeting, 27 December 1728, the Lodge made a rule as to the fees that would be payable for each degree:

> That each who shall be received Members of this Lodge shall pay into the Box when entered as Apprentices One pound ten shillings Scotts,

twelve shillings when passed Fellow-Craft, and twenty shillings Scotts when raised Master Mason, besides paying the expenses of the night's entertainment . . .

I doubt that the word 'passing' in its original Masonic usage had anything to do with passing up a winding stair. At its first appearance *in England* it was certainly used more often in connection with the M.M. degree than with the F.C., and it does not seem to have come into general use for the second degree until after the third, the 'raising', had become general practice in all the English Lodges, around the 1750s.

---

112.   UNRECOGNIZED GRAND LODGES

Q. In course of conversation with an American Brother, I discovered that several Grand Lodges recognized in the U.S.A. are not recognized by the United Grand Lodge of England, e.g., Italy, Japan, Turkey, etc. Is this correct, and if so, why? Are the reasons for non-recognition ever published?

A. [When this question was received, in 1967, the three Grand Lodges named in the question were not recognized by our Grand Lodge. Since that time the Grand Lodge of Turkey and the Grand Orient of Italy have been recognized; but the question is of such broad interest that both question and answer are reproduced as originally printed.]

I have consulted the President of the Board of General Purposes and the Grand Secretary on this matter and am authorized by them to give the following general answer, which will, I hope, be of particular interest to our members from other Jurisdictions.

The three Grand Lodges named above are not recognized by our own Grand Lodge, although they are indeed widely recognized among the U.S.A. Masonic jurisdictions. The United Grand Lodge of England very rightly pursues an extremely cautious approach in these matters. It publishes its *Basic Principles for Grand Lodge Recognition*, which may be summarized very briefly, as follows:

Regularity of origin and constitution. Belief in the G.A.O.T.U. The use of the V.S.L. Exclusively male membership and no connection with mixed or irregular bodies. A Grand Lodge must have sovereign and sole jurisdiction over the Craft Degrees. Essential presence of the 'Three Great Lights'. The ban on religious and political discussion. Observance of the Ancient Landmarks.

It would not be proper to discuss details of specific cases and the following notes represent only my personal views. Broadly speaking, I believe that the unrecognized Grand Lodges generally fall into one or more of the following categories:

(a) Those which, for various reasons, do not conform to our strict requirements under the 'Basic Principles . . .' outlined above.

(b) Jurisdictions which contain several rival Grand Lodges, each claiming to be *the* Grand Lodge of that country, where it is not certain which of them is the real, responsible authority.

(c) Small and newly-developing jurisdictions, where Masonry is, so-to-speak, still on trial, or where, as in some cases, the home-grown Masonry is largely maintained by the *temporary presence* of foreign military personnel.

(d) Irregularly self-constituted Grand Lodges, or newly-formed jurisdictions of dubious origin.

There are, of course, many other reasons which might delay, or prevent recognition but, apart from natural and inevitable delays, all the conditions for recognition are fully covered in the official 'Basic Principles . . .'.

As regards the publication of the reasons for non-recognition: when the Grand Lodge decides to withdraw recognition from a previously-recognized jurisdiction, the details are usually reported very carefully, in the Grand Lodge *Proceedings*. No announcements are made regarding jurisdictions that still await recognition.

---

113. PILLARS OF BRASS, OR BRONZE?

Q. Were the Pillars of Solomon's Temple made of brass, or bronze?

A. The Hebrew word which appears in connection with the story of the Temple Pillars in I Kings, chap. vii, is *'nehoshet'* and it is translated 'brass' in the Geneva Bible, and in the Authorized Version.

> Brass is an alloy consisting mainly if not exclusively of copper and zinc; in its older use the term was applied rather to alloys of copper and tin, now known as bronze.
> The brass of the Bible was probably bronze, and so also was much of the brass of later times, until the distinction between zinc and tin became clearly recognized. (*Encyclopaedia Britannica* 14th Edn.)

The use of bronze is believed to date back before 2000 B.C., in Egypt and the Near East, and it seems probable, therefore, that, despite the use of the word brass in the biblical account, the Pillars were made of bronze.

---

114. THE LENGTH OF MY CABLE-TOW

A Cable's Length From The Shore

Q. The word 'cable' appears several times in the course of the ritual, and it seems to have a different meaning in each case.

(a) In the initiation the cable-tow is to prevent any attempt at retreat.

(b) Later, during the Ob. of the M.M. degree the Cand. promises 'to answer and obey all lawful . . . Summonses . . . if within the length of my cable-tow . . .'. This surely refers to a specific distance, but no precise distance is mentioned.

(c) At another stage there is a warning of something to be buried 'at least a cable's length from the shore, where the tide, etc. . . .'. This seems to indicate a specific measurement, but the distance is not stated. What is the meaning of a 'cable's length' in this instance?

It is all very confusing; can you explain and define?

A. Ropes and cables appear in several degrees outside those of the Craft. My answers are confined to the three cases quoted above:

(a) The cable-tow in the first example has a primarily practical purpose which is defined in the ritual and I cannot trace a single text in which its length is prescribed. In addition to its practical use, it is also capable of a wide-ranging symbolism, e.g., submission, and the bondage of ignorance.

The *Dumfries No. 4 MS.*, *c.* 1710, has two 'rope' questions in its catechism:

Q. hou were you brought in
A. shamfully w^t a rope about my neck . . .
Q. whay a rop about your neck
A. to hang me If I should Betry may trust

This is believed to be the earliest allusion to a rope, as a piece of equipment then used in the preparation of the Candidate. It did not appear again in early ritual documents until 1760, when it was first described as a 'cable-tow'.

(b) The Length of my Cable-tow. This is really a modern symbolical allusion to one of the oldest of the operative regulations, which obliged the medieval masons to attend the annual or triennial 'Assemblies', except in sickness, or 'in peril of death' The later versions of the Old Charges often mentioned the distance within which attendance was obligatory, and the variations on this point range from three to fifty miles!

Nowadays the Candidate's obligation to answer a Lodge Summons 'if within the length of his cable-tow' is a simple promise to attend the Lodge so long as it is in his power to do so, and no specific distance is involved.

(c) A Cable's Length from the Shore. The *cable*, or *cable's length*, is indeed a unit of marine measurement, defined in the *Oxford English*

Dictionary as 'about 100 fathoms; in marine charts 607.56 feet, or one-tenth of a sea-mile'. The same work quotes several examples of the early use of this term, the earliest being dated 1555. It may be assumed that this distance from shore was specified in our ritual to ensure that whatever was buried there would be irrecoverable.

It is interesting to notice that this idea of burial 'a cable's length from the shore' appears in our earliest ritual documents, though the actual words 'cable's length' came in later. According to the *Edinburgh Register House MS.*, 1696, and its two sister texts, the candidate—after taking his E.A. obligation—went out of the Lodge room and was there entrusted with the 'signe and the postures and words of his entrie'. He returned to the Lodge and introduced himself at length: the key words are shown in italics:

> Here come I the youngest and last entered apprentice As I am sworn . . . under no less pain then haveing my tongue cut out under my chin and of being *buried, within the flood mark* where no man shall know . . .

The same theme appears in somewhat similar context in another Scottish text, the *Dumfries No. 4 MS., c.* 1710, again without the, cable tow':

> y^r bodys to be *buried in ye sea mark* & not in any place Q^r christians are buried

These two quotations show that there was already some difference of opinion as to what was to be buried, and the numerous early texts are by no means unanimous on this point.

The 'cable's length' does not make its appearance until *c.* 1727, in the *Wilkinson MS.*, which has the words:

> & buryed in the Sands of the Sea, a *Cables Length from the Land* where the tide Ebbs & flows . . .

Lastly, *Masonry Dissected*, 1730, in the most elaborate version of the E.A. obligation that had appeared till that time, had:

> them to be buried in the Sands of the Sea, *the length of a Cable-rope from Shore*, where the Tide ebbs and flows . . .

Incidentally, the *O.E.D.* cites a number of 'special combinations' with the word 'cable', e.g., cable-rope, cable-range, cable-stock, etc., but it does not give 'cable-tow'.

---

115.   COMPASS OR COMPASSES

Q. I am an officer at an American 'Square and Compass' Club, in Suffolk. A visiting English Grand Officer recently pointed out that it should be 'Compasses'. Which is correct?

A. According to the *Oxford English Dictionary* the history of the word 'compass' presents many points of uncertainty; and the history of the various senses in which the noun is now used is also obscure. But as regards the mathematical instrument which is the subject of this question, *O.E.D.* is quite explicit. Its definition runs:

> Compass. 'An instrument for taking measurements and describing circles, consisting (in its simplest form) of two straight and equal legs connected at one end by a movable joint.'

It then quotes several uses of the word 'compas' from *c.* 1340 onwards in our present '*pair* of compasses' sense of the word. I cite one of its later examples however (dated 1570) for obvious reasons:

> Geometrie. . . . teacheth the Vse of the Rule and the Cumpasse' (Dee, *Math*. Pref. 40).

There is no doubt, therefore, that the use of the singular form 'compass' to describe the mathematical instrument was quite common originally, and *O.E.D.* adds a note that the word is generally used now in its plural form (compasses); also *pair of compasses*. Its earliest quotation for the use of the word in this form is 1555:

> 'We tooke owre compases [sic] and beganne to measure the sea coastes.'

There can be no doubt that the singular word 'compass' to describe the mathematical instrument is a perfectly correct (though rather archaic) use of the term, and the evidence from *O.E.D.* seems to indicate very definitely that our modern usage, 'pair of compasses', came in considerably later.

So far as I am aware, the Americans have always used the term 'Square and Compass' for their Masonic Clubs and it is possible that several of their jurisdictions also use the same term in their rituals. Remembering that we, in our English ritual, have also retained many old archaic words, using them in their ancient rather than their modern sense, I can see no objection at all to the American usage.

---

116.   'YORK RITE'

Q. My Lodge works in the 'York Rite' and there is a dearth of information concerning this Rite in Guyana. Can you throw any light on its origin, history, etc.? Is there any printed ritual for this Rite? (From Bro. C. R. Hopkinson, Guyana.)

A. The title 'York Rite' presents many difficulties, because it arises NOT from fact, but from a tradition (in the *Old Charges*) that a great Masonic assembly was held in York by Prince Edwin, under a Charter granted by King Athelstan. Anderson, in his *Book of Constitutions, 1738,* said that this took place in A.D. 926.

It is true, of course, that York is one of the oldest centres of Freemasonry in Britain but, although many of the *Old Charges* and other rare Masonic documents have come down to us from York, none of them relates to early or medieval ritual, and none of them could be described as forming the whole or part of a Rite. Indeed, the ritual now practised even in the oldest Lodges at York, while it contains various slight local differences from the more-or-less standardized versions, is largely identical with our modern rituals which were developed mainly in the 16th to 18th centuries.

Laurence Dermott, who was Secretary of the Antients' Grand Lodge, fostered the idea that the Antients were preserving the ritual of the York (and Scottish) Masons, but despite his efforts to emphasize the notion that there were vast differences between the 'workings' of the Antients' and the Moderns' Grand Lodges, the main differences were only two:

    (a) The Antients adhered to the original sequence of the 'words' of the first and second degrees, which the Moderns had reversed.

    (b) The Antients held that the Royal Arch was an integral part of the Craft degree system; (the Moderns treated it, correctly, as a new addition).

Neither of these differences had anything to do with York, and the title 'York Rite' as the description of a system of Craft degrees has not been commonly used in England at any time. When it is so used, it is rather misleading.

In 1725 there was an old Lodge in the City of York, which constituted itself into 'The Grand Lodge of ALL England'. Its influence was confined to the counties of York, Cheshire and Lancashire. It did not warrant or authorize dependent lodges until 1761; it was dormant from 1740 to 1761 and it finally ceased to exist in 1792.

In 1780, it gave its sanction to the working of five separate degrees, i.e., the three Craft Degrees, the Royal Arch, and the Knight Templar. On this basis it might seem possible to raise an argument for the existence of a genuine 'York Rite', but it must be emphasized that those degrees were all in existence before 1780 and they were by no means peculiar to York.

The York Grand Lodge constituted some thirteen Lodges during the whole period of its existence and one Grand Lodge. The latter was the 'Grand Lodge South of the River Trent', William Preston's break-away organization which he erected in 1779; it lasted only ten years.

In the U.S.A. and other countries where the Ancient and Accepted Scottish Rite has established itself very strongly, the title 'York Rite' is applied to the older system of additional degrees which comprise the Mark Degree, with a cluster of degrees belonging to the Royal Arch and the Orders of the Red Cross, Knights of Malta, Knights Templar, etc., each with separate Statutes or Regulations. The A. & A.S.R. is *bound by its Constitutions to have no jurisdiction whatever over the Craft Degrees.* For both Rites the only link with 'blue' Masonry is that Brethren are unable to enter their Orders unless they have already acquired the three regular degrees of Craft Masonry.

Nowadays, therefore, the title 'York Rite' *when applied to Craft ritual*, represents an implicit claim that those who practise it are using the oldest and purest forms of the ritual. Unfortunately it is a claim that is virtually beyond proof.

Finally, so far as I am aware, there is no English printed ritual claiming to reproduce the whole of the York Rite, as understood in the U.S.A. The rituals for the individual degrees or stages are certainly obtainable in England, but it would not be possible to confirm that they are identical with their American counterparts.

---

117.   GUTTURAL, PECTORAL, MANUAL, PEDESTAL

Q. In the Lectures of the Three Degrees in Craft Masonry, in the First Lecture, Sixth Section, the following question is posed:

'How many original forms have we in Freemasonry?'

The answer is given in abbreviations which I cannot understand. Can you tell me what these letters stand for?

A. The four abbreviations represent the four words shown at the head of this question. They made their first appearance in a Masonic context, in slightly different sequence, in an anonymous twelve-page pamphlet exposure, published in London, in 1724, under the title *The Grand Mystery of Free-Masons Discover'd*.

The question, in the modern Lecture, refers to these four words as 'original forms', but the exposure calls them 'signs', and lists them as follows:

THE FREE-MASON'S SIGNS

A Gutteral (*sic*)	>
A Pedestal	∠
A Manual	7
A Pectoral	X

(The four words mean respectively, 'pertaining to the throat, the foot, the hand, the heart'.)

The exposure does not attempt to elaborate on the manner of making the so-called 'signs'. A close examination of earlier and contemporary documents may provide the answers to the first and last; but 'Pedestal' and 'Manual' are rather doubtful, because each of them involves several possibilities.

This print appeared at a time when (so far as we know) only two degrees were practised, and it affords no evidence as to which of the signs belonged to each degree. At a later stage, the same text has the question, 'How many proper points?', and the answer is a variant of the 'Points of Fellowship' which had appeared regularly in most of the seven catechisms and exposures that had preceded this publication.

I have used the word 'Pedestal' hitherto, because that is how it was printed in the exposure. It should, of course, be 'pedal', pronounced 'pee-dal'.

Perhaps the most interesting puzzle in the extract quoted above, is in the four 'geometrical' diagrams, which are presumably intended to illustrate the 'signs'; I have never seen a satisfactory explanation of them.

---

118.   THE 24-INCH GAUGE
IN THE DECIMAL SYSTEM: AS A 'WORKING TOOL'

Q. We seem to be moving rapidly towards the decimal system; how shall we moralize on the 24 inch gauge when we have to deal with centimetres instead of inches?

A. We are informed that the 24-inch gauge is not moralized in all the French ritual workings, but in those rituals that use the tool and explain its symbolism, centimetres are not mentioned, and English practice is followed. They use the old French word for inch, which is 'pouce'; thus, *'la règle de vingt-quatre pouces . . .'*. (We are indebted to Bro. C. N. Batham, an Officer of the Grande Loge Nationale Française for these details.)

Some German Lodges use the word 'zoll' which means inch, and both 'pouce' and 'zoll' are of course much older than the metric system.

Rest assured; even when the whole world has 'gone decimal' we shall not give up the 24-inch gauge!

THE 24-INCH GAUGE AS A 'WORKING TOOL'

The advent of the '24-inch gauge' provides an interesting example of the rather slow development of English symbolical or speculative ritual. In the seven catechisms and exposures that appeared between 1696 and 1723 there is no trace whatever of the 'Rule' or the '24-inch gauge'. The 'Rule' made its first appearance in *The Grand Mystery of Free-Masons Discover'd*, in 1724:

> Q. How is it [i.e. the Lodge] governed?
> A. Of Square and Rule.

In the next three years, the 'Rule' is mentioned in five other texts, always without symbolical explanation and never a word regarding the number of inches.

In the fullest and most interesting exposure of that era, *Masonry Dissected*, 1730, which contains references to the Compass, Square, Level, Plumb-Rule, Setting Maul, Setting Tool, and Setting Beadle, there is still no hint of the 'Rule' or the '24-inch gauge'. We know virtually nothing of English ritual developments between 1730 and 1760, because of the absence of any new information during that thirty-year gap, but the '24-Inch Gauge' did appear, at last, in *Three Distinct Knocks*, 1760, in the course of the E.A. catechism or 'Lecture':

> Ans. I was set down by the Master's Right-hand, and he shew'd me the working Tools of an enter'd Apprentice.
> Mas. What were they?
> Ans. The 24-Inch Gauge, the Square and common Gavel, or Setting Maul.
> Mas. What are their Uses?
> Ans. The Square to square my Work, the 24-Inch Gauge to measure my Work, the common Gavel to knock off all superfluous Matters, whereby the Square may sit easy and iust.
> Mas. Brother, as we are not all working Masons, we apply them to our Morals, which we call spiritualizing; explain them.
> Ans. The 24-Inch Gauge represents the 24 Hours of the Day.

Mas. How do you spend them Brother?

Ans. Six Hours to work in, Six Hours to serve God, and Six to serve a Friend or a Brother, as far as lies in my Power, without being detrimental to myself or Family.

The symbolism is, by this time, so advanced, and the words are so familiar, that it is hard to believe that the whole piece could have been so fully detailed when it first came into use. It seems far more likely that it had developed slowly during the preceding thirty years.

---

119. CORRECT SEATING IN LODGE

The following questions occur frequently among the enquiries addressed to us. We furnish the official rulings, as given in 'Points of Procedure: Board of General Purposes', and printed in the *Masonic Year Book*.

INITIATE

(a) Where should the Initiate be seated in Lodge after the ceremony?

In the north-east immediately on the right of the Senior Deacon.

(b) Has the Initiate any precedence in the outgoing procession from the Lodge?

No.

POSITION OF OFFICERS IN THE LODGE

Where should (a) the Immediate Past Master, and (b) the Chaplain normally sit in Lodge?

The I.P.M. should sit on the immediate left of the Master and the Chaplain on the immediate left of the I.P.M.

Where should (a) the Master, (b) the I.P.M., (c) the Chaplain sit when some other qualified Brother is temporarily presiding?

The Master should sit on the immediate left of the Brother presiding, the I.P.M. on the immediate left of the Master, and the Chaplain on the immediate left of the I.P.M.

---

120. THE CHARGE TO THE INITIATE

Q. I have seen a copy of William Preston's *Illustrations of Masonry* which contains a version of the Charge to the Initiate that is very near to our modern form. Did Preston write it, or is our Charge descended from the *Old Charges*?

A. As to the possibility of its descent from the *Old Charges*, there are a few points which might suggest that some of our modern themes may have had their sources in the earlier texts, but the links are so remote that it would be quite impossible to prove the line of descent. The reasons are fairly obvious when we compare their objects. Our modern Charge is a moral exhortation, designed for Speculative Masons, and it is given after the whole procedure of the Initiation is finished.

The *Old Charges* had a much wider range and purpose. They were primarily 'rule-books', prefaced by a history of the craft. There are some 130 versions, which begin in *c.* 1390 and run well into the 18th century. Apart from an opening prayer and occasional instructions relating to the Obligation, their general structure follows a fairly standard pattern consisting of two main parts:

1. A history of the craft of masonry, tracing its rise in Bible lands and showing how the craft was brought across Europe into France, and finally established in England. The importance of the 'Seven Liberal Arts and Sciences', especially geometry, is stressed, and the story tells of the Kings and other biblical and historical and legendary characters who 'loved masons well and gave them Charges' (i.e., codes of regulations by which they might govern themselves). This was all designed to provide a traditional background to the craft and to give the masons a pride in its antiquity. It must be admitted, however, that the history would not withstand any critical test as to its accuracy.

2. The 'Charges' or regulations for masters, fellows and apprentices. The majority of these were 'operative' regulations based on well-established customs of the mason trade; but there were also several items of a moral character, prescribing a code of self-discipline which would prevent the craft from being put to shame. They may be summarized as follows:

(a) Love God and Holy Church.
(b) Be faithful to the craft and to your master and fellows.
(c) Keep secret your master's affairs and teachings, and all that is seen or heard in Lodge.
(d) Avoid lechery; always respect the womenfolk of your master and fellows.
(e) Be not a thief or nightwalker and have no contact with thieves or robbers.
(f) Do not gamble or play at dice, or at any unlawful games.

A glance at these ancient guidelines of conduct will suffice to show how far they differ from those in our modern 'Charge to the Initiate'. It might be argued that the ideas embodied in the first three (a, b, and c) are reflected in our present-day version, but the language in which they are framed nowadays is so far from the early texts that it would not be possible to prove any connection. Their moral purpose may have been the same, but their contents are entirely different.

As regards Preston's 'Charge at Initiation into the First Degree', it appears in all editions of his *Illustrations of Masonry* from 1772 onwards. It was, however, his custom to make alterations and additions from time to time, so that they are not all identical. But although he may have been responsible for some minor parts of the Charge, and more perhaps for the language in which they are framed, it would be manifestly wrong to credit him with the whole work. Preston never made any secret of the trouble he had taken in collecting earlier materials, which he polished, arranged, and interpreted before incorporating them in his own work. The 'Charge to the Initiate' is an excellent example of this, especially when we compare his version with the earliest-known Speculative 'Charge'. It was composed by an anonymous author and first published in 1735, in W. Smith's *Pocket Companion*. Here, seven years before Preston was born and almost forty years before he had published anything on Masonry, is a version of the Charge which contains—in beautiful language—every theme that survives in our modern usage:

A SHORT

CHARGE

To be given to new admitted

BRETHREN.

YOU are now admitted by the unanimous Consent of our Lodge, a *Fellow* of our most Antient and Honourable SOCIETY; *Antient*, as having subsisted from times immemorial, and *Honourable*, as tending in every Particular to render a Man so that will be but conformable to its glorious Precepts. The greatest Monarchs in all Ages, as well of *Asia* and *Africa* as of *Europe*, have been Encouragers of the *Royal Art*; and many of them have presided as *Grand-Masters* over the *Masons* in their respective Territories, not thinking it any lessening to their Imperial Dignities to Level themselves with their *Brethren* in MASONRY, and to act as they did.

The World's great *Architect* is our *Supreme Master*, and the unerring Rule he has given us, is that by which we Work.

Religious Disputes are never suffered in the Lodge; for as MASONS, we only pursue the universal Religion or the Religion of Nature. This is the Cement which unites Men of the most different Principles in one sacred Band, and brings together those who were the most distant from one another.

There are three general Heads of Duty which MASONS ought always to inculcate, *viz.*, to God, our *Neighbours* and *ourselves*.

To God, in never mentioning his Name but with that Reverential Awe which becomes a Creature to bear to his Creator, and to look upon him always as the *Sumum Bonum* which we came into the World to enjoy; and according to that View to regulate all our Pursuits.

To our Neighbours, in acting upon the Square, or doing as we would be done by.

To ourselves, in avoiding all Intemperances and Excesses, whereby we may be rendered incapable of following our Work, or led into Behaviour unbecoming our laudable Profession, and in always keeping within due Bounds, and free from all Pollution.

In the State, a MASON is to behave as a peaceable and dutiful Subject, conforming chearfully to the Government under which he lives.

He is to pay a due Deference to his Superiors, and from his Inferiors he is rather to receive Honour with some Reluctance, than to extort it.

He is to be a Man of Benevolence and Charity, not sitting down contented while his Fellow Creatures, but much more his *Brethren*, are in Want, when it is in his Power (without prejudicing himself or Family) to relieve them.

In the Lodge, he is to behave with all due Decorum, lest the Beauty and Harmony thereof should be disturbed or broke.

He is to be Obedient to the Master and presiding Officers, and to apply himself closely to the Business of Masonry, that he may sooner become a Proficient therein, both for his own Credit and for that of the Lodge.

He is not to neglect his own necessary Avocations for the sake of MASONRY, nor to involve himself in quarrels with those who through Ignorance may speak evil of, or ridicule it.

He is to be a Lover of the Arts and Sciences, and to take all Opportunities of improving himself therein.

If he recommends a Friend to be made a MASON, he must vouch him to be such as he really believes will conform to the aforesaid Duties, lest by his Misconduct at any time the Lodge should pass under some evil Imputations. Nothing can prove more shocking to all faithful MASONS, than to see any of their *Brethren* profane or break through the sacred Rules of their Order, and such as can do it they wish had never been admitted.

---

121.   'MONARCHS THEMSELVES HAVE BEEN
PROMOTERS OF THE ART'

Q. In your Lodge Summons dated 30 Sept. 1968, you reproduced the earliest Charge to the Initiate, of 1735. The opening paragraph contained the following lines:

'. . . The greatest Monarchs in all ages, as well of *Asia* and *Africa* as of *Europe*, have been Encouragers of the *Royal Art*; and many of them have presided as *Grand Masters* over the *Masons* in their respective Territories . . .'.

What are your views on these lines as statements of history?

A. The short answer is that they are without historical foundation and, regardless of the motives that prompted such statements, they cannot have been particularly beneficial to the Craft in 1735, and may have done a great deal of harm to the unwary since then. But, in order to judge the words fairly, it is essential to understand the background against which such statements were made—or the purpose that prompted them.

It was William Smith who first published this Charge, in his *Pocket Companion* of 1735, which was in fact a pirated version of Anderson's *Book of Constitutions* of 1723; but the Charge had not appeared in the *B. of C.*, although it is written very much in Anderson's style. Indeed, he had used almost identical words:

> . . . Kings and great *Men* encourag'd the *Royal Art.*

Whoever the author may have been, the ideas expressed in the quotation above were not new. They were a re-statement, in 18th century language, of ideas, stories or legends concerning the outstanding figures in the Craft, biblical, historical and traditional, who are woven into the very fabric of its foundation, in the earliest of our Masonic documents, the *Old Charges*, of which the two earliest are dated *c.* 1390 and *c.* 1410, with a stream of about 130 versions from 1583 onwards.

In the 'historical' sections of these texts we find Euclid as a founder of Geometry, Jabal the builder of tents (or houses), Tubal Cain, the artificer in metals, with many others who had their places in the traditional evolution of the craft of masonry. Of the Royal characters with whom we are mainly concerned in this quotation, Nimrod, 'King of Babylon' usually heads the list of those who 'loved masons well and gave them a Charge'; then David and Solomon, followed by an unidentified King of France, Carolus Secundus (sometimes called Charles Martel).

The earliest of the English Kings in the list is Athelstan under whose reign a great assembly of Masons was said to have been held at York. Prince Edwin, his 'son', presided (but Athelstan had no sons).

All these characters appear regularly in the *Old Charges* and, in the earliest version which gives textual sources for its statements, i.e., the *Cooke MS.*, of *c.* 1410, six separate authors are cited, though it seems very doubtful if the compiler had actually read the books he was supposed to be quoting. The point is that the compilers of the *Old Charges* were eager to establish an ancient and respectable ancestry for the story of their craft. They were not deliberately inventing their history, but compiling it from the best materials available to them, whether from tradition, or memory, or from their limited reading. The regularity with which the same names appear throughout three centuries, from *c.* 1400 onwards, suggests that the operative masons—at least—had no reasons to doubt the authenticity of their craft heroes.

When, around 1720–1723 Dr. James Anderson prepared to write and publish the first *Book of Constitutions*, he took the *Old Charges* as his model and, like them, his work was divided, broadly, into two sections, the first containing a history of the Craft since the beginning of time, and the second containing the Regulations which were to be approved and adopted by the Grand Lodge. But Anderson had the advantage of education and he set out to fill the numerous gaps in the earlier versions, and to give an account of the Craft which would be a real work of Masonic 'history'. His opening lines set the pattern:

> *Adam*, our first Parent, created after the Image of God, *the great Architect of the Universe*, must have had the Liberal Sciences, particularly *Geometry*, written on his Heart. . . .

According to Anderson, Noah and his three sons were 'all Masons True'; Moses 'became the GENERAL MASTER-MASON' (also described as 'GRAND MASTER MOSES'). Later, '*King* SOLOMON was GRAND MASTER of the Lodge at Jerusalem, . . . *King* HIRAM was the GRAND MASTER of the *Lodge* at *Tyre*', and 'HIRAM ABIF was *Master of Work* and *Masonry*'.

In case these were not sufficient, Nebuchadnezar, Zerubbabel. Ptolomeus Philadelphus of Egypt and Augustus Caesar at Rome all became Grand Master-Masons or General Master-Masons and their stories are linked by details of many others who promoted the building arts.

Dealing with Athelstan, Anderson says that he improved 'the Constitution of the English Lodges . . . to increase the wages of working Masons'; but it was his 'youngest son, Prince Edwin' who summoned the assembly at York 'and composed a General Lodge of which he was Grand Master'.

One cannot help wondering how far Anderson believed in his own 'history', but legend and tradition die hard. In my view, the only way to treat these statements *when they appear in the ritual* is to view them as part of the allegorical or traditional background of the Craft, against which our teachings are displayed. If they were not historically accurate in ancient times, they are certainly true of Freemasonry today, for during the last two hundred years and more, many Monarchs and Royal Princes have played prominent and active roles as leaders in the Craft.

---

122.   THE POINT WITHIN A CIRCLE

Q. How would you explain the symbolism of the 'Point within a Circle'?

A. The ideal symbolism is that which is simple and immediately obvious, so that the word or picture instantly conveys its own interpretation, e.g., the lily for purity, the lamb for innocence, the level for equality. In most cases—and especially for the 'working tools'—the ritual itself gives an explanation, which is all the more satisfying because it is usually simple and clear.

Occasionally, as in this question, the symbolism is obscure, or it may bear a wide range of meanings; often the accompanying ritual gives only a faint hint as to the interpretation. In all such cases it seems to me that the best symbolism is that which a Brother can work out for himself. When, in an incautious moment, I said this aloud in Masonic company, I was challenged with the question above and, as a penance, I must answer it now without reference to any of the numerous works on Masonic symbolism.

The relevant passages, from the explanation of the First Tracing Board, may vary in different 'workings' but they generally run roughly as follows:

> The point within a circle is the centre, the point from which every part of the circumference is equidistant; it is the point from which a Master Mason cannot err . . .

The words in the second part of this passage indicate that the 'point' is an ethical one. It implies the specific foundation upon which the Mason should base his standard of conduct and, so long as he adheres to it, he 'cannot err'. To define that standard in simple Masonic terms, the words that come instantly to mind are from Dr. Anderson's First Charge, in 1723, '. . . to be good Men and true, or Men of Honour and Honesty . . .'.

The first part of the passage under discussion is more difficult to interpret. It appears to be a plain statement of geometrical fact, but we may perhaps assume that a moral or symbolical lesson is embodied in it. The Prophet Isaiah, (Chap. 40, v. 22) used the circle to symbolize the world, and it has been similarly used ever since. If we visualize the 'point' at the centre as the individual Mason, and the world at large on the circumference, where all are equidistant from him, this might be interpreted as a Masonic lesson in equality. There are two items in the ritual which, in my view, are directly related to this 'equidistant' theme. First, '. . . to keep in due bounds with all mankind . . .'; the other is more explicit:

> Let no eminence of situation make us forget that we are Brothers, and he who is on the lowest spoke of fortune's wheel is equally entitled to our regard.

The 'point within a circle' has an immediate religious significance (which parallels the point, or 'Yod' within the equilateral triangle) as the symbol of the Deity. The 'point and circle' call to mind the many illustrations, in the early Bibles, of the Creator with the Compasses, so that we see the symbol as a clear emblem of the Great Architect of the Universe. The ideas and lessons to be drawn from this starting point are unlimited but the simple themes outlined here are very satisfying.

The 'point and circle' convey other lessons too. The point—without length or breadth—implies man's insignificance, and his dependence on his fellow man. The circle is, indeed, a symbol of perfection, a divine attribute; without beginning or end, it is the symbol of infinity and eternity. When we take these two ideas together, the helplessness of man in relation to the Infinite, or the Eternal, we approach a religious theme, the relation of man to God, and here we touch on mystery so obscure, or problems so difficult to answer in plain logic, that we find refuge, or understanding, in faith.

I am by no means adept in the subject of symbolism, but in my experience too many of the writers in this field tend to give explanations which are so devious and far-fetched that they confuse their readers instead of enlightening them. I hope to escape that accusation.

---

123.   THE FIVE PLATONIC BODIES AND THE
ROYAL ARCH

Q. What is the reason for the 'Five Regular Platonic Bodies' usually to be found displayed in a R.A. Chapter. There is a very short reference to them in the Symbolical Lecture and the *Hornsey R.A. Ritual* gives a 'Lecture on the Platonic Bodies and the R.A. Jewel' in extension and explanation of the Symbolical Lecture. Can the early history of this Lecture be traced?

A. This question first appeared in the pages of *Misc. Lat.* vol. XV in 1931 and was answered in the same publication vol. XVIII, pp. 8–9, in 1934. That answer is reproduced here:

The Platonic Bodies.—The passing reference to the Platonic Bodies which will be found in the Symbolical Lecture is sufficiently cryptic. But the *Perfect Ceremonies* also prints an Explanation of the Jewel which would seem to correspond to the Hornsey Lecture [mentioned above], as it contains a long mathematical explanation of the Platonic Bodies and their angles. This does not, however, correspond to the reference in the Lecture, as it only mentions four of them, and assigns the Tetrahedron to fire, the Octahedron to air, the Cube to earth, and the Icosahedron to water, the Dodecahedron being omitted.

In the Introduction to the second edition, 1930, of the privately printed *Hull R.A. Ceremonies*, the text of which goes back at least a century, a much more satisfactory explanation is given. The text itself contains no more than the brief reference in the Lecture. But this explanation concludes by saying that Plato took the Tetrahedron as the symbol of the element fire, the Cube as that of earth, the Octahedron as that of water, and the Icosahedron as that of air; whilst he took the Dodecahedron as the symbol of the universe itself. This probably explains how the five regular polyhedra came to be known as the five regular Platonic Bodies. This fits in with the statement in the Lecture, but it was, of course, written quite recently. The longer explanation of the Jewel and the Platonic Bodies, in the *Perfect Ceremonies* is not only not accurate, but seems to me to be an afterthought. In any case, the fact that the original phrase is found at Hull indicates a considerable antiquity for it.

In an analysis of twenty R.A. Rituals, compiled by Bro. R. A. Wells in *AQC* 81, p. 358, eleven texts contain only a brief reference to the platonic bodies, as follows:

. . . these may be taken in five several combinations and when reduced to their amount in right angles, will be found equal to the five regular platonic bodies, which represent the four elements and the sphere of the universe.

(Is it really possible that a given number of angles can 'equal' five regular platonic bodies?)

Only six texts have the brief reference *with a full explanation of the platonic bodies*, always given as part of the Lecture on the R.A. Jewel. They are, *Complete*, 1925; *Hornsey* 4th edn. n.d.; *Metropolitan*, 1897; *Midland*, 1929; *Perfect Ceremonies*, 1877 and *Sussex*, 1932.

In an attempt to discuss the 'early history', the Hull and Hornsey 'workings' referred to in our quotations from *Misc. Lat.*, above, are not very helpful. The Hull version may have just claims to antiquity, but that working only contains the customary 'brief reference', and its 'satisfactory explanation' of them is simply a modern note which was prepared and printed in 1930.

There is a note in the Hornsey version stating that their explanation was derived from a lecture first published in Madras in 1870, based on materials compiled and expanded by at least two earlier writers. (*AQC*, Vol. 72, *Misc. Lat.* section, p. 5). This might imply a mid-19th century date for its compilation, but it would be difficult to justify an earlier date than that. A search through a collection of 18th century R.A. manuscript rituals has failed to reveal any reference to 'platonic bodies' in R.A. ceremonies of those days.

Of the seventeen rituals that contain the 'brief reference' the oldest is *Bradshaw*, 1851, but there is a degree of uniformity in that section among all of them, which suggests very strongly that they are all descended from a common source. This would imply that the 'parent' text must have been a version which had some weight of authority to aid its acceptance. There was only one occasion in the history of the R.A., when this could have happened, i.e., in 1834, when, in order to stabilize the R.A. ritual, a Committee was formed, of which the Rev. George Adam Browne was one of the principal members. The work of the Committee progressed rapidly and was approved by Supreme Grand Chapter in November, 1834. In Feb. 1835, a special Chapter of Promulgation was formed for six months to rehearse and demonstrate the revised R.A. ceremonies, which was done regularly during that period, and in order to avoid misconception Supreme Grand Chapter resolved and declared, in November, 1835:

> . . . that the ceremonies adopted and promulgated by special Grand Chapter on the 21st and 25th Nov. 1834, are the ceremonies of our Order which it is the duty of every Chapter to adopt and obey.

It seems fairly certain that only a resolution of this kind could satisfactorily explain the general uniformity of our R.A. ritual and especially the 'brief reference' in nearly all of them to the 'platonic bodies'.

There is no evidence of any kind of *detailed explanation as part of the prescribed R.A. ritual in* 1835, and this implies that, in those Chapters where it was felt that such explanation was desirable, those expansions were drawn up by Companions more or less able to undertake the work. This may explain why there is no uniformity in the geometrical and alchemical explanations of the platonic bodies.

Finally, it is evident that several of the so-called explanations are incorrect in important details as is obvious from the *Misc. Lat.* answers quoted above. Personally, I find them utterly incomprehensible, and wholly irrelevant to the essential teachings of the R.A. Even if the explanations were complete and correct I would not mourn their passing, because I believe that it is our duty to instruct and enlighten Candidates, not to confuse them with matters which can only be understood by specialists and which have no genuine place in our teachings.

---

124.   THE COMPOSITION OF THE BOARD OF
                    GENERAL PURPOSES

PROVINCIAL REPRESENTATION

Q. How did the Board of General Purposes come into existence in its present form and when did the Provincial Lodges obtain the privilege of representation on the Board?

A. Prior to the Union of the Grand Lodges in 1813, most of the functions of the present-day Board of General Purposes were handled by the so-called 'Committee of Charity' which was first appointed on 17 March 1725. It was instituted, primarily, 'to regulate the Generall Charity' of Grand Lodge, and was limited at first to no more than thirteen members, all Master Masons, any seven of them to be a quorum. The first appointees included two former Grand Masters, several noblemen, and the Masters of only a few Lodges in the London area.

Gradually, the functions of the Committee of Charity were extended, so that it was empowered to conduct a great deal of the business of Grand Lodge. The constitution of its membership was also changed from time to time, and in November 1732 it was enlarged to consist of former Grand Officers with 'twenty Masters of Lodges'. The Provincial Lodges had no representation as of right.

In the Antients' Grand Lodge, a somewhat similar procedure obtained and their 1787 Book of Constitutions, for example, added the Masters of ten lodges to their Committee, 'five from the oldest lodges, and five from the youngest'.

The 1815 *B. of C.* specified that the B.G.P. should consist of the Grand Master, Deputy Grand Master and Grand Wardens of the year (these being members *ex-officio*) with 'twenty other members' ten of them *including the President* to be nominated by the G.M., and the other ten elected by the Grand Lodge from the 'actual Masters of lodges'. One third of the members at least were to go out of Office annually, and there was no provision for representation of the Provinces.

The 1841 *B. of C.* recorded that Past Masters were to be eligible for election to the Board; that was a major change.

In the 1873 *B. of C.* the main change was that fourteen members were to be elected (instead of ten) and they were to be Masters or P.M.s, but not more than seven of the latter. There was still no mention of Provinces. The G.M. nominated ten members including the President.

The *B. of C.* for 1896 enlarged the list of *ex-officio* members, by adding the G. Treasurer, G. Registrar, Dep. G. Registrar, Past President(s) of the B.G.P., the Pres. of the Bd. of Benevolence and the Grand D.C. The elected members were increased to eighteen and the Grand Master was permitted to nominate only six, including the President. An amendment dated 6 March 1901 specified that six of the eighteen elected members were to retire each year, the first group to be those who had polled the least votes at the election, and the second group those who had been elected by the next smallest number, etc. The Provinces were still without specific representation.

This procedure lasted until June 1917 when a new arrangement came into force. It appears that some time in 1915 a movement had begun to obtain Provincial representation on the Board of General Purposes and a Special Committee had been appointed by the Board to enquire and report on the subject (with powers to co-opt expert advisers). The Special Committee reported at great length (after massive correspondence with Provincial Grand Masters) at the Quarterly Communication on 7 June 1916.

After outlining the difficulties (and the report is well worth reading) Sir Alfred Robbins, as President of the Board, made it clear that the special Committee was agreed that there ought to be a suitable representation of the Provincial Lodges on the Board and the schemes for selection of suitable Provincial candidates was left to the Provincial Grand Masters themselves.

From June 1917 onwards the Grand Master would nominate eight members to the Board, as his personal appointees, so as to 'balance' the increase in elected members—but there was a gentle hint in the proposals that those two additional nominees might be chosen with a view to representing the Districts, i.e., Lodges overseas.

The London Lodges were to have twelve representatives on the Board (four retiring each year) and the Provinces were to have twelve (also with four retiring each year).

Rule 255b as then revised dealt with procedure for Provincial nominations and after necessary modification and simplification that Rule remains as No. 219 in our present *B. of C.*

Our present system as to the composition of the B.G.P. has been in use since 1917, and it must seem rather strange that 200 years elapsed after the foundation of the first Grand Lodge before the Provincial Lodges achieved representation on the Board of General Purposes.

---

125.   NAMING OF LODGES

Q. In what period did Lodges take their own names?

A. Before the first Grand Lodge was formed in 1717, and for several decades after its foundation, English Lodges were usually called by the name of the Tavern or Coffee House where they met. There was, as yet, no law requiring Lodges to take names; they were simply known by their place of meeting.

The first Lodge *in the English records* to take a distinctive title was University Lodge No. 54, which took this name from its inception in 1730. It met at the Bear and Harrow, Temple Bar, London, but lasted only until 1736 when it was erased from the Lists.

The present Lodge of Antiquity, No. 2, was No. 1 of the Four Old Lodges; it met at the Goose and Gridiron, St. Paul's Churchyard and was known by that name in 1717. It took its first name as West India and American Lodge in 1761 and its present title in 1770.

Several Lodges have a history of more than one name; an example is No. 3 of the Four Old Lodges, which, in 1717, was identified only by its meeting place, the Apple Tree Tavern, Covent Garden, London. It took its name as the Lodge of Fortitude in 1768 and in 1818 it merged with the Old Cumberland Lodge and added that name to the title; it is now Fortitude and Old Cumberland Lodge No. 12.

Two Lodges whose original meeting place is unknown were No. 6 and No. 8 in the year 1722. The former was not named until 1770, when it took the title British Lodge, and bears this name, but ranks as No. 8 on the present Register. The latter, the original No. 8 took the name Union Lodge in 1734 but lasted only until 1744 when it was erased.

In the Antients' Grand Lodge Minutes, Lodges were referred to by their numbers only, and very few had names until after the Union in 1813. Their numbering commenced at No. 2 and the first mention of No. 1 is in the Minutes dated 5 September 1759: 'The Grand Master's Lodge (was) Proclaimed and took first seat accordingly as No. 1'. This could be deemed an instance of naming.

The Antients' records show that St. David's Lodge No. 54(A) met at the Bear's Paw, London, in 1756, having taken that Saint's name from inception. This Lodge was erased in 1781. Lodge of Freedom No. 26(A), meeting at Dudley, Worcester, was named from inception in 1788, but this too was erased, in 1828.

It is surprising to notice that there was no official ruling on the naming of Lodges until 1815 and Rule 11 in the *Book of Constitutions* for that year states:

> Any lodge which may not be distinguished by a name or title, being desirous of taking one, must for that purpose, procure the approbation of the grand master, or provincial grand master, and the name must be registered with the grand secretary. No lodge shall be permitted to alter its name without the like approbation.

The Regulation even at this late date was only permissive. Although the vast majority of the Lodges had names, the naming of the Lodges was not yet mandatory, and that situation remained for nearly seventy years. The Regulation was at last made mandatory in 1884, in Rule 128 which is in force today as Rule 98:

> Every Lodge must be distinguished by a name or title, as well as a number, and no Lodge shall be permitted to make an alteration in its name or title without the approval of the Grand Master, and in Provinces or Districts, that of the Provincial Grand Master or District Grand Master also.

The tendency for Lodges to take names developed fairly strongly in the 1760s but it did not become general. When names became mandatory the choice was very wide, although the majority might be included under one of the following headings:

Commemorative—Saints, persons, events, e.g., Coronations, Jubilees, etc.

Places —Cities, Towns, localities, buildings, etc.

Association or 'Class Lodges'—Naval, Military, Schools, Livery Companies, professional, trade, etc.

Architectural styles or features, e.g., Doric, Architrave, Pillar, etc.

Classical —Roman or Greek gods, mythical characters.

Virtues —Cardinal, Moral and Accepted, e.g., Fortitude, Charity, Integrity, etc.

Masonic characteristics, such as Noble Brotherhood, Harmony, Fraternal Union, Grip of Friendship, etc.

Individuality has asserted itself, however, and the *Masonic Year Book* includes many examples which are outside any of these categories.

126.   CORN, WINE, OIL AND SALT
               IN THE CONSECRATION CEREMONY

Q. I have seen Corn, Wine, Oil and Salt used in the Consecration of a
Masonic Lodge. Why are these items used, especially Salt, and when
were they brought into Masonic practice?

A. There are several instances in the Bible in which all four 'elements'
are mentioned together in a single sentence, e.g., Ezra vi, v. 9 '... wheat,
salt, wine and oil . . .', and again in Ezra vii, v. 22, and I Esdras vi, 30.
In our present-day consecration ceremonies these 'elements' owe their
introduction, almost certainly, to their use in Biblical times as oblations,
offerings, and as bloodless sacrifices, in the Temple. Corn, Wine and Oil
are mentioned in Deut. xi, v. 14 among the rewards for those who
followed God's commandments. They were deemed the prime necessi-
ties of daily life; hence their use among the Hebrews as thank-offerings,
(i.e., non-animal) sacrifices.

Salt is also related to sacrifice but it has a variety of symbolic meanings
in the Bible. Its use is prescribed in Leviticus ii, 13.

> Every oblation of thy meat offering shalt thou season with salt ... With
> all thine offerings thou shalt offer salt.

Cruden in his *Concordance* interprets Salt, in this passage, as a symbol
of friendship, and it was a custom in Europe and the Near East in the
middle ages, to welcome distinguished visitors to a town or village with
Bread and Salt.

Because it helps to preserve from corruption and is itself impervious
to decay, Salt has become a symbol of incorruption. Brewer (*Dict. of
Phrase and Fable*) calls it a symbol of perpetuity and this association of
Salt with the idea of permanence appears frequently in the Bible:

> 'It is a covenant of salt for ever before the Lord' (Num. xviii, 19).

Rashi, one of the greatest among the Hebrew commentators, said of
this passage,

> 'As salt never decays, so will God's covenant . . . endure'.

On a theme nearer to Freemasonry,

> 'The Lord God of Israel gave the kingdom . . . to David . . . by a covenant
> of salt' (2 Chron. xiii, v. 5).

Here, again, the idea of permanence is emphasized, and that is
undoubtedly one of the main reasons for the use of Salt in our Masonic

consecration ceremonies. So far as I am aware, the theme of preservation and permanence is not usually mentioned by the Consecrating Officer but, in some of the numerous Consecration mementoes in our Library, the verse that is sung before the Salt is used in the ceremony, runs as follows:

> Now o'er our work this salt we shower,
> Emblem of Thy conservant power;
> And may Thy presence, Lord, we pray,
> Keep this our temple from decay.

It may be interesting to reproduce the symbolical explanations of the elements, as they are given in the English Consecration ceremony.

Corn,	symbol of Plenty.
Wine,	symbol of Joy & Cheerfulness.
Oil,	symbol of Peace and Unanimity.
Salt,	symbol of Fidelity and Friendship.

The *Masonic* symbolism for the elements seems to have varied considerably in different times and places. C. C. Hunt in his *Masonic Symbolism* (Iowa, 1939 pp. 100, 101) quotes the report of an English foundation-stone ceremony in the 1920s when the Provincial Grand Master for Nottinghamshire officiated; on that occasion Oil was 'the emblem of charity', and Salt 'the emblem of hospitality and friendship'. The same writer notes the curative or purifying powers of Salt, citing ii Kings, II vv. 20–21 in which Elisha with a cruse of Salt 'healed the waters'. Another reference in similar vein is in Exodus xxx, v. 35, 'Thou shalt make it a perfume . . . *seasoned with salt*, pure and holy'. (In this last instance the customary translation of the words in italics is 'tempered together', but the original Hebrew certainly means 'salted' or 'seasoned with salt'.)

The use of Salt in the Consecration of Masonic Lodges seems to be of modern introduction, probably after 1850. In the late 1780s, Preston's descriptions of Dedication Ceremonies mention Corn, Wine and Oil— but never Salt. In addition, Bro. T. O. Haunch, the Librarian of Grand Lodge, has checked a number of descriptions of Masonic Consecration and Dedication ceremonies up to the 1840s. None of them makes mention of Salt, and it seems impossible to say, with certainty, when that 'element' was brought in. Incidentally, the ceremony of Consecration as practised under the Grand Lodge of Scotland uses Corn, Wine, and Oil, but there is no mention of Salt.

127.   'PROGRESS' IN PLACING THE CANDIDATES
Turning The Candidate in The Third Degree

Q. In the Third degree the Candidate is placed in the N.E. for the Charge and then moved to the S.E. for the Entrusting. Why is this move made and would it not be easier to keep the Candidate in one place for both Charge and Entrusting? If there is no authoritative reason for this will you give your opinion?

A. The custom of moving the Candidate at this point in the proceedings dates back to early post-union times. Indeed we find evidence of this in the Claret ritual, 1st Edn: 1838, p. 140, where a rubric after the Raising and before the Entrusting directs:

> The W.M. now takes the right hand of the candidate with his right [sic] and gently turns him, so that they occupy each others places.

There appears to be no practical reason (or physical reason) why the M.M. Candidate should be moved at this stage and it seems possible that the movements of the Candidate from (roughly) N.E. to S.E. and subsequently to the 'centre' are directly related to the idea of progress, which is expressed very clearly in the ritual of the second degree. There the W.M. says:

> '. . . you are now placed in the S.E. part of the Lodge *to mark the progress you have made in the science* . . .'

The perambulations themselves, advancing by three, five and seven steps, the three E.A. steps each longer than its predecessor, are all examples of this 'progress'. Our E.A.s are placed in the N.E. corner; the F.C.s are further on in the round of progress, and they are placed in the S.E. Similarly, after raising, the Candidate in the North hears the solemn speech, and he moves 'up' to the South, for the entrusting. Later, he is brought to the centre, for the last part of the ceremony.

If this theory is acceptable, and I can see no other, then the three separate positions of the M.M. in the course of the Third Degree are virtually a complete 'symbolical' resumé of his craft career, finishing at the centre for the Sublime Degree.

---

128.   FIDELITY, FIDELITY, FIDELITY

Q. It is the practice of a number of Lodges in this Province to use the Sign of Reverence during the Ob. in the First Degree, and the Sign of F. in the Second and Third Degrees. This arrangement seemed to be in

order, as it was pointed out that E.A.s would not know the Sign of F.
But the question was then raised as to what sign is given in the Closing
Ceremony, when the I.P.M. says 'Fidelity, Fidelity, Fidelity'?

A. The main question is so interesting that I dare not embark on the
subsidiary problems of whether it is more 'correct' to use the Sn. of
Reverence, or the Sn. of F., or the appropriate penal-sign of each
Degree, during the Obligations. Four of my Lodges use the Sn. of F.
during all Obligations. Many Lodges throughout the country use the
penal sign, and both practices are so strongly established that it would
be almost impossible to determine which is the best or correct procedure.
I have only mentioned it here because this point becomes relevant in the
discussion below. (This question is discussed in greater detail under
'The W.M.'s Sign During The Obligation' on pp. 186–7, above.)

THE SIGN OF FIDELITY

The mention of two signs, Reverence and Fidelity, involves a number
of issues and it may help if we try to separate the wheat from the chaff.
Fundamentally the signs are alike, except for the position of one digit.
I have spent some time trying to ascertain when, how and why the
actual position of the digits was prescribed for either of these signs,
but with only limited success.

Two points may be made here with certainty:

(1) The earliest description of the F.C. sign in a trigradal system is in
Prichard's exposure of 1730 and it gives the r.h. in the then customary
place, but without any reference to digits.
(2) Prichard also indicates that this was the posture of the Wardens, while
the W.M. asked them 'their situations' etc., during several questions which
seem to belong to the closing of the Lodge. Possibly it was a mark of
respect (see below), but still no mention of digits.

Soon after this, from *c.* 1740 onwards, there is ample evidence that the
modern 'squared' form had been adopted. No reason or explanation is
given, but now the thumb is specifically mentioned in almost every
Craft ritual that survives, e.g.,

A Dialogue between Simon & Philip, c. 1740
Le Secret des Francs-Maçons, 1742
Le Catéchisme des Francs-Maçons, 1744
L'Ordre des Francs-Maçons Trahi, 1745
Three Distinct Knocks, 1760
J. & B. 1762

The two last-named, both famous English exposures, had a great run,
with numerous editions published up to the end of the 18th century
and later.

It is noteworthy that the *Dialogue*, of *c.* 1740, while describing the lay-out of the Lodge, etc. (presumably at the Opening), states that the Wardens stand in the Sn. of F. position *generally*, i.e. without reference to a specific Degree, and *Trahi* says that this 'squared' sign is always used 'when addressing the Worshipful'. (I take this posture as a mark of respect.)

From the brief details given above, we may safely agree that, though the earliest mention of the sign made no reference to digits, the 'squared' position has been established practice in England for well over 200 years, and *the same sign* was certainly in use in France and England during portions of other ceremonies, e.g., in Opening and Closing and *when addressing the Master in any Degree.* Thus the sign, almost from its earliest appearance, seems to have served a dual purpose:

    (I) As a mode of recognition.
    (II) As a mark of respect.

It seems possible that the latter usage may have led to its being adopted, in some Lodges, as a general posture for all Brethren during Prayers or Obligations, and in that case it was probably modified (in the 19th century) by the 'loss of a digit', simply to draw a distinction between the postures for different parts of the proceedings.

   It is strange that, although many of our early documents give full details of the posture of the Candidates during each of the Obligations, there is no mention anywhere of a sign or posture by the remaining Brethren during Prayers or Obligations. This suggests that there was no particular sign or posture in general use, or that there was no uniform practice in this respect.

THE SIGN OF REVERENCE

It is certain that throughout the 18th century there is no trace, in *ritual or rubric*, of a 'Sign of Reverence'. That so-called 'sign' may have acquired some sort of status in many workings, simply because its origins have not been questioned, but I hold that *it is not a sign*, because it has no place as a mode of recognition in our 'entrusting'. This view was very strongly supported by the late Dr. E. H. Cartwright[1] who was a great specialist in such matters.

I agree, readily, that this posture is widely used (during Prayers) in many English workings, but that does not make it correct, nor have we any right to introduce this practice as a new and wholly unauthorized sign, regardless of what title we give it, or the purpose for which it is used.

---

[1] *A Commentary on the Freemasonic Ritual*, pp. 56/7.

Uses of The Sign of Fidelity

Having disposed of the 'Sn. of Reverence' as an unauthorized practice, it seems that we must now accept the fact that nowadays we use the posture or Sn. of F. *for several purposes*, e.g.,

(1) As a prescribed mode of recognition.
(2) In Lodges where the Brn. make the Sn. of F. during all three Obligations, the Sign is presumably an affirmation of our own fidelity.
(3) It may also be interpreted as a mark of respect, while the V.S.L. is actually in use.
(4) In many workings the Sn. of F. is used (momentarily) at the mention of the name of God, e.g. at the end of the lecture on the second T.B., and at the end of the Address to the W.M. on his Installation.
(5) In nearly all workings, at the final closing of the Lodge.

This brings me, at last, to the main question, and the problems arising from it, i.e., 'What Sn. is given when we utter the F.F.F.?' Whatever sign is given, I am convinced that with those words, *it ought to be* the posture or 'Sn. of F.'. This raises the difficult and oft-repeated questions:

(a) Is it right to give the Sn. of F. in the presence of E.A.s?
(b) Is it right to make (or give) a Masonic sign after the Lodge has been closed?

On the first question, it is perfectly clear that we do use that posture for several different purposes. The E.A. accepts it as a Masonic *custom*, and he cannot possibly know—until later on in his career—that he has seen something which ultimately proves to be *part* of one of the modes of recognition.

On (b) there is a difficulty, which depends largely on the problem 'When is the Lodge actually closed?' Perhaps the simplest guide on this point is to ask another question 'When is the Lodge actually open?' and the answer to that is surely, 'Not until the V.S.L. has been opened'. Using this as a fairly safe guide, I would argue that the Lodge is not finally closed until the V.S.L. has been closed; and for those Brethren who are worried about the F.F.F. being made after the V.S.L. has been closed (as is done in most Lodges) I would suggest a very simple alteration in procedure:

After the W.M., S.W., and J.W. have made their 'Closing' announcements, the I.P.M. lays his hand on the *open* V.S.L. and says:

'Brethren, nothing now remains . . . F.F.F.'

and then he closes the Book.

On this point, (b), I quote from a letter received after this article was published in *AQC* 81:

> When the initiate is being entrusted with the signs, he is told that they are the marks by which we are known to each other, and distinguished from the rest of the world. If they are only to be used when the Lodge is open, how can he make himself known to another Mason outside the Lodge? Further, a stranger, visiting a Lodge, is proved either by the Tyler or the J.W., before entering the Lodge room. He must make use of the Sign, Token and Word to prove himself.

Incidentally, it seems strange that although many of our correspondents have queried the use of a Masonic sign after the Lodge is closed, nobody has ever queried our practice in Opening the Lodge, where all the Brn. prove that 'none but Freemasons are present' before the Lodge is opened!

---

129. CORRECT SEQUENCE OF THE LOYAL TOAST

Q. Which is the correct sequence when giving the Loyal Toast? Is it 'Toast, Drink, Fire, National Anthem?' or should it be 'Toast, Drink, National Anthem and Fire?'.

A. The official ruling, from the Grand Secretary's Office, is as follows: 'Toast, Drink, Fire, and National Anthem'.

One further note may be added. If the National Anthem has been sung in Lodge, as is often done, it would not be repeated at Table.

---

130. WARDENS' TESTS IN THE SECOND DEGREE AND ON THE WINDING STAIRS

Q. In the explanation of the Second Degree Tracing Board we are told that the ascent of our ancient Brethren 'was opposed by the J.W. who demanded of them the p.g. and p.w. leading from the First to the Second Degree,' whereas in the actual ceremony of passing it is the S.W. to whom the p.g. and p.w. are communicated. How do you explain this difference?

A. Let us be clear about the nature of the question you have posed. The *tests* on the 'Winding Stairs' *are a piece of pure legend* relating to the builders of Solomon's Temple. The tests conducted in the Lodge are a part of the actual ceremony of 'Passing' and, when the J.W. asks for the E.A. test, and the S.W. asks for the p.g. and p.w., they are examining the E.A. Candidate *to ensure that he is qualified to receive the Second Degree.*

In the Lecture on the Second T.B. (at the point which gives rise to your query) we are dealing with qualified F.C.s who went to receive their wages in the 'Middle chamber' (or treasury?) where, so our story goes, they were paid in specie. (Elsewhere, the T.B. Lecture states that the E.A.s received their wages in corn, wine and oil, implying that they received those items in some other place and had no cause to go to the 'Middle chamber').

Thus, the tests in the Second Degree (prior to the Obligation) *are concerned with the E.A.*, whereas the T.B. tests deal with F.C.s only, and those two procedures cannot be reconciled (nor, indeed, do they need to be).

The compilers of the ritual were clearly at great pains to divide parts of the ceremonial work in lodge between J.W. and S.W. and so they each get a part of the test in the pre-Obligation portion of the Second Degree. Later, towards the end of the Ceremony (after the Cand. has been entrusted) he is somewhat similarly examined by the J.W. and S.W.

This division of the work between the Wardens is reflected in the legend of the ascent of the winding stairs; but now, because they are dealing with acknowledged F.C.s, the tests are re-arranged for that purpose. Presumably it would have been enough to have had the S.W. test alone, i.e., the F.C.s Sn. Tn. and Wd. but, in order to share the work, the J.W. is brought in first for the test on the p.g. and p.w.

To sum up:

(1) The designers of the Tracing Boards were not at all concerned with the veracity of our legend about the place in which the craftsmen received their wages.

(2) The compilers of the T.B. Lecture were trying to construct a clear simple story.

(3) The revisers of the Ritual, *c.* 1813 and later, were not overmuch concerned with the need to reconcile their ceremonial procedures with the details contained in the legend, which could have been done quite easily had they so desired, but they were concerned to divide the work in the Lodge between the J.W. and S.W. at the point on which your query is raised and so they gave one part of the test to the J.W., with the main test to the S.W.

This kind of difficulty arises regularly out of a misguided desire to treat particular items in our *legendary* materials as though they are established facts. In the present instance you are comparing fact with fiction, i.e., the actual procedure in conferring the Degree with the *legendary* procedure in the ascent of the Winding Stair. They do not match, probably because nobody really tried to make them match. It would be simple enough to organize this but, needless to say, I am not suggesting this change.

---

131.   LANDMARKS: TENETS AND PRINCIPLES

Q. We frequently refer in the ritual to the Landmarks of the Order, yet they are nowhere specified or listed. What constitutes a Masonic Landmark, and can you furnish a list of them?

A. This is one of the most debatable subjects in Masonry and it gives rise to very wide differences of opinion. Any good dictionary will define a 'Landmark', but Masonically the term requires a stricter definition. The best writers on the subject are unanimous on two essential points:

(a) A landmark must have existed from the 'time whereof the memory of man runneth not to the contrary'.
(b) A landmark is an element in the form or essence of the Society of such importance that Freemasonry would no longer be Freemasonry if it were removed.

If these two qualifications are used strictly to test whether certain practices, systems, principles, or regulations can be admitted as land-marks it will be found that there are in fact very few items that will pass this rigid test.

Nevertheless the tendency, even among prominent writers who try to compile lists of landmarks, seems to be to incorporate items which really come under the heading of regulations, or customs, or principles, and tentative lists of landmarks range from five to fifty separate items.

Without the least desire to be dogmatic, the following is an attempt to compile a list of acceptable landmarks that would conform to the two-point test:

1. That a Mason professes a belief in God (the Supreme Being), the G.A.O.T.U.
2. That the V.S.L. is an essential and indispensable part of the Lodge, to be open in full view when the Brethren are at labour.
3. That a Mason must be male, free-born, and of mature age.
4. That a Mason, by his tenure, owes allegiance to the Sovereign and to the Craft.
5. That a Mason believes in the immortality of the soul.

The first four items listed above are derived directly from the *Old Charges*, which date back to *c*. 1390 and are the oldest documents in the world belonging to the Craft. The last item in the list, 'immortality', is implicit in the religious beliefs of that period.

English Masons may be interested to know that many Grand Lodges overseas have adopted specific codes of landmarks, usually printed as preambles to their Constitutions, and the brief list above is in close accord (though not identical) with the code adopted by the Grand Lodge of Massachusetts.

One of the most interesting lists was drawn up by Albert Mackey, a great American student (1807–1881). Although he based his selection on the two essential points noted above, quoting them almost word for word, his list ran to twenty-five items, most of which could never have passed as landmarks if he had applied his own test. Limitations of space do not permit a detailed analysis and only a few of Mackey's landmarks are examined here, with comments to illustrate the pitfalls.

Mackey's No. 1. 'The modes of recognition. They admit of no variation . . .' These cannot be landmarks. Several of the most important of them did not make their appearance in the Craft until the 18th century.

Mackey's No. 2. 'The division of symbolic Masonry into three degrees . . .' The trigradal system did not emerge until some time between 1711 and 1725. Prior to this period there is no evidence of anything more than two degrees.

Mackey's No. 3. 'The legend of the Third Degree . . .' The earliest evidence of this legend concerns Noah, not Hiram Abif. There is good evidence of the F.P.O.F., in 1696, as a part of the then second degree (for Master or fellow-craft) and the legend in one of its early forms *may have been in existence at that time*, but there is no evidence of it in the ritual until 1726.

Mackey's No. 4. 'The government of the Fraternity by a presiding Officer called a Grand Master who is elected . . .' The first Grand Lodge was founded in 1717. There was no Grand Master of Masons before that time. This item is a very proper regulation in the *Book of Constitutions*, but it cannot be a landmark.

Mackey's Nos. 5, 6, 7, 8. Various prerogatives of the Grand Master, but all of them are, in fact, privileges vested in him by the Grand Lodge over which he presides. They are regulations, or customs, *not* landmarks.

Mackey's No. 9. 'The necessity of Masons to congregate in Lodges . . .' This extremely interesting item may well be a landmark, but if we try to go back to 'time immemorial' practice, the operative masons seem to have had the right to congregate for Lodge purposes when any five or six of them came together anywhere. Nowadays, however, the mode of congregation for Lodge purposes is governed by regulations.

Mackey's No. 10. The government of the Craft in a (Lodge) by a Master and two Wardens . . .' Another doubtful landmark. There was a time when the Lodge was governed by the Master and one Warden.

Several of Mackey's landmarks deal with the rights of individual Masons, rights which are all governed nowadays by regulations and some of them are certainly not of time immemorial status.

Of course it is quite impossible to discuss such a wide-ranging subject within an article of a 1000 words or so, and these brief notes are designed mainly to open up the subject and to point the way to discussion.

TENETS AND PRINCIPLES

Q. We discussed your recent Lodge Summons on the subject of Landmarks at our Lodge of Instruction and one of our younger members asked for a definition of 'Tenets' and 'Principles'. The Dictionaries suggest that the two latter are synonymous. Can you help?

A. The *Masonic* definitions of 'Landmark' are given in (a) and (b) in the answer above.

Tenet —The principal definition in the *Oxford English Dictionary* is 'A doctrine, dogma, principle, or opinion in religion, philosophy, politics or the like, held by a school, sect, party, or person'.

Principle—The best definition for our purpose in the *O.E.D.* is '. . . a primary element, force, or law, which produces or determines particular results; the ultimate basis upon which the existence of something depends; cause, in the widest sense'.

From the above it would seem that 'tenets' and 'principles' could be in some respects alike so that a 'tenet' in certain instances might have the force of a 'principle'. For the sake of a sharper distinction, we may perhaps ignore this aspect of the definition, and rely more strongly on the definition of 'tenet' as 'doctrine or dogma'. The essential element of those two words is that they represent an idea, a belief, or a conviction, which cannot necessarily be proved, *but is held by faith*, and perhaps one of the best examples that one can give of a Masonic tenet is the doctrine of the immortality of the soul.

The *O.E.D.* definition of 'principle' is a very strong one, 'a primary element, force, or law . . .' etc., and one might quote, as an example, the oft-repeated maxim, 'All men are equal in the sight of God'. This could well be a Masonic principle. In the Craft, however, the term has a more specialized significa̅nce. The Code of 'Basic Principles for Grand Lodge Recognition' illustrates this, e.g., No. 7:

> That the discussion of religion and politics within the Lodge shall be strictly prohibited.

This item could very well have been a Rule in our *Book of Constitutions*. The Grand Lodge *has made it* one of the 'Basic Principles' of Free-masonry and this leads me to my summing up of the whole question.

'Landmarks', in our sense of the term, are something perpetual and unchanging.

'Tenets' are beliefs that we hold, even though they are beyond proof. They may be of our own invention, or inherited, but we do not question them because they are founded in our faith.

'Principles' may have their roots in natural law, or in ethics and philosophies which shape our code of conduct. But they may also be invented or adopted rules, or beliefs, which have their basic force as 'principles' simply because we choose to acknowledge them as such.

---

132.   IS SYMBOLISM A LANDMARK?

Q. As I understand it, 'Landmarks' are those fundamental principles which characterize Masonry; and Freemasonry is defined as 'a peculiar system of morality, veiled in allegory and illustrated by symbols'. Since 'illustrating by symbols' constitutes an integral part of the 'peculiar system' would I be right in saying that symbolism is a Landmark of Freemasonry?

A. The definition you have quoted is a widely accepted one, but I would suggest that it is the system of morality which is the essential characteristic of the Craft, while the manner in which we illustrate it, i.e., by symbols, is incidental. Indeed, I think it would be fair to say that the major part of our teaching is by precept, example and exhortation.

It is true that we use symbols throughout our ceremonies, etc. in the preparation of Candidates, steps, signs, working tools, clothing and furnishings, right down to the chequered flooring of the Lodge. Practically all of them are 'moralized' in a few words of the ritual, designed to teach their immediate symbolism. But that is only the foundation; the experts in that field could add a chapter where we use only a few words, and they could find meanings for those same symbols vastly different from those that we accept.

In short, symbolism is not precise; it is an art, not an exact science, and it has no boundaries. For all these reasons, I believe that it cannot properly be described as a Landmark.

---

133.   THE CONSENT AND CO-OPERATION OF
                  THE OTHER TWO

Q. In the Third Degree legend, Hiram Abif told his assailants that the secrets of a M.M. were known to but three in the world and that 'without the consent and co-operation of the other two he neither could nor would divulge them'.

Later in the same legend Solomon said that 'by the untimely death of our Master the genuine secrets . . . were lost'.

How could they be lost by the death of one man if they were known to two others? What is meant here, 'by consent and co-operation of the other two'?

A. This part of the legend is concerned with a tradition that there were three Grand Masters at the building of the Temple, namely, Solomon, Hiram King of Tyre and H.A., *who were the sole repositories of the genuine secrets*; it also emphasizes that those secrets could only be conferred by the three Grand Masters *acting in co-operation*. Hence, the genuine secrets were, to all intents and purposes, 'lost' by the death of H.A. and this resulted in the adoption of the 'substituted' secrets.

This is the essence of the legend, in a nutshell, and *the solution to the problem actually appears in the Royal Arch Ceremony where the Candidate learns the precise nature of the 'co-operation' during his entrusting.* In effect our M.M. legend is incomplete so far as the Candidate is concerned until he has taken the Royal Arch.

But there are other extremely interesting problems that arise from this two-part procedure, with half the story in one Degree and the remainder in a later Ceremony. It is perfectly clear that our Third Degree legend in its present form is deliberately shaped so as to link it with an essential element in the Royal Arch, which suggests the remote possibility that originally the whole story was included in the Third Degree, so that the loss of the secrets and their subsequent recovery might have formed a single Ceremony.

It must be admitted that when the Third Degree made its first appearance in Britain, *c.* 1725, there was no evidence of any kind of Royal Arch theme and when Prichard's exposure of 1730 appeared with an extremely good early version of the Hiramic legend, there was *still no evidence of the R.A. completion theme*. A substitute word was adopted and the story is complete in itself, because, as the text says, '. . . that which was lost . . . is now found'.

The earliest hint that might be taken to suggest a link between the Third Degree and the Royal Arch appears in *Le Catéchisme des Francs-Maçons*, 1744, in which one of the Names of God is mentioned in the legend and displayed on the Tracing Board as 'the former word of a Master' [i.e. M.M.]. *In that legend* (repeated in several later French texts), *the word was not lost*; the searchers only adopted a substitute out of fear that H.A. had been forced to divulge the original. This version of the legend is complete in itself and, in many respects, more logical than our modern Hiramic legend. It appeared at a time when there was no evidence of the Royal Arch in French practice, though there is useful evidence in England and Ireland that a *separate* Royal Arch ceremony was already in existence.

We still await a complete solution to this interesting problem of the 'Relationship between the Third Degree and the R.A.' which is examined in greater detail in a paper by the present writer in *AQC* 86.

---

134.   MONEY AND METALLIC SUBSTANCES

Q. What is the origin and significance of our procedure in this part of the preparation of the Candidate?

A. The polluting influence of metal is stressed several times in the Bible. Here are two examples:

> And if thou wilt make me an altar of stone, thou shalt not build it of hewn stone: for if thou lift up thy tool upon it, thou hast polluted it. (Exodus, xx, 25.)
> And the house, when it was in building, was built of stone made ready before it was brought thither: so that there was neither hammer nor axe nor any tool of iron heard in the house, while it was in building. (1 Kings, vi, 7.)

The idea of pollution by metal seems to have been common in many countries and we find it in various mythologies, e.g., in the Baldur myth, the mistletoe may not be cut with iron.

Although we have descriptions of ritual and ceremonial procedure in a number of documents from 1696 onwards, the earliest hint of this practice appears in the *Graham MS.* of 1726:

How came you into the Lodge—poor and penyless [sic] blind and ignorant of our secrets.

Prichard's exposure, *Masonry Dissected*, dated 1730, emphasized the 'metallic' aspects of the procedure of those days, but he gave no reason for it:

Q. How did he bring you?
A. Neither naked nor cloathed, barefoot nor shod, deprived of all Metal and in a right moving Posture.

The next description—from a similar source—*Le Secret des Francs- Maçons*, by the Abbé G. L. C. Perau, was published in France in 1742, and it is much more detailed:

After he has satisfied these questions, he is deprived of all metal articles he may have about him, such as buckles, buttons, rings, (snuff)-boxes, etc. There are some Lodges where they carry precision so far as to deprive a man of his clothes if they are ornamented with *galon* [i.e., a kind of gold or silver thread].

Another French exposure, *Le Catéchisme des Francs-Maçons*, seems to have been the first document of this kind to give the reasons for the procedure:

Q. Why were you deprived of all Metals?
A. Because when the Temple of Solomon was in building, the Cedars of Lebanon were sent all cut, ready for use, so that one heard no sound of hammer, nor of any other tool, when they used them.

(Note the Biblical quotation referred to stone; *Le Catéchisme* and later French texts speak of the Cedars of Lebanon.)

A more extended symbolism began to make its appearance towards the end of the 18th century and the following is an unusual interpretation from Preston's First Lecture, Section ii, Clause 1:

Why deprived of metal?
For three reasons: first reason, that no weapon be introduced into the Lodge to disturb the harmony; second reason, that metal, though of value, could have no influence in our initiation; third reason, that after our initiation metal could make no distinction amongst Masons, the Order being founded on peace, virtue and friendship.

There can be little doubt that the present-day procedure is a survival of the idea of pollution from metal and, since the Candidate for Initiation is symbolically erecting a Temple within himself, that is probably the reason why the 'deprivation' has remained a part of our practice throughout more than two centuries.

135.   THE ATTENDANCE (SIGNATURE) BOOK

Q. In our Lodge (in Victoria, Australia), the W.M. asks, 'Has every Brother signed the Appearance Book?' Why and what is the origin of the custom of signing the book?

A. The surviving (operative) minutes, from 1598 to *c.* 1700 show that Masons in Lodge usually signed their names, or marks, *in the minute book,* or their presence was recorded there by the Secretary. Often he gave only the name of the Master or presiding officer. There was no Grand Lodge and no rule on the subject.

Soon after the formation of the first Grand Lodge in 1717 the Craft was troubled with clandestine 'makings' of Masons. In 1723, a London newspaper, *The Flying Post or Post-Master,* printed a Masonic exposure, rather a paltry piece. A more interesting one, *The Grand Mystery of Free-Masons Discover'd,* appeared in 1724 and 1725, but none of them seems to have done much damage.

In October, 1730, however, Prichard published his sixpenny pamphlet *Masonry Dissected,* which must have caused a sensation. It was the first work that described a system of three degrees; it contained the first printed version of the Hiramic legend and much interesting material besides. It ran through three editions and two pirated versions before the end of that year! On 15 December 1730, Grand Lodge took steps:

> The Deputy Grand Master took notice of a Pamphlet lately published by one Pritchard who pretends to have been made a regular Mason: In Violation of the Obligation of a Mason wch he swears he has broke in order to do hurt to Masonry and expressing himself with the utmost Indignation against both him (stiling him an Impostor) and of his Book as a foolish thing not to be regarded. But in order to prevent the Lodges being imposed upon by false Brethren or Impostors: Proposed till otherwise Ordered by the Grand Lodge, that no Person whatsoever should be admitted into Lodges unless some Member of the Lodge then present would vouch for such visiting Brothers being a regular Mason, *and the Member's Name to be entred against the Visitor's Name in the Lodge Book,* which . . . was unanimously agreed to.

This was the origin of the Visitors' Book, but the Rule requiring a record *in the minutes for all Brethren attending* did not appear in the *B. of C.* until 1884. As a matter of convenience, most Lodges nowadays keep an Attendance Book (or Signature Book) which records signatures of all members and visitors with other requisite details, but the *B. of C.,* Rule 144, still requires, *inter alia,* that precise records be kept *in the Lodge minute-book.*

136.   THE TYLER'S TOAST

Q. When giving the final Toast after Lodge dinners, our Tyler habitually omits the phrase 'a speedy relief from all their sufferings' but goes straight on with 'wishing them a safe return ro their native land . . . etc.'. I have never heard the Toast abbreviated elsewhere in this way; are such variations permitted?

A. The Tyler's Toast is a part of our Table procedure; it is not ritual, and is presumably not governed by the rules applicable to a particular 'working'. The 'standard' formula is widely known, but it has often suffered from the idiosyncrasies of individual Brethren who have the duty of proposing the Toast. If there is any objection to the form used by the Tyler, a gentle hint from the Master or the Director of Ceremonies is surely the obvious remedy.

The drinking and Toasting routines which have become such an established part of our English Masonic banquets have a long and respectable history (though there may have been periods when 'respectable' was the wrong adjective). The evolution of these practices is discussed at length in Q. 146, pp. 313–319, and we need only deal here with what has now become the Tyler's Toast.

Dermott, in his *Ahiman Rezon*, 1756, printed a long collection of Masons' songs clearly designed for use at Table, each followed by a Toast; No. XXXVI (on pp. 148–50) has:

> *To all Ancient Masons, wheresoever dispers'd, or oppress'd, round the Globe, &c.*

and this seems to be the earliest version of what later became the Tyler's Toast.

In *J & B*, an exposure first published in 1762, the Toast appears in the middle of the E.A. Lecture. The third of three toasts at this point, is:

> 'To all Brethren wheresoever dispersed'

but the Tyler had no part in it at this date.

The two themes 'oppressed and dispersed' must have become regularly embodied in the Lectures during the last decades of the 18th century. Browne's *Master Key* gave a similarly brief version of the Toast in 1798, but we find it expanded into virtually its modern form in Claret's *Lectures* of 1840, still without reference to the Tyler (as a Charge at the end of Section III of the 1st Lecture) and it reappears regularly in all later versions:

To all poor and distressed Masons, wherever scattered over the face of Earth and Water, wishing them a speedy relief from their misfortunes, and a safe return to their native country if they require it:

'All Poor and Distressed Masons'

In this expanded form, ideal for a farewell toast, it probably became the Tyler's Toast in the 1850s, but it may have been a little earlier.

As a modern item of interest, the following is a Russian version of the Tyler's Toast, still used in France by Russian refugee Masons under the *Grande Loge Nationale Française*, who give it in their native tongue. It was first heard by the Brethren of Quatuor Coronati Lodge after the meeting on 5 January 1973, when it was given, in English translation, by the W.M., Bro. C. N. Batham, to whom I am indebted for the text:

Brethren, according to ancient custom among Freemasons, before rising from this festive board, let us turn our thoughts to those of our brethren who are scattered over the face of the earth. Let us wish solace to those who suffer, a speedy recovery to those in sickness, an improvement in their lot to those in misfortune, humility to the fortunate and, to those who stand before the Gates of Death, firmness of heart and peace in the Eternal East.

Reverting now to the original question, it is clear that the full 'speedy relief' version has been in Masonic practice for more than 130 years and it would seem a pity to discard it now. But, in case 130 years is not enough, there is a version of the same theme in the Hebrew Prayer Book, which was codified into its present form about 1,100 years ago (though most of its contents are much older). It is recited in Synagogue on most Mondays and Thursdays shortly after the reading of the Holy Scroll of the Law:

As for our Brethren, the whole house of Israel, such of them as are given over to trouble or captivity, whether they are on the sea, or on the dry land, —may the All-Present have mercy upon them, and bring them forth from trouble to deliverance, from darkness to light, and from subjection to redemption, now speedily and at a near time; and let us say, Amen.

---

137.   GLOBES ON THE PILLARS

MAPS, CELESTIAL AND TERRESTRIAL

Q. Why do we talk of the pillars, B. and J., being crowned with 'two spheres on which were delineated maps of the celestial and terrestrial globes' when everybody, at that time, believed the world to be flat?

A. The Biblical account of the objects which surmounted the pillars is by no means clear. The original Hebrew word is *goolot* (plural) or

Pillars with 'Bowls', not 'Globes'
Craft Apron, *c.* 1810

goolah (singular) and it may mean globes, bowls or vessels. Various forms of the same word are often used to describe anything circular or spherical. The *Geneva Bible* of 1560 was one of the early illustrated Bibles that contained a picture of the pillar surmounted by an *ornamental* sphere, *not a map*; but there are several illustrations, produced about the same time and later, showing the pillars surmounted by hemispheres or bowls, and the Authorized Version of the Bible at 1 Kings vii, v. 41, speaks of 'the two bowls of the chapiters that were on the top of the two pillars . . .'. Whether they were really bowls or globes cannot now be determined, but it is quite certain that they were not maps, either celestial or terrestrial.

Solomon's Temple was completed, according to Usher, in 1005 B.C. (Graetz, the Jewish historian, says 1007). The earliest known map of the world is believed to have been designed, some 400 years later, by Anaximander (*c*. 611–546 B.C.) who held that it was flat and shaped like a cylinder of great thickness, bounded round its circumference by water, and suspended in the circular vault of the heavens.

During the next 1500 years or so, the science of cartography made very little progress, although *celestial* globes were already known in the time of Bede, A.D. 637–735. The map-makers were generally agreed that the world was flat, though they differed as to whether it was an 'oblong-square', or oval, or circular. The fathers of the Christian Church did not encourage scientific pursuits and it was not until the period *c*. A.D. 1100–1250 that the sphericity of the globe began to find acceptance among philosophers and scholars. The earliest known 'global maps' (the Nuremberg globe, by Behaim, and another, known as the Laon globe) are both dated 1492, the year in which Columbus began his first major voyage.

Masonic interest in these matters seems to have developed in a very gradual and somewhat roundabout way. Most of our early ritual texts contain questions relating to the 'lights of the lodge', always three in number, at first denoting the Master, warden, and fellow-craft. Later, they are said to represent the 'Sun, Moon, and Master', and *c*. 1727–1730 we find the expansions 'Sun to rule the Day, Moon, the Night', the first faint hint of an interest in the celestial bodies. By this time, 1730, *Masonry Dissected* indicates in its catechism that the Lodge is 'as high as the Heavens' and as deep as 'the Centre of the Earth', and is covered by 'A cloudy Canopy of divers colours (or the Clouds)'.

The next main link in the chain of evolution is in the French exposure *L'Ordre des Francs-Maçons Trahi*, 1745, which repeated all the details summarized from *Masonry Dissected*, above, but added a new piece of interpretation to the dimensions:

    Q. Why do you answer thus?

    A. To indicate, that Free-Masons are spread over all the Earth, & all together they form nevertheless only one Lodge.

Here is the first hint, in any Masonic ritual, of the idea which was soon to be enshrined in the phrase 'Masonry universal'. In the French texts generally, the canopy is now 'studded with golden stars', but the *Trahi* has another embellishment of rather greater interest. At the centre of the combined E.A.–F.C. 'Floor-drawing' or Tracing Board, there is an 'armillary sphere', i.e., a kind of skeleton celestial globe consisting of metal strap rings or hoops, used in the study of astronomy. This was, apparently, the first precursor of the handsome globes which became a distinctive feature in the wealthier and well-equipped Lodges in the late 18th and 19th centuries.

The final evolutionary stages cannot be determined precisely, though they seem to be directly linked with the words 'Masonry universal' which appeared for the first time in *Three Distinct Knocks*, 1760, and then in *J. & B.*, 1762:

> *Mas.* Why . . . from the Surface to the Center of the Earth?
> *Ans.* Because that Masonry is Universal.

Both texts describe the Wardens' columns in detail and there is no hint, at this stage, that they were surmounted with globes. Many later editions of these and other English exposures contain an engraved frontispiece showing the furniture of the lodges of their day, in which the globes are a regular feature, and we cannot be sure which came first, i.e., the handsome globes or the words 'Masonry universal' which may well have inspired their introduction.

The evidence of Lodge minutes and inventories suggests that it was not until the last quarter of the 18th century that the Lodges began to acquire these costly items of furniture and there is a strong possibility that the *globes with maps* were added to the Wardens' columns as an economy measure, in place of the far more expensive globes on ornamental stands.

Eventually the term 'Masonry universal' made its appearance in the Lectures, and in the 'Explanation of the Second Tracing Board' in which the *Masonic* description of Solomon's pillars stated that they were 'further adorned with two spherical balls, on which were delineated maps of the celestial and terrestrial globes [symbolizing] . . . masonry universal'. The symbolism of the globes is wholly acceptable, but the statement that Solomon's pillars were adorned with globes depicting those two maps is nonsense, a flight of fancy, doubtless introduced by a fanatical 'improver' who was determined to make the ritual comply with his ill-founded theories.

---

138. **THE PRIEST WHO ASSISTED AT THE DEDICATION OF THE TEMPLE?**

Q. Why did the High Priest entrust the dedication of King Solomon's Temple to his Assistant instead of doing it himself?

A. There is a dreadful confusion in this question, largely caused by some of the compilers of our ritual who were never content to leave well alone. Determined to dot all the i's and cross all the t's, whenever they came to a problem they could not solve they invented—with disastrous results.

First, let it be clear that, according to the Bible, neither the High Priest nor 'his Assistant' played any part in the dedication of the Temple and, indeed, they are not mentioned at all in that context. Solomon presided alone; he spoke and he prayed. (I Kings, viii, and II Chron., vi and vii.)

The pillar Jachin appears in I Kings, vii, 21 and II Chron, iii, and it was named, according to custom in Bible lands, with an allusive or commemorative name, which means 'He [God] will establish'. Neither the pillar nor its name had anything to do with Jachin, the wrongly styled 'Assistant High Priest'. That name appears at the head of the 21st division of Priests, among the twenty-four divisions listed in I Chron., xxiv. It must be emphasized, however, that no Priest is named in the accounts of the dedication of the Temple, either in Kings or Chronicles.

Having established the facts of the Bible story, we may now turn to the offending phrases in the ritual, where, at the relevant point in the S.W.'s examination of the Candidate, we are told that the pillar, Jachin, was:

> so named after Jachin, a priest who assisted at its [the Temple's] dedication.

There are numerous versions of this statement, all in the same vein. Some rituals say 'who officiated'; some call him the 'Assistant High Priest', and every one of these attempts to fill in the details of the story simply adds to the confusion!

To summarize:

(a) The two pillars were completed and named *before* the dedication of the Temple and each of the names was designed to symbolize or express Solomon's gratitude to the Almighty. Neither of them was named after a Priest!

(b) Jachin certainly did *not* officiate at the dedication. If he assisted at all (and he was certainly not mentioned in that connection) he assisted only by his presence, in the same way as guests are deemed to 'assist'—by their presence—at a wedding!

(c) The Masonic use of the pillar name, belongs strictly to the pillar alone. The introduction of the 'priest who officiated' is an error arising from the excessive zeal of the compilers of the ritual.

139.   FREEMASONRY AND THE ROMAN
        CATHOLIC CHURCH

On 28 April 1738 Pope Clement XII promulgated the first Papal Bull, *In Eminenti*, against the Freemasons. The reasons for the ban were not stated very clearly, but they may be summarized briefly as follows:

1. The Society was comprised of men of any religion or sect.
2. The oath, with its grievous penalties, which bound them to inviolable secrecy and silence.
3. Masonic meetings, held in secret, aroused suspicions of depravity and perversion.
4. It was charged that the Freemasons did not hold themselves bound by either civil or canonical sanctions.

The vague character of these reasons was hardly clarified by further unspecified and therefore unanswerable charges described in the Bull as '. . . other just and reasonable motives known to Us'.

Masonry was only just beginning to take root in Italy at that time. The first Masonic Lodge in Florence was instituted in 1733 by the Earl of Middlesex, apparently self-constituted and certainly without Warrant from the Grand Lodge of England. Its membership in 1738 represented the best of local English and Italian society, men of liberal education, learning and culture, poets and painters, priests and politicians, including a few high-ranking but dubious or shady characters. The advanced views of some of the members had already attracted the attention of the Inquisition authorities and in June 1737, at a conference of Cardinals in Rome under the Chief Inquisitor of Florence, the Bull was drafted, though it was not issued until April 1738.[1]

The stated object of the Bull was 'to block the broad road that the influence of the Society might open to the uncorrected commission of sin'. The faithful were forbidden 'to enter, propagate or support the Freemasons . . . or to help them in any way, openly or in secret, directly or indirectly . . .' or to be present at any of their meetings, 'under pain of excommunication . . . from which none can obtain the benefit of absolution, other than at the hour of death . . .'.

To this day, it is impossible to be sure whether the Bull was promulgated for mainly moral, religious, or political reasons. Whatever the

---

[1] 'The Earl of Middlesex and the English Lodge in Florence', by J. Heron Lepper, *AQC* 58.

true reasons may have been in 1738, they hardly seem to have justified such a heavy steamroller procedure, to crack what must have been a very small nut in those days. Fifty or sixty years later, when a strong anti-clerical movement had begun to infect much of Freemasonry on the European continent, the successive Bulls might have had more solid justification.

The last three anti-Masonic Encyclicals were promulgated in 1884, 1894, and 1902, and it would be no exaggeration to say that their collective influence kept thousands of Roman Catholics from the Craft and, in many countries, imbued them with a wholly unfounded mistrust and even hatred of the Order. In 1884, and during the ninety years or so that have elapsed since that time, the gulf between Freemasonry and the Church of Rome must have seemed so wide that even the wildest optimist could not have envisaged the possibility of bridging it.

During recent years, however, the advent of the Second Ecumenical Council brought the wind of change into matters of religion. The various sects, hitherto separated by questions of dogma, but now inspired by a new spirit of tolerance amongst their leaders, were beginning to learn at last that no matter what path they choose in the expression and interpretation of their religious faith, they are all moving in the same direction and they have the same ultimate goals.

The warm effects of these new ideas of co-operation in religious matters began to spread beyond their original and limited objectives, and the new spirit became manifest in a number of incidents—isolated incidents, it is true—but all of the utmost importance to Freemasonry in its relation to the Roman Catholic Church.

This period seems to have marked a turning point in the attitude of the Church of Rome towards the Craft. Efforts were now being made, openly and behind the scenes, to bridge the gulf. There were promising reports from the U.S.A., France, Germany, Austria and Scandinavia, but no official pronouncements from the Holy See.

In 1968, a most important book was published in Spain under the title *La Masoneria Despues del Concilio* (Masonry since the [Vatican] Council). The author, Father J. A. Ferrer Benimeli, a Jesuit Priest, was at great pains to show that regular Freemasonry, *based on belief in God, could not and should not stand condemned under the Papal Bulls*, whose charges should be directed only against the irregular Grand Lodges which preach and practise atheism and anti-clericalism

The subject was one that had long been of high interest to me and, in February 1968, in a lecture on 'Freemasonry of the Future', given to

the London Grand Rank Association (a body of experienced Free-
masons, all Past Masters of at least five years standing) I spoke at some
length of our hopes of bridging the gulf which has so long separated the
Craft from the Church of Rome.

During question-time at the end of my talk, one of the Brethren asked
'How can you hope for accord between us and the Roman Catholic
Church, when the bookstall in Westminster Cathedral still sells those
horrible anti-Masonic pamphlets?' I was momentarily floored! Then I
asked if he had done anything to try to stop the sales. He said 'No' and
I promised (with some 500 Brethren as witnesses) that I would try.

I wrote to the late Cardinal Heenan explaining that the pamphlets
are both defamatory and inaccurate and begging him to use his
authority to get them removed. I enclosed that part of my L.G.R.A.
paper which dealt with 'Freemasonry and the Roman Catholic Church',
expressing my eagerness to see peace restored between the Craft and the
Vatican, and asked for an appointment when we might discuss these
matters. Cardinal Heenan replied and, in regard to the anti-Masonic
pamphlet, he promised that:

'. . . if, as I suspect, it is misleading, I shall see that it is withdrawn'.

He also asked me to arrange an appointment through his secretary and
I went to Archbishop's House, Westminster on 18 March 1968. I could
not have prayed for a kinder or more sympathetic reception. I first
explained that, as a Jew, I had high hopes from the Ecumenical movement and, as a Freemason, the evidence of wider tolerance in the Roman
Catholic Church had been a source of great joy to me. His Eminence
replied 'Yes, your letter to me was quite an extraordinary coincidence
because I am deeply interested in the whole matter, and have been for
a very long time—I shall show you a picture, later on'. Our talk ranged
over many aspects of the subject.

He told me that he would be reporting direct to Rome on Masonic
matters and he asked me a number of questions on side degrees and
other bodies and their supposed connections with the Craft. (I replied
later on eight sheets of typescript with a collection of Official printed
documents all of which were subsequently taken by him to the Holy See.)

The highlight of our conversation arose when I emphasized the
necessity to draw a sharp line between the Freemasonry recognized
by the United Grand Lodge of England and the atheistic or anti-
Christian Grand Orient type. I urged that the Church of Rome could
safely take the English standards as a yardstick for distinguishing

between the good and the bad, and I added 'But what we really need is an intermediary, to convince your authorities'. He answered, 'I am your intermediary'.

Then he led me into an adjoining Council-chamber, a lovely room, and showed me 'the picture', a large oil-painting of Cardinal Manning's last reception. It depicted the dying Cardinal seated on a settee, his face grey and haggard, speaking to several frock-coated men nearby, while the whole background was filled with similarly frock-coated figures. It was a 'portrait' picture of famous men, with a chart below giving their names.

His Eminence pointed to one heavily-bearded man leaning over the settee in the group surrounding the Cardinal, and asked 'Do you know who that is?' I pleaded ignorance and he pointed to No. 3 on the chart. 'No. 3', he said, 'is Lord Ripon; you know he was a Grand Master and he resigned from Freemasonry in order to become a Roman Catholic'.

(I did know, indeed. The first Marquess of Ripon, *K.G.* was Grand Master of the United Grand Lodge from 1870 to 1874 and, after a series of dreadful family troubles, he decided to adopt the Roman Catholic faith. He immediately resigned his Grand Mastership and was succeeded by H.R.H. Albert Edward, Prince of Wales, afterwards King Edward VII.)

His Eminence continued:

> You may not know, perhaps, that after he resigned he used to say that 'throughout his career in Freemasonry he had never heard a single word uttered against Altar or Throne'. Those words have always remained strong in my memory and so you can understand how eager I am to help.

Cardinal Heenan very kindly gave me another interview a few weeks later, when I was accompanied by a senior Grand Officer. It was a most promising conversation, because His Eminence was on the eve of his departure for Rome when it was hoped that all these matters were to be discussed at the highest level; but we were advised beforehand that 'the mills of God grind slowly'. And then, almost without warning, 'The Pill' exploded in Rome: it seemed that we would have to start all over again!

All this was written in 1969 and during the next two or three years there were no overt developments concerning the Craft. There were, indeed, rumours that the Vatican was conducting a revision of its Code of Canon Law, and especially Rule 2335, which relates to Freemasonry and similar societies. There was talk also of high-level negotiations between the Craft and representatives of the Holy See, but there were no official pronouncements. In the hope of obtaining further news, I sought and was granted an interview with Cardinal Heenan on 26 April 1971. Not surprisingly, he was unable to comment on the rumours, but something important had happened since my last visit, and he told me the story which I repeat here, as nearly as possible in his own words:

> We had a letter some time ago from one of my parish Priests—in the Eltham area—asking for guidance about a Protestant in his parish, married to a Roman Catholic lady, their children all being raised very respectably in the R.C. faith. The husband, a Freemason, out of love for his wife and family, was anxious to be received into the Catholic faith, but without having to give up his Freemasonry. The Priest spoke very highly of both the husband and the wife. I answered saying that this was a matter only for the Holy See and that I would write to ask for an official ruling, which I did.
>
> I am delighted to say that the reply was all that we could have desired. The husband could be received into the R.C. Church 'without restriction', which means that he would not have to give up his Masonry, and he would be deemed as good a Catholic as any born in that faith who have practised it all their lives.
>
> Within a few weeks after this, a Masonic friend of the husband, in the same parish, and in exactly the same circumstances, made a similar application, and both have now been received into the faith.

His Eminence then showed me the letter from the Holy Office; it requested that no undue publicity should be given to it 'for fear of creating misunderstanding'. The story is told here by kind permission of Cardinal Heenan. It is the first case of its kind in England and the first clear evidence of the possibility that we might one day bridge the gulf that separates the Craft from the Church of Rome.

Time passed and in July 1974 Cardinal Heenan received a communication from the Holy See, which was promulgated in due course by the (Roman Catholic) Bishops of England and Wales. The following brief extract must suffice:

> The Sacred Congregation for the Doctrine of the Faith . . . has ruled that Canon 2335 no longer automatically bars a Catholic from membership of masonic groups. . . . And so a Catholic who joins the Freemasons is excommunicated only if the policy and actions of the Freemasons in his area are known to be hostile to the Church.

There must be hundreds of dedicated Masons all over the world who have played some part in the achievement of this long desired end. We have seen Masonic history in the making and I make no apology for including this item in my book even though it is no longer news. The sad story which began in 1738 is now happily ended.

140.   WHY TYLERS?

Q. Can you explain why Tylers were chosen to serve as outer guards to the Lodge? They were not masons; why should men of an associated trade have been chosen when there must have been plenty of men in the mason trade who could have served equally well?

A. Apparently a simple question but a number of curious problems arise, and the reason why that particular officer should bear that title is by no means the first of them.

The *O.E.D.* shows, beyond doubt, that the tiler's craft got its name from the actual work of making tiles, or from the covering, or roofing, of buildings with tiles. (Incidentally, this also applies to the corresponding title in French Freemasonry, *le tuileur*.) The spelling 'Tyler' appears to be a purely Masonic usage and *O.E.D.* quotes from Hone's *Every-day Book* (1827), 'Two Tylers or Guarders . . . are to guard the Lodge with a drawn Sword, from all Cowens and Eves-droppers' [in *c*. 1742].

Early operative records are not very informative, but it is impossible to imagine that the masons on a large-scale building job would *continually* have the services of a tiler at their disposal to guard their lodge during meetings. The tilers only came on to the job at the end, when virtually all the structural work was finished; theirs was the final stage in the works.

This purely practical consideration leads to the conclusion that 'Tyler' in speculative Masonry was simply the *name* of the office; it was not the trade of the man who held the office. Moreover the name 'Tyler' was not universal. In the 1723 *Book of Constitutions* Anderson could not give a name to the Office but ruled on the subject as follows:

'Another Brother (who must be a *Fellow-Craft*) should be appointed to look after the Door of the *Grand-Lodge*; but shall be no member of it' (Reg. XIII, p. 63).

In the 1738 *Constitutions* he did use the title 'Tyler', but even in that year the celebrated portrait of the Grand Tyler, Montgomerie, calls him 'Garder of ye Grand Lodge'. Eventually the title 'Tyler' did come into general use for that office, which comprised a variety of duties in the 18th century, including the 'Drawing of the Floor Designs', delivering notice of meetings to members of the Lodge, and the preparation of the candidates. The Tyler was virtually a handyman or odd-job man for the Lodge; but I cannot trace the title being used in that sense, and the range of duties does not help at all in finding a reason why that officer was called Tyler.

I feel that the title of the Office had some more-or-less reasoned connection with the actual job of a tyler or tiler—to roof or cover—i.e. protection from the weather, or it may be simply that as the tiler was the last man to work on a building job, so the Tyler, in a speculative Lodge, is the last man to leave the Lodge, or to complete the team of officers; but this is pure speculation.

---

141.   WHEN TO PRODUCE THE WARRANT

Q. Rule 101 of the *Book of Constitutions* requires that the Master shall produce the Warrant at every meeting of the Lodge. In one of my Lodges the Master, before the Lodge is opened, announces:

'Brethren, in accordance with Rule 101 of the *B. of C.*, I produce the Warrant of the Lodge.'

Elsewhere, I have seen a Lodge opened first and the W.M. then announces:

'The Lodge having been formed just and perfect, in order to make it regular I produce the Warrant from the United Grand Lodge of England'.

Is there any rule as to when the Warrant is to be produced by the Master?

A. Neither Rule 101 nor the relevant paragraph of *Points of Procedure* under 'Custody and Production of Lodge Warrants' gives any instruction as to precisely when the Warrant must be produced. That paragraph is quoted here, with the Editor's italics:

It has come to the notice of the Board that Lodge meetings have taken place without the Warrant being present. *The Master is responsible not only for its safe custody but also for its production at every meeting.*

In my opinion, *since the Lodge may not be opened without the Warrant*, the best time to produce it is before the opening, and I see no fault in the first formula given above. The second formula seems to be open to criticism. The Lodge, *at its creation*, is made regular by the Seal of Grand Lodge upon its Warrant. Production of the Warrant, at best, could only regularize that particular meeting.

---

142.   THE EVOLUTION OF THE INSTALLATION
CEREMONY AND RITUAL

In the whole recorded history of Masonry in England, going back more than 600 years, there is no trace at all of even the most elementary ceremony of Installation until after the formation of the first Grand Lodge in 1717. The rare English minutes that have survived from the pre-Grand Lodge era contain no evidence on the subject. The old Scottish Lodge minutes, from *c.* 1600 onwards, provide ample records of the election of the principal officer (by whatever name, i.e., Deacon, Warden, *Preces*, or Master) but never a word to indicate that the election was followed by any kind of ceremony of induction or installation into the Chair.

Dr. Anderson published his first *Book of Constitutions* in 1723 and the Regulations, 'Compiled first by Mr. George Payne, *Anno* 1720, when he was Grand Master', had been digested in 1723 'into this new Method, with several proper Explications, for the Use of the Lodges in and about *London* and *Westminster*'. They contained, *inter alia*, the earliest rules relating to the formation of a new Lodge, which could not be done without first obtaining 'the Grand Master's Warrant', and without which the regular Lodges were 'not to countenance them, nor own them as fair *Brethren*'.

The book included a two-page section describing 'The Manner of constituting a New Lodge, as practis'd by his Grace the Duke of Wharton', Grand Master in 1722–3. It appeared at a time when the newly-formed Grand Lodge was trying to establish itself as the governing body of the Craft, eager to bring the existing Lodges under its wing and to ensure that new Lodges were encouraged to mark their allegiance by an official ceremony of 'constitution', a procedure that was unknown until that time.

WHARTON'S INSTALLATION CEREMONY

Wharton's 'Manner of Constituting . . .' laid down the procedure to be followed after all the preliminaries had been fulfilled, and it also contained the earliest description of *the Installation of the Master of a new Lodge*. The full text of this historic document is readily accessible to students and, to avoid unnecessary repetition, the whole procedure is summarized below, quoting the original words where they are of special significance:

(i)   The Grand Master asks his Deputy if he has examined the 'Candidate *Master*' and if he finds him 'well skill'd . . . and duly instructed in our *Mysteries &c.* . . .'

(ii) After an affirmative answer, the Candidate ('being yet among the *Fellow-Craft*') is presented to the Grand Master, as a '*worthy Brother . . . of good Morals and great Skill* . . .'

(iii) The G.M., placing 'the *Candidate* on his left Hand' asks and obtains 'the unanimous Consent of all the Brethren' and constitutes them into a new Lodge, 'with some Expressions that are . . . not proper to be written'.

(iv) The Dep.G.M. rehearses 'the *Charges* of a *Master*' (which are not printed, and are still unknown at this date) and the G.M. asks '*Do you submit to these* Charges, *as* Masters *have done in all Ages*?' The Candidate signifies his submission.

(v)   The G.M. installs him 'by certain significant Ceremonies and ancient Usages' [which are not described].

(vi) The Members, 'bowing all together' return thanks to the G.M., and 'do their *Homage* to their *new Master*, and signify their Promise of Subjection and Obedience to him by the usual *Congratulation*.

(vii) The Dep.G.M. and other non-Members congratulate the Master.

(viii) The W.M. chooses his Wardens. [The remaining business is not relevant to our study of Installation procedure.]

The text contains several notes which confirm that there were only two degrees in practice at that time, 1723, but there is no mention of the Lodge having been opened into a particular degree. It may be assumed, perhaps, that all present were 'among the Fellow-Craft', or 'Masters and Fellow-Craft' as Anderson had described them in Reg. xiii of this same *Book of Constitutions*. There is no trace of an Obligation being taken by the Master-designate, nor any hint of a sign, grip, or word being conferred in the Installation at this period. Two items are noteworthy:

(iii) In constituting, 'Expressions . . . not proper to be written'.
(v)   Installation, 'by certain significant Ceremonies and ancient Usages'.

Allowing that the Grand Lodge itself was only six years old; that nobody was excluded or even separated from the work in progress; that no Obligation is mentioned; that the ritual was still in its early formative stage and the third degree still unknown, it is difficult to accept that the ceremony had any esoteric content, or that the 'Expressions . . . and ancient Usages' were anything more than mere flowers of language, typical of Anderson's style, and perhaps of Wharton's too.

The Installation of Masters of Lodges did not become instantly popular. In those early days, when there was no other guidance on the subject, *Wharton's ceremony seems to have been treated as belonging only to the constitution of a new Lodge,* and surviving minutes show that the Lodges generally ignored it. Masters were elected 'and took the Chair accordingly', as recorded in the minutes of the Old King's Arms Lodge (now No. 28), on 6 May 1735. A typical minute of the period may be quoted from the records of the Lodge at the Blue Posts, Old Bond Street (now the Lodge of Felicity No. 58):

> [16 May 1739] This was Election Night and Bro Wright was elected Master Bro White Senr Warden Bro Wise Junr. Warden and Bro Kitchin Secr. and paid there two shillings each for the Honr. Done them. [Not a word about Installation.]

'Fees of Honour' were not unusual and fines for non-acceptance of office were quite normal. Many Lodges elected their Master twice yearly but, in the Lodges under the premier Grand Lodge, it is almost impossible in the first half of the 18th century to find any minutes that could be taken to imply *a ceremony of Installation.*

THREE DISTINCT KNOCKS, 1760

The earliest description of an Installation ceremony *unconnected with the constitution of a new Lodge* appeared nearly forty years after Wharton's text, in *Three Distinct Knocks,* 1760. It is headed *The Charge given to the Officers of a Lodge,* and begins:

> And first of the Master belonging to the Chair; which they call installing a Master for the Chair.

The Lodge is apparently in the third degree; there is no mention of election, presentation, reading of the Charges of a Master, or any of the routine procedures which may have been fairly well established at this date. The text seems to confine itself, deliberately, only to the esoteric portion of the ceremony. The new incumbent

> kneels down in the South, upon both Knees; and the late Master gives him the following Obligation, before he resigns the Chair.

The new Master solemnly swears that he 'will not deliver the Word and Gripe belonging to the Chair . . . except to a Master in the Chair, or past Master . . . after just Trial and due Examination'. He will act as Master and 'fill the Chair every Lodge Night'. He will not wrong the Lodge, nor 'reign arbitrarily', but 'will do all things for the good of Masonry in general' and 'keep good Orders' as far as lies in his Power. All this, *under the E.A., F.C., and M.M. penalties of those days.* The Penal Sign of an Installed Master is unknown at this date.

Then, still kneeling, he is invested with the 'Master's Jewel', raised from his kneeling posture by the 'Master's Gripe' [i.e., the M.M. grip]; a Word is whispered in his ear, and the Installing Master 'slips his Hand from the Master's Gripe to his Elbow' and presumably he installs the new Master in the Chair, but that point is not mentioned.

The next paragraph, still apparently part of the Installation details, is headed *The Master's Clap*. It describes 'the grand Sign of a Master Mason', which was a rowdy salutation 'holding both Hands above your Head and striking upon your Apron, and both Feet going at the same Time ready to shake the Floor down'. This seems to have been given by M.M.s to the newly-installed Master and the context suggests that the Lodge is still in the third degree.

The main elements of the ceremony may be summarized briefly:

(1) An Obligation relating to the duties of the Chair and to the secret 'Word and Gripe', with the penalties of all three degrees.

(2) The 'Word' given in a whisper, and the 'Gripe' (which was an extension of the M.M. Grip) followed by

(3) A rowdy salutation, known only to Master Masons.

This implies that only E.A.s and F.C.s were excluded, and that during the communication of the 'Word and Gripe' the Installed Masters would have formed a screen round the kneeling Master Elect. That would explain why the 'Word' was given in a whisper, and the salutation at the end.

Three Distinct Knocks represented Antients' working, probably imported into England by Irish Brethren; but *J. & B.*, a Moderns' exposure, reproduced it almost word for word, in 1762, though it is doubtful if many of their Lodges were using the Installation ceremony. The importance of these twin texts, in so far as we dare to trust them, is that they show that, in the earliest description of the *esoteric portion* of the Installation ceremony, both Antients and Moderns were using the same procedure. Indeed, there is valuable evidence to show that they did. When John Pennell compiled the first Irish *Book of Constitutions* in 1730, he reprinted Wharton's 'Manner of Constituting a New Lodge' word for word (though he omitted to mention Wharton's name, or the *B. of C.*, from which he had copied it).

Laurence Dermott, who later became Grand Secretary of the Antients, had been installed Master of a Dublin Lodge (No. 26) on 24 June 1746, before he arrived in England. Ten years later, in 1756, he published *Ahiman Rezon*, the first Book of Constitutions of the Antients'

Grand Lodge, in which he also reprinted Wharton's 'Manner of Constituting . . .' practically word for word, the differences being so slight that they do not in any way affect the synopsis given at p. 285.

The implication is that *Dermott himself must have been installed*, in Ireland, *by a ceremony which was to all intents and purposes identical with the English forms.*

The Antients, in their early years, were somewhat negligent about Installation and this is confirmed by their Grand Lodge minutes:

St John's Day, June 1755

The Grand Secretary [Dermott] was order'd to examine the Officers of particular lodges as to their Abilities in Instaling their successors Upon which Examination it was thought Necessary to Order the said Secretary to attend the Instalation of several Lodges, which the G.S. promised to perform.

A year later:

June 24th 1756

The Grand Secy. was Order'd to Examine several Masters in the Ceremony of Installing their Successors. and declared that *many of them were incapable of performance.* [My italics. H.C.] Order'd that the Grand Secretary shall attend such deficient lodges and having obtain'd the consent of Members of the said Lodges he shall solemnly Install and invest the several Officers according to the Antient Custom of the Craft.

PRESTON'S INSTALLATION CEREMONY

The next stage in the evolution of the Installation ceremony appeared in William Preston's *Illustrations of Masonry*, 1775, in which he outlined the ceremonies of Constitution, Consecration and Installation, under three separate headings. The latter still embodies virtually the whole of Wharton's procedures, but to avoid any misapprehension he added a footnote:

The same ceremony and charges attend every succeeding installation.

Preston also included *the first full text of the Charges of a Master*, almost identical with those in use today. They had only been mentioned in Wharton's version of 1723. In Preston's ceremony, after hearing them, the Master Elect promised submission, and then he was 'bound to his trust' (which may imply that he took an Obligation relating to his duties as Master, rather like the Master Elect's Obligation in the second degree nowadays). He was next invested 'with the badge of his office' by the Grand Master and presented with the Warrant, the V.S.L., *B. of C.,* tools, jewels, and the 'insignia of his different officers'. He was conducted to the left of the Grand Master, who received homage, after which the new Master received 'the usual congratulations in the different degrees of Masonry'. The remainder of this section deals with the appointment and investiture of the Officers (i.e., Wardens, Treasurer, Secretary, Stewards and Tyler) with the various Addresses, which, though quite short, are already very similar to those in use today. (Deacons were not mentioned in the list of Officers.)

Throughout this 1775 version of Preston's Installation, there is no note of the Master being 'Chaired', or that any secrets were communicated to him; nor is there any hint of an esoteric Obligation (i.e., one that contained secrets such as a penalty or Penal Sign).

There are useful indications of the adoption of Installation practices in the records of the Lodge at the Queen's Arms, later the Lodge of Antiquity, No. 1 on the Moderns' Roll. Their elections, half-yearly, were recorded regularly, without any mention of Installation, until 8 January 1753, when the minutes record:

> According to the minutes of Last Lodge Night Br Moses *was placed in the Chair, as Master of this Lodge*, Bro^r. Burgh, Senr, Warden, B^r. Humphreys, Junr. Warden . . .

The words in italics are open to wide interpretation, but they do imply, at the very least, some kind of induction ceremony, still apparently without secrets.

An Adjacent Room

A new stage in the Installation procedures is revealed, from 1792 onwards, in the records of the Lodge of Antiquity:

> Hitherto [i.e. up to 1792] the ceremony of Installation had been conducted in the Lodge Room. Now and henceforward the Installed Masters withdrew with the Master Elect to another room. The Minutes are not clear, but this practice would appear to have been continued until 1812, or perhaps later. It is not until 1822 that we find it stated that all the Brethren below the rank of Installed Masters retired.
> (Firebrace, *Records of the Lodge of Antiquity No. 2*, Vol. 2, p. 120n.)

The separate room, and a ceremony conducted in the presence of Installed Masters only, is the first clear evidence of an esoteric installation within a 'Board of Installed Masters' though that name had not yet made its appearance. The 'adjacent room' becomes a regular feature of Preston's *Illustrations*, from 1801 onwards, but he gives very little detail of what took place in there. The preliminaries began with the Lodge apparently in the third degree. The M.Elect was presented to the

Installing Master, with a brief list of his qualifications, '. . . of good morals, of great skill, true and trusty, and a lover of the whole fraternity . . .'. The Secretary was ordered to read the Ancient Charges and the Regulations, and the Master Elect promised 'to submit to . . . and support [them] as Masters have done in all ages':

> The new Master is then conducted to an adjacent room, where he is regularly installed, and bound to his trust in antient form, by his predecessor in office, in the presence of three installed Masters.

This is the whole of Preston's data on what we would call the Inner Working, and there is no hint of any opening or closing for that portion of the Installation ceremony. The remainder of the proceedings are summarized here, from the 1801 edition:

> 'On his return to the Lodge, the new Master . . . is invested with the badge of his office. [The presentations are made with suitable Charges to each, as listed on p. 288. Preston 'moralized' each item in very familiar language, in a long collection of footnotes.]
>
> 'He is chaired amidst acclamations'.
>
> 'He returns acknowledgements to the Grand Master' [or Installing Master] and the acting Officers, in order.
>
> 'The members . . . advance in procession, pay due homage . . . and signify their subjection and obedience by the usual salutations in the different Degrees.' [This implies that the salutations are well known, but there are no details as to what they were, or how many were given. It also means that the Lodge is closed after each salutation in the third and second degrees, and that the rest of the ceremony is conducted in the first.]
>
> The S.W. is invested with the 'ensign' of office, the J.W. with the 'badge' of office, with a summary of their duties to each; followed by an Address to them jointly.
>
> The Treasurer is invested.
>
> The Secretary is appointed, with an account of his duties.
>
> The Deacons are invested. The 'columns' [nowadays the emblems of the Wardens] are entrusted to the Deacons as 'badges' of their office.
>
> Stewards are invested with a brief Charge.
>
> The Tyler is appointed with a short Charge.
>
> The W.M. addresses the Lodge: 'Brethren, such is the nature of our constitution . . . and unite in the great design of communicating happiness'. [An early version of our third Address.]

Preston's ceremony in an 'adjacent room' in which the new Master was 'regularly installed', must have been a ceremony with secrets, but he gave no details in his *Illustrations*.

We may pause here to survey the situation at this stage. The ceremony just described was very new, and in no sense official. *We shall soon see that the majority of Moderns' Lodges were still without any kind of Installation*; their Grand Lodge had made no law on the subject. The Antients were certainly practising Installation, but we have no details and it is doubtful if their ceremony was as far advanced as Preston's version of 1801. *There was no standardization, and we still have no information about the 'Inner Working'.*

INSTALLATIONS IN THE LODGE OF PROMULGATION

The next stage in our study is a minute of the Lodge of Promulgation, dated 19 October 1810. This was the Lodge, created under the Grand Mastership of the Prince of Wales (afterwards George IV), Grand Master of the Moderns' Grand Lodge, to pave the way for the union of the rival Grand Lodges:

> Resolved, that it appears to this Lodge, that the ceremony of Installation of Masters of Lodges, is one of the two [true?] Land Marks of the Craft, and ought to be observed.

Here is evidence, if evidence were needed, to show how far the Moderns had lapsed in their neglect of the Installation ceremony, which had been zealously fostered among the Antients by their Grand Secretary, Laurence Dermott. The Resolution, which implied the reintroduction or revival of the Installation ceremony as a Landmark, was one of the major steps by the Moderns towards the standardization of their procedures, in readiness for the anticipated union. But this was not all. James Earnshaw, Master of the Lodge of Promulgation (and of another Lodge) *had never been installed*, and that had to be rectified. A further minute on the same day resolved:

> . . . that it be referred to those members of this Lodge who are Installed Masters, to install the R.W.M. of this Lodge, and under his direction take such measures as may appear necessary for Installing Masters of the Lodge.

It was arranged that the Installations would take place on 16 November 1810, and the record must be unique:

> November 16th [1810]. The proceedings in open Lodge preparatory to the Ceremony of Installation having been conducted in due form, Bros John Bayford, Grand Treasurer, Thomas Carr, Charles Valentine, and Charles Bonnor, being themselves Installed Masters, retired to an adjoining chamber, formed a Board of Installed Masters, according to the Ancient Constitution of the Order, and forthwith Installed Bro. James Earnshaw, the R.W.M. of this Lodge and of the Saint Alban's Lodge No. 22. They

then proceeded to Install Bro. James Deans, S.W., R.W.M., of the Jerusalem Lodge No. 263, and Bro. W. H. White, J.W., R.W.M. of the Lodge of Emulation No. 12.

There are several points of high interest in this minute. The W.M., S.W., and J.W., all Masters of other Lodges, were that night installed *for the first time*. Three of the four Brethren who were privileged to conduct the ceremonies and who had formed the 'Board of Installed Masters', were members of the Lodge of Antiquity, which had been using the 'adjoining chamber' for the principal part of the Installation ceremony since 1792. It must also be noted that the 'Board' was 'formed'; there is no hint of formal Opening or Closing.

The Installations on 16 November 1810 were the start of a whole series of meetings for the Installation of Masters of Moderns' Lodges, ceremonies which were conferred only to regularize their status as Masters. The Lodge of Promulgation was primarily concerned with the three Craft degrees. It was not teaching the Installation ceremony, only conferring it, and its labours ended in March 1811. Its post-union successor, the Lodge of Reconciliation, 1813–1816, was composed of representatives of both Antients and Moderns, but it was charged only with the duty of demonstrating the approved forms of the Craft degrees. In effect, no official attempt was made during the life of those two Lodges to revise or standardize the Installation procedures.

In April 1813, eight months before the union, the Duke of Sussex, as Dep. G.M. of the Moderns, considering the widespread neglect of the Installation ceremony among the Moderns' Lodges, and that many of their Masters had never been properly installed so that there were few Past Masters competent to assist in the ceremony, granted a one-year Warrant to a body of eminent Grand Officers and Masters of Lodges, forming them into a Lodge of Installed Masters

> . . . for the purpose of giving Instructions in the Mysteries and Ceremony of Installation and . . . Authority to instal such Brethren as now are or have been or hereafter may be Masters of Regular Lodges, and also any Past Grand Wardens and Provincial Grand Masters who may not yet have received the Benefit of Installation . . . (*A.Q.C.* 84, pp. 44–5).

The Warrant stated that these 'Instructions' were to be confined to Lodges in the London area only; there was no provision for similar instruction to be given in the Provinces.

Surprisingly, this Lodge of Installed Masters appears to have been stillborn; there is no shred of evidence that it ever met or acted upon the instructions embodied in its Warrant. It would seem that the birth was premature, because nobody had taken steps to ascertain the form of the Ceremony that was going to be approved by the Antients and adopted by the United Grand Lodge, when that would come into existence. It was not until 1827 that this much-needed instruction was undertaken by another 'Lodge or Board of Installed Masters'.

DEVELOPMENTS SHOWN IN THE *TURK MS.*, 1816

Nevertheless, there had been some useful unofficial developments in the Installation procedures during the preceding years, and this is shown by a deciphered copy of the *Turk MS.*,[1] of which the original, in cypher, is dated 1816. It is the only complete contemporary version of Preston's 'Third Lecture', and Section IX of this text, summarized below, deals with the Installation of that period:

(1) The M.Elect is presented; Ancient Charges and general Regulations are read to him and he expresses submission. A later note indicates that *this occurs in the second degree.*

(2) The M.Elect enters into the following 'engagement', covering his duties as Master and promising 'adherence to the constitutions . . . bye-laws; to preserve and keep in good condition . . . the books . . . charters . . . furniture, jewels . . . apparatus & property' etc., and to hand over in good condition etc. *This was a document to be signed and sealed by the M.Elect in Open Lodge, prior to Installation.*

(3) All M.M.s and P.M.s adjourn to the Installation room. The Lodge is opened in the third degree in the Installation room.

(4) All M.M.s are ordered to withdraw.

(5) 'The Board of installed masters *is formed.*'

(6) The M.Elect is presented to the Board of Installed Masters, to receive 'the benefit of installation . . .'

(7) The Installing Master addresses the M.Elect. 'From time imme-morial . . .' followed by the qualifications, 'of good repute, true & trusty, & in high estimation . . .' and he is asked to declare whether he 'can accept the trust on these conditions'.

(8) He assents and 'kneels on both knees, with *two installed masters joining hands, & forming the arch over him*'.

(9) All the brethren kneel.

(10) An invocation is made; 'Almighty father . . . vouchsafe thine aid . . . sanctify him by thy grace . . . & consecrate our mansion to the honour of thy name—Amen'.

(11) The Oath of Office is administered. This is *a clear combination of the two Obligations taken nowadays by the M.Elect in the second degree and later in the Inner working.* The first part of this Ob., contains all the themes of our present-day Ob. for the M.Elect. In the second part, he promises that he 'will never reveal the secret word & grip of

---

[1] P. R. James, 'Preston's Third Lecture of Free Masonry', *AQC 85.*

a master in the chair, . . . & not to him or them unless it be in the presence of three installed masters'. All this *under no less a penalty than what has been before specified in the three established degrees of the order.* So help me . . .'.

(12) The Installing Master raises him 'up by the right hand *with the grip & word of the master in the chair*', with the words 'In the name of the most high God under whose banner & auspices we act . . . & I pray God to preserve you in his holy keeping, & enable you to execute the duties of your office with fidelity'.

(13) The new Master is then 'chaired & saluted' [no details].

(14) 'The board of installed masters *is adjourned.*'

(15) M.M.s re-admitted and Lodge closed in third degree.

(16) The brethren return to the Lodge where the rest of the ceremony is completed.[1]

It may be helpful, at this point, to add a few observations on some of the items in Preston's 'Third Lecture' Installation (numbered here only for ease of reference; they are not numbered in the original):

Items 1 and 2. There is no hint, in this preliminary stage, of the M.Elect being *obligated* in the second degree.

Item 2. The M.Elect's 'engagement . . . signed in open Lodge'. This was the practice in the Lodge of Antiquity from 1788 onwards. (Firebrace, *Records of the Lodge of Antiquity,* Vol. 2, p. 79.)

Items 5 and 14. The Board of Installed Masters is 'formed', and at the end of the Inner Working, it is 'adjourned'. *There is no evidence of the formal Opening and Closing of the Board of Installed Masters including secret words and signs,* of which we have evidence in various parts of England (and more rarely in London) at a later date.

Items 9 and 10. This is the earliest version of Installation procedure that contains *an opening Prayer.* It is specifically related to the new Master and is almost word for word as we have it today.

Item 11. The two parts of Preston's combined Obligation are clearly defined, and they are in fact a much expanded and polished version of the Ob. in *Three Distinct Knocks,* 1760, and *J. & B.,* 1762 (summarized on pp. 286–287). The second part of Preston's version relates specifically to 'the secret word & grip of a master in the chair', and it carries the same penalties as in the two exposures; an unexpected confirmation! *Apparently the Penal Sign of an Installed Master was still unknown in 1816.*

---

[1] Throughout this summary, the italics are mine. H.C.

It is perhaps necessary to take note of one item of ritual and procedure that is conspicuously absent. I refer to the story of Solomon's inspection of the completed Temple and Adoniram's respectful greeting, which gave rise to a 'calling' Sn., the Tn. and Wd. and one of our 'Salutations'. In effect, Preston recorded the Tn. and Wd. of an Installed Master, but omitted the story that gave the supposed source for those items and for what is sometimes called the Sn. of Humility.

Preston's 'Third Lecture' deals, very inadequately, with the procedures *following* the Inner Working; they had appeared in many editions of the *Illustrations* and must have been widely known by this time. But this would not apply to the Inner Working *in its advanced form*, as given in the 'Third Lecture'. *That material had never been printed*; indeed, only five manuscript versions have survived and only one of those—the *Turk MS.*—is complete.

It is not easy to assess the importance of Preston's writing on the Inner Working, and the obvious question arises as to whether or how far he had invented the work of the Board of Installed Masters, as he had depicted it in this 'Third Lecture', or whether he had simply collected and arranged materials that were already in practice. The frequent references, from *c.* 1792 onwards, to the work conducted in 'an adjacent room', or in 'the installation room', indicate that certain esoteric elements must have been in existence and that Preston—as was usual with him in much of his Masonic writings—was responsible mainly for their arrangement, interpretation and embellishment. The more polished and elaborate ceremony depicted in the *Turk MS.* may have been familiar to a few of Preston's friends and followers within his own immediate circle; but, to the fraternity at large, the procedures in that form must have been virtually unknown. The 'Land Mark' resolution of the Lodge of Promulgation on 19 October 1810, and the numerous Installations that followed, show that many London Lodges had never practised the Installation ceremony. Others, especially in the Provinces, were following inherited practices, right or wrong, simply because they had never heard of any other forms.

DIVERSITIES OF PRACTICE: THE 1827 BOARD OF INSTALLED MASTERS

In the circumstances, it is not surprising to find that substantial diversities of practice had arisen, sufficient indeed to attract the notice of the Grand Master. The *Grand Lodge Proceedings* for 6 June 1827 announced:

The M.W. Grand Master stated that finding there was much diversity in the Ceremonial of the Installation of Masters of Lodges, and feeling it to be most desirable that uniformity should exist, His Royal Highness had deemed it expedient to issue a Warrant to certain intelligent Brothers, directing them . . . to hold meetings for the purpose of promulgating and giving instructions in this important Ceremony that conformity might be produced, and also at such meetings to instal any Masters of Lodges who had been duly elected to office . . .

The Warrant, dated 6 February 1827, was to run for 'Twelve Calendar Months, and no longer'. It is an important document, but not very well known, and its principal contents are reproduced here, because they enlarge on the information contained in the *Grand Lodge Proceedings* quoted above:

WHEREAS it hath been represented to us that, *from the want of immediate source for information and instruction*, there exists some diversity of practice in the Installation of Masters of Lodges; and feeling how important it is that all Rites and Ceremonies in the Craft should be conducted with uniformity and correctness; . . . We have thought it proper to appoint, and do accordingly nominate and appoint our trusty and well-beloved Brothers . . . [ten names in all, including the G.Sec., G. Registrar, and the Masters of seven senior Lodges] to make known to all who may be entitled to participate in such knowledge *the Rites and Ceremonies of Installation as the same have already been approved by us, upon the Report of a Special Committee appointed for that purpose*: And in order the more effectually to carry this our intention into execution and operation, We do constitute the before-named Brethren into a Lodge or Board of Installed Masters, authorizing and requiring them to hold meetings for the purpose of communicating Instructions in such Rites and Ceremonies, giving Notice thereof to the Masters of our several Lodges, enjoining their attendance, as well as the attendance of their several Past Masters at such meetings: And We do further authorize and empower the said Lodge, or Board of Installed Masters, when duly assembled, *to instal into office all such Masters of Lodges as may not heretofore have been regularly installed*, and who shall require the same: And We do declare that this our Warrant shall continue in force for the space of Twelve Calendar Months, and no longer.

Given at London, the Sixth Day of February, A.L. 5827, A.D. 1827,

DUNDAS, D.G.M.

Several points (shown in italics) in the Warrant are of special interest, notably, 'the want of . . . information and instruction'. Next, 'the Rites and Ceremonies of Installation as the same have *already been approved by us*, upon the Report of a Special Committee . . .'. This 'Lodge or Board of Installed Masters' was only required to give instruction in the Ceremony that had been revised, or arranged, by a Special Committee, *and already 'approved' by the Grand Master.* Apparently nobody outside the Special Committee had had any say in the matter.

The *Proceedings* had recorded that it would be the duty of the 'intelligent Brothers' to install any Masters of Lodges who had been duly elected. The Warrant authorized them 'to install into office all such Masters of Lodges as may not heretofore have been regularly installed'. This is a clear admission that many Masters had been installed with inadequate or irregular procedure, or had never been installed at all. Little wonder that the Grand Master had taken action.

The Grand Lodge issued a Circular on 10 December 1827, *to the Masters of Lodges in the London area,* announcing the constitution of the 'Lodge or Board of Installed Masters' authorized to hold 'Public Meetings' for the purposes set forth in the Warrant, a copy of which was included in the Circular. Three 'Public Meetings' were to be held on 17, 22 and 28 December 1827, at which the attendance of the (London) Masters and Past Masters was required.

It is surprising that this very necessary instruction was to be demonstrated at only three London meetings, and only for the benefit of London Masters and P.M.s. It may be that the Provincial Grand Masters were expected to make special arrangements for instruction in their own Provinces, but that is not known. There were approximately one hundred Lodges in the London area at that time, and some 400 in the Provinces. Attendance records for the three 'Public Meetings' (quoted by Henry Sadler in his *Notes on the Ceremony of Installation*) show that seventy-four Brethren were present at the first, thirty-three at the second, and twenty-one at the third, together representing some sixty Lodges in all; so that only two-thirds of the London Lodges obtained instruction, while the Provinces got none at all.

It will be useful, at this stage, to try to ascertain which items of procedure the 'Special Committee' found it necessary to revise. The preliminary business *before* the 'Inner Working' had been expanded and elaborated by Preston, who gave full details of the Charges of a Master, etc., so that we have a reasonably good account of established procedures, except that there may be some doubt as to whether those preliminaries (originally conducted in the second degree of the two-degree system) had been re-arranged in any way after the trigradal system was established.

As to the procedures that followed the 'Inner Working' (except in matters of esoteric detail, which will be discussed later) it is evident that they were already fairly well standardized, in the numerous editions of Preston's *Illustrations*. We know that the Brethren *in procession . . . in the three degrees* paid 'homage' and 'saluted'; but we lack details as to the number and kind of salutes that were given in each degree. We have lists of all the items that were presented to the W.M., but no details as to how those items were distributed between the three degrees; and we also have brief forms of the Addresses. It seems reasonably certain, therefore, that, for those Lodges that were eager to work to an established standard, the broad general forms were readily available.

In effect, the main work of the 'Special Committee' must have been directed towards the stabilization of the 'Inner Working'. Here, we meet with difficulties, because we cannot be sure what kind of esoteric ceremony the Lodges may have been working. At worst, in those Lodges that had no ceremony at all, the Master was elected and took the Chair. Many Lodges must have been using the esoteric Installation described in *Three Distinct Knocks*, or *J. & B.* (as outlined on pp. 286–287). Brethren familiar with our modern usages will not need to be told how inadequate those exposures were.

At best, there would have been a few Lodges, probably all in London, that were using an elaborate 'Inner Working', including a Board of Installed Masters, as described in Preston's 'Third Lecture', which is the only respectable account of the proceedings *inside the Installation room* available to us *before 1827*. Those advanced procedures can only have been known to a fairly limited and select number of Lodges and Brethren; but, allowing that the members of the 'Special Committee' had been specially chosen for their task, it may be safe to assume that they were reasonably well acquainted with that Lecture, and that they may well have used it as the best available framework upon which their revisions and recommendations were to be based.

MINUTES OF THE 'LODGE OR BOARD'—24 February 1827

The Report of the Special Committee, to which the Grand Master had given his approval before the Warrant was issued, does not exist. The wording of the Warrant implies that it would have been a fully detailed survey of the whole of the Rites and Ceremonies pertaining to the Installation; no such document has survived. There is a file of papers in the Grand Lodge Library relating to the 'Lodge or Board of Installed Masters' which contains copies of the Warrant, the Circular to Masters of the London Lodges, attendance records of the three 'Public Meetings' and other related documents; but only one paper remains that deals with the actual work of the 'Lodge or Board'. It is a single sheet, folded to form four foolscap pages, of which the last two are blank.

Page 1 is a record of what was probably the first working meeting after the Board was warranted and it is the only one that gives some idea of the procedures approved by the Special Committee. It is written largely in abbreviations and there are seven interlinear insertions, probably made after a careful check. In the following transcript they are shown in their proper places and distinguished by italics. There are also three lines of irrelevant material in mid-page which were obviously entered in the wrong place and crossed out by the scribe. They are omitted from the transcript. At the foot of the page there is a note headed 'Qy' (i.e., Query) and I have placed asterisks in the body of the text to mark the places where that line probably belongs:

[Page 1]   Installed Masters, 24th. Feb: 1827
                       Present
                    Bro. Meyrick

White	Cant
Bott [erased]	Taylor
Clere	Moore
Smith	Broadfoot
Percivall	

In ⬚ of 2°

Presentation—Address—Qualifications—Antient
Charges & regulations—1st p^t of Ob:—F.C. retire—
⬚ . op: in 3^d Deg:—M.M. retire—

In Board of Inst: M.—Prayer *according to the religious observance of the parties*—2^d pt. ob: Entrust ***
raise ***—Invest & place in Ch: *** then deliver Hir: as Emblem of Power—New Master then places Jewel on Past Master ***
[Three irrelevant lines of text crossed out]

Call in M.M. who go round & Sal: by Pen: Sin: then the Past Master proclaims the New M. after which all Sal: by 5.—*three prncl*: [?] *lights* & Tools presented and Cl:

Fellow Crafts called in, go round *alone* Sal: by Sn: second Procl: then *the whole* Sal: 5—Br: ha: ba: Tools presented— Cl:

E.A. called in, go round Sal: by Pen: Sin: 3 procl:
Sal: by 3   Pen: Sin: & ha: on Ba:—
The P.M. delivers Wart: Book of Const: & By Laws *Minute Books and Tools—Charge He then* calls upon the officers whom
he had appointed to surrender their Jewels of office that
the new Master may make his own Selection—The new officers
then appointed & invested *pledged* & saluted by 3—

Qy—Past Masters Grip—Sn: & Sal: of M. of A. & S.

[Page 2 contains minutes (or attendance records) of three further meetings, held on March 3, 31, and April 27, and the dates fixed for five more, on May 5, 15, 29, and June 2 and 11.]

[Page 2]

Installed Masters 3ᵈ March 1827

Bro. Meyrick	Percival
White	Cant
Bott	Moore
Cleere	Broadfoot
Smith	

Broʳ Broadfoot acted as Master
Bott as S.W.
Cleere as J.W.

Went thro the Ceremony of Installation as agreed
Bro Smith acting as M.E.

Private meetg. Friday 27 April [1827] ½ past 7

Saturday 5 ⎫
Thursday 15 ⎭ May at 7

Board to meet 31 March at 7

Saturday 31 March [1827]

Meyrick	Taylor
White	Moore
Bott	Broadfoot
Percival	
Cant	

Friday 27 April [1827]

Meyrick	The respective officers should be pledged
Percival	previous to investiture.[1]
Smith	
Cant	The Board to meet May 29 at 7 o'Clock P.M.
Taylor	for rehearsal

General meetings on Saturday June 2nd & 11 Monday
at 7 o'Clock

The Lodges to receive the Summonses at least
one month previous & Bro White is requested
to procure the extension of the Warrant that
it may be inserted in the general summonses.

[G.L. Library: Hist. Corresp. File, 12 B 14]

We may now return to the minutes of 24 February 1827, which are invaluable in relation to the procedures for the three degrees *after the Inner Working*. Most of those procedures were well known before 1827; but the 'Lodge or Board of Installed Masters' arranged them in a fixed form, much as we have them today.

The few lines devoted to the procedures within the Board of Installed Masters, even if we include the 'Query line' at the foot of the page, are not so helpful, and one could wish that the scribe had been more generous. The abbreviations do indeed provide an outline sketch of that part of the ceremony, but much of the detail is missing. It does, nevertheless furnish confirmation of several items that may previously have been in doubt. This is particularly noticeable when we compare these brief notes with the Inner Working details in Preston's 'Third Lecture'. Several of the preliminaries in Preston's 1816 'Board of I.M.s' are shown in the 1827 text *in the second degree*. His long 'combined Obligation' is now divided; its first part, which deals with the Master's duties, is put back into the second degree; the second part, which relates to the secrets of the Chair, remains in the Inner Working.

The 'Query line' poses several problems. Obviously it represents two (or perhaps three) separate items:

---

[1] This is the only item of Installation procedure in all the eight meetings recorded on this page. In our modern working it would be rather puzzling, but there is a note in the *Henderson Notebook*, c. 1835, indicating that officers—at their investiture—were required to pledge that they would faithfully discharge their duties, the pledge being signified by the E.A. Sn., in token of assent.

It will be noticed that this minute reverses the sequence of procedure shown in the penultimate line of the minutes of 24 February (on page 1).

(a) The Past Masters' Grip.

(b) The Sn: & Sal: of M. of A. & S.

but where precisely do they belong? the Grip undoubtedly belongs with the instruction 'raise', and the query on this point probably refers only to the manner of giving it. The stages in the ceremony are indicated very clearly up to the word 'Entrust'; but entrust with what? The text shows that the new Master was still kneeling at that stage. He might have received the Word and Penal Sign of an Installed Master, *but it is not certain that the Pen. Sn. existed at that date.*

The 'Sn. & Sal. of a M. of A. & S.' is somewhat ambiguous. Nowadays we might read it simply as a salutation; no Sn. has been mentioned in the body of the text and the salutation would probably be given immediately after the 'chairing'. It is possible, however, that the note refers to a salutation to be given by the whole assembly at the end of the proceedings. For all these reasons the asterisks have been inserted in the body of the text, to show where the various parts of the 'Query line' may probably belong.

The 'Query line' gives rise to another interesting point. It was written on 24 February 1827, eighteen days after the date of the Warrant, which stated that the 'Rites and Ceremonies' had already been approved by the Grand Master. Yet here, on an essential part of the Inner Working, there was a query. In the minutes of 27 April (shown on page 2 of the text) there is a record of yet another item of procedure that had not been settled until that date.

If the procedures had indeed been approved before 6 February, why did the 'Board' hold nine meetings for rehearsal, queries, and modifications during the following five months? And why was there a delay of ten months (February to December 1827) before the 'Board' started on its three Instruction-cum-Installation meetings? It seems obvious that the Special Committee can only have given the Grand Master a very rough draft of the proposed work, which they later proceeded to arrange in proper form. This implies that *we cannot accept the detailed minutes of 24 February 1827 as a final statement of the recommended procedures, and that applies especially to the Inner Working.*

Several important items have been omitted, deliberately perhaps, because changes were being made and the precise details were not yet settled. The 'Query line' would seem to support this view:

1. There is no mention of the procedure for forming, declaring, or constituting a Board of Installed Masters, and no hint of a formal Opening or Closing for the Board.

2. The word 'Entrust' implies that a 'Word' and Grip were given, but there are no details.

3. The Obligation probably contained a penalty clause, but no details are given; nor is there mention of the Penal Sign of an Installed Master.

4. There is no mention of Solomon's inspection of the Temple, and of the Adoniram incidents which gave rise to *several* esoteric items in the Inner work.

5. The salutation to be given by the whole assembly, is prescribed for each of the three degrees, but is apparently omitted from the Inner Working.

It is reasonably certain that all five of these items were settled to the Grand Master's satisfaction before the 'Lodge or Board of Installed Masters' had completed the three demonstrations in 1827. The absence of a written record of all their decisions may be due to the loss of minutes that had been carelessly scribbled on loose sheets, like those of 24 February 1827; but it may also be that they were never written, because esoteric matters were involved.

LATER EVIDENCE

If we are to reconstruct the ceremony which was promulgated, including the five points listed above, we can only do so from reliable evidence in documents that were compiled during the next ten years or so.

One of the most valuable documents for our purpose is the so-called *Henderson Notebook*, a manuscript volume of some 350 pages, mainly written by John Henderson, who was Dep. Master of the Lodge of Antiquity, No. 2, in 1832, and President of the Board of General Purposes of the United Grand Lodge in 1836-7. The book contains his decipherment of Preston's Third Lecture, from the *Turk MS.*, together with the Lectures of the Three Degrees and a large collection of notes on various ritual matters, including the Craft Installation ceremony There is evidence to show that these materials were compiled c. 1830-1835, only a few years after the 1827 'Board' had completed its duties.

In 1838, ten years after the 'Board' had finished its work, George Claret published his ritual, *The Ceremonies of Initiation, Passing . . .* etc., a detailed ritual for all three degrees and the Installation ceremony. It was a perfectly respectable publication, its esoteric and procedural matters being indicated by dots . . . , or by initial letters with dots, e.g., L . . . F . . . , or R . . . F . . . , etc. Claret was an enthusiastic Masonic ritualist. He had attended six of the demonstration meetings of the Lodge of Reconciliation and had served as candidate at several of them.

His ritual achieved a well deserved success; it was reprinted and there were several improved and enlarged editions. In short, Claret's ritual may be described as the first example (if not the direct ancestor) of the printed rituals that we use today. So far as our present study is concerned, his Installation ceremony is doubly valuable, because it must have reflected the work of the 1827 'Board of Installed Masters' (B. of I.M.).

In trying to gauge the trustworthiness of Claret's work, or of any other documents that describe Masonic ritual and ceremonial procedures (whether they are of reputable origin, or exposures published for profit or spite) there is one final test that is applicable to all of them; that is the degree of acceptance that they achieved within the actual practice of the Craft. Of Claret's status in this respect, there can be no doubt at all. We may safely use *Henderson* and *Claret* as guide and check on the omissions and doubtful items in the minutes of 24 February 1827.

Our present study is concerned only with the evolution of the Installation ceremony commonly practised in the vast majority of Lodges under English Constitution. Within that 'common form' there are numerous variations of procedural detail which do not affect the main contents and it is fair to say that, with a few rare exceptions, the ceremonies, despite variations, are virtually identical. After the Lodge has been opened in all three degrees, M.M.s retire, and the B. of I.M. is 'constituted' (in the presence of at least three Installed Masters) by a simple 'declaration'; there is no Opening or Closing ceremony.

There is, however, a so-called 'Extended working' of the B. of I.M. in use in a number of Provinces and a few London Lodges, which consists of lengthy Opening and Closing ceremonies which precede and follow the 'common form'. There is a p.g. and p.w. to the Opening, and the ceremonies contain, *inter alia*, several Sns. and other esoteric items. In Lodges that practise the 'Extended' form, the Installing Master of today must make a preliminary announcement that the Sns. and secrets are not necessarily known to Installed Masters and are not essential to the Installation of a Master; after this, all present pledge themselves not to reveal etc., except to an Installed Master.

We return now to the five items:

1. Preston, in the *Turk MS.*, had said 'The Board of installed masters is formed' and, at the end of the Inner work, 'The board of installed masters is adjourned'. There was no formal Opening or Closing. We have a valuable piece of evidence to confirm this, in the *Henderson Notebook*. After the Lodge has been opened in the third degree, he says:

[The Installing Master] . . . requests 2 P.M.s to take the Wardens' chairs
& then declares(*totidem verbis*) the Bⁿ. present to be a board of installed Ms.

The closing of the Board is also by 'declaration, *totidem verbis*'. The
Latin phrase, which means 'in as many words', may well be treated as
something more than a mere confirmation that the B. of I.M. was opened
and closed by a simple 'declaration'. *It also implies that if Henderson
had ever heard of any such 'Extended' procedure he had firmly rejected it.*
This argument may apply equally to Preston's 'formed' and 'adjourned',
because it is reasonably certain that if he had known of (or approved)
the formal Opening and Closing of the B. of I.M., he would certainly
have included them in his work.

For final confirmation on this point, we have Claret, 1838:

The Instg Master gives one knock, and declares the Board of Installed
Masters open.

At the end of the Inner Working, the I.M. 'gives one knock, and declares
the board of Installed Masters closed'.

It would be beyond the scope of this essay to discuss the many problems that relate to the rise of the 'Extended working', its contents and
the recurring question of its regularity, which came to a head in 1926
when *the Grand Lodge ruled that its use would be permitted*, subject to
the announcement outlined above. I will only add here, after a careful
study of the relevant documents, that there is useful evidence that some
such ceremony did exist in 1827, but that the Grand Master's 'Lodge or
Board of Installed Masters' either knew nothing about it, or decided
not to adopt it. My own view, based on Henderson's very emphatic
note, *totidem verbis* (quoted above), is that the 'Extended Working', in
one or more of its several forms, *was known* to the 'Board' in 1827, and
was firmly rejected by them.

2. The missing 'word' of an Installed Master was, almost certainly,
omitted for reasons of caution. We find it, in somewhat debased form,
in two catechisms of the 1720s, but neither of them allocates it to a
particular degree or grade, so that we cannot be sure how it was used.
It reappears, grossly debased, in texts of the 1760s, where it is allocated
to the Master, and there seems to be no doubt that the omission of the
'word' from the minutes of 1827 was deliberate.

3. The Penal Sign of an Installed Master is another missing item.
'Was it omitted for reasons of caution?' We must remember that
Preston's Obligation in the Inner Working of his Third Lecture, 1816,
had said:

... under no less a penalty than what has been before specified in the three established degrees of the order.

Clearly, Preston knew nothing of a Penal Sign for an Installed Master and there is no trace of that Sn. in any documents before 1827. Yet *Henderson's Notebook*, c. 1835, and Claret's 'Ceremony of Installing...' 1838, both contain adequate indications of a Penal Sign that had never been previously recorded.

It is impossible to believe that two writers so closely concerned with instruction in the ritual of their day would have dared to invent that Sn., or to describe one that was different from the routine prescribed by the 1827 'Board'. *On the firmly-based assumption that the 'Board's' minute of 24 February 1827 was not a final version*, there seems to be good reason to argue that the Penal Sign of an I.M. was introduced by the 'Board' some time between February and December 1827.

4. Solomon's inspection of the Temple. There is no trace of this story in any text before 1827; but the 'Query line' in the February 1827 minute contains a reference to the 'Sn: & Sal: of M. of A. & S.' and that Sn. & Sal. is actually a part of the story. *Henderson's Notebook* contains both Sn. and Sal., but with only a bare hint of the story in which they originated. Claret gives the whole story (including the Queen of Sheba, etc.), and both Sn. and Sal., are described in footnotes which have been deliberately obliterated in the print, apparently for reasons of caution. Taking all the evidence into account, I am inclined to believe that the 'Board' queried and considered both the Sign and Salutation, *as two separate items*, and adopted them, together with the story of Solomon's inspection of the Temple, which explained their origins.

5. Here we are concerned only with the 'multiple Salutation or Greeting' given nowadays by the whole assembly at the end of the Inner Working. Preston did not describe the Salutation or say if it was given by the Installing Master alone, or by the whole assembly. The 'Query line' implies that the subject was considered by the 'Board', but both Henderson and Claret seem to describe a single Salutation, given or only demonstrated by the Installing Master. I am inclined to believe that our 'multiple' Salutations are a more modern innovation.

So we have traced the rise of the Craft Installation ceremony, from its first appearance in print in 1723, through the early stages of its gradual adoption, and the later stages of its embellishment and expansion, up to the point when it was 'standardized' by command of the M.W.G.M. of the United Grand Lodge, and promulgated with his full approval, in 1827. We have also been able to identify—with some reasonable degree of accuracy—those items of procedure which were inadequately described, or totally omitted, from the only official document that survives as a record of the ritual and procedural work of the special 'Lodge or Board of Installed Masters.'

There can be no doubt that the Grand Master's objective in 1827 was standardization, *but the results were promulgated only to Lodges in the London area* and there was no provision at all for similar instruction in the Provinces. In the circumstances, the degree of uniformity that has been achieved, especially in the actual words of the Installation ritual, is really quite remarkable. The Queen of Sheba has disappeared from most modern workings; indeed, one wonders how she ever managed to come in! In the vast majority of English Lodges, the only real variations that have survived are purely procedural. They appear mainly in the Signs and Salutations, where the Lodges have tended to adopt practices which do not conform with those outlined in the minutes of 1827. This gives rise to constantly recurring questions as to which Signs and Salutations ought to be given in the Inner Working, and how many?

Other peculiarities have crept in, either because of inadequate promulgation, or in pursuit of long-established local custom, and a few of them deserve mention. Unfortunately it is not possible to discuss them in detail, and I can only indicate where they are to be found. For example, there are several different versions of the 'Extended Working' of the Board of Installed Masters, with the full Opening and Closing ceremonies. There are also substantial variations in the manner in which the G. of an I.M. is given, and in the way in which the G. is used when placing the new W.M. in the Chair. I have actually witnessed at least four different versions of the Sn. of Humility, one of which would require the agility of a contortionist! Apart from this last item, the variations do not matter at all; indeed, they help to make the ceremony more interesting, especially when visiting.

Installation is, above all, the highest honour a Lodge can confer, involving duties and responsibilities of deep significance for the happy recipient, and the ceremony is always interesting and beautiful so long as it is conducted with due dignity and decorum.

---

143.   SALUTATIONS AFTER INSTALLATION

IN THE INNER WORKING

Q. Why do we greet the new W.M. with 'five G. or R.' salutations in the Board of Installed Masters?

A. There are two questions here, i.e., 'Why the G. or R. Sn.?' and 'Why five?' The only official document on the subject, 24 February 1827 (see p. 300), queries the 'Sn: & Sal: of M. of A. & S.' but does not say who gave it, or how many times it was given. Since that time, variations of practice have arisen. *Emulation* and many other workings give 'five G. or R.', a Salutation which has belonged to M.M.s for over 200 years. The only explanation I can offer for the use of this procedure in the Inner Working is that it is closely associated with 'joy and exultation'.

Many other workings give 'five Humility', which belongs only to Installed Masters, and is only used in the Inner Working. Despite its late introduction, I believe that it is the proper Salutation for that purpose. It is only necessary to add that, in English practice, at the Consecration of a new Lodge nowadays, this Salutation is given five times to the new W.M.

Five is undoubtedly the most popular number, but *Ritus Oxoniensis* and *Logic* give only three.

In the Degrees

Q. When we greet the new W.M. after Installation, we salute with three as M.M.s; five as F.C.s; and three as E.A.s. It has been suggested that these should be seven, five, and three respectively. Can you explain which is correct, and why?

A. Your 'three—five—three' is customary in all the modern rituals that I have been able to check, but it does not agree with the 1827 minutes, which gave 'five—five—three' (see p. 299). But it was not always like that.

The earliest record of the *number* of Salutations *in the Degrees* is in an annotated copy of *J. & B.*, 1777. The notes were written by Emanuel Zimmerman, a Swiss settler in Dublin, a Masonic enthusiast who was also an occasional visitor to London, but it is probable that his notes represent only Irish practice, *in this respect*, of about 1790. (P.A. Tunbridge, *AQC*, Vol. 79, p. 128.)

Against the *J. & B.* description of the Installation ceremony (which is very brief) he wrote of the processions after the Master had been installed:

> . . . they go two and two round ye Lodge three time, ye first tourns passin ne[a]r him they throw ye apprentice Sing [= sign].
> they stop at ye end of ye Lodge and Clap 5 &c
> > ye Crafte 7
> > ye Master 9.

In modern terms, the E.A.s went two by two in procession round the Lodge, and at the end of their tour they saluted with 'five Claps &c.'. The '&c.' suggests that they may have given five Salutes as well, because it is certain that *the 'M.M. Clap' was a Salutation in those days.* (See *Three Distinct Knocks,* on p. 287). In this Zimmerman version the Salutations are 'nine—seven—five' respectively.

Henderson's Notebook of *c.* 1835 is a rather late version of Prestonian material, and its details conform to the 1827 ruling:

For the M.M.   Five, "Exultation & centre' [*sic*]

„   „   F.C.   Five, B.H.B. "and Penal"

„   „   E.A.   Three.

Claret's Ritual in the first edn., of 1838, made no mention of salutes. The 3rd edition, of 1847, listed:

For the M.M.   Five Grand or Royal (described)

„   „   F.C.   Five

„   „   E.A.   Three.

The *Humber* working is unusual. It gives three 'Grand and Royal' for the M.M., five 'Ht. Ap., & Hd.,' for the F.C., and only one E.A. sign by the E.A.s.

On the question of numbers, the best guidance is our Grand Lodge practice after the Consecration of a new Lodge, when the relevant salutes are 'Three—five—three'.

As to the suggestion that the Salutes ought to be seven, five and three, it seems likely that, when they were first introduced, the numbers were chosen because they had some special Masonic significance, or were related to other numbered items in ritual practice, e.g., three steps in the first degree, five in the second and seven in the third; or to the old dictum 'three form a lodge, five hold a lodge, seven or more make it perfect'. This query was discussed by eminent members of Q.C. in 1916 (*Misc. Lat.,* vol. iv, p. 122) and it was generally agreed that 'three—five —three' was the 'correct' procedure. It was also agreed that the salute of three in the M.M. degree must have been adopted in place of seven because the latter belongs to Provincial and District Grand Masters and certain other R.W. Brethren.

THE SALUTATIONS—AUDIBLE OR NOT?

This question arises frequently, especially in relation to the 'G. or R. sign'. It is nearly always described as a sign, which suggests that it is not audible. But it is constantly used as a salutation and, in its earliest form, it was certainly noisy. The rituals of the 1840s and later seem to indicate a more sedate approach.

Personally I believe the inaudible salute is preferable, and among the most popular present-day rituals, I know of only one, *Emulation*, that requires the salutations to be made audibly.

---

144. THE LONG CLOSING

Q. On several occasions in recent years, just before the final words used in closing the lodge, I have heard the I.P.M. give an address which begins:

Brethren, you are now about to quit this safe retreat of peace and friendship to mix again with the busy world...

Who wrote it; where did it come from; is this 'official' ritual?

A. A long search through 18th and 19th century texts which may be the source for this 'Charge at Closing' proved wholly unsuccessful[1] and I am unable to find any trace of it in early English usage. It appears in several modern (20th century) workings, e.g., *Taylor's, Universal, Benefactum*, and *New London*, and others perhaps, but there is no evidence to show who compiled it, or where it first appeared.

Soon after this question was printed in *AQC* 82, we received a letter from Bro. R. H. Brown, Editor of the *Transactions of the American Lodge of Research*, New York. He had found the answer and we reproduce the relevant extracts from his letter, with a copy of the earliest version of the Charge, dated 1792:

. . . The earliest appearance of it, I find, is in Thaddeus Mason Harris's *Constitutions*, published under the sanction of the Grand Lodge of Massachusetts, in 1792. Coil's *Encyclopedia* calls Harris a writer of 'high but not wide reputation'. The *Constitutions* is monitorial in form and contains a great deal of material from Anderson, Entick and Preston, with some original work by Harris himself. It includes a 'Charge at the Closing of a Lodge' which is credited as 'by Brother T.M.H.' (Also, the quotation in the penultimate paragraph is here credited to Isaiah xlix, 4; this does not appear in later printings.) This, I believe, is the first appearance of this piece of work. Slightly amended, it was included in Frederick Dalcho's *Ahiman Rezon* (Charleston, S.C., U.S.A., 1807), and Dalcho's version appears in many later American monitors; Cole's *Ahiman Rezon*, Baltimore 1817, Sickels's *Ahiman Rezon* NY. 1864; (*Ahiman Rezon* was a popular American title for monitors in the 19th century—no debt to Dermott, save the name . . .).

When I became a Mason in 1921, the Simons-Macoy *Monitor* was a popular book, and the 'Charge' appears therein. It is still included in some Grand

---

[1] Wm. Preston, in his *Illustrations*, 1775, printed a Charge 'To be rehearsed at closing the Lodge' but it bears no resemblance to the Charge in question.

Lodge monitors, including Florida, Pennsylvania, and the State of Washington, so it has been far-flung. . . . it has never been used in New York during the fifty years I have been a Mason and so far as I am aware *it is never obligatory* in any of the jurisdictions where it is allowed.

A CHARGE AT THE CLOSING OF A LODGE

(By Brother T.M.H.)

Brethren, you are now about to quit this sacred retreat of friendship and virtue, to mix again with the world. Amidst its concerns and employments, forget not the duties you have heard so frequently inculcated, and forcibly recommended in this Lodge. Be, therefore, diligent, prudent, temperate, discreet. And remember also, that around this altar you have solemnly and repeatedly promised to befriend and relieve, with unhesitating cordiality, so far as shall be in your power, every Brother who shall need your assistance: That you have promised to remind him, in the most tender manner, of his failings, and aid his reformation: To vindicate his character when wrongfully traduced; and to suggest in his behalf the most candid, favorable, and palliating circumstances, even when his conduct is justly reprehended. That the world may observe how Masons love one another.

And these generous principles are to extend farther. Every human being has a claim upon your kind offices. So that we enjoin it upon you to 'to do good unto all', while we recommend it more 'especially to the household of the faithful'.

By diligence in the duties of your respective callings, by liberal benevolence, and diffusive charity, by constancy and fidelity in your friendships, by uniformly just, amiable, and virtuous deportment, discover the beneficial and happy effects of this ancient and honourable institution.

Let it not be supposed that you have here 'Laboured in vain, and spens your strength for nought; for your work is with the Lord, and your recompense with your God.'*   (*Isaiah xlix, 4)

Finally, Brethren, be ye all of one mind, live in peace, and may the God of love and peace delight to dwell with, and to bless you.

The English versions of this Charge are almost word for word identical with the original Massachusetts version, printed above. I have heard it often and see no objection to it, except the un-Masonic and embarrassing passage which says that we have 'promised to remind a Brother of his failings . . .'. There is no such promise in our English ritual.

As to the final question, 'is this "official" ritual?' The answer is 'No!' All the workings I have named that print it give it as a kind of optional addition to the Closing of the Lodge. I imagine it was first compiled as a graceful addition to the Closing in one particular lodge, and was subsequently adopted by other workings.

Most interesting of all, is the fact that this 'Charge at Closing' appears to be a very rare example of U.S.A. ritual establishing itself in English practice; normally, the traffic was in the opposite direction.

---

145.   THE SQUARE AND COMPASSES, AND THE POINTS

Q. A great deal of importance seems to be attached to the business of the Square and Compasses with two points exposed, one point exposed, etc. When and why did this practice arise?

A. In the answer that follows, it must be emphasized that, for obvious reasons, it is impracticable to discuss our present-day procedures. Fortunately, that will not be necessary, because reference will be made to the earliest known evidence on the subject and the reader will find no difficulty in comparing the procedure with that of the present day.

Early references to the Square and Compasses are plentiful in the exposures from 1696 onwards, but none of the early texts says anything about the 'variations' with the points.

Those variations were almost certainly introduced in order to draw a distinction between the work of three different degrees. If that is so, then the practice cannot have been older than the evolution of the three-degree system, i.e., some time between 1711 and *c.* 1725 when we find the earliest hints of trigradal practice. But none of our documents up to 1760, English or French, gives any information at all on the subject of variations with the points.

The earliest description of the 'points' procedure made its appearance in 1760 in an English exposure, *Three Distinct Knocks*, which claimed to describe the practices of the Masons under the Antients' Grand Lodge. It is known that this (and other English exposures of the 1760s) betrayed evidence of French influence, and if *T.D.K.* was indeed describing Antients' practice it probably represented some Irish practices too. For these reasons, it must be noted that the *origins* of the procedures cannot definitely be ascribed to any particular country, though we may be reasonably certain that they were current in England —not necessarily widespread—from 1760 onwards. The relevant extract is quoted below, without comment on present-day English procedure:

> The Master always sits in the East, or stands with the Bible before him; and if it is the Apprentices Lecture, he opens it about the Second Epistle of

Peter, with the Compasses laid thereon, and the Points of them covered with a little Box Square or *Lignum Vita*, about 4 Inches each Way, and the Points of the Compasses points to the West, and the Two Points of the Square points to the East. If it is the Craft's Lecture, the Master shews one Point of the Compasses, the Bible being open at the 12th Chapter of *Judges*. If it is the Master's Lecture, the Bible is opened about the Seventh Chapter of the First Book of *Kings*, and both the Points of the Compasses is shewn upon the Square. This is the Form they sit in when they work, as they call it

Finally—and this may help to answer the question 'Why'—it is said that in many of our old Lodges it is customary for the square and compasses to be displayed, *outside the door of the Lodge*, in positions which will indicate to knowledgeable Brethren the Degree that is being worked, and in several jurisdictions in the U.S.A. one of the tests for examining an unknown visitor is to ask him to arrange those tools so as to indicate a particular Degree.

---

146.   MASONIC TOASTS

Q. Can you sketch the history of Masonic Toasts? I have never seen a study of the subject and, in particular, I would like to know the meaning of one in the *Lectures of the Three Degrees* (*Perfect Ceremonies*) published by Lewis, which runs 'Golden eggs to every Brother and goldfinches to our Lodges'.

A. The rise of the practice of Masonic Toasting is closely linked with Masonic feasting generally, a practice doubtless inherited from the Gilds and other medieval societies in which a proportion of admission fees, fines, etc., were usually devoted 'to the Ale'.

The earliest surviving minutes of an operative lodge are those of Aitchison's Haven (near Edinburgh) beginning in 1598 and they make no mention of any kind of feasting but, in the Kilwinning section of the Schaw Statutes issued in 1599, precise rules were laid down for the 'banquets' that were to be provided, or paid for, by apprentices at their admission, and by fellow-crafts at their promotion to that grade. In that same year, 1599, the Lodge of Edinburgh, Mary's Chapel (now No. 1 S.C.) ordered that John Watt was to be entered apprentice and *to make his banquet*,[1] within 14 days.

The regulations of the Lodge of Aberdeen, in 1670, required that non-operative apprentices were to provide in addition to their entry

---

[1] Author's italics throughout.

money *a dinner with a speaking pint*.[1] Operative apprentices might be admitted for lower fees but they still had to provide refreshment, and there were similar rules for fellow-crafts. At Melrose, in 1674, an apprentice had to pay a fee of £2 'to the Box' (i.e., to the Lodge funds) and £8 *for meat and drink*. (These sums are in Scots money; the relative equivalents in sterling are 16p and 66p.)

In 1682, Ashmole wrote of the 'noble dinner he attended [at the London Masons' Company's Hall] given at the expense of the new accepted masons . . .', and in 1686, Dr. Plot wrote of the '. . . collations . . . when any are admitted . . .'. There is no mention of drink in these two items, but it was a drinking age.

It must be admitted that the Lodge minutes of this period afford no indication of the convivialities that accompanied these banquets, and it is probable that the word 'Toast' in the sense of 'drinking of healths' had not yet made its appearance in English usage. One of the earliest terms describing the practice was 'to pledge', conveying an expression of goodwill, friendship, etc., and the *O.E.D.* quotes examples from 1546 onwards. 'A health', in the same sense, also made its appearance at about this time and the earliest example in *O.E.D.* is quoted (from Shakespeare) in 1596.

According to *O.E.D.*, the verb to 'toast', in the particular sense now under discussion, came into use '*ante* 1700' and it quotes a number of the earliest examples, none of them earlier than 1700. In view of what follows below on the subject of 'sentiments' the *O.E.D.* definition is given here:

> To name a person to whose health or in whose honour, or a thing or sentiment to the success of which, or in honour of which, the company is requested to drink; to propose or drink a toast.

The earliest official records of toasting that I can trace *in a Masonic context* are in the first two editions of the *Book of Constitutions*. In the 1738 edition, Dr. Anderson supplemented his record of the Grand Masters etc., from 1717 onwards, with various historical notes which are extremely interesting, and he described Dr. John T. Desaguliers's Installation as Grand Master, on 24 June 1719 when he '. . . forthwith reviv'd the old regular and peculiar Toasts or Healths of the *Free Masons*'.

This little tit-bit of Masonic history may be accepted as reliable, more particularly because it is supported by evidence in the first *Book*

---

[1] The old Scottish pint was equal to three pints of our standard measure.

of Constitutions of 1723 which contained a collection of the Masons' songs at the end of the book, including two which were compiled by Dr. Anderson himself. The first of these, 'The Master's Song' (described by Bro. Knoop and his colleagues as 'a tedious verse history of masonry'), acquires some importance in our study because at intervals throughout the song he added toasting instructions in the form of footnotes, as follows:

[Stop here to drink the present Grand Master's health]

[Stop here to drink the Health of the Master and Wardens of this particular Lodge]

[Stop here to drink to the glorious Memory of Emperors, Kings, Princes, Nobles, Gentry, Clergy, and learned Scholars, that ever propagated the Art]

[Stop here to drink to the happy Memory of all the Revivers of the ancient Augustan Stile]

The last song in Anderson's collection was the 'Enter'd Prentice's Song' attributed by him to 'Mr. Birkhead, Deceas'd'. A version of this piece had appeared as early as *c.* 1710 under the title 'The Free Mason's Health', and it contained the well-known lines:

'Let's Drink Laugh and Sing, our Wine has a Spring,
'tis a Health to an Accepted Mason'.

We cannot be sure, but it seems possible that the complete list of Anderson's 'Healths' may represent a formal toast-list of that period, 1723, though one may wonder how many Lodges in those days actually drank to 'The Revivers of the Augustan Stile'. It is certain, however, that the 'drinking of healths' was regular practice at this time and the oldest minutes of the first Grand Lodge, 24 June 1723, confirm this:

'. . . After Dinner, *and some of the regular Healths* drank, the Earl of Dalkeith was Declared Grand-Master . . .'

and on 27 February 1727,

'. . . After Dinner the Grand Ma^r. drank all the publick healths, then proceeded in form as Usuall . . .'

One of the most important of the Masonic Toasts made its first appearance in print in Anderson's *Constitutions* of 1723 (p. 37), where he spoke of the love and loyalty of the Masons for their Kings:

'from whence sprung the old Toast among the *Scots* Masons, *viz*
GOD BLESS THE KING AND THE CRAFT'

It is certain therefore that this toast was already in general Masonic use in 1723.

Early minutes are scarce, and on the subject of toasting they are extremely rare, but the following brief extracts may serve to indicate that the practice was not confined to Grand Lodge. In the minutes of the Old King's Arms Lodge (now No. 28) for 7 April 1735:

'The D.G.M. [Sir Cecil Wray] was pleased to recommend the Rt. Honble John Lord Viscount Tyrconnel to be admitted a Mason at their convenience. This was seconded in the warmest manner and supported *and his health was drank to* with a partial regard'.

This was an early example of toast-drinking within the Lodge room, unusual only because they were toasting a *prospective* candidate. The incident had an amusing ending, however, because at the next meeting of the Lodge four days later, his Lordship:

'having changed his mind, did not appear, and it being suggested . . . that his Lordship desired to withdraw his claim the Lodge . . . ordered the Restitution of his Deposit'.

Soon after this there is evidence of the custom of toasting the Master-elect on the night of his election:

[6 March 1738] 'Our Brother Sir Robert Lawley, Bart, was this Evening chose Master of this Lodge unanimously and his Health was drank with the greatest regard in due form'.

At the Lodge of Friendship, now No. 6, the minutes of 13 March 1738 record a Lecture on 'Education' by Brother Clare after which the Brethren '. . . drank to his Health & return'd him Thanks for his Instructive Lecture'. On 12 June 1738 'Particular Business' having caused the Master to be absent 'His Worshipl. Health was drank to with Ceremony and Affection'.

From 1737 onwards we find the first description of 'Masonic Fire' in the French exposures, and soon after this the fuller versions begin to supply lists of toasts customary in the French Lodges. They are compiled in narrative form (i.e., not as carefully tabulated lists) and, in the absence of better evidence, they deserve consideration. *Le Secret des Francs-Maçons*, 1742, is the first work (so far as I am aware) that gives a proper list of Toasts indicating their sequence, as follows:

1. The King
2. The Very Worshipful (i.e., the Grand Master)
3. The Worshipful (i.e., the W.M.)
4. The first and second Wardens
5. The Initiate (if any)
6. The Visitors (if any)
7. The Brethren of the Lodge

This work also gives an excellent description of Masonic 'Fire' (see Q. 56 above, and *AQC*, Vol. 79, p. 276) and it also gives the formula for the opening words of the toast:

> Whoever desires to propose a toast strikes a blow on the table; all become silent. Then the Proposer says: *Worshipful, First and Second Wardens, Brethren and Fellows of this Lodge, I give you the health of so and so*. If it is one of the Officers whose health one is proposing, his title is *not* included in the opening list of titles, for example when toasting the Worshipful one would begin by saying: *First and Second Wardens, Brethren etc*. When toasting the First Warden, one would begin: *Worshipful, Second Warden, Brethren etc*.
>
> He whose health is being drunk remains seated while they drink; he does not rise until the ceremony is ended and they are all seated. Then he thanks the Worshipful, the First and Second Wardens, Brethren etc., and announces that he will pledge them for the pleasure they gave him in drinking his health. Then he goes through the whole exercise that I have described [i.e., the Fire] entirely alone.

For later developments in the Toasting practices we return to England. Here, in 1760 and 1762, two interesting exposures were published—admittedly showing marks of French influence—but they are useful because they confirm certain practices hitherto unrecorded in England. *Three Distinct Knocks*, 1760, has a note at the beginning of the book describing *inter alia* 'a Toast to the King and the Craft, with Three Times Three in the Prentice's' followed by the 'Fire' almost identical with that of *le Secret*.

The catechisms of the three degrees were interspersed with Masonic songs each of which contains some reference to wine [or the drinking of healths]. In *J. & B.*, published in 1762, there is a paragraph inserted in the middle of the catechism, from which the following is an extract:

> '. . . as the Ceremony of drinking Healths among the Masons takes up much of their Time, we must stop a little, in order to introduce some of them. The first is,
> "To the Heart that conceals and the Tongue that never reveals";
> then, "The King and Royal Family";
> and, "To all Brethren wheresoever dispersed".'

Having regard to the widespread publication of the many editions of *le Secret* it is reasonable to assume that the Lodges generally were practising a fairly standardized list of Toasts at their banquets in the 1760s, both in France and England. No opportunity was missed to enlarge the number of Toasts and 'Sentiments' which began to make their appearance in Masonic publications from 1766 onwards.

The 'Sentiments' were usually expressions of goodwill, or admiration, towards persons or groups of persons selected because of their status, rank, virtues, or other qualifications.

One of the earliest lists of this kind appeared in *Mahhabone*, an English exposure of 1766, and a similar and slightly fuller list appeared in the same year in *Hiram*. A few of them are reproduced here as a useful example of what was happening at Masonic banquets in those days:

Toasts used by Masons

To the King and the Craft, as Master Masons
To his Imperial Majesty (our Brother) Francis, Emperor of Germany
To the Right Worshipful the Grand Master
To all the Noble Lords, and Right Worshipful Brethren that have been Grand Masters
To the Worshipful Grand Wardens
To the Masters and Wardens of all Regular Lodges
To the Memory of him who first planted a vine
To Masons and to Masons Bairns
    And Women with both Wit and Charms,
    That love to lie in Masons Arms
To the Memory of the Tyrian Artist
To the Memory of Vitruvius, Angelo, Wren, and other noble artists
The Prince God bless, The Fleet success, The Lodge no less.
To him that did the Temple rear, &c.
To all those who live within Compass and Square
To all true Masons and upright, Who saw the East where rose the Light
To each charming Fair, and faithful she, That loves the Craft of Masonry
To each faithful Brother, both antient and young
    Who governs his Passions and bridles his Tongue
To the Memory of P.H.Z.L. and I.A. [i.e., Prophet Haggai, ZerubabeL, and IoshuA].

This was really a very sedate list, though, in the permissive society of the 18th century, there are several examples in Masonic collections which display lively imagination. Incidentally, several of the Sentiments above were drawn from the Masonic songs which were in vogue at that time.

In a long collection of Songs published in Preston's *Illustrations of Masonry*, 1796 (the 9th edition), there is one by Bro. Stansfield of Sunderland, which clearly gives the sequence of Toasts customary at lodge banquets in those days. The same song appears regularly in several of the later editions without alteration to the sequence of toasts which may be extracted as follows:

1. The King & the Craft
2. The Grand Master

3. The Provincial [G.M.]
4. The Absent [Brethren]
5. The Silent and Secret [i.e., the Brethren generally]
6. The Guests [one *honour'd guest* being called to reply]

The formal stereotyped lists were rapidly gaining ground and this can be shown by the numerous Toast-lists-cum-menu that survive from 19th century Masonic banquets. It is all the more strange, therefore, to find a fairly modern edition of *The Lectures* (published by Lewis) which contains a fantastic list of 'Toasts and Sentiments' including the one which prompted this enquiry:

'Golden eggs to every Brother and goldfinches to our Lodges'.
Golden eggs present no difficulty but 'goldfinches' are a problem, solved in this instance by *O.E.D.* which gives two suitable definitions:

(a) (Slang) 'One who has plenty of gold'. Now obsolete, but examples are cited from 1603 onwards.
(b) 'A gold coin, guinea, or sovereign', with examples from 1602 onwards.

Armed with these details the Toast or Sentiment may be interpreted as:
'Great profits to every Brother and wealthy Candidates to our Lodges'
or
'Great wealth to every Brother and golden guineas to our Lodges'.

The earliest occurrence of this toast (so far) traced is in a section devoted to Masonic Toasts in *The Social and Convivial Toast-Master and Compendium of Sentiments*, published by C. Daly, 19 Red Lion Square, London, in 1841. It appeared again in *The Masonic Minstrel, a Collection of Songs, Odes, Anthems etc.*, published by Spencer's Masonic Depot, *c.* 1877. This was a reprint of a publication of 1828 but that edition did not contain the 'Sentiment' under discussion. [We are indebted to Bro. T. O. Haunch, Librarian of Grand Lodge for the details in this paragraph. Ed.]

---

147.   PRESENTATION OF GLOVES

Q. Our lodge has resolved that a pair of White Gloves be presented to each of our Candidates on the night of his being raised. Could you supply us with material for a few brief words explaining how our Glove customs arose?

A. The gloves, which form part of our regalia nowadays, were originally a necessary part of the operative masons' protective clothing, being specially important to prevent injury. Numerous early records show that they were *supplied to the masons by their employers*.

At Ely, in 1322, the Sacrist bought gloves for the masons engaged on the 'new work', and at Eton College, in 1456, five pairs of gloves were provided for 'layers' of the walls 'as custom may have required'. (Knoop & Jones, *The Mediaeval Mason*, 1949, p. 69.) At York, in 1423, ten pairs of gloves were supplied to the mason 'setters' at a total cost of eighteen pence (Salzman, *Building in England* . . . p. 80). At Ayr, Edinburgh and St. Andrews there are a large number of records of gloves supplied to 'hewers' and 'layers' from 1598 to 1688. (Knoop and Jones, *The Scottish Mason,* pp. 42–3.)

All these records relate to masons 'on the job'. But for the masons in their lodges there was another source of supply. From 1599 onwards there is evidence that masons were obliged to furnish a pair of gloves to each of the Brethren on the day of their entry into the lodge, as part of their admission fees. The earliest official record on the subject is in the Schaw Statutes addressed to the Kilwinning Lodge in 1599, re-quiring that all Fellows of Craft at their admission to that grade were to pay £10 Scots with 10/- worth of gloves. (These fees must be divided by twelve to find the corresponding English sums. F.C.s therefore paid the equivalent of 83p plus 4p for gloves.)

Records of the Lodge of Melrose for 1674 and 1675 show that both apprentices and Fellows at their entry were to pay the requisite fees with 'sufficient gloves to ye whole company . . .'. (Vernon, pp. 12/13.) At Aberdeen, in 1670, the apprentice was called upon to pay '4 rex dollars', with '. . . Ane *linen* apron and a pair of good gloves . . .' to each of the Brethren. (Miller, p. 61.) The *linen* apron is rather surprising, but linen was probably a local product and therefore economical.

At Dunblane, in 1724, the Lodge presented gloves and aprons to its 'intrants'. (Lyon, *Hist. of the L. of Edinburgh*. . . Tercent. edn., p. 204.) At Haughfoot, as late as 1754, the Lodge enacted

'. . . that none can Enter here in time Comeing without a pair of Gloves to each member of the sᵈ Lodge'. (Carr, *Haughfoot, AQC* 64, p. 34.)

In 1723, a Masonic exposure, now known as 'A Mason's Examination', was published in a London newspaper, *The Flying Post*. Its opening words run:

'When a Free-Mason is enter'd, after having given to all present of the Fraternity a Pair of Men and Women's Gloves and Leathern Apron. . . .'

This is the earliest known reference to women's gloves in connection with non-operative Masonic practice, but from this time onwards they become a regular part of admission procedure. The *Hérault Letter*, the earliest known French exposure, 1737, records that an apprentice received an apron of white skin, a pair of gloves for himself and a pair of ladies' gloves 'for her whom he esteems the most'. The same practice appears, in more or less gallant language, in practically all the French 18th century accounts of the initiation ceremony.

In England (and Scotland) the actual provision of gloves fell gradually out of fashion, and their cost (i.e., 'glove-money') was usually added to the entry-fees. After the dawn of the 19th century gloves virtually disappear from Lodge minutes and regulations.

When *your lodge* presents a pair of gloves to the Candidate, it will be reviving a custom practised in Britain since 1724, if not earlier; but some of our glove customs go back over 600 years, into the very beginnings of English Craft history.

---

148.   THE CHEQUERED CARPET AND
                INDENTED BORDER

Q. In our lodge (*Emulation* ritual) the carpet has black and white squares bordered by blue and red 'dentilations' of the Chapter. It is argued by some that all Craft floor-work must be carried out within the area of the black and white squares, and that the I.G., when reporting Brethren who seek admission, should come on to the squares, i.e., not merely on to the edge of the carpet.

Is this view pedantic or is there some allegorical explanation?

A. I begin with the official answer for 'Emulation' workers, for which I am indebted to Bro. C. F. W. Dyer:

> In the demonstrations of the Emulation Lodge of Improvement the place of the I.G., when making any report, is in front of his chair. He makes no movement forward so as to be on the carpet: he will only stand on the carpet if the normal position of his chair requires this. This position is stated in the *Emulation Ritual* book (p. 11 in the 1972 edn.).

The arguments mentioned in the question seem to have arisen from the comments of Brn. who do not follow *Emulation*, and the following brief notes may serve to trace the evolution of 'carpet and indented border', and should help to show how some of our modern views arose.

In the days of our earliest records of lodge procedure, i.e., when the floor-drawing (or T.B.) was actually drawn on the floor, there would have been no black and white chequered carpet—probably only bare boards—and the drawing would have occupied only a section of the floor. I think we may safely assume that nobody walked on the 'drawing' (except the candidate with his escort in the third degree). When, around the 1730s, the ready-made floor-cloths came into use, the same rule probably applied, hence the origin of the custom of 'squaring' the lodge, and the Brethren stood around the drawing or floor-cloth during the ceremonies. (See illustration on p. ii.)

The earliest surviving printed illustrations of the Tracing Boards, in 1744 and 1745, show a combined design for the first and second degrees. A small part of these Boards is covered with 'chequered flooring', but each picture is framed by straight ruled lines, i.e., without an indented design.

So much for the earliest *illustrations*. Against this, we have the mysterious 'Indented Tarsel', mentioned by Prichard (in his exposure of 1730) as part of the 'Furniture' of the lodge. He describes it as 'the Border round about it', i.e., round the lodge and, if Prichard is to be trusted on this point, it was an 'Indented' Border!

From 1751 onwards we have (in *Le Maçon Démasqué* and later versions) illustrations showing indented borders and when, at a much later date, the chequered carpets were introduced, covering the whole of the working area, the ornamental border became a regular but more-or-less variable feature of the design, generally made up of triangular indentations. (See Q. 87, p. 197.)

The notes hitherto are intended only to show the probable line of development and it may be interesting to add that in our Grand Lodge building, with some twenty Temples, the majority—if not all of them—now have a chequered design entirely *without* ornamental or indented borders. The Indented Border has become a standard part of our Tracing Boards, but it is not deemed an essential part of the carpet.

The 'First Lecture, Section V' explains the symbolism of the 'Mosaic Pavement' and the 'Indented Border', but offers no suggestion as to the use of the edge of the carpet (chequered or indented) in the course of our proceedings:

> The Mosaic Pavement . . . points out the diversity of objects which decorate and adorn the creation . . . The Blazing Star . . . refers us to the Sun, which . . . by its benign influence dispenses its blessings to mankind . . . The Indented or Tesselated Border refers us to the Planets, which . . . form a beautiful border or skirtwork round . . . the Sun, as the other does round that of a F. Mason's Lodge.

It is obvious that a great deal of importance is attached to the carpet, with or without the indented border, and it is easy to understand how the idea arose that all lodge work must be conducted, as far as possible, on the carpet. It follows from this, that the I.G., in announcing a report etc., is required, in some workings, to come forward on to the carpet. For the same reason, Brethren on entering the lodge after it has been opened, take up that position before saluting the W.M., and Candidates on entering the lodge are brought there. No symbolism is involved; it is simply deemed to be the best position for their purpose.

There is no doubt that many workings follow the *Emulation* practice as described at the beginning of the answer, above. Many others use the 'edge of the carpet'. All are equally correct if they follow the rubric in their ritual, or adhere to inherited custom.

---

149.   TASSELS ON THE CARPET

Q. Our lodge carpet has a Tassel design *round the very outer edge.* Is this a punning allusion to the tesselated (tasselated) pavement?

A. One would hesitate to comment on the design without having seen a sketch, but a tasselled design *all round* the carpet is perhaps unusual. Many Masonic carpets nowadays have a tassel in each of the four corners and in some 'Lectures' they are said to symbolize the four cardinal virtues, but this interpretation probably belongs to the end of the 18th century. (See illustrations on p. 119.)

The tassel design is not a pun. Tessellated means 'Of or resembling mosaic, having finely chequered surface'. (*O.E.D.*) The word is from the Greek *tessares* = four. It has nothing to do with tassels, which seem to have arisen from a misunderstanding of the 'Indented Tarsel' in Prichard's exposure of 1730. That work became the basis of the catechisms in all the early French exposures, which translated the 'Indented Tarsel' as *Houppe dentelée. Houppe* means tuft or tassel; *dentelée*, with one *l*, means 'indented'; *dentellée*, with two *ll*s, means 'lacy' or 'laced'. The exposure *Le Catéchisme des Francs-Maçons*, 1744, in its combined Tracing Board for the 1st and 2nd Degrees, was the first text to *illustrate* the *Houppe dentelée* as a long cord with two tasselled ends forming a kind of ornamental headpiece across the top of the design. This was the first appearance of tassels in a Masonic context. They may have been in use on English Tracing Boards of that period, but there is no evidence to support this. (See illustration on p. ii. Tasselled Cord or 'lacy tuft' on the Floor-cloth.)

Thus, the immediate source of the tassels was probably a misinterpretation of the English text. But the cord with tassels also has a curious French derivation, based on the Biblical statement that *H.A. was a widow's son*. In Masonic ritual, all Masons are Brothers to H.A., and are therefore called '*sons of the widow*'. In French heraldry, *the Arms of a widow are surrounded or framed by a wavy (indented) tasselled cord*, a *Cordon de veuve*, i.e., a widow's cord, and from 1747 onwards, the cord with tassels is described as the *Cordon de veuve*. (See p. ii and *E.F.E.*, pp. 95, 320–1, 336–7.)

There has always been a strong element of uncertainty about Prichard's 'Indented Tarsel', with many explanations, none of them completely satisfying. Thus, *Le Maçon Démasqué* of 1751 gives the combined E.A.-F.C. 'floorcloth' *without the 'widow's cord'*, and with an indented border formed of triangles alternately blank and shaded, and this *border* is called *Houppe dentelée*. In its 1757 edition, the same work illustrates *both* the widow's cord and the indented border, but the text makes no mention of the '*widow's cord*' (or tassels): The 'indented border' is called *Houppe dentelée*, and is explained as 'empty and filled' triangles, as before. Thus, the French texts translate the *Houppe dentelée*, either as a widow's cord (with tassels) or as an indented border. Prichard may have been wrong in his use of the term 'Indented Tarsel', but there can be no doubt at all that he meant it to refer to a border.

All very confusing, but we do know at least how the tassels arose, as a heraldic and symbolical allusion to 'the widow', i.e., the Craft itself, whose sons we are.

---

150. HEBREW INSCRIPTIONS ON TRACING BOARDS OF THE THIRD DEGREE

There have been numerous enquiries recently as to the meaning of the Hebrew inscriptions to be found on several versions of the 3° Tracing Board, some of them doubtless arising from the excellent picture in the newly-published *Emulation Ritual*. There are several versions of that design, which may be described briefly as a scroll arranged across a coffin. *The ends of the scroll are invariably rolled up so that only fragmentary portions of the inscriptions remain visible.* They are generally sufficient, however, to enable us to reconstruct the whole text.

Third Degree Tracing Board
With a complete Hebrew inscription

The *Emulation* inscription may be reconstructed as follows, but it should be noted that only the words in italics are visible:

[At right   The *Temple* of *Jerusalem* was built by Solomon
of scroll]   King of *Israel*, Hiram King of *Tyre* and
                 Hiram *Abi*[f] in the year *2992*

[At left foot
of scroll]   *In the year 3 thousands*
Presumably the 2992 and 3000 are starting and finishing dates.

For the benefit of many enquirers, we reproduce the Third Degree Tracing Board of a set newly designed by Bro. Esmond Jeffries, on behalf of the Logic Ritual Association. It is one of the few versions that contains a complete and perfect Hebrew inscription and the translation follows line by line:

lines 1 and 2	= The Holy Temple
line 3	= at Jerusalem
line 4	= was built by [lit. by the hands of]
line 5	= Solomon King of
line 6	= Israel,
line 7	= Hiram King of
line 8	= Tyre
line 9	= and Hiram of the Tribe of Naphtali, the Builder, in the year 3 thousands.

The cypher on the left of the Tracing Board is all fairly obvious except the last two lines and we are indebted to Bro. T. O. Haunch for the solution of the unusual problem which they present. The cypher on the penultimate line reads C. C. C. and below it, reading from right to left, are the characters F. F. Z. They represent Chalk, Charcoal and Clay, and they denote Freedom, Fervency and Zeal. These phrases, which originated in Prichard's *Masonry Dissected*, were repeated with variations in several of the later French Exposures and eventually found their way into the English 'Lectures' of the 18th century; they are still preserved in the present-day versions.

---

151.   HELE, CONCEAL . . .

Q. What is the correct meaning and pronunciation of the word 'hele' and how did it get into the Masonic ritual?

A. Hele, Heal. *The Oxford English Dictionary* gives two basic definitions:

1. (Obsolete except in dialect) To hide, conceal; to keep secret (with examples from c. 825.)
2. To cover, cover in. Still in local use, especially in the senses:
    (a) to cover (roots, seeds, etc.) with earth (with examples from c. 1200);
    (b) to cover with slates or tiles, to roof (with examples from 1387).

While several early English variations indicate a 'hayl' pronunciation, *O.E.D.* now gives the pronunciation as heel (so that it rhymes with keel or kneel).

It will be noted that the definition under 2(*b*) has a slight relationship with the mason trade but, since it refers to the specialized skills of a kindred trade and not to the mason trade itself, I believe that it was not used in our ritual in that sense but, more probably in the meaning as given in 1 above, 'To hide, conceal; keep secret'.

The main question, however, is how the word ought to be pronounced as one of the trio of words 'hele, conceal and never reveal'. The earliest appearance of all three together is in Prichard's *Masonry Dissected*, 1730, but prior to that the old documents show that only two words were used, and some of the variations are very interesting:

1696	*The Edinburgh Register House MS.*	'. . . to heill and conceall . . .'
c.1700	*The Chetwode Crawley MS.*	'. . . Hear & Conceal . . .'
c.1700	*The Sloane MS.*	'. . . heal and Conceal or Conceal and keep secret . . .'
c.1710	*The Dumfries No. 4 MS.*	'. . . heall & conceall . . .'
c.1714	*The Kevan MS.*	'. . . hear & Conseal . . .'
1723	'A Mason's Examination'	'. . . Hear and conceal . . '
1724	*The Grand Mystery of Free-Masons Discover'd*	'. . . Hear and conceal . . .'
1724	*The Whole Institution of Masonry*	'. . . Hold and conceal . . .'
c.1725	*Institution of Free Masons*	'. . . hide & conceal . . .'
1725	*The Whole Institutions of Free-Masons Opened*	'. . . Heal and Conceal . . .'
1726	*The Graham MS.*	'. . . hale and conceall . . .'
1730	Prichard's *Masonry Dissected*	'. . . Hail and Conceal, and never Reveal . . .'
c.1727	*The Wilkinson MS.*	'. . . heal and Conceal . . .'
c.1740	*Dialogue Between Simon and Philip*	'. . . Heal and Conceal . . .'
c.1750	*The Essex MS.*	'. . . heal & conceal . . .'
1760	*Three Distinct Knocks*	'. . . always hail, conceal, and never will reveal . . .'
1762	*J & B.*	'. . . always hale, conceal, and never reveal . . .'

Although it is likely that Masonic secrets were in use in the Craft in the early 1500s, the earliest reference to secret 'words & signes' in a Masonic context is in the *Harleian MS.* No. 2054, a version of the Old Charges, dated *c.* 1650. In that text *there is no hele, conceal and never reveal*, but simply the instruction (which I reproduce in modern spelling) 'you keep secret and not to reveal the same in the ears of any person . . .'.

The variants 'hear, hold, hide' in six of the earliest examples seem to imply that in the period 1696-*c.*1725 there was still some doubt as to the 'correct' word, and this tends to confirm that it was a comparatively late introduction of around that period.

We know very little of the precise detail of English ritual in the period 1730–1760, but it is evident that Prichard's 'Hail and Conceal, and never Reveal' had taken root during those thirty years. From 1760 onwards *Three Distinct Knocks*, *J. & B.*, and all the principal exposures, without exception, follow Prichard's triad, but with occasional variations in spelling. It must be agreed that 'Hail' in 1730 and 1760, and 'hale' in 1762, all seem to suggest that the 'hail' pronunciation was common in the 18th century, so that the triad would have been recited as 'hale, consale and never revale'. There seems to be no doubt, however, that *the original meaning* was 'hele' = to conceal or hide (not 'hail', = to salute or greet) and our only problem is pronunciation.

According to Claret, the Grand Master, the Duke of Sussex, directed in about 1816 that the word to be used was 'hele' and he stated its meaning. Claret's rituals use the word 'hele', on 'the authority of the G.M.', but the pronunciation is not recorded.

The *Shadbolt MS.*, and the *Williams/Arden MS.*, both deriving from prominent members of the Lodge of Reconciliation, give the word 'hail'. *The majority of our modern rituals print the word 'hele' without any direction as to pronunciation. Emulation*, 1969, prints the abbreviation 'h*' and insists on the pronunciation 'hail'. *Universal*, 1968, uses the word 'hele', and prints the rubric 'heel'. Frankly, the conflicting evidence makes it difficult to decide what the correct pronunciation should be today, but I would be inclined to follow the guidance given in *O.E.D.*, with the pronunciation 'heel'. We use an archaic word, out of sentiment perhaps, but I see no reason for maintaining an archaic (or doubtful) pronunciation, when all the rest of our ritual is in modern usage.

---

152.   THE 47TH PROPOSITION ON THE
             PAST MASTER'S JEWEL

Q. When and why was the 47th Proposition chosen as one of the features of the P.M. jewel? Has it any particular symbolism?

A. The modern P.M. jewel was officially prescribed for the use of Past Masters in the first *Book of Constitutions* following the Union, i.e., 1815, as follows:

> Past Masters . . . The square and the diagram of the 47th prop. 1st B. of
> Euclid, engraven on a silver plate pendent within it.

But there is good evidence of the popularity of the 47th proposition in the Speculative Craft long before that time. Anderson used it in the frontispiece to his 1723 and 1738 *Constitutions* and it also appeared in Smith's *Pocket Companion* of 1735, an Edinburgh edition of 1752, and in *Multa Paucis*, 1764. There is no early evidence, however, of its use as *part of a Masonic jewel* until the last decades of the 18th century.

Those early versions are all of the so-called 'gallows' type, i.e., the square hangs with its short arm horizontally and the diagram of the 47th proposition is suspended from that; hence the 'gallows' effect.

Throughout the 18th century there was no official rule for a Past Master's jewel and we have to look further afield for evidence on the subject, e.g.,

> *Three Distinct Knocks*, 1760: The Pass-Master hath a Compasses and Sun, with a Line of Cords, about his Neck, viz. 65 Degrees.
>
> *J. & B.*, 1762: Pass Master, with a Sun and Compasses, and a String of Cords.
>
> *Mahhabone*, 1766: A Pass'd Master, with the Sun and Compass, and a String of Cords.

There are, moreover, numerous portraits of famous 18th century Masons wearing jewels which seem to correspond to these descriptions, and there is a splendid collection of jewels in the Grand Lodge museum containing combinations of emblems, e.g., Square, Compasses, Sector and Sun, occasionally with other symbols, which were almost certainly worn as P.M. jewels, although they had no *official* sanction.

Even in official circles there seems to have been real doubt as to the correct or most suitable jewel for Past Masters and, only nineteen months before the 1815 *B. of C.* was published, specifying the 'Sq. and 47th proposition' for the P.M. jewel, the Order of Proceedings of Grand Lodge, dated 2 May 1814, ruled:

> . . . that the following Masonic clothing and insignia be worn by the Craft and that no other be permitted in the Grand Lodge or any subordinate Lodge. . . .
>
> Jewels . . . Past Masters . . . The Square within a Quadrant.

There is no known record of the reasons which prompted the adoption of a new design so soon after the 'Square and Quadrant' ruling. One might hazard a suggestion that the quadrant was abandoned because a similar feature, 'the Sector' soon became a part of the jewel of the Grand Master and Past Grand Masters, a distinction nowadays extended to Pro Grand Masters and Past Pro G.M.s.

Our main concern, however, is the reason for the selection of the 47th proposition, and here too there is room for speculation because no official reason was ever given.

Geometry, in the designing of buildings and in the practice of the mason trade, had always been closely linked with the Craft. Indeed the *Old Charges* constantly re-iterate the link between Geometry and Masonry even to the extent of outright declarations that 'Geometry is now called Masonry'.

When Dr. Anderson, in his 1723 *Constitutions* (pp. 20–21) averred that '. . . the 47th Proposition of Euclid's first book . . . is the foundation of all Masonry, sacred, civil, and military' he was treating the 47th proposition as *the symbol of all Geometry*, and proclaiming the age-old link between that science and the Craft. This must have been the reason why he displayed the 'diagram' so prominently on the flooring of his frontispiece and why it was so readily adopted by similar writers in the following decades.

When the time arrived, after the Union of the Grand Lodges, to establish a design for the P.M. jewel, Anderson's idea cannot have been far from the minds of the designers. They needed a Master's jewel plus some special distinguishing mark, and Anderson's favoured design was selected.

Many papers have been published on the 'Symbolism of the P.M. Jewel', but I cannot forget the words of our late Bro. Speth (the first Secretary of the Q.C. Lodge) that *the jewel itself is not a symbol; it is the badge of a P.M.* For the symbolism, I suggest that we disregard the jewel and concentrate on the 47th proposition, which is universally acclaimed by the specialists in that field as the *quintessence of perfection and truth*.

153.   ECCLESIASTES XII AND THE THIRD DEGREE

Q. At a Lodge that I visited recently, the Chaplain—during the most solemn moment in the Third Degree—read verses from Ecclesiastes. Can you furnish a simple interpretation which would also explain their relationship to the ceremony?

A. Verses 1–7 of Ecclesiastes XII are used in many Lodges during the Third Degree, and some of them certainly need interpretation. Personally I greatly admire the revised version as given in *The Bible to be Read as Literature* (Heinemann, p. 769). Only a few words have been altered in it as compared, say, with the Authorized Version, but with excellent results.

As regards interpretation, we are much indebted to V.W. Bro. The Rev. Canon Richard Tydeman, M.A., P.G. Chaplain, for the following notes which he very kindly compiled in response to our request:

> The Book called Ecclesiastes, popularly attributed to King Solomon, was probably written some five hundred years later, i.e., 200–300 B.C.

The outlook of the Book is fatalistic rather than pessimistic. All is vanity, because what is to be will be and nothing man can do will change it. The author has much in common with Omar Khayam.

Chapter XII, verses 1–7, sometimes read in lodges during the Third Degree, gives a picture of old age, the helplessness of senility, and death. It is written in highly picturesque and poetic language, the pictures mixing into one another with bewildering rapidity. Just as Omar Khayam speaks at one moment of flinging the stone of morning into the bowl of night, and the next minute catching the Sultan's turret in a noose of light, so in Ecclesiastes, as one commentator has said, 'the metaphors change and intermingle in accord with the richness of an oriental imagination'.

The passage could be roughly paraphrased thus:

Make the most of youth while the sun still shines, for as life advances there is less to look forward to. Arms ('keepers') and legs ('strong men') grow weak and weary; teeth ('grinders') are few and cease to work, eyes ('windows') grow dim. One by one the senses fail ('doors shut'); sleep is difficult and the old man wakes at the first sound of the dawn chorus ('voice of the bird') though he is deaf to other music. He becomes scared of heights and open places; his hair is white as almond-blossom, the lightest of insects would weigh him down, and he has lost all desires and interests. Man's departure to the grave ('his long home') is like the breaking of the golden lamp-bowl (see Zechariah ch. 4, v. 2) when the silver chain snaps and the flame is put out; it is like the spilling of water when the pitcher breaks, like the stillness that follows the breaking of a water-wheel. Body and soul thus part; for the body, dust to dust; for the spirit, a return to God who gave it.

The value of this passage to Masons, at that particular part of the Third Degree ceremony, is that it adds point and emphasis to the Charge which follows. The opening of the passage—'Let me now beg you to observe . . .'—in effect, is saying 'Be careful to perform your allotted task while it is yet day' and it continues by expressing 'that gloom which rests on the prospect of futurity . . . unless assisted by that Light which is from above'.

---

154.   OPENING A LODGE—SYMBOLISM, IF ANY?

Q. What is the actual significance of the ceremony of opening a Lodge; is there any symbolical explanation, or is it just an age-old custom? Why are the Officers asked their situations and duties every time a Lodge is opened?

A. There is no evidence of formal Opening in English working before 1760, but we can perhaps trace some of the stages which led up to the Opening ceremony, as follows:

(1) In the *Edinburgh Register House MS.*, 1696, which gives the earliest details of actual ceremonies, there is a question on 'What makes a true and perfect lodge', i.e., the number of men and situation of the lodge.

(2) In the *Trinity College, Dublin MS.*, 1711, a question 'Where sits ye master?' The earliest question on this subject.

(3) In 'A Mason's Examination', 1723, we have the first symbolic tools, in addition to the required numbers for a lodge, i.e., '. . . with Square, Compass, and common Gudge' (i.e., gauge or rule). In the same text, there is a reference to the situation of the Master, Wardens and Fellows, in answer to the question 'How do Masons take their Place in the Work?'

(4) Later exposures from 1724 onwards begin to discuss the situation and duties of the Master and Wardens, until we come to Prichard's *Masonry Dissected*, 1730, with the familiar Q. & A.:

Q. Where stands your Master?
A. In the East.

Q. Why so?
A. As the sun rises in the East and opens the Day . . .

Q. Where stands your Wardens?
A. In the West.

Q. What's their Business?
A. As the sun sets in the West . . .

Q. Where stands the Senior Enter'd 'Prentice?
A. In the South.

Q. What is his Business?
A. To hear and receive instructions and welcome strange Brothers, [while the Junior E.A., in the North, had to keep off all Cowans and Eavesdroppers].

These questions, in 1730, were apparently part of the Catechism, and it is not at all certain that they were used as part of an Opening ceremony. All we can say on this point is that much of the verbal material of that ceremony was already in existence in 1730.

There is a very brief Opening of a 'Master's Lodge' in *Le Catéchisme*, 1744, but the earliest records of any formal opening of Lodges appear in England at a comparatively late date in two famous Exposures, *Three Distinct Knocks*, 1760, and *J. & B.*, 1762, in both cases under the heading—'How to open a Lodge, to set the Men to work' and practically the whole of our present-day Opening ceremony is to be found there, in the language of that day, together with a few lines at the end (which have now been discarded) forbidding swearing, cursing, etc., under penalty.

The questions to the Officers on their situation and duties were clearly designed to ensure that the Lodge had its full complement, properly stationed, and the evolution of the Opening ceremony can have been only the result of a natural desire among masons to give formal shape to their proceedings.

It seems doubtful if there was any symbolism attaching to the Opening ceremony itself, until the Tracing Board was drawn or displayed and the V.S.L. was opened. *Those were the items which transformed the room into a Temple*, but although the V.S.L., Square, Compasses, and most of the emblems on the 1st T.B. were known and in use in *c.* 1730, symbolical explanations were still at a very rudimentary stage.

---

155.   SYMBOLISM OF THE INNER GUARD?

Q. A question was asked some time ago—'What in life does the Inner Guard represent when he admits a candidate?' I made a somewhat hazardous guess, suggesting that he may represent humanity and its resistance to revolutionary change. The lesson to be learned is 'not to rush in with an idea that would change an established way of living'. I hope this does not sound too far-fetched and would appreciate your guidance on this question.

A. There can be no objection to your interpretation of the admission of the Candidate by the I.G., as quoted above, but the question seems to be a good example of trying to find symbolism where none was originally intended. You start from the assumption that the mere presence of the I.G. represents something in our daily life, and I doubt if that was ever intended, more especially because the I.G., as such, is of comparatively late introduction. There was a time when the Cand. at the door would have been received by a Warden, or by the most junior member of the degree that was going to be conferred. They discharged the duties of the present-day I.G.

This, and my views on the subject generally, leads me to the conclusion that the symbolism attaches NOT to the I.G., but to the particular task which he performs in each of the degrees conferred. Thus, the point of a s . . . i . . . is usually explained as a warning '. . . never improperly to reveal'.

To find your own interpretation of our symbols is the very best kind
of Masonic exercise. The only danger is that it may lead too far from
the normally simple explanations that were intended. Many of us have
seen extraordinary and far-fetched examples that have no relationship
to Freemasonry, and which could never have been in the minds of those
who compiled or approved the actual words and procedures that are in
use today.

---

156.   SYMBOLISM
            INTERPRETATION AND LIMITATIONS

Q. My questions arise after reading W. H. Rylands's Paper in *AQC* 8,
which contained comments about the interpretation of symbols.

1. I believe that every Mason is free to interpret the symbols and
ceremonies of Masonry according to the light which he has received.
It is frustrating, consequently, to be told that an interpretation can't
possibly be accepted because it was never intended. For example—the
'Three Ages of Man' interpretation of our ceremonies appears to have
rather general acceptance, but when the spiritual interpretation is pro-
pounded, someone is likely to say that it cannot be accepted because
there is nothing in the early records to indicate that the Three Ages
interpretation was intended. It seems reasonable to believe that it could
not have had significance *before the Three Degree system was established,*
which means that real hoary antiquity cannot be attributed to it? I
would like your views on *an interpretation never intended.*

2. The Lectures of the Three Degrees give interpretations of many
things such as 'slipshod', 'hoodwinked' etc. Would a person be out of
bounds in saying that they indicate interpretations *which ought to be
accepted*?

A. 1. Symbols are a mode of communication; they teach by implication, or recollection, or interpretation. But symbolism is not an exact
science; so far as I know, there are no rules by which we can measure
the authenticity, or logic, or the accuracy of one's interpretations. Our
estimation of truth or accuracy, in dealing with symbols, will be
governed entirely by how far a particular explanation or interpretation
is in accord with our previous convictions, or how far it may succeed in
satisfying us in our search for understanding.

Hence I agree that every man is fully entitled (and should be encouraged) to work out his own symbolism and, when he has done this

to his own satisfaction, his symbolism is *valid for him*, regardless of the arguments of extraneous logic.

For myself, I prefer interpretation at its simplest level and, whenever possible, *in the actual words of the ritual*, e.g., 'The Square teaches us to regulate our lives and actions . . .', but it is obvious that teaching can be conducted on different levels, and should be, if that will give the most effective results. To illustrate the necessity for this kind of approach, imagine the teacher-child relationship. There may be many different ways in which a particular point or problem could be explained. One of them may be the generally accepted one, on which most teachers are agreed. Good; but for the child of slower perception it is the teacher's bounden duty to try another and another until the point is clarified.

For the brilliant child, it would be *the teacher's duty* to go beyond the normally accepted interpretation, especially if that would enable the child to achieve a wider understanding. No teacher could justify neglecting a particular level of instruction if it enables him to teach a lesson effectively.

I have only used the 'teacher-child' relationship in order to emphasize my point. The same reasoning would apply to one's own interpretation of symbolism, i.e., *a system of self-teaching* which has, and should have, no specific limits, no object except enlightenment and understanding.

As to the symbolism that was 'never intended', I believe that the chronological objection cannot fairly be raised or sustained, e.g., we all accept the symbolism of the Hiramic Legend as a basic part of our teachings, regardless of its late introduction.

Nevertheless, I must still put on record a deep-rooted dislike for aberrations in symbolism, extremes of interpretation which have no justification in the symbol itself and only mislead the reader or succeed in bemusing him. Some time ago a paper on the Meaning of Masonry was submitted to me for criticism. The writer was clearly a 'teetotaller' with strong views on the drink question and in two separate pieces of interpretation of Masonic ritual he showed that they meant, respectively, 'the virtues of teetotalism' and 'the evils of drink'. He was probably astonished when I pointed out that he was not giving an interpretation of Masonry, but of himself! Similarly I am convinced that real damage is done by those inveterate symbolists who need the dimensions of the pyramids, the mysteries of the heavenly bodies, the Tarot Cards, the Zodiac and other equally complex paths towards truth.

A. 2. '. . . which ought to be accepted?' No 'Working' and no authority can compel a man to believe something. It seems to me that he will only believe, or accept an argument that satisfies him as to its veracity or historical accuracy, or as a convincing explanation of something he does not understand. The Lectures (whether *Emulation* or any other version) are not obligatory in any of the Lodges with which I am connected. As a result, I am able to view them without that awe and veneration which they receive in some places. I have said this only to explain why there are some parts of the ritual and Lectures that I simply could not and cannot accept, remembering that their only justification is that they are supposed to explain or illustrate the meaning of our ceremonies and especially the meaning of those parts which are obscure. As examples, and to avoid repetition, I would ask you to read my notes on 'Inaccuracies in the Ritual' in Q. 178, p. 368.

---

157.   THE GRAND PURSUIVANT

Q. When was the Office of Grand Pursuivant first created and what is a Pursuivant? I have just been appointed Grand Pursuivant for the G.L. of Quebec. My Apron is the only one with a colourful crest. Assuming that our Aprons follow the designs of the United Grand Lodge of England, can you tell me something of the origin and meaning of the crest or badge?

A. The *O.E.D.* gives three main definitions of Pursuivant. The Masonic meaning would be under (c) below:

- (a) A Junior heraldic officer; an officer of the College of Arms ranking below a Herald.
- (b) A royal or state messenger with power to execute warrants. (A warrant officer—obsolete.)
- (c) A follower—an attendant.

EARLIEST RECORDS OF THE OFFICE AND ITS DUTIES

The first mention of Pursuivant in English Grand Lodge records is in the minutes of a Grand Committee of the Antients' Grand Lodge on 1 April 1752, at the Griffin [Tavern], Holborn:

> Brother Christopher Byrne Master of No. 6 in the Chair
>
> The Pursuivant Bro[r] William Lilly gave notice that Bro[r] John Gaunt Master of No. 5 desired admittance, and upon his admission the Worshipful President Resign'd the Chair to him . . . Not as his Right, but for his acknowledged skill and Judgement.

(Quatuor Coronatorum Antigrapha, xi, p. 32)

The earliest record of the regular appointment of Pursuivant in the United Grand Lodge was in 1833 when *it was a paid appointment*. The holder of that Office was Robert Miller until he died in 1839. In 1840 'Pursuivant' became an Honorary Office carrying Grand Rank status, and the first holder of that Office was William Rule, who remained Grand Pursuivant from 1840 to 1849. The 1847 *Book of Constitutions*, p. 41, described the duties of the Office:

> The grand pursuivant is to preside over the brethren nominated to attend within the porch of the grand lodge. He is at every meeting of the grand lodge to preserve order in the porch, and with the assistance of the brethren nominated for attendance there, to see that none, except those who are qualified, and who have their proper clothing and jewels, and have signed their names to the accustomed papers, and are in all respects entitled to admission, be admitted.

We are indebted to Bro. J. W. Redyhoff of Leeds, Yorkshire, for an early Provincial reference. He writes:

> At the first meeting of the Provincial Grand Lodge of Yorkshire, West Riding, on 1 November 1822, no Prov. G. Pursuivant was appointed, but a resolution was passed:
>
> > That the Assistant Grand Secretary, Pursuivant and Tylers be paid out of the funds of the Provincial Grand Lodge.
>
> After this, the accounts contain a number of records, up to 1834, of the payment of Ten Shillings to the Prov. G. Pursuivant for each attendance and all this had begun at least eleven years before the United Grand Lodge had made any such appointment.

Jewel of the Grand Pursuivant
By courtesy of the Board of General Purposes

THE BADGE OR CREST OF THE GRAND PURSUIVANT

The badge or crest of the Grand Pursuivant is described as 'Arms of the Grand Lodge with Rod and Sword crossed'. The Arms are a combination of those of the first Grand Lodge, 1717, and of the Antients' Grand Lodge, founded in 1751. (See illustrations on pp. 15, 17, 19.)

As to the query on your 'colourful crest': originally, the Grand Lodge of Quebec used the English Arms as its Seal and their Pursuivant's Jewel etc., copied the English design. But the Arms were abandoned in their 1953 *Constitutions*, and the badge became simply the 'Rod and Sword crossed'. You have apparently inherited a pre-1953 Apron and I hope you may be permitted to wear it; if not, it should go into your Grand Lodge Museum.

---

158.   THE V.S.L. IN OUR CEREMONIES

Q. There are several things that puzzle me about the V.S.L.

(a) How or why did it come into our ceremonies?

(b) What about Indian or Turkish Freemasons; don't they have *their own sacred writings* open in their lodges?

(c) How do Brethren of those other religions accept the numerous allusions, legends etc., which belong to—or occur—only in the Old Testament; for example King Solomon's Temple and all the references, legends and persons connected with it.

A. (a) The Bible can hardly be said to have 'come in': it was almost certainly in use from the first beginnings of Freemasonry. From *c.* 1390 onwards every one of the *Old Charges* (our oldest documents) indicates that the Masons' oath was the 'Heart and marrow' of the admission ceremony, e.g., *The Regius MS.*, *c.* 1390 says, in modern English:

> And all shall swear the same oath
> Of the Masons,
> Be they willing, be they loth . . .

Clearly the oath required the use of the Holy Book, and most of our 130 versions of the *Old Charges* (but not all of them) prescribe the manner in which the Holy Book was used for that purpose.

(b) In Asiatic countries—and indeed in all countries of the world where regular Masonry is practised, arrangements *must be made* to furnish the Candidate with a V.S.L. that is sacred *to him*. Lodge Singapore No. 7178 (E.C.) has four different V.S.L.s open on the pedestal at any one time. In the Grand Lodge of Iran there are three versions in use, i.e., the *Koran*, the *Zend Avesta* of the Zorastrian faith, and the *Holy Bible* in the Authorized Version.

(c) *Allusions in the ritual to matters only contained in our V.S.L.*, etc. I see no reason why this should cause difficulty or embarrassment. Our Masonic teaching is based entirely on the Old Testament, but I've never heard a Christian Brother complain about this, and the reason for this tolerance arises from the manner of our teaching.

We use the Temple of Solomon as the glorious background to our legends; we use the Hiramic legend in the same way as Christ used parables, i.e., to teach moral and spiritual lessons. *But we do not require that our Candidates accept these legends as Truth.* They are legend—and we do not claim any more than that. Solomon, Hiram, King of Tyre, and Hiram Abif, are part of 'world literature'. Nobody breaks his vows, or abandons his faith, when he learns a spiritual lesson by such means; and our legends would have been equally valid for us if they had been about Mohammed, or Christ.

Turkish Lodges do exist and their Grand Lodge was recognized by us in 1970. Apropos the preceding paragraph you will be interested to hear that at least one of their Lodges works *Emulation* translated into Turkish!

---

159.   ORATORS IN FREEMASONRY

Q. Did the English Lodges ever appoint an Orator (as in several European jurisdictions), and when was the first reference to Orators in Masonry?

A. There are three London Lodges that appoint Orators. Two of them are 'Time Immemorial', i.e., Antiquity No. 2, and Fortitude and Old Cumberland No. 12. The third is the German speaking Pilgrim Lodge No. 238, which uses the Schroeder working. Constitutional Lodge No. 294, at Beverley, Yorkshire, appointed Orators since its foundation in 1793, but all such records are very scarce, even in the 18th century lodges which regularly heard lectures on a variety of Masonic and non-Masonic subjects.

The earliest reference to the office of Masonic Orator appears to be in the *Réception d'un Frey-Maçon*,[1] 1737, the first of all the French exposures. According to that text, it was his duty to address the Candidate immediately before the Obligation, and the address—comprised in a single sentence—is curiously reminiscent of the Master's remarks at the same point in the Initiation today:

> Brother Orator says to him, you are about to embrace a respectable Order, which is more serious than you imagine; there is nothing in it against the Law, against Religion, against the King, nor against Manners; the Worshipful Grand Master will tell you the rest.

The Orator appears again in several other exposures, using precisely the same formula, but *Le Sceau Rompu*, 1744, gives a new form[2]:

> Sir, the fearlessness that you have shown in surmounting & overcoming the obstacles that you have encountered, during the mysterious journey that you were made to undergo in this august Lodge: the desire you have so long evinced, to be admitted into a Society as ancient as it is honourable, proves to us conclusively that you have trampled underfoot the prejudices of the vulgar Profane.
>
> You are about to enter into a solemn engagement with us, which will unite you in bonds of tender & sincere affection to an Order, in which the Greatest Kings have not disdained to be initiated.
>
> It is at the foot of the Tribunal of prudence, that you are about to promise in the presence of the great Architect of the Universe, to keep inviolate the Secret of Masonry. Consummate this great Work, by repeating with attention the obligation which our Worshipful Master will now dictate to you.

The first substantial change in procedure appeared in *Le Maçon Démasqué*, 1751. In this text, there was no pre-obligation address, and the Orator's duties began at the end of the entrusting in the Fellow's degree.[3] After a brief reference to the darkness which enveloped the Profane, the orator continued:

> But now . . . the *light* appears, & our mysteries are unveiled to your astonished sight. Look at these noble designs portrayed in chalk, these steps, these columns, it is the Temple . . . so renowned in History, destroyed by the Romans, & raised again by Brother Masons. . . . it is to give a new lustre to this Temple that no longer exists except in our hearts, that we assemble under the auspices of Wisdom to recreate in a loving fraternity the virtues of the Golden age . . . Armed with the square & Compass, we regulate our actions, we measure our steps; . . . & this level that we carry in our hand teaches us to appraise men in order to do honour to their humanity; . . . never does the poisoned breath of discord tarnish its brightness nor mar its

---

[1] *Early French Exposures*, p. 7 (publ. by the Quatuor Coronati Lodge).
[2] Ibid, p. 212.
[3] Ibid, p. 437–8.

beauty. In whatever distant climes fortune may take you, . . . you will see the Mason divest himself in Lodge of the pompous titles which decorate him, admiring the virtues in his Brethren, . . . helping them in their difficulties, sharing their woes, . . . showing gentleness & kindness in his countenance, disdaining the contemptuous looks of pride that create gulfs between men, forgiving wrongs & never offering any, loving goodness & hating only vice . . . a faithful subject, a constant friend . . . & opening his heart to enjoy with his Brethren pleasures that are always Innocent & lawful.

That, my dear Brother, is a lightly-sketched outline of the portrait of a Free-Mason. The dignity with which you have just been invested gives you a right to his virtues; put them into use throughout the entire universe of which you now become a citizen. You are a Brother, enjoy with us the happy privilege of being one. [Only a few extracts from a very long Oration.]

When we recall that this piece was published in the early developing years of Speculative Freemasonry, it seems to contain a number of sentiments that would deserve mention in a modern 'Toast to the Initiate'. But the author of *Démasqué* had no real affection for the Craft and his own summing up of the Orator's address is:

This is virtually the same as all speeches made by Orators of Lodges. Nothing of truth, plenty of tinsel, & little Solidity.

The Office of Orator has no place in our English system, more's the pity, especially since the gentle art of oratory occupies such a large part of our Masonic after-proceedings. Indeed, it seems likely that if more of our after-dinner speakers were trained in the art a far higher proportion of our members and their guests would remain at table till the Tyler's toast, instead of pleading that they had a train to catch.

In some of the European jurisdictions, e.g., France, Holland and Belgium, and also in the U.S.A., the Orator plays a variable—but often important—part in the ceremonies. In Austria and Germany especially, where the Schroeder Ritual is deservedly popular, it is the Orator's duty, in that system, towards the end of the Initiation ceremony, to deliver a full explanation and interpretation of the whole ceremony including the symbolism of the '*tapis*' (a carpet woven with designs of tools, symbols etc., the counterpart of our modern Tracing Boards). The Orator's duty in these cases is all the more interesting and important because he is not merely reciting the printed word; indeed, every word he utters is of his own free choice and, having recently witnessed a Schroeder Initiation in Vienna, I must say that it was one of the most beautiful and inspiring ceremonies I have ever seen.

160.   MUST ALL THREE CHAIRS BE OCCUPIED THROUGHOUT THE CRAFT CEREMONIES?

Q. In our Lodge (Cathay No. 4373, Hong Kong) when the J.W. leaves his Chair to give the Lecture on the 2° Tracing Board, the Chair is always filled by someone, usually the Director of Ceremonies. Is it possible that the reason for this is to have someone there ready to sound the Gavel when the J.W. gets to the part where he explains the letter G?

A. There is no law in the Craft that requires all three Chairs in the Lodge to be permanently occupied (or filled) throughout every moment of every ceremony! We know the J.W.'s place is in the south, but we do not have to nail him down in his seat. He leaves his Chair in the 3° without having someone to sit on it during his absence, and similarly in the Closing in the 3°.

I do not say that your Lodge is wrong in this particular practice; only that it is quite unnecessary.

As to who is going to give the knock at the proper moment, could not the Master or the S.W. sound the Gavel?

So much for the specific question. It may be helpful, however, to give a more general answer. When any of the three Principal Officers leaves his Chair momentarily *to continue his duties on the floor of the Lodge*, there is no need to replace him. When any one of them has to withdraw from the Lodge for reasons of health, or comfort, or to answer a telephone call, the vacant Chair should be filled.

---

161.   QUESTIONS BEFORE PASSING AND RAISING
WHO MAY STAY TO HEAR THEM?

Q. There is an argument here as to when or whether E.A.s should be asked to leave the Lodge when a Candidate is about to answer the Questions leading to the 2°. Some of our senior P.M.s argue that all E.A.s (except the Candidate) should retire *before the Questions*. Other Brethren believe that E.A.s should be allowed to stay *during the Questions only*. May we have your views?

A. Without doubt I urge that all E.A.s should be permitted to stay, for obvious reasons. It gives them the opportunity to hear the Questions and Answers once more than they would otherwise, and it serves them virtually as an additional rehearsal. I would add (as an old Preceptor) that, if the watching E.A.s are of a nervous disposition, so that being present actually gives them the encouragement that they need, this one experience could make a lifelong difference to them in their enjoyment and appreciation of Masonry. Of course let them stay—and similarly with F.C.s and the Questions leading to the 3°.

I suggest that the proper time to ask them to retire would be (in each case) after the Questions had been answered and the Candidates have been taken up to the W.M. for the entrusting, *but before the entrusting begins*; the Brethren should salute before they retire.

A friendly critic has written to say that this suggestion 'is heresy to most ritual workings'. If that is really so, then there are some heretical Lodges both in London and the Provinces. I will only add that *The Universal Book of Craft Masonry*, one of the popular workings, especially in the London area, in its 7th edition, 1968, permits E.A.s and F.C.s to stay in lodge for the examination, and prints a special rubric *at the end of the questions and before the entrusting*, exactly on the lines I have outlined here.

---

162.   NON-CONFORMING CANDIDATES

Q. Are the following people eligible as Candidates for Initiation and if the circumstances described here raise any special problems will you please say how you would deal with them:

    (a) One who believes in a Supreme Being, but professes and practises no religion.

    (b) One who will not take an oath but agrees to make a declaration instead.

A. Certainly these are complex questions. Let us deal with (a).

'One who believes in a Supreme Being' etc. etc.

This fulfils 'the first condition of admission into the Order' according to the Official statement in 'Aims and Relationships of the Craft', Clause 3. Under Charge 1 of 'The Charges of a Free-Mason', still printed as a preamble to our present-day *Book of Constitutions*, we read:

> Let a man's religion or mode or worship be what it may, he is not excluded from the order, provided he believe in the glorious architect of heaven and earth . . .

and on those words alone it would seem arguable that so long as a man professes belief in a Supreme Being we are really not entitled to ask what religion he professes, or whether he practises any at all.

But at this stage we are governed by another major item (No. 4) in the catalogue of 'Aims and Relationships', which says:

> The Bible, referred to by Freemasons as the Volume of the Sacred Law, is always open in the Lodges. *Every candidate is required to take his Obligation on that book or on the Volume which is held by his particular creed* to impart sanctity to an oath or promise taken upon it. [Editor's italics.]

It is clear that this item orders that we provide a Bible or V.S.L. for the Candidate for the Obligation that he 'is required to take . . .', and it must be that version which '. . . is held *by his particular creed* to impart sanctity to an oath or promise taken upon it'.

Whether the Candidate likes it or not, we are bound to exact an oath or declaration from him at his admission, and it must be taken on the particular book of his particular creed. If he says at the outset that he has no creed or acknowledges no particular form of religion he makes himself ineligible because we—in our procedures—have no option.

I would go one step further on this question, however. It may well be that the Candidate, eager for admission, will stretch a point (that is always easy) and say, 'Well, if I must; I must: you can put me down as Methodist (or Anglican or what-not) and I'll take the Obligation on a Bible'. I firmly believe that that Candidate should be rejected. The Craft will be better off without him.

I am reminded of a story, within my own experience, of a bright young Candidate, who on being asked 'Do you believe in God?' hesitated a moment and said 'Well, it depends on what you mean by God'. The Committee were momentarily shocked by what seemed to be a rather careless or casual reply. But the W.M. remained unruffled —and very quietly he continued:

'No, Mr. . . . . it depends on what *you* mean by God.'

The Candidate was a good talker, but he talked himself out of that lodge, and was not admitted.

(b) The same Clause 4 which is quoted above makes provision, in its final words, for the problem raised by your Question (b), i.e., by making allowance for 'an oath or promise taken upon it'. This means, in fact, that the Obligation may be administered so that it forms a 'solemn promise' instead of an oath.

It may be added that this procedure, generally described as 'affirmation' is considered to be the correct procedure (or the prerogative) for Quakers, a strict Christian sect whose faith forbids them from taking oaths. The Biblical law on oaths is very complex, and the modern interpretations of the practice vary considerably, but there is no doubt that many religious people—and others perhaps—have very strong objections to swearing an oath. My own view, therefore, is that 'permission to affirm' should not be the prerogative of any particular faith, but ought to be available to anyone who asks for it.

I have never seen that ceremony but, as I understand it, Quakers have no objection to *affirming on the Holy Bible* so long as they are not required to take an oath.

Question (b) asks whether the candidate may make a declaration instead of an oath. Assuming that 'declaration' and 'affirmation' are the same thing, I feel sure that the candidate may make such a declaration on a V.S.L.

But suppose (a) and (b) above were the same man: a 'declaration' without a V.S.L. would not be valid.

Virtually every case arising out of these questions will require a measure of tact and caution, and I would urge that guidance should be sought in all such cases from the Grand Secretary, or the Provincial or District Grand Secretaries, preferably before the Candidate is interviewed.

---

163.   U.S.A. LODGES WORKING IN THE
THIRD DEGREE

Q. I have heard that in the U.S.A. the lodges generally conduct all their lodge business in the Third Degree and that they only go into the 1st or 2nd degrees when they have to confer those ceremonies. Is this true, and if so, why?

A. Personal observation enables me to confirm that this is the practice in several (if not all) U.S.A. jurisdictions. There is one major difference between English and U.S.A. practice which seems to indicate a possible explanation. Under English Masonic law, a Candidate *after his initiation* is a member of the lodge with all rights and privileges of membership, except that he may not remain in lodge during any degree work beyond the First.

In most (if not all) U.S.A. jurisdictions the Candidate *does not become a member of the lodge until after he has taken his Third Degree.* Some jurisdictions actually require that he must also have passed his 'Proficiency Test' in the Third Degree (involving the answers to a catechism of some forty or more questions—plus the Obligation by heart!). At this stage, whether with or without the Proficiency Test, the Candidate is allowed to 'sign the Register' and becomes a member of the lodge.

On several occasions in trying to answer the question, I have suggested that this may be the reason for all business being conducted in the Third Degree, i.e., to keep the E.A.s and F.C.s out, but I was never wholly satisfied with that answer, or even sure that it was correct.

I have just heard from a good friend in New York, W.Bro. Herbert H. Stafford, Past Master of the Lodge *L'Union Française*, No. 17, N.Y. confirming my theory. He writes:

> . . . I discovered the source of the practice in the United States to hold meetings in the third degree. This—deplorable—custom stems from the National Masonic Convention held at Baltimore in May, 1843 during which Grand Lodges assembled there decided to hold all meetings in the third degree, which decision was then incorporated in the different Constitutions and carried through without further thoughts on it. It must be borne in mind that this Baltimore Convention was a kind of revival for the Craft after the Morgan affair and the subsequent hysteria which swept the Country for most of the 1830s . . .

Bro. Stafford has very kindly sent a copy of the relevant section of the Convention Report for 5–17 May 1843, p. 34:

> The impropriety of transacting business in Lodges below the Degree of Master Mason, except such as appertains to the conferring of the inferior Degrees and the instruction therein, is a subject which has recently been presented to the consideration of the Grand Lodges in the United States by the Grand Lodge of Missouri, and in the opinion of the Committee ought to be adopted. *Entered Apprentices and Fellow Crafts are not members of Lodges, nor are they entitled to the franchises of members.* To prevent, therefore, the possibility of any improper interference in, or knowledge of, the transactions of the Lodge, the confining of all business to Master Lodges will be found most advantageous and undoubtedly is the only course of practice. [Editor's italics.]

It is always easy 'to be wise after the event' and since the arrival of Bro. Stafford's letter I had the opportunity to examine the Massachusetts *Book of Constitutions* on the subject of lodge membership. Section 317 reads:

> 'The Lodge shall admit as members such only as are Master Masons'.

I need only add that the U.S.A. lodges can open from zero directly into the Third Degree. They do not have to open in all three Degrees as is the practice in England.

164. THE WARDENS' COLUMNS

A PAIR, OR PART OF A SET OF THREE?

Q. Are the Wardens' Columns intended to represent the two Pillars at the Porch of K.S.T., or are they part of the set of three Pillars which we symbolize as Wisdom, Strength and Beauty?

A. The answer to this question is not a simple one and, for fear of offending those who believe that our system came down from Heaven all ready-made as it is today, it is important to emphasize that it developed slowly through the centuries from very small and modest beginnings.

If we go back to our earliest documents of the Craft, the *Old Charges* which run from *c.* 1400 onwards, the *two earliest and only pillars* in our literature were not those of K.S.T., but the pillars built by the children of Lamech, on which were engraved all the then-known sciences, to preserve them from destruction in case the world was to be destroyed by flood or fire. In all those documents (some 130 separate versions) Solomon's Temple played only a very small part and his two pillars do not appear at all!

It is not until *c.* 1700 that we find Solomon's Pillars named in our earliest ritual documents, at first by chapter and verse Biblical references, later by initials and with further expansions. In *c.* 1710 the *Dumfries No. 4 MS.* has a reference to those same Pillars giving strong Christian religious symbolism to them, and in 1724–5 two other ritual texts, *The Grand Mystery of Free-Masons Discover'd* and the *Institution of Free-Masons*, say that they represent 'Strength and Stability of the Church in all ages'.

We go back to *Dumfries c.* 1710 for the first appearance of a set of 'Three Pillars', but with an unusual significance:

Q. How many pillars is in your Lodge? A. Three.
Q. What are these? A. ye Square, the Compas and ye bible.

In Prichard's *Masonry Dissected*, 1730, and the *Wilkinson MS.* of about the same date we find the first mention of the 'Three Pillars' that 'support the Lodge . . . [i.e.] Wisdom, Strength and Beauty'. There can be no doubt that these were *a separate set of three which were purely symbolical*; they were not yet part of the lodge furniture. Moreover, they had nothing to do with the two in the *Old Charges*, or with those of K.S.T.

It must be emphasized that throughout this period the Wardens were 'floor-officers', discharging duties comparable to those of our Deacons today. It is very doubtful if they had seats during the ceremonies and it is certain that they had no Pedestals or Pillars; the latter were simply drawn on the floor, or 'floor-cloth', and though they had a place in the ritual they were not part of the Wardens' equipment.

It is not until 1760–2, with the appearance of *Three Distinct Knocks* and *J. & B.*, which are believed to represent Antients' and Moderns' practice, that we have evidence of the Wardens *each carrying in his hand* one of the two Pillars representing the B. and J. of Solomon's Temple. In addition to their verbal and ritual significance, they had now become portable emblems of the Wardens' Offices.

In those same texts of 1760 and 1762 we find (for the first time so far as I am aware) that the 'Wisdom' Pillar *represents* the Master in the E; the 'Strength' Pillar *represents* the S.W. in the W; and the 'Beauty' Pillar *represents* the J.W. in the S., implying almost certainly that these three Pillars were now something more than a piece of verbal symbolism; they were actually three pieces of solid furniture with specific positions in the layout of the lodge. It was our mass-production furniture manufacturers who turned them into Candlesticks, combining them with the 'Three Lesser Lights'.

In effect, the W.M. has only one Pillar; the Wardens have two each but those which stand on their pedestals are, strictly speaking, their personal emblems of Office, a tradition now more than 200 years old.

---

165.   ADMISSION OF CANDIDATES IN THE
                              SECOND DEGREE

Q. When the I.G. admits the Candidate in the 2°, how should he apply the Square, i.e.,

    (a) With the point of the angle?
    (b) With the tip of one arm?
    (c) With the tips of both arms?

A. The correct answer depends on whether your particular 'working' has a rubric on the subject. If it has not, I would personally favour (c). But *Emulation, West End, Benefactum* and Dr. E. H. Cartwright's *English Ritual* prescribe that the 'angle of the square' be used—so there seems to be a solid weight of custom in favour of (a).

---

166.   'THE ASSISTANCE OF THE SQUARE'

Q. In one of the ceremonies it is stated that the Candidate hopes to obtain the privileges of the Degree by 'the assistance of the Square' and the Square is included by the W.M. in the term 'powerful aid'. What form does the assistance take?

A. There seems no doubt, if the words mean what they say, that at some stage either before or during the ceremony the Square will have been used to 'assist' the Cand. in becoming a F.C. I see this, however, as a purely symbolical 'usage and assistance', but it is still necessary, in answering the question, to review briefly all the occasions in the 1° in which the Square has played (or should have played) some important part in the ceremony *thereby qualifying the Cand. to receive his 2°.*

The first of these cases that I would cite is a practice that has virtually disappeared from general Craft usage, though it certainly existed in England and Scotland from *c.* 1730 throughout the rest of the 18th century at least. I refer to the ancient custom of the E.A. Candidate *kneeling within a square* for his Obligation. There is no limit to the symbolical explanations that might be adduced for this practice; I will quote only one simple piece from 'The First Lecture of Free Masonry by William Preston' (*AQC*, Vol. 82, p. 125, Sec. II, Clause VI). One of the early answers in this clause describes the posture of the E.A. during the Obligation as 'Kneeling . . . body erect within the square . . .'. A later answer explains that this is

> 'To remind us that being *obligated within the square*, we are ever afterwards bound to act upon it'.

Only one more instance from the 1° involving the Square need be quoted, i.e., the posture of the Candidate at the N.E. corner in readiness for the homily from the Master.

> In what form does he appear?
> With his feet formed into a square, body erect. . . .
> What recommendation does he then receive?
> That as he then stood . . . before God and the Lodge a just and upright man and Mason, so to maintain that character through life (*ibid.* Sec. III Clause IV, p. 129).

In the 2° the Square will be used mainly (a) at the moment of admission, (b) during the Ob., (c) in the subsequent entrusting, for several signs or postures pertaining to that ceremony which cannot be discussed here in detail, (d) at the S.E. corner, and finally (e) when the W.M.

explains its use as one of the tools of the 2°. I have no hesitation in saying that in all these cases (as in the 1°) the Square is used, or was used, to inculcate moral lessons by the method which is peculiarly Masonic, i.e., veiled in allegory and illustrated by symbols.

---

167.   THE HAILING SIGN
                    WHEN DIT IT APPEAR?

Q. In one of your recent lectures you mentioned that the Hailing Sign was not yet known in Masonry in 1730. How can you or anyone be certain that it was not known?

A. 'Certain' is indeed a strong word and should not be used lightly; in this case, however, there are reasonably good grounds for the statement; but first, a cautionary note. In the answer that follows, reference is made to two signs (the Sn. of Fidelity, and the Hailing Sign), and it is necessary to emphasize that we are discussing those signs *as they were given at the various dates that are quoted*, ranging from 1730 to 1760. We are not describing present-day practice.

In 1730, when Samuel Prichard's *Masonry Dissected* was published, it contained the earliest description of a set of three degrees, and although the Sn. of F. was described (in what was then its proper place) there was no mention of a Hailing Sign.

During the next thirty years, 1730–1760, apart from the 'Charge to the Initiate' and the transposition, by the premier Grand Lodge, of certain words in the first two degrees, there are no written or printed records of any Craft ritual developments in Britain. Prichard's work proved so popular that it seemed to put all other English Masonic exposures out of business, and our only records of ritual developments during that period come from across the Channel, and notably from France.

Thus, from 1737 to 1751 we find the Sn. of F. in regular use in France, as a 'sign' and also as the proper attitude for every Mason (E.A. or upwards) when addressing the Master. But there is no trace of a Hailing Sign.

In 1742 (*Le Secret des Francs-Maçons*) we have an excellent description of the Initiation Ceremony of that period, and a rather weak hint of a Second Degree. This contains the Sn. of F. but again no Hailing Sign.

From 1744 onwards there are several really splendid descriptions of the First and Third Degrees and one or two moderately satisfying descriptions of the Fellow's Degree (i.e., the second—which was always the weakest of the three) but still there is no Hailing Sign.

Of course we have to be careful when discussing exposures. Some of them were rubbish, admittedly, but the good ones were really remarkably good, and one only has to read those to realize that their authors, for whatever reason, were genuinely trying to give all the information at their command. If there was a Hailing Sign at that time one of these exposures would have got hold of it and described it—but that sign never appeared in print until 1760 and then, in an English exposure! I believe it is absolutely safe to say that the Hailing Sign did not exist in 1730 and probably did not come into use until the 1750s.

Finally, there are indeed several instances of somewhat similar postures in ancient Egyptian wall-paintings and carvings, and in archaeological remains in other parts of the world, but it must be emphasized that we are only concerned with the sign in Craft usage.

---

168.   AT, ON, WITH, or IN, 'THE CENTRE'

Q. In the Third Degree Opening we have the question—'Where do you (we) hope to find them?' The given answer is 'With the Centre'. Why not 'At the Centre?'

A. There is reason to believe that the answer 'With the centre' was authorized by the Lodge of Reconciliation shortly after the Union of the Grand Lodges in 1813. No official record survives of their decision on this point, but William Shadbolt, who served that Lodge as J.W., left cypher notes of the Openings and Closings, and his answer gives the words 'With the centre'.

Many Brethren whose workings have retained that answer would say that your question simply does not arise, or else they deem it purely academic. My own view is that this is a perfectly proper question and it should not be brushed aside. We ought to know the meaning of the words when we utter them, and I shall try to answer accordingly.

The 'centre', in this case, is almost certainly a piece of symbolism, and there is a quite remarkable degree of variation among the different rituals on this subject. In your question you have quoted *Emulation*, and that same formula appears in *Claret* (1838), *Irish* (1910), *Exeter* (1932), *Standard* ('Stability'), Sussex (1965), *West End* (1967). Here I have named only a few examples taken almost at random, and it must be clear that the answer is either in very bad English or it is simply not the answer to that question. If the question is 'Where', the answer should begin 'In, Within, At, On, Around, Near' etc., i.e., a location, and so long as the answer begins 'With', something must be wrong.

In all fairness I quote a few correct versions, e.g., *Veritas* (1937)—'Where do you . . .'—'At the Centre'; *Complete*—'Within a Centre'; *Castle,* (Northumbrian, 1927)—'On the Centre'.

There are a number of workings, old and new, in which *the question* is different. *York,* the so-called *Britannia* (Sheffield), *Oxford, Logic, Universal* and *New London*, all ask 'How do you hope to find them?' and their answer 'With the Centre' is wholly acceptable.

By way of an interesting variation I quote an extract from the *Turk MS.*, an exact copy of one of Preston's versions of the Third Lecture *c.* 1816 (in a Paper by Bro. P. R. James in *AQC*, Vol. 85):

M.   Bro. J.W. how do you hope to find them?
J.W.   By Working towards the centre.

If we look at the question *in its proper context*, there may be a clue as to how the question and answer should run. At that point in the ritual at which the question arises, we are talking—of course—about finding the 'genuine secrets of a M.M.' which were 'lost' through the untimely death of H.A. Our earliest English version of the legend in *Masonry Dissected*, 1730, tells how the searchers decided that:

'. . . if they did not find the Word in him or about him, the first Word should be the Master's Word';

In this version there is no hint of what the *original* Master's Word was.

Several of the early French versions of the same legend tell the story in better detail. They show that the searchers, all Master Masons, *knew the Word* but, when they discovered the body of H.A. and found that he had been murdered, they were afraid that the assassins had forced him to divulge it and they resolved that 'the first Word that any of them might utter while disinterring the Corpse' would thenceforward be the Master's Word. The texts indicate that the Word was adopted to replace the 'sacred and mysterious Name', i.e., the Tetragrammaton, which appears clearly written in several 18th century Tracing Boards of the third degree; the illustration on p. 197, above, from *Le Maçon Démasqué*, 1751, is a typical example. Obviously that was never lost; it was the Ineffable Name, and therefore unpronounceable, but not lost. [There is—of course—a stage beyond the Craft in which the

Candidate learns the manner in which it may be pronounced and conferred.] Thus the French documents supply the earliest clue to the so-called lost Word of a M.M. and where it is to be found. (The other secrets need not concern us here.)

If we return to the original question 'Where do we hope to find them?', there is another clue that has been foreshadowed in the Closing in the second degree, where we teach that another Name of the G.G.O.T.U. is situated 'In the Centre of the building'. So, without disrespect to any of the workings which use different forms, I suggest that the Questions and Answers might be clearer if they ran:

Q. Where do you (we) hope to find them?
A. In (or AT, or On) the Centre.

or

Q. How do you (we) hope to find them?
A. With the Centre.

---

169.   SALUTING THE GRAND OFFICERS
AND OTHERS

Q. When is the proper time to salute the Grand Officers, or Provincial Grand Officers?

A. Customs vary and, in the Provinces especially, the procedure will usually be governed by the expressed views of the Prov. G.M. The general practice in London, and also my own preference, is for the Salutations to be made as the last business of the meeting before the 'Risings'. Thus the salutations are made when everyone is in the lodge including the E.A.s if any.

If the visitor is the Prov. G.M. or (on a state occasion) one of the most senior Grand Officers who is invariably accompanied by his personal D.C., the Salutation will usually be given immediately after arrival, and the aforementioned D.C. will be in charge of that part of the proceedings.

---

170.   POSITION OF THE ROUGH AND
SMOOTH ASHLARS

Q. What, do you consider, is the correct position of the Rough and Smooth Ashlars in the Lodge Room?

A. As to 'What is correct?', since there is no Grand Lodge rule on the subject, the answer may be simply a matter of custom in your Jurisdiction or Province, or in your particular ritual 'Working' if it rules on that subject. In England nowadays, they are generally to be found on the J.W.'s and S.W.'s pedestals; they are also to be seen, occasionally, on the floor, immediately in front of the pedestals.

If we go back to our earliest *ritual evidence* on this subject (i.e., the *Edinburgh Register House MS.* of 1696 with the *Chetwode Crawley* and *Kevan MSS.* which are virtually identical), there is some real doubt as to the kind of stones that were used in the Lodge. Their earliest description is in the catechism of 1696:

> Q. Are there any jewells in your lodge
> A. Yes, three, Perpend Esler a Square pavement and a broad ovall

The texts are unanimous about the square pavement, which appears continuously in later texts and in illustrations of the 'floor-drawings' and Tracing Boards right up to the present day.

The 'Perpend Esler' was a dressed block of stone, shaped so that it extended right through a wall from one side to the other, to serve as a binding stone.

The 'broad ovall' (or Broked Mall in the *Chetwode Crawley MS.*) is the problem. It may have been a 'broached ornel', i.e., a stone that had been 'broached' (pricked, indented, or furrowed), but it may also have been a broaching maul', i.e., a mallet or maul used for indenting or furrowing the stone.

Prichard, in 1730, had the question in a different form:

> Q. What are the Immoveable Jewels?
> A. Trasel Board, Rough Ashler, and Broach'd Thurnel.
> Q. What are their uses?
> A. Trasel Board for the Master to draw his Designs upon, Rough Ashler for the Fellow-Craft to try their Jewels upon, and the Broach'd Thurnel *for the Enter'd Prentice to learn to work upon.* [My italics.]

Evidently Prichard was satisfied that his 'Broach'd Thurnel' was another stone and not a mason's tool, and this is probably the earliest text from which we may safely deduce that there were two stones in the lodge-room. In the early years of the first Grand Lodge the stones would probably have been drawn on the floor of the lodge, but they might have been actual stones laid out on the 'drawing' and since practices were not standardized we cannot be sure.

The minutes of the Old King's Arms Lodge (now No. 28) on 1 December 1735 speak of 'the . . . . Foot Cloth made use of at the Initiation of new members' and this must have been an early version of our modern Tracing Board.[1] On the other hand, the records of the Old Dundee Lodge (now No. 18), London, show a host of entries from 1748 to the end of the 18th century of payments made to the Tyler for 'Drawing the Lodge' and 'floor-drawings' seem to have been the more general practice.[2]

From 1744 onwards, when the *printed* pictures of the 'Floorcloths' begin to appear frequently in the French exposures (and later from the 1760s in the English exposures) the Rough and Smooth Ashlars[3] are usually shown in the designs, though not in any fixed position. The earliest version in *Le Catéchisme des Francs-Maçons*, 1744, has the rough stone towards the N.E. corner of the design and the polished stone towards the S.E., but later versions do not follow the same layout.

Towards the end of the 18th century and in many of the old English lodges today, we find the Rough and Smooth Ashlars placed respectively in the N.E. and S.E. corners of the lodge floor and, from the nature of the exhortations which the Candidates receive when placed in those positions, I am convinced that these are their proper positions. Preston's *First Lecture of Freemasonry* supports this view:

> [After the E.A. has been] Entrusted and invested . . . what is his proper situation in the Lodge?
>
> At the north-east corner . . . or at the right hand of the Master [*AQC* 82, p. 128]
>
> Why . . . at the north-east rather than at any other part of the Lodge? Because there he treads on the foundation stone of the building.
>
> To what does it allude?
>
> To an established custom of laying the foundation stone . . . at the north-east corner . . .
>
> In what form does he appear?
>
> With his feet formed in a square, body erect and eyes fixed on the Master [ibid., p. 129]

Later:

> Name the immoveable jewels.
>
> The rough ashlar, smooth ashlar and the tracing board.
>
> What is their use?

---

[1] A. F. Calvert, *History of Old King's Arms Lodge, No.* 28, p. 5.

[2] A. Heiron, *Ancient Freemasonry and the Old Dundee Lodge, No.* 18, pp. 126–7.

[3] In the French drawings the Smooth Ashlar was a 'pointed cubic-stone for the Fellows to sharpen their tools on'. *Early French Exposures*, p. 95, published by the Quatuor Coronati Lodge.

The first is the representation of the brute stone taken from the quarry, which is assigned to the apprentices . . . that by their industry it might be brought into due form and made fit for use. The second is the smooth stone, or polished ashlar, which has undergone the skill of the Craftsman and is used by him to adjust his tools . . . The rough ashlar is an emblem of the human mind in its pristine state . . . The smooth ashlar is a representation of the mind improved by culture . . . [ibid., pp. 139/140]

At this stage, the position of the Fellow-Craft is not yet specified. That item appears in Preston's Second Lecture (*AQC*, Vol. 83, p. 207):

What is the proper situation of the newly accepted Fellow-Craft?
In the S.E. corner of the Lodge . . .
Why?
To mark a distinction from the preceding Degree . . .

Thus we find the N.E. corner as the place for the Rough Ashlar, the E.A.'s foundation stone, symbolically the foundation stone of the spiritual temple which we, as Masons, are to build within ourselves. The position of the Smooth Ashlar—allocated to the Fellow-Craft—is not mentioned by Preston, but the F.C.'s special position is confirmed and I believe that these are indeed, by long-standing custom, the traditional position of the Ashlars, N.E. and S.E. (See illustration, p. 20.)

---

171. THE IMMEDIATE PAST MASTER'S CHAIR

Q. When the Master of a lodge is absent through illness and the I.P.M. acts as W.M. under Rule 119, *B. of C.*, who acts as I.P.M.?

A. First let it be clear that the status of *I.P.M. is not an office and nobody can act for him*, so we need only discuss the question of who is to occupy the I.P.M.'s Chair when the I.P.M. is absent or is acting as Master.

There appears to be no Rule that deals with this specific question, but Rule 119(b) in the *Book of Constitutions* suggests that some form of seniority should prevail. This would imply that the senior P.M. might be chosen to occupy the I.P.M. Chair. For purely practical purposes it might be preferable to select the Brother with the most recent experience of those duties, i.e., the junior P.M.; but I think the lodge would best be served by choosing the Brother who can be relied on to discharge the duty satisfactorily.

---

172.   THE STAR-SPANGLED CANOPY IN
                        FREEMASONRY

Q. Our lodge-room for the First Degree (in Charlottenlund, Denmark) has a blue star-spangled ceiling. Where did this idea originate?

A. Star-spangled *ceilings* are comparatively rare in London lodge-rooms nowadays. They are to be found more frequently in Provincial and European Masonic Temples, and were fairly common in London fifty years ago. It should be added that this was simply a matter of decoration, because there was nothing in the ceremonies or in the Regulations that prescribed a star-spangled *ceiling* as part of lodge décor.

Most of the *Old Charges*, from the 14th century onwards, discuss the 'Seven Liberal Arts and Sciences' (with special emphasis on Geometry) and Astronomy appears regularly.

The *Dumfries MS. No. 4, c.* 1710, has the questions:

Q. how high is your lodge?
A. inches & spans Inumberable.
Q. how Inumberable?
A. the material heavens & stary [*sic*] firmament.

Trinity College, Dublin, MS. 1711, has:

Q. W^t sits he there for
A. To observe the suns rising to see to set his men to work
Q. How high is y^r lodge?
A. As high as ye stars inches, & feet innumerable

But stars and clouds have a place in later Masonic ritual since the early Speculative years of the 18th century. In Samuel Prichard's *Masonry Dissected*, 1730, we find:

Q. What Covering have you to the Lodge?
A. A clouded Canopy of divers Colours (or the Clouds)
Q. Have you any Furniture in your Lodge?
A. Yes
Q. What is it?
A. *Mosaick* Pavement, Blazing Star and Indented Tarsel

Here, in *Masonry Dissected*, 1730, we have the *first appearance in ritual*, of the 'Blazing Star' and the 'clouded Canopy'. The next stage appears in an exposure of *c.* 1740, *A Dialogue between Simon and Philip* which shows two diagrams of the 'Lodge' that might be described as early ancestors of our modern Tracing Boards. Both show the Letter G in the centre of the diagram; in one case the G is enclosed in a 'diamond' outline; in the other the G is at the centre of a sun in glory, roughly a 'Blazing Star'. The progress seems to be slow indeed but the next stage of development moves more rapidly. It appears in one of the early French Exposures. *Le Secret des Francs-Maçons*, 1742, compiled by the Abbé Gabriel Perau. In a rambling description of the 'Floor-drawing' of those days, he mentions the Pillars, a Mosaic Palace, an Indented Tuft, a Plumb-line and a 'star-spangled Canopy' (*Dais parsemé d'étoiles*). This is the earliest reference I can trace to the 'star-spangled' theme.

L'Ordre des Francs-Maçons Trahi . . . , 1745, repeats the 'star-spangled Canopy' from Perau's text, and in the catechism the lodge is covered:

'By a celestial Canopy, spangled with golden Stars'

In *La Désolation des Entrepreneurs* . . . (2nd Edn. 1747) the author, Louis Travenol, brought into his catechism a Question and Answer which he had omitted in his first venture:

Q. What covered it? [i.e. the Lodge]
A. A celestial Canopy, adorned with stars.

Le Maçon Démasqué, 1751, has:

Q. by what was your lodge surmounted?
A. by a canopy of celestial blue, spangled with golden stars

In 1760 the 'Cloudy Canopy' reappears in *Three Distinct Knocks*, and again in *J. & B.* of 1762, but the stars are not mentioned in either of them.

In 1801, there is an engraved set of Tracing Boards designed by John Cole and the 1st Degree Board depicts a cluster of clouds, with Sun, Moon and seven Stars.

Around 1800 the Tracing Boards were beginning to show coloured drawings of the 'Clouds with Stars' and they became embodied in some of the best designs which were produced *c.* 1820–1840; these are still in use to this day.

Nowadays the references to the 'Cloudy Canopy' and 'Stars' are shown on the Tracing Boards but they do not appear in the course of the ceremonies. They do appear, however, in the *Lectures of the Three Degrees* and I quote from the First Lecture (Fourth Section):

'. . . The Heavens He has stretched forth as a canopy; the earth He has planted as a footstool; He crowns His Temple with Stars as with a diadem, and with His hand He extends their power and glory.'

and from the Second Lecture (Second Section):

> ... Besides the Sun and the Moon the Almighty was pleased to bespangle the ethereal concave with a multitude of Stars, that man, whom He intended to make, might contemplate thereon, and justly admire the majesty and glory of His creator.

---

173.   '. . . DO HEREBY AND HEREON . . .'

Q. In dictating the Obligations the Master uses the words 'do hereby and hereon' and at the same time he places his hand(s) on the hand(s) of the Candidate and on the V.S.L. Should the Master's hand be placed *first* on the V.S.L. or on that of the Candidate?

A. I would suggest—as a preliminary to the answer—that the 'hereby' is a direct allusion to the pledge which the Candidate makes with his r.h. on the V.S.L.; the 'hereon' refers, of course, to the V.S.L. itself (or whichever Sacred Writ is being used for that particular Candidate).

I have seen many Masters who obviously agree with this view, and first press the Candidate's hand(s) for the 'hereby', but touch the V.S.L with their own hand for the 'hereon'. That would seem to be perfectly satisfactory procedure for the Obligations in the Second and Third Degrees, when the Candidate is able to observe the action. During an Initiation, however, the Candidate would not easily appreciate the significance of the 'hereon' movement.

As a Preceptor of many years' standing, I have always taught that the W.M. during the Initiation Ob. should rest his hand on the back of the Candidate's hand for the 'hereby' and press *again* for the 'hereon', thereby indicating that the Candidate is avowing the solemnity of his Obligation 'by' and 'on' the V.S.L.

---

174.   THE GRAVE
ITS DIMENSIONS AND LOCATION

Q. [From Oregon, U.S.A.] Why is the grave in the 3rd Degree said to be six feet long, six feet deep and no mention of width? The standard grave is $6 \times 4 \times 6$.

A. It appears that your Oregon ritual differs in several respects from the majority of English rituals, because we do generally specify all three dimensions. Your question is, in fact, a very interesting one, and the

answer to it—if we try to find acceptable reasons for both the dimensions and location of the grave—is not at all easy.

The *Graham MS.*, 1726, contains the *earliest known version of a
'raising', within a Masonic context*, but there are no measurements for
the grave.

The *Wilkinson MS.* has been dated *c.* 1727 (though I am inclined to
think it is a little later). It does not have the Hiramic legend, but there
is a reference to Hiram's grave, which mentions the shape, also without
measurements, as follows:

Q. What is the form of your Lodge
A. An oblong square
Q. Why so
A. The manner of our Great Master Hirams grave.

The measurements, when they first appeared in our ritual, were
probably intended to be quite a genuine description of a large grave,
without any particular mystery or symbolism attached. I have collected
below the earliest references to the grave that have a bearing on your
question.

In Prichard's exposure *Masonry Dissected*, published in 1730, we
have the earliest version of the Hiramic legend and it states that he was
buried

'. . . in a handsome Grave 6 foot East, 6 West, and 6 Foot perpendicular,
and his Covering was green Moss and Turf, which surprised them; . . .'

The French exposures, 1737-*c.*1760, do not give any dimensions for
the grave but the next English exposure, *Three Distinct Knocks*, 1760,
said he was buried in a handsome grave

'. . . Six Foot East and West, and Six Foot perpendicular.'

Two years later in 1762 another exposure, *J. & B.*, stated that they

'. . . buried him on the side of a Hill, in a Grave Six Foot perpendicular
dug due East and West.'

It is clear that the measurements as given, i.e., '6 Foot East, 6 West',
imply that they were taken from a single fixed point, though its precise
location is unspecified.

It seems to me quite impossible to draw any particular symbolism
from the details in these earlier forms of the Masonic legend. By the
time we reach the 1840s, with standardized and printed rituals, it would
seem that an attempt was being made to create some kind of mystical
symbolism around the grave by relating it to the 'Centre'. The modern
words 'from the centre three feet East, three feet West, three feet

between north and south and five feet or more perpendicular' seem to represent the majority of versions in English usage today. If the words mean anything at all they describe a grave 6' × 3', at least 5' deep and if, as I believe, those figures have no special significance the only point in our modern wording which would seem to carry any weight at all is that which places the grave at or near the 'Centre'.

As to the statement, in most English rituals, that the body was not buried in the *Sanctum Sanctorum*, that goes without saying. Our ritual does imply, however, that the burial was somewhere 'in the Centre' of the Temple area—and that is quite incredible; neither Jews, nor half-Jews are buried within Temple premises.

---

175.   FORTY AND TWO THOUSAND

Q. Following a lodge meeting at which we had heard an explanation of the Second Degree Tracing Board, a discussion arose as to the story of Jephtha's battle and the death of 'forty and two thousand' warriors. Some said the figure was 2,040 and others that it should be 42,000. Which is correct?

A. The King James 'Authorized Version' of the Bible (at Judges XII, 6) gives the number as 'forty and two thousand' and that is the source of some confusion, although *it is a precise translation from the original Hebrew*, with each word in its correct place. It is perhaps necessary to explain that it is not possible in Hebrew to say 'forty-two'; one could say 'two and forty' (as in German) or 'forty and two', but the 'and' must be there.

For the remainder of the argument, I quote from a recent Lodge News-letter by Bro. C. T. Holmes, Secretary of United Technical Lodge No. 8027:

> The 1st Chapter of the Book of Numbers gives an unequivocal answer to this problem. The Lord commanded Moses to number each of the twelve tribes of the children of Israel 'every male from twenty years old and upward, all that were able to go forth to war'. Verse 21 says: 'Those that were numbered of them even of the tribe of Reuben were forty and six thousand and five hundred.' Verse 46 gives the final figures of all the tribes 'So were all those that were numbered of the children of Israel, by the house of their fathers, from twenty years old and upward, all that were able to go forth to war in Israel. Even all they that were numbered were six hundred thousand and three thousand and five hundred and fifty.'

The figures for each of the twelve tribes are given in verses 21 to 43, and the wording of the final total leaves no room for error, 603,550. That total can only be achieved when we calculate the census of the individual tribes by the same method as we use for the 42,000 in Jephtha's battle.

Finally, one hears a great deal of criticism, nowadays, of the *New English Bible* and it is only fair to add a word of praise. In its account of the slaughter of the Ephraimites (Judges XII, 6) it gives the figure in modern terms—'forty-two thousand'.

---

176.   THE DUE GUARD

Q. 1. I have seen a Scottish visitor to an English lodge give an un-usual sign in the First Degree and I was told that it is the 'Due Guard'. Will you please explain this?

2. Is it used anywhere in English practice?

3. What is its symbolism, if any?

A. 1. For the answer to the first question, i.e., the 'Due Guard' in present-day Scottish practice, I am indebted to R.W. Bro. G. S. Draffen, Depute Grand Master of Scotland, who writes:

> In Lodges under the Grand Lodge of Scotland and in certain jurisdictions overseas the Obligation in the First Degree is taken while the Candidate holds the V.S.L. in both hands in a particular manner which cannot be described here. This does *not* apply in the 2nd Degree.
>
> At the end of the Obligation are the words 'God keep me steadfast in this my solemn Obligation as an Entered Apprentice Freemason'. Later, at the 'entrusting' the Candidate is told that the first Sign is called the '*Dieu Garde*' and the position of the hands is as they were when taking the Obligation, only now there is no V.S.L. Note that the name of the Sign is made up of the French words which mean 'God keep', i.e., the '*Dieu Garde*' (or Due Guard) is a direct reference in French to the words of the Obligation. It should be added that the Sign is discharged in the normal manner of the Entered Apprentice Penal Sign.
>
> It may also be noted that when the Lodge is opened in the First Degree, the Master, at the end of the opening, says 'I declare the Lodge open in the First or Entered Apprentice Degree and this (giving the Due Guard and discharging it) shall be your Sign'. It is also given by Brethren coming into the Lodge after it has been opened, or leaving it before it has been closed. In a few Scottish Lodges Brethren entering the Lodge, after it has been opened, salute

not only the Master but also the Wardens. This latter point applies to all three Degrees.

There is also a Due Guard in the 3rd Degree (but not in the 2nd) which is discharged in the normal manner of the Master Mason Degree Penal Sign. Here again at the 'entrusting' an explanation is given that the hands are in the position they were in while the Candidate was taking his Obligation. Some Scottish Lodges do not make the distinction in the 3rd Degree and instead refer to the Penal Sign as being in two parts; the final result is, however, the same.

2. As to the 'Due Guard' in English practice, that title is used in several present-day workings (mainly in the Provinces), but in English usage it now has an entirely different meaning and purpose. I believe the best way to explain the different procedures is to go back to their beginnings. The earliest records, however, are Scottish and we begin with those.

The Edinburgh Register House MS., dated 1696, is the earliest Masonic document that mentions the 'due guard', and the words appear only once, at the moment when the Candidate (for the E.A. degree) has taken his Obligation and is removed out of the lodge

'. . . with the youngest mason . . . [where] . . . he is to learn . . . the manner of making his due guard whis [= which] is the signe and the postures and words of his entrie which are as follows'.[1]

The 'words of entrie' were a form of greeting that ended with the E.A. Sn., but did not contain the E.A. 'word(s)'. Incidentally, the text does not mention the G. or T. The 'posture' may have included the position of the hands before the Sn. was made, as noted in Bro. Draffen's first paragraph, above.

The *Chetwode Crawley MS.*, *c.* 1700, is virtually identical, but speaks of 'making Guard, which is the Sign, Word & Postures of his Entry . . .'[2]

Another text, 'A Mason's Confession' was published in *The Scots Magazine* in March 1755-6, and it claimed to represent Scottish practice of *c.* 1727. Here the 'due guard' is directly related to a sign—but the possible mis-spelling of the word 'breath' makes the description of the sign rather doubtful:

. . . he gives the sign, by the right hand above the breath, [*sic*] which is called the fellow-crafts due guard[3]

There is no mention of a due guard for the E.A.

All the references to the 'due guard' quoted up to this point are of Scottish origin and because all the remaining ritual documents up to

[1] *Early Masonic Catechisms*, by Knoop Jones & Hamer, 2nd Edn., p. 33.
[2] Ibid, p. 36.   [3] Ibid, p. 105.

1730—mainly of English origin—make no mention at all of the 'due guard', there would seem to be fair grounds to accept that the practice stemmed originally from Scotland. Since there is rather a long interval between the 1727 quotation and the next in the series (1760) and most of our ritual information throughout that period comes from France, it must be emphasized that *none of the early French exposures contains any hint of the 'due guard'*—or of words in the original French that might suggest that they had any such practice.

The first reference to the 'Due Guard' in an English text is in *Three Distinct Knocks*, published in 1760, a popular exposure that was frequently re-printed.

> 'Mas. What was the next Thing that was shewn to you?
> Ans. The due Guard, or Sign, of an enter'd Apprentice'
> . . . [Duly described, *and it is not Bro. Draffen's two-handed sign.*]
> Mas. Have you got that due Guard, or Sign, of an enter'd Apprentice?
> . . . (op. cit., p. 23)

In *T.D.K.* the 'due Guard' follows the conferment of the 'Gripe and Word' (p. 23) but there is a note saying that this procedure is sometimes reversed (p. 22). The text, however, is definite in saying that *the Due Guard is only the Sign of an E.A., and nothing more.*

The next English exposure, and one of the most popular texts for some forty years, was *J. & B.*, published in 1762; its Due Guard details agree with *T.D.K.*

Towards the end of the 18th century, Preston's 'First Lecture of Free Masonry' contains a series of questions and answers which show that 'the first secret' is 'The due guard of an E.A.M.' and that sign is given by way of explanation. Some years later, the *Shadbolt MS.*, *c.* 1817, also speaks of 'the sign of dueguard' [*sic*].

It may be helpful, at this point, to summarize the evidence on the *early meanings* of the 'Due Guard' in Scottish and English practice:

Scotland, 1696: The D.G. is the E.A. Sn., possibly including a preliminary 'posture' for the hands.

    ,,   *c.* 1700: The D.G. is the E.A. 'Sn., Word & Postures'.

    ,,   *c.* 1727: The D.G. is a Sn. associated with the F.C.

England, 1760: *T.D.K.*, Antients' practice, says that the D.G. is the E.A. Sn., (and nothing more).

    ,,   1762: *J. & B.*, Moderns' practice, is the same.

    ,,   *c.* 1800-*c.*1817. Preston's 'First Lecture' and the *Shadbolt MS.*, confirm that the D.G. is the E.A. Sn., both without the two-handed posture.

In spite of the evidence from Preston and *Shadbolt*, the words 'Due Guard' seem to have gone out of fashion during the early decades of the 19th century, especially in the London area. It is not to be found in Browne's *Master Key*, 1802, or in Carlile's *Republican*, 1825, or in Claret's *Ritual*, 1838, and I have been unable to find any evidence that the 'Due Guard' was used in 'Emulation' or 'Stability', two of our earliest post-Union workings.

When it finally reappeared in English usage, it had acquired a completely new meaning and purpose, and the evidence for this change comes from authentic ritual workings in several widespread Provinces. The following examples will serve to illustrate the new procedures and some of its variations.

The 'Bristol' working is one of the oldest and most distinctive rituals still in use to this day. In its E.A. ceremony, the W.M. explains that the E.A. Sn begins (as in Scottish and U.S.A. fashion) with two hands, a reminder of the posture in which the candidate took his Ob., and it finishes with the normal E.A. Sn. The W.M. continues:

> This Sn. demands a G. or T., which is given . . . always with the due guard [using the L.H.] to prevent any unqualified . . .

At the appropriate part of the second degree, he says:

> The G. or T., is given by . . . covered with the due guard . . .

The *Exeter Ritual of Craft Masonry* exhibits many interesting variations from the general run of workings, and the 'Due Guard' is one of them. The W.M., while giving the G. or T., uses familiar phrases, but with an additional sentence:

> . . . serves to distinguish a Brother by night as well as by day. It should always be given with the due guard, to hide it from the eyes of the cowan or insidious.

Exeter prescribes similar procedure for the F.C.

The Hull ritual, commonly known as the '*Humber Use*', claims to be of early post-Union date and it bears the marks of antiquity in several of its procedures and phrases. In this working, after the W.M. finishes the normal entrusting, and immediately before the candidate is led away to be tested by the J.W., the W.M. warns him that if he wants to greet a Brother with the G. or T., *outside the lodge*, he must

> . . . observe this necessary caution, or due guard, to prevent the eye of the insidious from prying into the S's. of Freemasonry.

The 'Due Guard' at Hull is a cautionary addition to the G. or T., although it is not required as a precaution inside the Lodge. (The same procedures apply to the second degree.)

In the Province of Dorset, two of the oldest Lodges, Amity No. 137, Poole, and All Souls No. 170, Weymouth, also use the 'Due Guard' in the same precautionary manner. There is no trace of the D.G. in any version of the third degree.

The date of the introduction of the 'Due Guard' in its 'covering' form is a mystery because of the lack of early dated documents that would prove its existence. All the examples I have quoted, however, are from workings that enjoy a very respectable antiquity.

It would be difficult to find comparable examples, in Craft practice, in which a specific item of established procedure has retained its original name but has totally altered its meaning and purpose. In this respect, the 'Due Guard' seems to be unique, and that is my sole justification for dealing with it at such length.

3. Symbolism? In its Scottish and U.S.A. form, in which the two hands are held in a posture before the E.A. Sn., the symbolism is a plain reminder of the solemnity of the Ob., and of the duties that have been undertaken, while the E.A. Sn., is a reminder of the traditional penalty.

In its later sense, the 'Due Guard' is a purely practical precaution, and I doubt if there is any symbolism involved.

---

177.   TESTS OF 'MERIT AND ABILITY'

Q. The W.M. informs the Initiate that there are several degrees, with peculiar secrets restricted to each, which are not communicated indiscriminately but conferred *according to merit and ability*. Why then are our Candidates passed and raised without reference to merit or ability?

A. It is true that we, in England, are singularly lax in our efforts to ascertain how ready a Candidate may be for progress in the degrees. Having satisfied themselves that Candidates are worthy of admission and Initiation, the lodges practically take it for granted that progress and promotion go simply according to their time-table, i.e., according to the lodge's programme of work for the year.

As to the requirement of a 'test of merit', in most English lodges our Candidates need to answer only twelve Questions leading from the First to the Second Degree, and only nine Questions from the Second to the Third and, though the Questions and Answers are very brief indeed, the Candidates who falter are usually prompted in their replies.

Moreover, where some of the Answers are necessarily somewhat obscure, requiring, at the least, a certain amount of explanation, nobody ever bothers to explain what those answers mean, so that the Candidates—unless they are really eager and inquisitive—have to be satisfied with a meaningless babble of words!

In this matter of preparing our Candidates for progress, or of ensuring that they have the requisite 'merit and ability' to entitle them to promotion, we lag far behind many of the jurisdictions overseas. Several of the European Grand Lodges require the Candidate to write an essay—short or long—on the last degree he has taken, and what that ceremony means to him; and the essay will be read *in lodge before* he is allowed to take the next step.

In most of the forty-nine jurisdictions in the U.S.A. the Proficiency Tests (as they are called) form a complete survey of the preceding ceremony in the form of Question and Answer, including all the procedural details and their symbolism, and generally the Obligation as well, *all recited from memory*.

In May 1972, in the course of a Lecture tour in U.S.A., I attended the Kanawha Lodge No. 20 at Charleston, W. Virginia, when the only business of the evening was the examination of a Candidate for Passing. The Candidate, a young man perhaps twenty-five years old, stood at the Altar in the centre of the Lodge, facing east; the examiner, a white-haired Past Grand Master, stood facing west and the examination lasted nearly an hour, without a halt. The questions were all extremely brief, never more than a single sentence. Many of the answers were really quite lengthy, including the Obligation, all from memory. Throughout this ordeal, the Candidate stumbled only twice, halted, and recovered the missing word.

This would have been a remarkable achievement even if the Candidate had learned his work from a ritual printed in clear language. But most of the U.S.A. rituals are printed in cypher of various kinds, and several jurisdictions allow no printed ritual at all, so that all teaching and learning of Masonic ritual is, as they say, 'from mouth to ear' and the Candidate must attend rehearsals continuously until he learns his answers simply from hearing them repeated over and over again.

Similar Proficiency Tests are required after the Second and Third Degrees. (See Q. 28, Questions after Raising, pp. 71–72.) Suffice it to say that the Candidates who have endured and passed these enormously difficult tests acquire a knowledge and understanding of the Three Degrees which is to be envied and which deserves emulation.

What can we do to bridge this educational gap in our system? As a first step, I would suggest that it should be made obligatory for the Candidate to attend at least one rehearsal of the Questions and Answers at Lodge of Instruction and, after the rehearsal, it should be the Preceptor's duty to explain the answers in full detail adding, particularly in the case of an Initiate, an 'Explanation of the Preparation of the Candidate'. The latter will help to give the newcomer useful answers to some of the points that must have puzzled him.

In those lodges that habitually work the 'Lectures for the Three Degrees' (in Question and Answer) there is some hope that the Candidates and junior members will eventually acquire an inkling of what Masonry means—but only a tiny fraction of our lodges work the Lectures regularly.

There is, indeed, so much more that could and should be taught, of Craft History, Ritual, Organization, Constitutions, and Customs. It is in this field that Preceptors and Past Masters can best serve their lodges by guiding the newly-admitted Brethren to the books and papers that will stimulate and encourage their interest.

---

178. INACCURACIES IN THE RITUAL

Q. Science has established that the world was created over 700 million years ago and that even primitive man did not appear on it until about a million years ago. Is it not ludicrous, therefore, to speak of '. . . the . . . death of our M., . . . who was slain 3,000 years after the creation of the world'? I suggest that we add 'This is based on the 17th century belief that the world was created 4,000 years B.C.'

To make statements that do not mean what they say, or say what they mean, obscures reality and is mentally dishonest. This belittles the intelligence of Candidates and is Masonically and morally wrong. What are your views, please?

A. One cannot help sympathizing with the point of view expressed in your letter or at least with your natural desire to add an explanatory sentence to the ritual. But there are too many items of this kind, and they are often too closely woven into the fabric of our ceremonies to be cured, either by the addition of explanations, or by the excision of offending passages.

To answer your question properly the ritual may be divided into two parts:

(a) The procedural portions, i.e., the actual business of entering, passing, and raising.

(b) The ethical or educational portions, which illustrate and teach, mainly by Biblical history and legend, the moral and spiritual lessons of Masonry.

It would be in the sections under (b) that your criticism arises, although your attack is not aimed at the legends in the Craft, but at the supposedly factual statements that accompany them. There is no difficulty in compiling a list of the subjects that would automatically earn your displeasure; I simply choose some of those that irritate *me*; and there is no need for a complete list; a few selected items will serve our purpose:

1. In the Second Degree we speak of K.S.T., and of a Pillar which was named after 'a Priest . . . who officiated at its dedication'. (*It was not and he did not.*)

2. Two Pillars were 'formed hollow . . . to serve as archives to Free-masonry, for therein were deposited the constitutional rolls'. (*There was no Freemasonry then, and there were no 'rolls'.*)

3. '. . . spherical balls on which were delineated maps of the celestial and terrestrial globes . . .' (*The spherical world was still unknown then.*)

4. The 'middle chamber' of K.S.T., where the builders 'went to receive their wages'. (*Some chamber! There were more than 180,000 men engaged in the work!*)

5. Their ascent was 'opposed by the J.W., who demanded . . . the pass grip and . . . leading to . . .' (*Did he really check every man?*)

6. Miscellaneous expansions of the Hiramic legend that add nothing of historical or ethical value to the story, e.g. '. . . to pay his adoration to the Most High, as was his wonted custom at the hour of high twelve'.

'. . . buried three feet East, three feet West, three feet between North and South and five . . .'

It seems likely that all the items listed are the results of over-active imagination and, allowing that the death of H.A. is pure legend, the details of his burial are scarcely to be trusted, even if they were comprehensible.

I would like you to accept my assurance that the above list of items was chosen entirely at random and with no ulterior motive; simply a collection of statements in the ritual and Lectures that are without historical or biblical foundation and are for that reason repugnant. It is pure coincidence, therefore, that a close examination of their context shows that they could all be removed without loss; indeed, the ritual would be vastly improved by their omission.

Nevertheless, there are many items in the ritual that cannot be cured by simple removal, and the ceremonies would become quite unbearable if they were to be interspersed with comments qualifying or rectifying each statement that needed such treatment.

As to the charge that our statements are 'Masonically and morally wrong'; we confer the degrees as we do because we know none better. The system, we are agreed, is 'veiled in allegory', and that would not normally imply a cast-iron guarantee of historical accuracy.

Clearly there is room for improvement and there can be little doubt that, if the Grand Lodge were to appoint a commission to remodel the ritual, the results would justify the effort. But if any action is to be taken, it will have to be on an official basis. It is impossible to imagine that any individual or committee could achieve *practicable and acceptable results* without official authorization. Meanwhile we do the best we can with what we have: despite the occasional blemish it is really very good.

---

179. WHY LEAVE THE EAST AND GO TO THE WEST?

Q. Why, when we open the lodge in the third degree, do we leave the East and go to the West to seek for that which was lost? Nobody seems to be certain what this really means. It seems to me quite logical to connect this with the Royal Arch, if one accepts that in the old days the Royal Arch formed part of the Lodge (or Craft) workings, but was restricted to those who had 'pass'd Master'. Presumably, the Master would leave his exalted place in the East and go to the West, where the Candidates start in all our degrees.

In *Masonry Dissected* the question is asked:

Ex. You're an heroick Fellow: from whence came you?
R. From the East.
Ex. Where are you going?
R. To the West.
Ex. What are you going to do there?
R. To seek for that which was lost and is now found.
Ex. What was that which was lost and is now found?
R. The Master-Mason's Word.

This seems to me to suggest a word of rather more significance than one which designates Excellent Mason or Stone Squarer.

A. I wish I could help you with your 'towards the West' problem. It is always difficult to give a practical answer to a 'speculative' problem. I have read your extracts from Prichard and of course I know them well. The reference to 'the Master Mason's word . . . lost and is now found' is a very interesting hint of the later development of the Royal Arch; but the very words—'To seek for that which was lost and is now found' suggest that there is something wrong here. Why seek for something 'which is now found'? I think there is a more correct, or at least a far more satisfying series of questions and answers which may also furnish the solution to your problem 'Why to the West?' You know that from 1730 to 1760 there were no new exposures published in England and for any information on what was happening in ritual we have to go to the French exposures starting from 1737 onwards.

Several of those documents contain lengthy catechisms, largely based on (or similar to) Prichard's work, but with additions and improvements. *Le Catéchisme des Francs-Maçons* of 1744, contains the following:

> Q. How do the Apprentice Fellows travel?
> A. From West to East.
> Q. Why?
> A. To seek the Light.

and later:

> Q. How do the Masters (i.e., M.M.s) travel?
> A. From East to West.
> Q. Why?
> A. To spread the Light.

These Questions and Answers preserve the idea of all knowledge (wisdom or light) being found in the East, but they emphasize the Master Mason's duty, after having acquired the requisite knowledge, *to travel towards the West to spread the light.*

I need only add that all the best surviving texts from the great formative period (1744–1751) contain these questions and answers with the same explanation—'To spread the Light'.

I trust this answer will serve until I can find a better one. Your hint that the Royal Arch might yield an answer would perhaps have been acceptable if the R.A. had actually been in existence in 1730, when Prichard's work was first published. I prefer to reply with Craft arguments even though they imply that one of Prichard's answers was wrong!

180.   'RAVENOUS' OR 'RAVENING'

Q. We work the Emulation Lodge of Improvement ritual. In the Ob. in the Second Degree, in my fifty years of Masonic experience, certain words have always been 'the devouring beasts . . . and *ravenous* birds . . .'. In some lodges the word '*ravening*' has come into use. Can you tell me which is correct, or if there is now also a 'permissive' use of the word. If it still *is* 'ravenous' I shall take energetic steps to stop these innovations of those 'who know better(?)'.

A. I fear I cannot really tell you which is 'correct'. If you follow *Emulation* strictly, I am officially informed that they use *ravenous* and that is *correct for Emulation*. I can only help by presenting the arguments in favour of both and expressing my own preference based on those details.

From the *Oxford English Dictionary*, under the verb 'to raven' and the forms 'ravening' and 'ravenous', I have selected some of the definitions which are related to the particular sense in which we use the words, i.e., to devour (or eat) voraciously, to go about in search of food, to prey on. Of animals, given to seizing in order to devour, etc.

> The earliest quoted use of the form 'ravening' is in 1526.
> The earliest quoted use of 'ravenous' is 1412–20.

Before we go into further detail, I would suggest that the two words do not mean precisely the same thing, i.e., a ravening bird is not necessarily always ravenous.

Now as regards Masonic usage; as you know, all the regular, accepted rituals print dots . . . in place of the penalties so that it is difficult to answer your question with certainty.

Three Distinct Knocks, 1760, and *J. & B.*, 1762, both say '. . . given to the Vultures of the Air as a Prey', and all the other 18th century *texts* that I have been able to check say the same.

An interesting exception comes from a cipher text of William Preston's Lecture of the Second Degree, First Section, Clause 111 where he says

> '. . . given to the ravenous vultures of the air . . .' (*AQC* 83, p. 204)

One of the earliest *Exposures* that gives a new form is Richard Carlile's *Republican* of 1825 and there we find:

> '. . . given to the ravenous birds of the air, or the devouring beasts of the field, as a prey . . .'

Unless there is some genuine reason to the contrary, I always prefer to go back to the oldest known usage and, so long as you seek a choice between ravening and ravenous, I suggest that the latter is preferable.

Soon after this item was published (in the Q.C. Summons for May 1972) I received a most interesting letter from R.W. Bro. Sir Lionel Brett, P.Dist. G.M. Nigeria, from which I quote:

> According to Cruden's *Concordance* 'beasts of the field' occurs twenty-five times in the Authorized Version. 'Bird(s) of the air' is less common, but [see] Matt., 8, 20 and Luke, 9, 58. The 'ravenous' quotation in our ritual must surely be based on Ezekiel, 39, 4:
>
>> I will give thee unto the ravenous birds of every sort and to the beasts of the field to be devoured.
>
> The ritual of the Royal Arch draws on Ezekiel, and so does the Mark ritual, and the Arms of the Antients' Grand Lodge are further evidence that the book was well known to Brethren at the time when the ritual was taking its present form.

The letter continues with five quotations for 'ravening' and two more for 'ravenous', and concludes, 'all this [i.e., the Ezekiel extract above] supports your preference for 'ravenous'.

In thanking Bro. Brett, I would only add that his letter is a most useful commentary on some of the Biblical sources of our ritual and on the unknown compilers who used them so aptly.

---

181. THE EARLIEST RECORDS OF CONFERMENT OF E.A., F.C., AND M.M. DEGREES

Q. Can you give me the dates of the earliest records of the conferment of the Entered Apprentice, Fellow Craft and Master Mason degrees?

A. Before answering the specific questions, and to ensure that there is no misunderstanding of the answers, it is perhaps advisable to point out that the earliest records of *conferment* of a particular degree—or ceremony—must not be confused with the date when it first came into practice. If we could go back to the time when there was only one degree (or admission ceremony) however brief, in the operative lodges, it was, in my opinion, almost certainly for the 'fellow of craft', i.e., the fully trained mason, and we might date it around the 1300s, though we have no real documentary evidence to prove it. Apprentices were still the chattels of their masters in those days and it is extremely unlikely that they had any kind of status in the earliest operative lodges.

In the early 1500s, there is reasonable evidence (Statutes of Labourers in England, and the 'Seal of Cause of the Masons and Wrights' in Edinburgh read in conjunction with the 'Schaw Statutes' and Lodge Minutes of 1598 and 1599) which point very clearly to the existence of a system of two degrees, one for the Entered Apprentice and the other for the Fellow Craft (or Master).

The third degree made its appearance at some date between *c.* 1711 and *c.* 1725. Having said all this by way of introduction you may find it interesting to compare the dates above with the dates of the actual records below:

The first *recorded* conferment of the E.A. degree was on 9 January 1598 in the Minutes of the Aitchison's Haven Lodge (near Edinburgh, Scotland)—'. . . Upon quhilk day Alexander Cubie was enterit prenteis to Georg Aytone .   .' (*AQC*, Vol. 24, p. 34).

The first *recorded* conferment of the F.C. degree is 9 January 1598 also in the Minutes of the Aitchison's Haven Lodge:

> . . . Robert Widderspone was maid fellow of Craft in ye presens of Wilzam Aytone Elder . . . (*AQC*, Vol. 24, p. 34.)

The earliest *record* of conferment of the third degree was almost certainly in a London Musical Society, the *Philo-Musicae et Architecturae Societas Apollini* (The Apollonian Society for lovers of Music and Architecture). It was not a Lodge. though all its members were or had to be made Masons:

> The 12th day of May 1725—Our Beloved Brothers
> . . . Brother Charles Cotton Esq^e
>   Broth^r Papillon Ball
> were regulaily passed Masters. (*Q.C.A.* Vol. IX, p. 41)

There has been a great deal of scholarly dispute about the correct interpretation of the Minutes of this Societv. In my view, this, *though highly irregular*, was certainly a third degree because we have separate records of the Initiation and Passing of Bro. Charles Cotton.

If I had to quote the earliest date for a *regular third degree* I would say Lodge Dumbarton Kilwinning (now No. 18 S.C.); the Lodge was erected in January 1726 and at its foundation meeting there were present the 'Grand Master' (i.e., the W.M.) with seven Master Masons, six Fellow-crafts, and three Entered Apprentices. At the meeting on 25 March 1726:

> . . . Gabrael Porterfield who appeared in the January meeting as a Fellow Craft was unanimously admitted and received a Master of the Fraternity and renewed his oath and gave in his entry money . . .

This Minute shows that the third degree, the step from F.C. to M.M. was an esoteric one, requiring the renewal of an oath (and, in Scotland, the payment of a separate fee).

All the above Minutes are *records of the earliest known dates*; they do not represent the actual date of introduction of the ceremonies.

---

182.   WHEN TO TURN THE TRACING BOARD
IN CLOSING THE LODGE

Q. In the *Commonsense Working* of my lodge it has been customary, ever since even the oldest Brother can remember, for the Tracing Board to be covered by the A.D.C. after the I.P.M. has declared: 'Nothing now remains but to put away our W.T.s . . . uniting with me in the act F. F. F.'. It is felt that the A.D.C. should perform his duty *before* the Closing words of the I.P.M.

Many years ago it was customary, as the very last act after the 'ritual' closing of the lodge, for the Candidate to eradicate all trace of the T.B., which used to be sketched on the floor of the lodge-room. Is there some link between this old custom and our practice today?

A. There is certainly a link between the old custom of the 'Mop and Pail' for washing away the 'floor-drawing' and our present custom of closing the T.B., but the modern custom is by no means standard practice.

Before venturing to give my own views on this point I examined a large number of 19th century rituals to establish our early English practice, and was surprised to find no instruction as to when the T.B. was to be closed (or indeed if it was to be closed at all!).

On present-day practice I quote the 1969 *Emulation Ritual* which directs that the T.B. shall be turned after the J.W. has spoken his final words and *before the I.P.M. says 'Nothing now remains . . .'.*

The *English Ritual* (1956 Edn.), compiled by the late Dr. E. H. Cartwright, gives precisely the same instructions. This is also the practice in *Universal, Logic, West End,* and *Sussex* Workings. I feel confident in supporting all these, chiefly because every Working I have examined (whether it gives instructions on the closing of the T.B. or not) finishes with the I.P.M.'s speech 'Nothing now remains . . .'. If the T.B. was still open at that moment, i.e., some item of Lodge duty still to be performed, he could never say correctly, 'Nothing now remains . . .'.

---

183. H.R.H. THE LATE DUKE OF WINDSOR 1894–1972

Q. Was the Duke of Windsor a Freemason?

A. The Duke of Windsor was a very active member of the Craft—and of the Royal Arch—from the date of his initiation in 1919, at the age of 25, until his death in 1972. His splendid record in those two bodies may be summarized briefly as follows:

UNDER THE UNITED GRAND LODGE OF ENGLAND

Initiated 2 May 1919 Household Brigade Lodge No. 2614
W.Master   1921   ,,   ,,   ,,   ,,   ,,
Joined   1923 St. Mary Magdalen Lodge No. 1523
W.Master   1925   ,,   ,,   ,,   ,,   ,,   ,,
Joined   1924 Lodge of Friendship & Harmony No. 1616 (Surrey)
W.Master   1935   ,,   ,,   ,,   ,,
Joined   1932 Royal Alpha Lodge No. 16

In 1922 he was appointed Senior Grand Warden and was invested at an Especial Grand Lodge held at the Royal Albert Hall, London.

In 1924 he was appointed Provincial Grand Master for Surrey.

On his accession to the throne he was appointed Past Grand Master.

UNDER SUPREME GRAND CHAPTER OF ENGLAND

Exalted   1921 United Chapter No. 1629 (which joined with Studholme
               Chapter and is now United Studholme Chapter No. 1591)
M.E.Z.   1927 United Chapter No. 1629
Joined   1930 Grove Chapter No. 410 (Surrey)

In 1930 he was appointed Grand Superintendent (Royal Arch) in and over Surrey.

A few notes may be added in amplification of the above details. The Prince of Wales studied at Magdalen College while an undergraduate at Oxford; hence his membership and mastership of St. Mary Magdalen Lodge No. 1523.

The Prince's Installation as Provincial Grand Master of Surrey was conducted by the M.W. Grand Master, H.R.H. The Duke of Connaught and Strathearn, K.G., and took place at the Central Hall, Westminster, on 22 July 1924.

He accepted Honorary Membership of the Grand Lodge of Scotland in December 1923 and the rank of Past Senior Grand Warden of the Grand Lodge of Ireland in 1924.

He was exalted into the Royal Arch in 1921, together with his younger brother, H.R.H. The Duke of York (afterwards King George VI), at No. 10 Duke Street, St. James's, London.

Under English practice Provincial Grand Masters in rotation are invited to preside over one of the Annual Festivals for the three great Masonic Institutions, at which the total sums subscribed for that year are announced. In 1927 the Duke of Windsor, then Prince of Wales, as Provincial Grand Master for Surrey, presided over the 139th Anniversary Festival of the Royal Masonic Institution for Girls, which was held at the Royal Albert Hall, London, and on that occasion he announced that his List totalled a record sum of £201,046.

Finally, an interesting extract from the *Yorkshire Herald* of 3 June 1924:

> An event without parallel in the history of the Craft; four members of the Royal Family are now holding high Masonic office, through the appointment by the Duke of Connaught, the Grand Master of England, of the Prince of Wales as Provincial Grand Master of Surrey, the Duke of York for Middlesex, and Prince Arthur of Connaught for Berkshire.

Members of the English Royal Family have been prominently associated with Freemasonry ever since 1737, when Frederick Lewis, Prince of Wales, eldest son of George II, became a member of the Craft.

---

184.   TYING THE APRONS—
         STRINGS AT FRONT OR BACK?

Q. How should the E.A. and F.C. Aprons be tied?

A. My preference is the old traditional method of tying an operative mason's apron, i.e., with the strings knotted at the front so that the ends of the strings hang on the front of the apron. Those 'ends' are the ancestors of the ornamental fringe seen on 18th century Masons' aprons, and of the 'tassels' on our aprons of today.

Nowadays, when nearly all aprons are fastened at the back with a snake buckle, that might be a good argument for tying the E.A. and F.C. aprons at the back; but, since most Brethren, at some time or other, want to know the 'why and when' for the tassels, I suggest that we might try to preserve old custom, so that on at least two occasions in their Masonic careers they (as E.A. and F.C.) actually see the answer to that question.

---

185.   THE JUNIOR WARDEN AS
                        OSTENSIBLE STEWARD

Q. I was recently appointed Junior Warden of my lodge and I am left wondering why that Officer is described as the 'ostensible Steward of the Lodge'. He is surely not a Steward; can you explain?

A. The answer hinges on the fact that from about 1600 onwards, when we begin to have *two* Wardens in each lodge, the J.W.'s principal duty seems to have related to itinerant masons, visitors, etc. Much later, in the 1770s when we get first details of the actual words of the Investiture of Officers, those duties relating to the care of visitors, etc., are allocated to the J.W. *in print*, and this continues into the middle decades of the 19th century.

Stewards, responsible for the organization of lodge feasting and feeding are recorded in the 1720s and this suggests the possibility of confusion in the duties of Stewards and Junior Wardens. I am indebted to Bro. C. F. W. Dyer, Secretary of the Emulation Lodge of Improvement, for the information that the first appearance in Masonic ritual of the J.W. as the '*Ostensible* Steward' was in a version of the *Emulation Lectures of the Three Degrees of Craft Masonry*, published in 1890 by John Hogg, but that was an unauthorized publication. The official *Emulation Ritual*, first printed in 1969, also calls the J.W. the 'ostensible Steward', in relation to his duties of calling the lodge from labour to refreshment.

I now quote the *Oxford English Dictionary* definition of the word 'ostensible', i.e., the definition that seems most apt to your question and to the above argument.

> Ostensible (*O.E.D.*): Declared, avowed, professed, exhibited or put forth as actual and genuine: often implicitly or explicitly opposed to 'actual', 'real', and so = merely professed, pretended

The word is of comparatively modern usage. The *O.E.D.* quotes its earliest use in a work by Horace Walpole written between 1762 and 1771. The word seems to have been first used *in our sense* in 1771 and *O.E.D.* quotes other examples in 1783, 1798, 1805.

Finally, I am assured that the 'ostensible' phrase is used in the *Castle* (Northumbrian) working and it also appeared in the *Perfect Ceremonies* and *Nigerian* rituals.

186.　　　THE NATIONAL ANTHEM AND THE
CLOSING ODE

Q. At the close of our Ceremonies we sing the National Anthem, followed by the Closing Ode. This would appear to be the wrong order, yet it is universally done; is there any good reason for it?

A. There is no official reason for singing the National Anthem before the Closing Ode. There is, however, a good commonsense reason and I suggest that as most Lodges sing the Closing Ode while the D.C. goes round with the Officers forming up his procession, that is why it is deliberately left to the last.

If the procession were formed first (with the Closing Ode) and the National Anthem was called for afterwards, the whole procession would have to stand rooted in the middle of the floor, while the Anthem was being sung. I feel sure that your present system, 'Anthem followed by Closing Ode', is far the better method.

187.　　　　　SALUTE IN PASSING

Q. In the course of procedure after the new W.M. has been installed, a number of Brethren are called upon to salute him on three separate occasions 'in passing'. In my own lodge each of the Brethren halts at the proper moment, takes a step and salutes; but I have seen the salutes given in other lodges without the 'halt and step': the Brethren simply give the requisite salute while they continue to march. Which is correct?

A. The question of 'correctness' in this matter depends on which particular 'working' your lodge follows—i.e., if your 'working' prescribes 'halt and step', then that is correct. In effect, if the lodge claims to adhere to a particular ritual it should observe the appropriate rubrics.

Personally, I draw a distinction between the 'signs' used as a mode of recognition (e.g., when instructing a Candidate or when the sign is made as a mark of respect, when addressing the W.M.), and the '*Salutes in Passing*'. In the two former instances the Brethren making the sign are standing, not marching, and the step is, of course, the proper preliminary to the sign.

But for the 'Salutes in Passing' in the Installation procedure, and especially when there are a number of Brethren in the procession, I find the 'halt and step' procedure is very slow and tiresome. That is the reason—I feel sure—why many or most of the London lodges do not 'halt and step', but give the requisite salute while marching. It is perfectly respectful and avoids three tedious delays.

---

188. FORMAL INVESTITURE OF OFFICERS

Q. When and where were the words now found in the *Emulation Ritual* first used for the Investiture of the various officers in the lodge?

A. *Emulation* is one of the oldest forms of English ritual to have been under a governing body since it first came into practice, but the 1969 version of *Emulation Ritual* was the *first official printing*, 'Compiled by and published with the approval of the Committee of the Emulation Lodge of Improvement'. The *modern* words of the Investiture in many versions, all virtually identical, have been *in print* for a hundred years or so, and there have been numerous changes even within that comparatively short period. To give some idea of the difficulties involved in tracing the slow evolution of our present procedures the Investiture of the S.W. may serve as a useful example.

William Preston was probably the first notable Masonic writer to give the actual words of the Investiture in the Appendix to his *Illustrations of Masonry*, 1772, p. 225:

> Brother C.D. I appoint you Senior Warden of this lodge; and invest you with the ensign of your office. Your regular and early attendance I particularly request, as in my absence you are to govern the lodge, and in my presence to assist me in the government of it. Your zeal for masonry, joined to your extensive abilities, will, no doubt, enable you to discharge the duties of this important station to your own reputation, and to the honor of those over whom you are now appointed to preside.

There were trifling changes in the 1775 and later editions up to his death, but the latest of those still contained the same ideas as those expressed above without the introduction of any new themes.

It was not until Claret published his ritual in 1838 that we find the introduction of the duty to attend Grand Lodge as a representative of the lodge. The text indicates that the Installing Master (not the W.M.) is conducting the Investiture:

> Br. A.B. The W. Master has appointed you the Senior Warden of this Lodge; it will be your duty to attend punctually the meetings of the Lodge, to assist the Master, in the discharge of the important duties of his office. You are also to attend the Communications of the Grand Lodge; in order that this Lodge may be properly represented.

There were no important changes during the next forty years and a printed ritual of 1872 is almost identical with the above; there is still no mention of Collar, Jewel, Gavel or Column.

It was not until the 1880s that various rituals began to provide something approaching the modern wording, e.g., the third edition of the *Text Book of Freemasonry*, Reeves & Turner, 1881, mentioned the Jewel, Collar, and the Level, in a very brief formula which omitted the Column, Gavel and all the customary injunctions except regular attendance at lodge and Grand Lodge.

The *Revised Ritual of Craft Freemasonry* (A. Lewis, London), 1888, pp. 309 *et seq.*, contained the Investiture of Officers which gave the S.W.'s piece as follows:

> Bro. . . . . . ., I have great pleasure in investing you as Senior Warden. Your Jewel, the Level, the emblem of equality, points out to you the just and equal measures which you are bound to pursue, to assist the Worshipful Master in ruling and directing the Lodge. In his absence it may become your duty to summon the Brethren to their Masonic labours. (Takes him by the right hand and conducts him to the West.) I place you in your chair, which is situated in the West, the position from which you are enabled to observe the setting sun, denoting the time for closing the Lodge at the Worshipful Master's command: I present to you this Gavel, the emblem of authority, which you will always use in answer to that of the Worshipful Master, so that order may be preserved in the West. I place under your care this Column, the position of which will always indicate the occupation of the Brethren for the time being. When they are at refreshment, your Column will be placed horizontally upon your Pedestal but when they are at labour, as at the present time, it will be raised to the perpendicular, to show that they are then under your care and superintendence. Your Column is of the Doric order, denoting strength. It implies that all your strength and energies of mind are to be devoted to the attainment and the preservation of order and regularity, harmony and industry, in the Lodge.

In 1895, Lewis published *The Lectures of the Three Degrees* (under the unauthorized heading 'Emulation' Working) with an Appendix entitled 'Form of Addresses to the Officers . . .'. The formula for the Investiture of the S.W. in this version contains most of the points in our present-day usage, but it seems that the S.W. received both a Column *and a Pillar*. I quote only the relevant words:

> This Column is the emblem of your office, and you will keep it in its erect position whilst the Brethren are at labour, as they are then under your superintendence; but place it in a horizontal position whilst at refreshment. I also intrust to your care this pillar of the Doric Order; it is an emblem of strength, and directs that you are to use all your strength of mind and powers of intellect to preserve peace, order, and harmony among the Brethren. . .

It would be tiresome to pursue the subject further, because, apart from *Emulation* and *Stability* which lay good claims to having been in use since shortly after the Union of the Grand Lodges in 1813, the principal London 'workings', *Logic, Taylor's, Universal* and *West End* all made their appearance in the three or four decades from *c.* 1880 onwards. They generally follow a fairly standardized pattern and the variations are usually trivial. The three last-named versions did not acquire controlling Committees until 1965 and, allowing for the fact that the *United Grand Lodge of England does not prescribe any fixed form of words for the Investiture*, it is surprising that the differences are so slight. The remaining officers may be discussed very briefly.

When Dr. Anderson, in his 1723 *Constitutions*, described the Constitution of a 'New Lodge' the only officers that were 'installed', besides the Master, were the two Wardens.

Preston's *Illustrations* of 1772, 1775, 1781 and 1788 gave the form of words of the Investiture for the S.W., J.W., Secretary, and Stewards, the latter being addressed jointly. The Treasurer and Tyler were also invested but without a specific address for either of them.

In the 1792 edition Deacons made their first appearance in the Investiture and *there was one address to both of them.* The words are extremely interesting:

Brothers . . . and . . . I appoint you Deacons of this lodge. It is your province to attend on the Master and Wardens, and to act as their proxies in the active duties of the lodge; such as in the reception of candidates into the different degrees of masonry, and in the immediate practice of our rites. *Those columns, as badges of your office, I entrust to your care,* not doubting your vigilance and attention. [My italics.]

It may be noted that every edition of the *Constitutions* of the United Grand Lodge up to and including that of 1873 had listed, among the officers of the lodge, 'the Wardens, and their two assistants, the deacons . . .'. It was not until 1896 that 'two Deacons' appeared as officers in their own right, i.e., no longer as 'assistants'. It is therefore particularly interesting to see that the Columns, nowadays presented to the Wardens 'as emblems of their office', were treated here as 'badges of office' for the Deacons.

ADDITIONAL OFFICERS

The 'regular Officers of a Lodge' are the Master, Treasurer, Secretary, two Wardens, two Deacons, Inner Guard and a Tyler. Rule 104(a) of the *B. of C.* permits the W.M. to appoint 'additional officers', but the emergence of the full modern team has been a very slow development.

The first *B. of C.* 1723, speaks of the Master and Wardens 'of each particular Lodge' and the only hint of a possible extension of this list is the requirement in Regulation III.

> The Master of each particular *Lodge*, or one of the *Wardens*, or some other Brother by his Order, shall keep a Book containing their *By-Laws*, the Names of their Members, with a List of all the *Lodges* in Town, and the usual Times and Places of their forming, and all their Transactions that are proper to be written.

This is a clear hint of the appointment of a Brother who was to conduct the secretarial work of the lodge and perhaps the Treasurer's duties too; but the Brother so appointed was apparently not to be an Officer of the lodge. (The idea of keeping a list of all the lodges in town with their 'Times and Places of meeting' may have been useful in 1723, but might be a little more difficult today, with some 1700 lodges in London alone!)

Later versions of the *Constitutions* contain a similar regulation to that quoted above and there is not a single version of the *B. of C.* until 1815 that has a specific rule *listing the Officers* of a Private Lodge.

As we go through the surviving minutes of some of our oldest lodges, Secretary and Treasurer appear as officers from the 1730s onwards. Deacons appear from about 1760 onwards, but they are very rare until the end of the century. Tylers are more frequent, but Inner Guards are also scarce until the late pre-Union minutes. All these were purely optional officers; there was no rule requiring the Master to appoint them.

In 1815, the first post-Union *Book of Constitutions* was published and it contained a whole section on 'Private Lodges', under which heading it ruled:

> The masonic officers of a lodge are the master and his two wardens, with their assistants [*sic*], the two deacons, inner guard, and tyler; to which, for the better regulation of the private concerns of the lodge, may be added other officers, such as chaplain, treasurer, secretary, &c.

It is interesting to see how many of our present-day officers were still optional in 1815. The *et cetera* might have provided scope for a number of peculiarities, but the rule remained unchanged until 1841 when the '&c.' disappeared and the new version ran:

> ... for the better regulation of the private concerns of the lodge are to be added a treasurer and secretary and other officers, viz. a chaplain, master of ceremonies, and stewards may also be added. (*B. of C.* 1841.)

It was not until 1884 that we have the Director of Ceremonies with his full title, capital letters and all:

... The Master may also appoint a Chaplain, a Director of Ceremonies, an Organist, and Stewards. No Brother can hold more than one regular office ...' (*B. of C.* 1884, 1896.)

The Asst. D. of C. made his appearance in 1911, with several other new officers:

... The Master may also appoint a Chaplain, a Director of Ceremonies, an Assistant Director of Ceremonies, an Almoner, an Organist, an Assistant Secretary and Stewards. No Brother can hold ...

Finally, in 1975, another office was added to the list, that of 'Charity Steward'.

---

189.   THE CHISEL AND ITS SYMBOLISM

Q. When did the Chisel come into our Craft ritual with its symbolism relating to the advantages of education?

A. The Chisel appears in three curiously assorted lists of working tools and other items, in English exposures of 1724–1726, in response to a question:

Q. How many Lights in a Lodge?
A. Twelve.
Q. What are they?
A. Father. Son. Holy Ghost. Sun. Moon. Master Mason. Square. Rule. Plum. Mall [= Maul] and Chizzel [Note: only eleven].
(From a manuscript entitled *The Whole Institution of Masonry.* 1724.)

In 1725, a longer version appeared as a printed broadsheet entitled *The Whole Institutions of Free-Masons Opened.* The answer in this is slightly different:

Father, Son, Holy Ghost, Sun, Moon, Master, Mason, [*sic*] Square, Rule, Plum, Line, Mall and Chiesal.
[Note as printed there are thirteen here.]

The latter answer appeared again, but without punctuation, in the *Graham MS.* of 1726, but none of these three texts added explanation or symbolism. After 1726 those lists of twelve items disappear altogether, perhaps because of the rapid expansion of the catechisms at that period, e.g., in 1696–1700 the E.A. catechism consisted of some fifteen questions and answers; in 1730 there were nearly a hundred for the E.A. alone!

Far more surprising is that the chisel itself seems to disappear from our ritual documents during the next sixty years or so, and we find no trace of it again until 1792. Prichard, in *Masonry Dissected*, 1730, gave only three tools for the E.A., calling them Moveable Jewels, 'Square, Level and Plumb-Rule'.

Three Distinct Knocks, 1760, gives:

24 Inch Gauge, the Square and Common Gavel, or setting Maul.

These are now 'moralized' in familiar fashion and there are no tools at all for the F.C. or M.M.

J. & B., published in 1762, and *Mahhabone*, 1766, are identical in this respect and this seems to have been general practice up to the end of the 18th century. Preston in his 'First Lecture' (with all the known versions collected in the late Bro. P. R. James's reproduction in *AQC*, Vol. 82) still gave 'plumb, level and square' as the 'moveable jewels' [=working tools] for the First Degree, and Browne, in his *Master Key*, 1802, still used only the same three tools, both writers moralizing on them in a manner that would be recognizable today.

The chisel reappears, in unusual surroundings, in the 1792 edition of Preston's *Illustrations* (p. 105), in his section on the Ceremony of Installation. Towards the end of the ceremony, in those days, the warrant was presented to the new W.M., and then:

the Sacred Law, with the square and compasses, the constitutions, the minute-book, the rule and line, the trowel, the chisel, the mallet, the moveable and immoveable jewels, and all the insignia of his different Officers, are presented to him, with suitable charges to each.

We may assume that this was the sequence in which the various items were presented. The 'suitable charges' were not printed in the body of the text, which might imply that they were optional, but Preston added a long and verbose set of footnotes, consisting of 'moral observations' on each of the tools, many of them in very familiar language. On the chisel, he wrote:

The Chissel demonstrates, the advantages of discipline and education· The mind, like a diamond, in its-original state, is unpolished; but as the effects of the chissel on the external coat, soon presents to view the latent beauties of the diamond; so education discovers the latent virtues of the mind, and draws them forth to range the large field of matter and space, to display the summit of human knowledge, our duty to God, and to man. [Note: Preston's own punctuation and spelling.]

The writers of those days were very willing to make use of each other's work, and this is noticeable in the next appearance of the 'moralized chisel', in the 3rd edition of William Hutchinson's *Spirit of Masonry*, 1802, p. 306, which included a lecture entitled 'A Lesson for

Free-Masons: or a series of Moral Observations on the Instruments of Masonry—By a Brother'. It was simply a florid expansion of Preston's themes.

Carlile, in *The Republican*, 8 July 1825, pp. 26–7, took a slightly different line:

> From the chisel, we learn, that perseverance is necessary to establish perfection, that the rude material can receive its fine polish but from repeated efforts alone, that nothing short of indefatigable exertion can induce the habit of virtue, enlighten the mind, and render the soul pure.
>
> From the whole we deduce this moral, that knowledge grounded on accuracy, aided by labour, prompted by perseverance, will finally overcome all difficulties, raise ignorance from despair, and establish happiness in the paths of science.

Finally, Claret, in his ritual, 1838, established the wording which is in general use today, and which was probably the form approved by the Lodge of Promulgation before the Union of the Grand Lodges in 1813:

> W.M. I now present to you the working tools of an E.A. Free Mason, which are the 24 inch gage, the common gavil [*sic*], and chisel. The 24 in. ga[u]ge is to measure our work, the common gavil is to knock off all superfluous knobs and excrescences, and the Chisel is to further smoothe and prepare the stone, and render it fit . . .

---

190.   ABSENT BRETHREN:
                  THE NINE O'CLOCK TOAST

Q. When Table procedure runs late, may we give the Toast to Absent Brethren at nine o'clock, *before the Loyal Toast* has been given, and may we follow it with the 'Fire'?

What is the earliest record of the Toast to Absent Brethren?

A. *No Toast may be given before the Loyal Toast*, and no 'Fire' until after that Toast has been given. The Master may have written to ailing or absent members saying 'We will drink your health at nine o'clock' and if he knows that they will be watching the clock at that hour he could simply 'take wine' with them (without 'Fire').

The nine o'clock idea is based on the fact that the hands of the clock form a perfect square at that moment; but that angle occurs forty-eight times in every twenty-four hours, and the Toast at that hour is custom, not law. By all means take it at nine if you can, but there is no need to break any rules for that purpose.

THE EARLIEST RECORDS OF THE TOAST

The Toast 'To all Brethren wherever dispersed' appeared in English exposures of 1762 and 1766 but we are indebted to Bro. T. O. Haunch for what may be the earliest known version, in the Minutes of the Lodge of Antiquity No. 2 (then called the Queen's Arms Lodge):

> 1759, April 10, Bror. Hammond in the Chair a Lecture in the Enter'd Apprentices part was given . . . the Health of our Absent members was drunk & no other business being proposed the Lodge was closed.
> (*Records of the Lodge of Antiquity, No.* 2 (Vol. 1, p. 195), by W. H. Rylands.)

Bro. Haunch adds the following notes:

> I think it very likely that toasts for absent brethren were originally associated with the sentiments expressed in what is now the Charge after the Third Section of the First Lecture, the present 'Tyler's Toast'—although just when the Charge was appropriated to this particular usage I have not been able to discover. The substance of this Charge certainly goes back into the eighteenth century.
> It seems to be generally accepted that 'Absent Brethren', *as a formal toast at a stated hour* came into widespread use during and after the 1914–1918 War.

---

191. SOLOMON AND HIS TEMPLE
IN THE MASONIC SYSTEM

Q. When did King Solomon and his Temple come into the Masonic System? Did this happen when the Hiramic legend was adopted in the ritual, or was it connected with the exhibitions of models of the Temple in the early 18th century? And why did the masons in a Christian country use Jewish themes?

A. David and Solomon (with many other Biblical characters) all appear in the *Old Charges* from *c.* 1390 onwards, but that was only because 'David loved masons well and gave them Charges' and Solomon 'confirmed the Charges that David his father had given to masons, etc.' The *Old Charges*, indeed, do not make any great fuss of either of them, but they were within the Masonic tradition from the beginning of our earliest records.

Christian interest in the Bible was not confined, in the 14th to 18th centuries, to the New Testament; they were equally interested in the Old Testament, and the Gentiles regularly quote the Old Testament (Isaiah especially) as predicting the coming of Christ. The Old Testament is *their* Book as well as the New.

Our oldest surviving ritual documents, 1696—c.1710, belong to the late operative period of Masonic history in Britain. The first of these texts, the *Edinburgh Register House MS.*, 1696, contains two questions in its catechism, repeated regularly in many of the later versions, which display an interest in Solomon's Temple, sufficient to show—at the very least—that Solomon and his Temple had their place in the ritual in operative days, and long before the Hiramic legend came into use:

Q.   How stands your lodge
An: east and west as the temple of jerusalem
Q.   Where wes the first lodge
An: in the porch of Solomons Temple

(E.M.C., 2nd Edn., p. 32.)

In 1659 Samuel Lee published his *Orbis Miraculum* which dealt at great length with the Temple and its equipment, and in 1688 John Bunyan published his *Solomon's Temple Spiritualized*, both of which excited much interest in the subject, but there were also many others (see *AQC*, Vol. 12, pp. 135–164, which contains a mass of information on 16th–17th century illustrations, etc., of K.S.T.). I do *not* believe that the London exhibitions of the models of K.S.T. created the Masonic interest in the Temple. I believe it was the interest of cultured men in the subject that helped to make the exhibitions successful. The models appeared in London in 1723, 1730, 1759–60.

When at the beginning of the 18th century the Craft began to acquire its speculative character, it was inevitable that the Temple should be adopted as the spiritual background to our ceremonies and ritual, in the same way as a theatrical producer selects suitable backgrounds for the play he produces.

The Hiramic legend did not appear *in print* until 1730, but we have hints of several streams of Masonic legend (about Noah and Bezaleel) from which our ritual builders were able to compile it. I believe that it existed (perhaps in several forms) *outside the ritual*, i.e., in folklore and craft-lore, before it was actually embodied in our ritual some few years before 1730.

---

192.   PRESENTATION TO THE BOARD OF
INSTALLED MASTERS

Q. It has been the practice in this lodge *at the Committee Meeting which precedes the Installation Meeting of the Lodge* to convene a Board of Installed Masters at which the Master Elect is presented. Such a meeting took place last week and several of the members queried whether it was in fact necessary to have this presentation as the Master Elect was known to all Past Masters and had, in any event, been freely elected in Open Lodge. Some of us were of the opinion that this presentation was done to conform with that part of the Installation Ritual which says '. . . and presented to a Board of Installed Masters'. For the benefit of the Members of the lodge would you care to give your comments?

A. In the course of a very long Masonic career I have never heard of a Board of Installed Masters formed at a lodge Committee meeting! Indeed, I believe that the usual way to form a Board of Installed Masters is by opening a lodge in all three degrees and, after M.M.s retire, the assembly is then constituted as a Board of Installed Masters. There are, of course, many English lodges that work the Extended Form of Opening and Closing a Board of Installed Masters, but that also requires that the lodge be opened in all three degrees. Needless to say, we are only discussing English practice, and it seems to me that your preliminary Board is at least redundant and perhaps irregular.

This question of presenting the Master Elect has arisen in various forms on many occasions. Although the word 'present' is not normally used, *the M.Elect is actually presented at the moment when he is admitted to the Board and he is presented specifically for the purpose of being regularly installed. The Board of Installed Masters has no other function at all.*

To satisfy many questioners, I suggest that the Master Elect goes out of the lodge with all the M.M.s, and when, a moment later, he is brought into the Board, which is already constituted, the Director of Ceremonies might begin the ceremony with a new sentence:

W.M. and Brethren of the Board of Installed Masters, I present Bro. . . . . . ., S.W. and M.Elect of this Lodge, to receive at your hands the benefit of Installation.

And then the Installing Master takes over.

Immediately after this item was published in the Q.C. Summons for January 1973, we received a number of letters from Brn. in English Provinces (Worcestershire, Suffolk, Surrey, E. Kent, W. Kent, and Warwickshire) all describing almost identical procedures of constituting a so-called Board of Installed Masters *at a Committee meeting held before the date of Installation, primarily for the purpose of presenting the Master Elect to the Board.*

One letter, from a Brother in Essex, confirmed that in his lodge the 'presentation' takes place *at the Election meeting, and in the first degree.* Immediately after the new W.M. has been elected, and without any other preliminaries,

> ... the W.M. declares the B. of I.M. with one knock. *No one leaves the room, nor do they turn their backs. No prayer, signs, or ceremonial takes place. ... All P.M.s gather in the East.* The D.C. presents the M.Elect to each P.M. starting with the W.M. 'He [i.e., the M.Elect] is greeted well.' The B. of I.M.s is declared closed with one knock by the W.M. and all return to their seats—and business is continued.

Another member of the Q.C. Correspondence Circle wrote describing almost identical procedure, but in his case, *after all the P.M.s have assembled in the East, all others (E.A.s, F.C.s, and M.M.s), assemble in the West, standing, and facing West, so that they cannot see the actual presentation.*

Before discussing the outcome of this correspondence, it may be helpful to describe the relevant details of our English Installation procedure for the benefit of Brethren of other jurisdictions who are not familiar with them.

On Installation night, after the lodge has been opened in the second degree, the M.Elect is brought before the W.M. for the first part of the ceremony, which deals with the essential qualifications for the Chair, and ends with the M.Elect's first Obligation relating to his duties as Master. The W.M. begins by addressing the lodge on the ancient custom of Installation, outlining some of the constitutional qualifications, e.g.:

> He [the M.Elect] must have been regularly elected by Master Wardens and Brethren in open Lodge assembled, *and presented before a Board of Installed Masters*, to receive from a predecessor the benefit of Installation, the better to qualify him to discharge the duties of that important trust.

In many of our modern workings the W.M. continues as follows:

> Bro. ... you having been so elected, before you are presented, I must claim your attention while I recite those qualifications which are ...

There are many workings, however, including two of the oldest, in which the W.M. uses a different formula:

> You, having been so elected *and presented*, I must claim your attention while I recite ... [various personal qualities and attainments] which are essential in every Candidate for the Master's Chair ...

The words shown in italics in this last extract imply that the M.Elect has already been presented to a Board of Installed Masters; but it must be emphasized that *at this stage he has only been presented before the*

W.M. (or the Installing Master) *for the preliminaries of his Installation.* The real presentation to a Board of Installed Masters takes place *at a later stage in the proceedings, after the lodge has been opened in the third degree, M.M.s have retired, and the B. of I.M. is formally constituted, or opened.*

It is not necessary here to discuss the origin of the words '*and presented*'. They belong, almost certainly, to the period before our Installation procedures were standardized. They are an archaic survival in the ritual, apparently in direct contradiction to the actual practice of the ceremony. Many lodges that use those words are well aware of this conflict but, being unwilling to alter or amend their ritual, they arrange for a more-or-less formal presentation *at a Committee meeting which they describe, quite improperly, as a Board of Installed Masters,* under the impression that this rectifies the situation. In effect, they have introduced an artificial (or irregular) B. of I.M. in order to make their practice conform with an archaic passage in the ritual, which has already been altered in many if not most of our modern workings.

In defence of their old established usage, I add a note from Bro. C. F. W. Dyer, Secretary of the Emulation Lodge of Improvement, which outlines their views on this problem. In their Installation procedure, as in most other workings, two Installed Masters are invited to occupy the Wardens' chairs before the lodge is opened in the second degree. I quote the note, but cannot accept the argument:

> Emulation claim that the inference of the placing of Installed Masters in the Wardens' chairs before the presentation of the Master Elect is to create a minimum Board of Installed Masters at that point for the public presentation of the Master Elect.

No such argument could apply to the so-called Boards of Installed Masters which are constituted at lodge Committee meetings and, being greatly disturbed by the many letters from the Provinces describing those extraordinary practices, I wrote to the Grand Secretary, asking for an official statement by the Board of General Purposes on the functions of the Board of Installed Masters, how it is formed or constituted, the necessary quorum, and whether it had any other function besides that of constituting the lawful environment for Installation of the Master Elect.

The ruling of the Board of General Purposes was printed in the *Grand Lodge Proceedings* for 12 September 1973. It is a lengthy document, and the following is a summary of its principal points:

1. *No one who is not an Installed Master . . . may take part in or be present at a Board of Installed Masters . . .* even under the pretext that they are unable to see or hear what takes place.
2. *The Board of Installed Masters is opened out of the third degree after all brethren below the rank of Installed Master have retired from the Lodge Room.*
3. *The Board of Installed Masters is employed solely for the purpose of installing the Master* (and investing the Immediate Past Master . . .).
4. *The Board of Installed Masters has no other function and cannot by any pretext be opened at any other time or occasion. Equally no Master can be regularly installed except in a Board of Installed Masters.*
5. *The quorum for a Board of Installed Masters is three,* apart from the Master Elect and a brother acting as Tyler, who need not of course be an Installed Master. (My italics. H.C.)

---

193.   GRAND HONOURS

Q. What is the origin of Grand Honours?

What is the explanation for the movements of the hands and arms?

What is the significance of the various numbers of salutes given as Grand Honours to the different ranks from Worshipful Master up to Grand Master? [From Saskatchewan, Canada.]

A. Grand Honours owe their origin to the first *Book of Constitutions* of 1723, Regulation XXIII, in which the new Grand Master was to be saluted 'in due form' after he had been proclaimed.

The 1738 *B. of C.*, which then contained details of the Annual Installations of Grand Masters from 1717 onwards, refers to:

Anthony Sayer, G.M., 1717. When the Assembly '. . . pay'd him the homage'.

George Payne, G.M., 1718. When the G. Wardens were 'congratulated and homaged'.

George Payne, G.M. again in 1720. When '. . . it was agreed . . . that the Brother proposed [for election as G.M.] if present, shall be kindly saluted. . . .'

There can be no doubt that 'paying the homage' and 'saluting' were the early fore-runners of our present-day Grand Honours, and the records show Salutations only for the M.W.G.M. and the Grand Wardens, who were the only Grand Officers in those early days.

By the time of the Union of the two Grand Lodges the list of Grand Officers had increased enormously, and there was still *no rule in the B. of C.* (1815) as to the number of Salutes, or who received them. But hitherto we have only discussed Salutes at the *Annual Festival for the Installation of the M.W.G.M.*

It was not until 4 June 1930 that Salutes for the various Grand Officers (with varying numbers of Salutes according to Rank) were agreed by the Grand Lodge, as an amendment to the 1926 *B. of C.* It was now proper to Salute visiting Grand Officers on private lodge occasions; that might have been customary before 1930, but the correct numbers of Salutes were not prescribed until 1930.

There is no explanation for the movement of 'hands and arms' apart from what is given *in the ritual*. The E.A. or F.C. 'Salutes' are the *signs* of those degrees, simply used as a Salutation. The G. or R. Sign in the Third Degree and in Grand Lodge (and sometimes in the inner Working of Craft Lodges) is simply the appropriate sign used as a Salute.

The number of Salutes allocated to the various ranks of Grand and Past Grand Officers is purely arbitrary and without any particular symbolism. It would be easy enough to write pages on the significance of the 3, 5, 7, 9, 11, but the numbers were designed to distinguish different ranks, without any symbolical intention.

Finally, it may be noted that, in English practice, the Worshipful Master only receives these 'multiple Salutes' on the night of his Installation.

It is proper to add that the corresponding 'Honours' in Ireland and Scotland differ vastly in numbers, etc., from English practice.

---

194. VISITORS' GREETINGS TO THE MASTER

Q. (Victoria, Australia.) During the Third Rising it is usually the custom in our lodges for the visiting Brethren to rise and 'give greetings' to the Master. What is the origin of this custom?

A. I believe our earliest record of conveying greetings to the Worshipful Master is in 'the Edinburgh group' of rituals, 1696—*c.* 1714, when the F.C. *Candidate*, after leaving the lodge to be 'entrusted' outside, came back and (after certain preliminaries) gave greetings to the assembly with the formula that he had been taught:

> The Worthy Masons & Honourable Company that I came from, Greet yow [*sic*] well, Greet yow well.

These words are from the *Chetwode Crawley MS.* of *c.* 1700; the *Kevan MS.* of *c.* 1714 gives the 'Greete you well' three times; the *E.R.H. MS.* also greets thrice, but omits the words 'that I came from'.

From the words and the manner in which those words were spoken, i.e., by a Candidate *in the middle of his ceremony*, it seems likely that this greeting was really part of a lesson teaching him how the greeting was to be given if he visited another lodge.

The next item in the story (actual early records are very scarce) is in Regulation XI of the 1723 *Book of Constitutions*:

> All *particular* [i.e. private] *Lodges* are to observe the same *Usages* as much as possible; in order to which, and for cultivating a good Understanding among *Free-Masons*, some members out of *every Lodge* shall be deputed to visit the *other Lodges* as often as shall be thought convenient.

Obviously, this kind of visiting—whether on a small or large scale—would demand some formal means of identification, not merely to show that the visitors were Masons, *but also what lodges they represented*, and I am satisfied that this was the earliest basis of the practice of giving greetings in lodge.

The custom, rarely seen in London nowadays, is practised in many if not most of the Provincial lodges. The greetings are usually given by the Master or senior member of a visiting group of Brethren from one lodge, and when he rises, all members of his lodge rise with him and they all stand to order while he says 'Hearty Greetings, Worshipful Master, from the ... Lodge No. ...'. The greetings continue from little groups all round the lodge and finally from individual visitors.

---

195.   OVERLOADING THE CEREMONIES?

Q. I am to give the Charge to the Initiate at our next meeting; would it be in order for me to begin with the formal Explanation of the Preparation for Initiation?

A. I would advise firmly against this, for two reasons:

1. There could be substantial objections to the inclusion of a lengthy piece of explanatory material—no matter how interesting—right in the middle of the ceremony, which has been practised in its present form for at least 160 years.
2. The Initiation needs approximately one hour, if it is to be conducted with proper solemnity. That is already something of a strain even for the most intelligent Candidate. To give details of the 'Preparation' on the same night would be overloading the ceremony and would leave him quite bewildered!

I suggest you save the Explanation for a later meeting, best perhaps when the same Candidate takes his 2°.

---

196. THE FAMILY TREE
OF THE
CRAFT, ROYAL ARCH AND MARK

Q. I am comparatively new in Masonry. Would it be possible for you to furnish a kind of 'family tree' of Masonry, covering the Craft, Royal Arch and the Mark degrees?

A. A fully detailed answer to this question would fill a fair sized volume. Here, it is only possible to outline the rise of the ceremonies, without furnishing the masses of documents, minutes, etc., by which these developments can be traced and proved.

At the time when Grand Lodge was founded in 1717 only two Degrees were in general usage in England and Scotland, the first for the 'Entered Apprentice' and the second for the 'Master *or* Fellow Craft'. The Third Degree, when it eventually appeared in 1725, *was not a new invention*. It arose by a splitting of the original First Degree into two parts, i.e., for the E.A., and the F.C., so that the original Second Degree then became the Third in the new Three-Degree system. (For recorded dates of the Craft Degrees see Q. 181, above.)

When the contents of the Third Degree, now including the Hiramic legend, appeared in print (for the first time) in Samuel Prichard's *Masonry Dissected*, in 1730, it is clear that the ceremony already contained material (i.e., a reference to a 'lost word') which subsequently formed one of the elements of the Royal Arch story. I must emphasize, however, that this does not mean that the Royal Arch existed in 1730.

The earliest clear evidence of the existence of the Royal Arch, as a degree or ceremony, is in a rather rare Irish work entitled *A Serious and Impartial Enquiry into the Causes of the present Decay of Free-Masonry in the Kingdom of Ireland*, by Dr. Fifield Dassigny, in 1744. He wrote that the Royal Arch was a separate Degree for 'men who have passed the chair'.

It would be quite impossible to discuss the contents of the Royal Arch ceremony at that date because we have no ritual documents, but there seems to be little doubt that soon after its appearance in England it began to embody various links with the legend of the Third Degree. Apparently both 'ceremonies' were verbally modified so that a more or less tenuous relationship was established. Thus, if your question is to be answered in the terms in which you framed it, I would say that the R.A. did not grow naturally on the tree of the Craft degrees, but it was 'grafted' on to one of its three branches. So, one might say that the Royal Arch nowadays does have a faint link with ordinary Craft working. Much was added to the original material during the second half of the 18th century, and our modern R.A. is generally described as the completion of the Third Degree, though I would prefer to call it an extension.

The 'Mark'. As early as 1598 we have a regulation in the *Schaw Statutes*, relating to operative masonry in Scotland, requiring that the 'Master or fellow of craft' should have his name and mark regularly inserted in the Lodge Book on the date of admission to that grade. Thereafter there are numerous records, in the Minutes of the early Scottish operative lodges, of masons who 'took their mark and paid for it'. *This was a purely operative practice*, enabling masons to mark their stones in a simple and recognizable manner. *In those days it was certainly not a ceremony or a degree.* When it did finally become a ceremony it had lost all operative connexion.

The Mark seems to have developed into a Degree or ceremony during the 1750s, and there is an interesting rule, made by an unattached Craft Lodge at Newcastle on 19 January 1756:

> That no member of the Saide Lodge Shall be Made a Mark Mason without paying the Sum of on[e] Mark Scots . . . (*AQC* 81, p. 264).

The 'one Mark Scots' suggests a Scottish source for this Degree, and there is evidence showing that this Lodge had some contact with the Grand Lodge of Scotland.

The earliest record of the making of 'Mark Masons and Mark Masters' is in the minutes of the Chapter of Friendship, Portsmouth, dated 1 September 1769. Because these are our earliest records, we have to treat the Mark Degree as a new ceremony, but it was certainly founded on good old operative practice.

---

197.   KNOCKS WHEN CALLING THE TYLER

Q. Why does the W.M. in Lodge on Installation night give two knocks when summoning the Tyler to come into the Temple to be invested? Why does he give two knocks at the end of the 'After-Proceedings' when signalling the Tyler to come to the Top Table to give the Tyler's Toast? Is there any particular symbolism for the double knock?

A. The two-knock procedure, right or wrong, is generally practised in most (if not all) lodges under English Constitution. As to its correctness, I would quote the late Dr. E. H. Cartwright who, in his *Commentary on* *the Freemasonic Ritual* (Chapter III) under the heading 'Knocks, Reports and Alarms', dealt with the matter in his customary forthright style, referring to

> . . . the curious custom, . . . of the Master giving a resounding double knock (which is not repeated by the Wardens) when the presence of the Tyler is required in the Lodge, for instance when he is about to be invested on Installation night. The custom is, strictly speaking, irregular. In the first place it is a knock that has no Freemasonic significance. Secondly, the fact that the Wardens do not repeat it contravenes the old-established rule that *every* knock given by the Master should be 'answered' by the Wardens. Further, while the obvious reason for the knock being given so loudly as is invariably the case is that the Tyler may hear it and take it as a summons to enter, that Officer cannot possibly act on it until the Inner Guard opens the door to admit him. Although, in view of the wide prevalence that the practice has now obtained, the writer is not prepared incontinently to condemn it, it does appear to him that it is an unnecessary innovation and that it would be more seemly for the Master, instead of knocking, simply to request the Inner Guard to call in the Tyler, . . .

My own view is that this criticism is too harsh. The variations in the different knocks used in the degrees, and in the Openings and Closings were undoubtedly introduced to mark distinctions between degrees, or between different parts of a ceremony. *The variations have no symbolical significance* and this applies, likewise, to the double-knock. It is now so widely accepted as being the customary knock for calling the Tyler, that there is not the least danger of its being misunderstood. It serves its purpose perfectly.

---

198.   THE PRELIMINARY STEP
              To 'Entrusting' And 'Communication'

Q. We were discussing at Lodge of Instruction the curious step which the Candidate takes before he is 'entrusted' by the W.M., who later informs him that that particular step is the position in which the S . . . of the degree are communicated; my question is 'Why that particular step; is there any known reason?'

A. A very difficult question, because there is absolutely no early evidence of any kind on this matter. In the dozens of catechisms, exposures and other—more respectable—documents of the 18th century, which furnish useful information on contemporary ritual and procedure, there is never any trace of an instruction that the Candidate is *to step or stand in a particular way as a preliminary to the 'entrusting'*, nor is there any kind of warning that such a step or stance is requisite as a preliminary to the communication of secrets at other times.

As late as *c.* 1800, in Preston's First Lecture, which gives an enormous amount of detail about the Initiation, the Candidate at the 'entrusting' stage was simply asked to 'advance one step', with no mention at all of how the feet were to be placed. I believe that the special position was introduced simply *to distinguish that step* from any of the others taken in the three degrees; i.e., the position for receiving or giving the sign, etc., was to be *a special one always.* It may even be that the 'awkward position' was specially chosen so that a Mason would recognize at a glance that someone he was testing was ignorant of this particular practice. (Incidentally, in many European and overseas jurisdictions, *each Degree has its own particular step.*)

Finally, and because that practice does not make its appearance in ritual texts until after the Union of the two Grand Lodges in 1813, I am inclined to believe that it was introduced at the time of the Union.

---

199.   THE IMMEDIATE PAST MASTER'S SALUTES
In Closing After Each Degree

Q. (From a Provincial Brother.) In my lodge, after the Closing of the lodge in each degree, and after the requisite knocks have been given and the Tracing Boards have been altered, the I.P.M. approaches the Master's pedestal, salutes in the degree which has just been closed, arranges the V.S.L., etc., and salutes in the lower degree before resuming his place. (Reverse procedure in the Openings, of course.)

Our Director of Ceremonies, who is from another Province, says this is incorrect, since the I.P.M. is saluting in the wrong degree, and that the correct procedure would be the 'Sn. of Reverence'. As W.M. of the lodge, I would be grateful for your guidance on this point.

A. On matters of this kind it is a very good rule to put the question to your Provincial Grand Secretary, because quite often there is a form of procedure laid down by the Provincial Grand Master, not necessarily as a law, but simply as a guide to the practice that he favours. If the Prov.G.Sec. says there is no ruling on the subject, there may be a ruling in the particular 'working' that your lodge follows.

On the assumption that no ruling can be obtained from those sources, I am glad you have not mentioned your particular 'working' because that leaves me free to express my views without fear of offending any-one.

I would say, first of all, that it is quite unnecessary for the I.P.M. to salute twice for the tiny piece of business that he has to do; one salute is quite enough, and I would suggest that he makes it after he has finished his duty, i.e., after the 3° Closing he makes the F.C. sign. After the 2° Closing he would give the E.A. sign. After Closing in the 1° he would simply bow (a 'Court bow', i.e., chin to chest with body held erect).

In my view, there are strong objections to the Sign of Reverence (widely used during Prayers), and really unsuitable in the present case. (See p. 259 above.)

---

200.   MASONIC STATISTICS
How Many Lodges, Grand Lodges, Freemasons?

Q. Is there a sort of world directory for Freemasonry? I would like to know:

1. How many Regular Grand Lodges there are?
2. How many Lodges?
3. What is the world-population of Freemasons?

A. Interesting questions but, for reasons which will be explained shortly, they cannot be answered completely. There is one book, a small annual publication, which deals with all these matters on a truly international scale. Its modest title is a marvel of understatement:

1980
LIST OF LODGES
Masonic

It is published by the Pantagraph Printing & Stationery Co., Bloomington, Illinois, U.S.A., price $4.25 post paid. In England, among those who use it regularly, it is known as the 'Pantagraph'. The book is an unassuming paper-back of nearly 300 pages and it is a veritable mine of information. It lists some 157 Grand Lodges in alphabetical order, from Alabama to the York Grand Lodge of Mexico, giving the full title in each case, with the date of its foundation, the names and addresses of the Grand Master and Grand Secretary, with the address and telephone number of the Headquarters building — or the Grand Secretary's office, and dates of Grand Lodge Communications.

All this information is contained in the heading for each of the Grand Lodges. There is also a figure for the number of lodges in each jurisdic-tion and generally another figure for the total number of members on its registers.

The heading is followed by a complete list of all lodges in that jurisdiction, by name and number, grouped under a location heading, i.e., under towns in which those lodges meet. Occasionally the lists will contain supplementary information.[1]

At the end of the entry for each of the Grand Lodges there are copious notes of 'recognition' details, showing for the 'senior' Grand Lodges, the jurisdictions they do not recognize. For the newly erected or very small jurisdictions the notes usually furnish a list of the Grand Lodges which have already recognized them.

On this matter of recognition, it is perhaps necessary to emphasize the obvious point that not all the Grand Lodges recognize all the others. Of the 157 Grand Lodges listed in the 'Pantagraph', the United Grand Lodge of England recognizes only some 107. This does not necessarily imply that the others are irregular, but simply that the 'senior' Grand Lodge always exercises more than average caution in awarding what may be deemed the hall-mark of Masonic stability and regularity. Thus, of the seventeen Grand Lodges listed for Brazil (all but one being 'State' Grand Lodges) the English constitution recognizes only the Grand Orient of Brazil; and of the eight Grand Lodges listed for Mexico, it recognizes only the York Grand Lodge of Mexico. Hence the oft-repeated warning to English Brethren that they must check-with the Grand Secretary's office, whether an overseas lodge that they propose to visit is regular or not. Alternatively, they should obtain a list of regular lodges in the area they are visiting and leave all others severely alone.

How Many Lodges Are There?

It is impossible to furnish completely accurate or even up-to-date figures. The latest edition of the 'Pantagraph' as I write these notes is 1980 and its statistics are already some six months late when the book appears. Meanwhile new lodges are coming into existence in almost every part of the world and these are not recorded until a year later. Analysis, mainly from the 'Pantagraph' data for 1980 with certain details extracted from

[1] There are several pages of charts giving further valuable information, especially on the subject of 'single, dual, and plural membership'.

[2] Under the United Grand Lodge of England the Brethren enjoy total freedom as to the number of lodges they may join; but many overseas jurisdictions exercise a strict control in this respect, e.g., in the U.S.A., some fifteen jurisdictions permit only single membership, so that a Brother may belong to no more than one Craft lodge within his own jurisdiction. Some of them permit 'dual membership', i.e., to join two Craft lodges under his own Grand Lodge. Most of them permit 'dual' membership outside the State, so that, quoting examples only, a Mason in Ohio may belong to only one Craft lodge in Ohio but he may join one lodge in any regular jurisdiction outside. Massachusetts permits plural membership inside and outside the State, i.e., no restrictions, as under Grand Lodge of England.

Year Books, shows a 'world total' of approximately 33,948 *lodges under jurisdictions recognized by the United Grand Lodge of England.*

England is the largest jurisdiction, and its latest figures (from the 1980/81 *Year Book*) are:

Lodges in London... 1676
Lodges in *47 English Provinces* 5595
Lodges *Overseas in 38 Districts etc*........................   780

                                                    TOTAL 8051

(The 1980 'Pantagraph' shows 7998 lodges and 600,000 members in all.)

To round off the information, the following is a list of the world's largest jurisdictions including all those which have 500 or more lodges on their rolls:

	Lodges		*Lodges*		*Lodges*
California	644	Italy (G.O.)	519	Ohio	681
Canada-Ontario	645	Michigan	512	Pennsylvania	587
Illinois	761	Missouri	549	Scotland	1095
Indiana	552	New South Wales	834	Texas	973
Ireland	854	New York	893	Victoria	
				(Australia)	810

WORLD POPULATION OF FREEMASONS?

This question is even more difficult to answer than the preceding one, simply because the full information is not available. Of the 157 jurisdictions listed in the 'Pantagraph' about one in every ten had not supplied *membership* details. The majority of these are the small South American jurisdictions, but several of the larger bodies also omit those figures. If we are to estimate the missing membership data *only for those Grand Lodges which enjoy English recognition,* they represent altogether some 4014 lodges. In the total absence of reliable data, it may be reasonable to take an outside estimate of say seventy members per lodge, yielding a round figure of 281,000 for the unrecorded memberships.

The total figures are further complicated by the 'single, dual and plural' membership regulations. The three senior jurisdictions, England, Ireland and Scotland, all permit plural membership, i.e., their members may join as many lodges as they please, and the majority of all other jurisdictions permit dual membership within their own territories and outside. This means that an English Mason who is a member of two lodges becomes, statistically, two members. The same applies to a Mason in New York who joins a lodge in Massachusetts, and it is quite impossible to ascertain how many Brethren are recorded *at least* twice over.[2]

There are approximately 3,332,000 Masons in the forty-nine Grand Lodges in the U.S.A., and roughly 736,000 under the three senior Grand Lodges, England, Ireland and Scotland. The 'world population of Masons' based mainly on the 'Pantagraph' data and including estimated figures for the jurisdictions that do not supply details is, in round figures, 4,732,000. If only 1% of these Brethren hold dual membership, this total would be reduced by 47,000. Opportunities for error are considerable but, since they only affect a fraction of the total number of lodges, they do not materially affect the final results, which seem to be much smaller than one might have expected.

During the past ten years, the membership records for the U.S.A. jurisdictions have shown a steady annual decrease of approximately 1% to $1\frac{1}{2}$% and, although precise figures are not available, similar falls are reflected in many of the older and strongly established jurisdictions. The reasons, whether social, economic, or political, may vary in the different countries, and the remedy is still to be found.

201.   THE ORIGIN OF THE POINTS OF FELLOWSHIP

Q. What is the origin of the Points of Fellowship?

A. A summary of the seventeen oldest ritual texts, from 1696 to 1730, shows the Points, variously described, in fourteen of them, including five of the earliest versions from 1696 to c.1714. They certainly date back into operative times, most of them belonging to the second degree in the two-degree system, perhaps as early as the mid-1500s. (See details on pp. 27 to 30, above).

As to the question of origin, twelve of our fourteen texts are without a single word to indicate where the Points came from, or what they mean. Only two of the latest versions, dated 1726 and 1730, contain clues as to their purpose. They appear, in each case, as part of our earliest legends, the first concerning Noah, and the second relating to Hiram Abif. The Points, in both stories, describe the actual mechanics of exhuming corpses from their graves, and the legends suggest that the participants were trying to obtain a secret from the dead body.

The Points, with some much-improved versions of the Hiramic legend, appear again in several French exposures from 1744 to 1751, but none of

[2] See footnotes on page 400.

them, English or French, gives a word of explanation of what the Points really meant. Yet their complexity alone implies that there must have been an explanation; nobody would have used them if they were utterly meaningless. Dealing with this problem in his Prestonian Lecture, 1938,[1] Douglas Knoop cited three Biblical examples of 'miraculous restoration of life', in each case by something closely resembling the Points:

I. Kings, XVII, v.21, in which Elijah raised the son of the widow in whose house he lived.

II. Kings, IV, v.34, in which Elisha revived the child of the Shunamite woman.

Acts, XX, vv.9-10, in which St. Paul resuscitated a young man who was taken up dead after a fall.

They are all interesting, but the second, with Elisha, gives the story in useful detail:

"And he [Elisha] went up, and lay upon the child, and put his mouth upon his mouth, and his eyes upon his eyes, and his hands upon his hands; and he stretched himself upon the child; and the flesh of the child waxed warm".

Bro. Knoop was suggesting that the Points are closely akin to what we describe nowadays as the 'Kiss of Life'. But he carried his argument a stage further, saying that in the 16th and 17th centuries these Bible stories would have developed into 'necromantic practices', i.e., the art of foretelling the future by means of communication with the dead. Here, I have to abandon his theory. One may well imagine the kind of person who would become involved in 'black magic' after reading those verses in the Old and New Testament, but it is difficult to believe that they could have affected the whole of the mason craft during several centuries. We are dealing with operative masonry, long before the appearance of speculative interpretation, and in a problem of this kind a practical explanation would be much more helpful.

Regardless of the precise words in which the Points appear in the various early versions (or in the standardized versions that came later), it seems likely, if they ever had a practical purpose, that they were taught and used originally as a means of raising a broken body, or reviving someone who had been killed by a fall in the course of his work. Accidents of this kind must have been common in operative times and, searching for early documentary evidence on the subject, I went back to the Schaw Statutes, 1598. They were promulgated by William Schaw, Master of Works to the Crown of Scotland and Warden-General of the Mason Craft, 'to be observed by all the master masons within this realm'. They are the earliest official regulations for the management of operative lodges, and contain incidentally, the oldest official regulation on scaffolding: Here it is, word-for-word, in modern spelling, but three obsolete terms are shown in [. . .]:

> Item, that all masters, enterprisers of works, be very careful to see their scaffolds and walkways [futegangis] surely set and placed, to the effect that through their negligence and sloth no hurt or harm [skaith] come to any persons that work at the said work, under penalty of *being forbidden* [dischargeing of them] *thereafter to work as masters having charge of any work, but they shall be subject all the rest of their days to work under or with another principal master having charge of the work.* (My italics. H.C.)[2]

This was the strictest rule in the whole of the 1598 code. All other offences could be satisfied by a fine, but not this one. A master, at the peak of his career, found guilty after an accident of careless scaffolding, was condemned for the rest of his life never to use scaffolding again, except under or with another principal master. He could not blame an underling; it was his personal responsibility.

I believe that this rule explains the origin and purpose of the Points, and it also solves the biggest problem of all, i.e., why the twelve oldest versions of the Points are without any kind of explanation. The masons did not need it. They learned those procedures in the normal course of their training, just as a child learns the alphabet as a preliminary to reading. The Points were simply the masons' 'Kiss of Life'.

[1] *Collected Prestonian Lectures,* pp.255-7. Published by the Quatuor Coronati Lodge.

[2] Dashwood & Carr. *Minutes of the Lodge of Edinburgh, (Mary's Chapel) No. 1, p.38.*

INDEX

Compiled by Frederick Smyth, Member of the Society of Indexers,
Junior Deacon of the Quatuor Coronati Lodge No. 2076, and
Fellow of the American Lodge of Research, New York

Page numbers in **bold type** denote complete articles or sections, or the more important references; page numbers in *italics* denote illustrations; *bis* after a page number indicates two separate references on that page; *passim* (e.g. 40–50 *passim*) denotes that the subject is referred to not continuously but in scattered passages throughout the pages; q. stands for 'quoted', q.v. for *quod vide* (which see); *n.* refers to a footnote on the page. The alphabetical arrangement is according to the word-by-word system.

Lodges mentioned are under the English Constitution unless otherwise designated and, unless a location is given (or indicated in the name), are (or were) London lodges. (IC) refers to the Irish Constitution, (SC) to the Scottish, and (A) to the 'Antients'. Lodges still in existence are in most cases indexed under their modern titles, numbers and Constitutions, and cross-references are made where appropriate. * against an English lodge number indicates that it derived from a period before the final numbering of 1863 and, usually, that the lodge has been erased or is no longer on the English Register.